A Unified Electro-Gravity (UEG) Theory of Nature

Nirod K. Das

New York University

Copyright © 2018 by Nirod K. Das. All Rights Reserved.

US Copyright
Registration Number: TXu 2-128-436
Effective Date: December 20, 2018

First Published Edition, October 2022
ISBN: 978-1-7340-6301-1
UEGM Publishing

(See http://wp.nyu.edu/ueg for any supplementary material or updates)

Table of Contents

Introduction

A collection of papers, describing a new theory unifying electrical, gravitational as well as mechanical concepts are presented. The papers demonstrate the generality and validity of the unified theory, as applied to a diverse set of fundamental problems, covering elementary particles in the small scale, as well as stellar, galactic and cosmological models in the large scale. The papers are listed in three major sub-groups:

The Part-I covers three papers applied to problems in the smallest scale of nature. The first paper introduces the new unified electro-gravity (UEG) theory to the most basic elementary particle - the electron. The UEG theory allows the electron to be modeled first as a static charge, without any spinning effects, which is self-consistently balanced as a stable particle. The second paper extends the static UEG theory, by including higher-order UEG effects, to model other elementary particles, which may be made of a single spherical charge layer located at different specific radii, or may consist of multiple charge layers to form composite charged or neutral particles. These particles may include all known particles - fermions or bosons - of the standard model of particle physics, such as a proton, neutron, neutrino and possibly even a Higgs, W or Z boson. The static UEG theory of the first paper is extended in the third paper, to model a dynamic electron structure that includes spinning, where the spinning motion is self-supported by new UEG effects due to the moving charge. Although the third paper explicitly models the electron, the basic concepts can be extended and generalized as well to other elementary particles. This electrodynamic UEG model is consistent with the basic quantum mechanics, and can consistently explain many quantum electrodynamic phenomena without having to simply accept them as some "special quantum effects", as they are currently understood. These include discovery of the origin of the fine-structure constant and the Planck's constant, explaining charge quantization, wave-particle duality and the photon concept.

The Part II of the papers extends the UEG theory to problems in the large scales of nature, presented in four papers. The fist paper models stellar gravitation, as per the new UEG theory, in order to re-evaluate the stellar mass-luminosity relation (MLR). This is accomplished by modeling UEG effects of stellar radiation on gravitation between binary stars, which determines the orbital dynamics of the binary stars, as well as on self-gravitation of a star, which determines the star's light output through nuclear reaction. Measured luminosity and orbital parameters of binary stars, supported by the new theory, lead to a revised MLR, where the actual mass of a star is found to be less - significantly less for highly luminous stars - than the currently believed mass. It is discovered that the actual mass of Sun, the lone star in our solar system, is about half of the gravitational mass which is currently estimated based on Newtonian gravitation. The other half of the Sun's gravitational mass is the result of the new UEG effect due to the Sun's radiation. The theory is similarly extended in the following two papers, in order to model gravitation in a spiral galaxy by including the new UEG effect due to the galaxy's light distribution. The new UEG effect would explain galactic rotation without need for any hypothetical "dark matter" (second paper) as well as explain gravitation at the galactic center without requiring any "super-massive black hole (SMBH)" (third paper). The fourth paper extends the UEG theory in the largest possible scale of nature, to model cosmic expansion without need for any hypothetical "dark matter" or "dark energy". This is possible by including the new UEG effects due to the cosmic back-ground (CMB) radiation, as well as due to future radiation from any new stars made from collapsing of the remaining hydrogen in the universe.

As per the new UEG theory, the electric charge and its force fields are the origin of all material mass, as well as of all forms of forces and energy. Accordingly, one may expect that the fundamental electro-magnetic fields of an electrical charge, which is governed by Gauss' law and certain basic principle of charge invariance, must be consistent with and supersede all mechanical principles. This is because the mass, force and energy, upon which all mechanical principles are empirically founded, trace their physical origin to the basic electro-magnetic fields. The above expectation is examined in two steps, as presented in the two papers of Part-III. The first paper was written as a tutorial on a "derivation" of Maxwell's equations, established from first principles, based on the discovery of a new concept of charge invariance, which is relativistically consistent across different inertial frames. The new concept of charge invariance allows a direct derivation of Maxwell's equations from first principles, based only on the basic definition of a charge using Gauss' law, and simple relativistic space-time transformation. This is accomplished without any apriori knowledge of the mechanical theory of Newton's laws, or on the associated principles of relativistic transformation of mass, energy and momentum. Instead, the mechanical principles of Newton's laws can now be "derived" from Maxwell's equations, as presented in the second paper, by deriving and relating the forces between specific charges under different conditions of motion, as they are observed in two inertial frames. The resulting transformation relations for the forces, so derived directly from Maxwell's equations, would dictate the basic relations of Newton's laws, that must be satisfied in order to be consistent with the electrical principles of Maxwell's equations. The combined results of the two papers essentially unify the basic electrical principles with the mechanical principles of Newton's laws, making Newton's laws theoretically redundant.

The unification of electrical or electromagnetic concepts with Newton's laws in Part-III, together with the unification of electricity and gravitation in Parts I and II, would establish a new unified paradigm to model any physical phenomena of nature. This would make the weak, strong forces and quantum theory of elementary particles, and the hypothetical dark matter and dark energy of astrophysics and cosmology, theoretically redundant. This is the closest we have come to a complete unified theory of everything (TOE), which has been the ultimate aspiration of physical sciences. The basic UEG theory is remarkably validated in all the collected papers, but it is still not fully rigorous. A fully rigorous UEG theory would require future development of a complete, dynamic unified electro-gravito-magnetic (UEGM) theory, including all possible higher-order UEG static as well as dynamic effects.

Nirod K. Das
New York, May 2018

Part-I: Unified Electro-Gravity (UEG) Theory in the Small Scale: Particle Physics and Quantum Mechanics

A New Unified Electro-Gravity Theory for the Electron

Nirod K. Das

Department of Electrical and Computer Engineering, Tandon School of Engineering,
New York University, 5 Metrotech Center, Brooklyn, NY 11201
(Dated: May 9, 2018, Revised July 15, 2019)

A rigorous model for an electron is presented by generalizing the Coulomb's Law or Gauss's Law of electrostatics, using a unified theory of electricity and gravity. The permittivity of the free-space is allowed to be variable, dependent on the energy density associated with the electric field at a given location, employing generalized concepts of gravity and mass/energy density. The electric field becomes a non-linear function of the source charge, where concept of the energy density needs to be properly defined. Stable solutions are derived for a spherically symmetric, surface-charge distribution of an elementary charge. This is implemented by assuming that the gravitational field and its equivalent permittivity function is proportional to the energy density, as a simple first-order approximation, with the constant of proportionality referred to as the Unifield Electro-Gravity (UEG) constant. The stable solution with the lowest mass/energy is assumed to represent a "static" electron without any spin. Further, assuming that the mass/energy of a static electron is half of the total mass/energy of an electron including its spin contribution, the required UEG constant is estimated. More fundamentally, the lowest stable mass of a static elementary charged particle, its associated classical radius, and the UEG constant are related to each other by a dimensionless constant, independent of any specific value of the charge or mass of the particle. This dimensionless constant is numerologically suspected to be closely related to the the fine structure constant. This finding may carry greater fundamental significance, with scope of the UEG theory covering other elementary particles in the standard model of particle physics.

I. INTRODUCTION

The electron is the most fundamental charged particle of nature [1], carrying the smallest mass among all known charged particles, and is classified as a lepton in the standard model of particle physics [2, 3]. It plays a fundamental role in our everyday nature as a basic building block of all chemical elements, which consist of one or more electrons orbiting in different spatial forms around an oppositely charged, massive central nucleus [4, 5]. Different physical parameters of the electron - its charge, mass, as well as the spin angular momentum and the magnetic moment [6–8]- have been measured in great precision. The electron's characteristics in an electromagnetic field have also been successfully modeled using quantum mechanical wave functions [9–11] and quantum electro-dynamics [12]. However, any internal structure of the electron, and the origin of its mass, remain mysterious. It is sometimes considered to be a "point particle" with no particular internal structure [13]. However, the electromagnetic energy, or its equivalent mass, for the point-particle would be infinite [14], which is unphysical and inconsistent with the finite measured mass of the electron [6]. Further, the question of how the electronic charge could withstand the repulsive force due to its own electric field [14], which is infinite for the point-structure with a zero radius (or even a finite value if the electron had a non-zero radius), can not be properly answered.

In this paper we model an electron using a new Unified Electro-Gravity (UEG) theory. The theory attempts to unify the concept of the electric field surrounding a source charge, as defined by the Coulomb's Law or Gauss' Law of electrostatics [15–17], together with a general-

ized concept of gravity produced due to energy density associated with the electric field, that would be consistent with the Newton's Law of Gravity [18, 19]. The permittivity of the "free-space" around a charge, which is conventionally assumed to be a fixed constant in the Coulomb's Law or Gauss' Law, is now modeled as a functional distribution, dependent on the distribution of the electric field or its associated energy density. The permittivity function needs to be consistent with the Newton's Law of gravity, where a gravitational field is recognized to be directly proportional to the gradient of the inverse-permittivity function. Accordingly, such an "unified electo-gravitational (UEG)" field may be modeled as a non-linear field, where the permittivity distribution is a general function of the source charge, or equivalently the electric field is a non-linear function of the source charge. Under this non-linear condition, the definition of energy density and its expression in terms of the source charge or the electric field, used in conventional electromagnetic theory, may have to be properly modified.

With a proper definition of the energy density associated with the non-linear UEG field, and a suitable relationship between the gravitational field and the energy density, the permittivity function surrounding a spherically symmetric surface-charge distribution may be solved, either analytically or numerically. Consequently, the total energy, or its equivalent mass as per special relativity, may be derived as a function of the charge radius. It is discovered that stable solutions, where the first derivative of the total energy with respect to the charge radius is zero, and the second derivative positive, are possible for certain discrete values of the charge radius. The derivation assumes a simple proportional relationship between the energy density and the UEG field, with the constant of proportionality referred to as the UEG constant. It may be reasonable to assume that the stable solution having the smallest possible mass/energy is associated with the mass/energy of an ideal "static electron" that does not spin around itself. Further, the mass of the static electron may be ideally assumed to be half of the total mass of an electron that includes its spin contribution. Accordingly, by reverse deduction, the UEG constant can be calculated, and is recognized as a new fundamental constant of nature. This is a significant fundamental development.

The new UEG constant is defined as the gravitational acceleration per unit energy density, carrying a dimension of $(m/s^2)/(J/m^3)$. More significantly, a dimensionless constant relating the UEG constant, the stable static mass, and its associated classical radius, is identified which would apply to any basic charge particle, independent of the specific charge or mass of the particle. The value of this dimensionless constant is numerologically recognized to be closely related to the fine structure constant [20]. This general finding may suggest a much broader scope of application of the UEG theory to other known elementary particles in the standard model of particle physics [2, 3, 21, 22], which might be associated with different effective values of the UEG constant, resulting in different mass and classical radii of the particles, while they carry the same value of the elementary charge as the electron. Considering the broad reach of the fine structure constant in quantum mechanics and electro-dynamics [20, 23, 24], the recognition that the fine-structure constant may have its fundamental origin in the UEG theory may carry profound theoretical and fundamental implications.

II. GRAVITY AS GRADIENT OF FREE-SPACE PERMITTIVITY

A massive body in a gravitational field $\overline{E}_g$ experiences a force $\overline{F}$ in a certain direction in space. In the theory of general relativity this force is seen as a result of curvature of the surrounding "free-space" [25]. The force may be alternatively modeled by considering the permittivity ϵ of the surrounding "free-space" to be a non-uniform function $\epsilon(\bar{r})$ of the location $\bar{r}$ (unlike a constant value $\epsilon = \epsilon_0$ normally used) [26], and assuming that the mass of a given body at a particular location is a function of the local permittivity (see Fig.1). As the mass is displaced from one location over an incremental distance along a given direction, its mass or equivalent energy is also incrementally changed due to the incremental change in the permittivity associated with the displacement. This change in energy per unit displacement in the given direction would be equal to the force component one needs to apply to move the body, or negative of the gravitational force component the body experiences, in the particular direction. Accordingly, the gravitational field is modeled in terms of gradient of the permittivity function of the

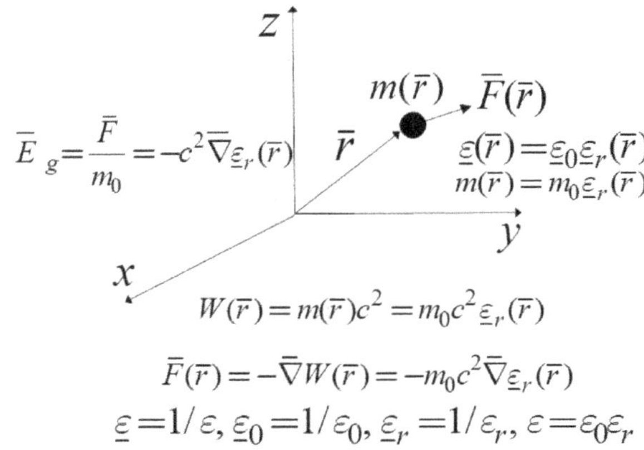

FIG. 1.

"free-space" medium.

We assume that the mass m or the equivalent energy $W = mc^2$, where c is the speed of light in an isolated free-space, is inversely proportional to the permittivity ϵ, or directly proportional to $\underline{\epsilon} = 1/\epsilon$. This is in consistency with the energy $W = \dfrac{q^2}{8\pi\epsilon r_q}$ of a spherical surface charge q of radius r_q, placed in a medium with permittivity ϵ.

$$\underline{\epsilon}(\bar{r}) = \underline{\epsilon}_0 \underline{\epsilon}_r(\bar{r}),\ \epsilon = \epsilon_0 \epsilon_r,\ \underline{\epsilon} = \frac{1}{\epsilon} = \frac{1}{\epsilon_0 \epsilon_r} = \underline{\epsilon}_0 \underline{\epsilon}_r,$$

$$\underline{\epsilon}_0 = \frac{1}{\epsilon_0},\ \underline{\epsilon}_r = \frac{1}{\epsilon_r};$$

$$m(\bar{r})\ \alpha\ \underline{\epsilon}(\bar{r}),\ m(\bar{r}) = m_0 \underline{\epsilon}_r(\bar{r}),$$

$$m_0 = m(\underline{\epsilon} \rightarrow \underline{\epsilon}_0,\ \underline{\epsilon}_r \rightarrow 1),\ \underline{\epsilon}_r = \frac{1}{\epsilon_r} = \frac{\underline{\epsilon}}{\underline{\epsilon}_0} = \frac{m}{m_0};$$

$$\overline{E}_g = \frac{\overline{F}}{m_0} = \frac{-\overline{\nabla}W(\bar{r})}{m_0} = \frac{-\overline{\nabla}[m(\bar{r})c^2]}{m_0}$$

$$= \frac{-\overline{\nabla}[m_0\underline{\epsilon}_r(\bar{r})c^2]}{m_0} = -c^2\overline{\nabla}\underline{\epsilon}_r(\bar{r}). \tag{1}$$

A. Gravitational Field and Permittivity Function in a Region with Energy/Mass Distribution

Consider the gravitational field produced by a body of mass of m_0, as per the Newton's Law of Gravitation, exerting a force on an external mass δm_0. The permittivity function around the mass m_0 may be expressed using the model (1) developed above.

$$\overline{F} = -\frac{Gm_0\delta m_0}{r^2}\hat{r},$$

$$\overline{E}_g = \frac{\overline{F}}{\delta m_0} = -\frac{Gm_0}{r^2}\hat{r} = -c^2\overline{\nabla}\underline{\epsilon}_r(\bar{r}) = -c^2\frac{\partial\underline{\epsilon}_r(r)}{\partial r}\hat{r},$$

$$\frac{\partial\underline{\epsilon}_r(r)}{\partial r} = \frac{Gm_0}{c^2 r^2},\ \underline{\epsilon}_r = 1 - \frac{Gm_0}{c^2 r},\ \underline{\epsilon}_r(r \rightarrow \infty) = 1\ . \tag{2}$$

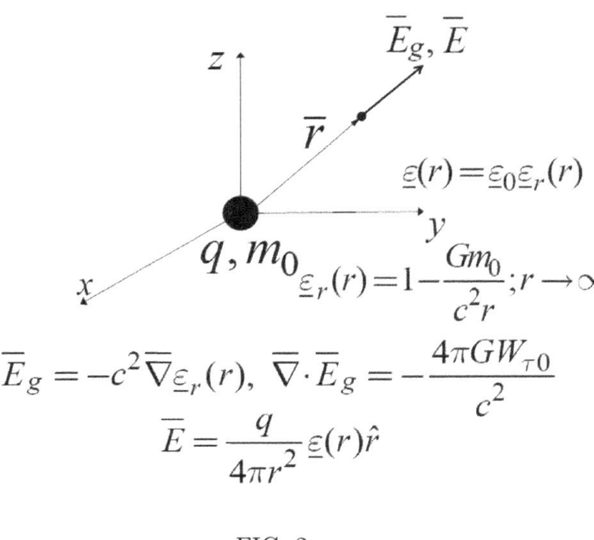

$$\overline{E}_g = -c^2 \overline{\nabla} \underline{\varepsilon}_r(r), \quad \overline{\nabla} \cdot \overline{E}_g = -\frac{4\pi G W_{\tau 0}}{c^2}$$

$$\overline{E} = \frac{q}{4\pi r^2} \underline{\varepsilon}(r) \hat{r}$$

FIG. 2.

The above result would be applicable for all distances $r > 0$ for an ideal point-body, and would apply only outside the body for a body of non-zero radius.

The permittivity function for a body with distributed mass/energy, such as an electric charge, may be similarly developed (see Fig.2), by relating the divergence of the gravitational field $\overline{E}_g$ in (2) to the mass-density $m_{\tau 0}$. The mass-density $m_{\tau 0}$ of a distributed body at a particular location is defined as the mass per a unit elemental volume $d\tau = 1$ at the given location. The equivalent energy-density $W_{\tau 0} = c^2 m_{\tau 0}$.

$$\overline{\nabla} \cdot \overline{E}_g = -4\pi G m_{\tau 0} = \overline{\nabla} \cdot (-c^2 \overline{\nabla} \underline{\varepsilon}_r),$$
$$\overline{\nabla} \cdot \overline{\nabla} \underline{\varepsilon}_r = \frac{4\pi G m_{\tau 0}}{c^2} = \frac{4\pi G W_{\tau 0}}{c^4} . \qquad (3)$$

III. MODELING ENERGY DENSITY IN A NON-LINEAR MEDIUM AROUND AN ELECTRIC CHARGE

In the unified electro-gravity (UEG) model, the permittivity distribution of the free-space is dependent upon the energy density distribution, which is dependent upon the source charge. This is unlike a linear dielectric medium where the permittivity function is independent of the field strength or the source charge. Having the permittivity distribution to be a function of the source charge, is equivalent to having the electric field distribution to be a non-linear function of the source charge. The energy density in such a non-linear medium needs to be properly modeled, starting from the fundamentals. This would result in a general expression for the energy density for a non-linear medium, which may be verified with a standard expression of the energy density for a

linear medium, as a special case when the permittivity is a constant independent of the charge.

The electric field $\overline{E}$ and the electric flux density $\overline{D}$ produced due to a charge q, at a distance r from the center of the charge, in the presence of a permittivity distribution $\epsilon(r) = 1/\underline{\epsilon}(r)$ may be expressed using the Coulomb's Law.

$$\overline{E} = \frac{q}{4\pi r^2 \epsilon(r)} \hat{r}, \ \ \overline{D} = \frac{q}{4\pi r^2} \hat{r}, \ \ \overline{E} = \frac{\overline{D}}{\epsilon(r)} = \underline{\epsilon}(r)\overline{D}. \quad (4)$$

Let us calculate an incremental energy dW required in moving an incremental charge dq from infinity to a radius $r = r_q$, using the above electric field. This is equivalent to having $dW = V(q)dq$ using a potential concept, where $V(q)$ is the potential (function of q) at the radius $r = r_q$. Integrating the dW over the total charge q would give the total energy W.

$$dW = dq \int_{r_q}^{\infty} \overline{E}(q) \cdot \overline{dr}$$
$$= V(q; r = r_q)dq = \int \int \int_{\tau; r > r_q} dW_\tau d\tau,$$
$$W = \int_{q=0}^{q} dW = \int \int \int_{\tau; r > r_q} (\int_{q=0}^{q} dW_\tau) d\tau. \quad (5)$$

The incremental charge dq may be expressed in terms of an incremental change in the electric flux density $d\overline{D}$ using Gauss Law. The incremental energy dW can then be expressed as an integral over the external volume $\tau; r > r_q$ using the divergence theorem.

$$dW = V(q; r = r_q)dq = \int \int_{S, r = r_q + \delta} V(q) d\overline{D} \cdot \overline{ds}$$
$$= \int \int \int_{\tau; r > r_q} \overline{\nabla} \cdot (-V(q)d\overline{D})d\tau$$
$$= \Big[\int \int \int_{\tau; r > r_q} (-\overline{\nabla} V(q) \cdot d\overline{D})d\tau$$
$$+ \ \int \int \int_{\tau; r > r_q} -V(q)(\overline{\nabla} \cdot d\overline{D})d\tau \Big]$$
$$= \int \int \int_{\tau; r > r_q} \overline{E}(q) \cdot d\overline{D} d\tau$$
$$= \int \int \int_{\tau; r > r_q} \underline{\epsilon}(q)\overline{D}(q) \cdot d\overline{D} d\tau$$
$$= \int \int \int_{\tau; r > r_q} \underline{\epsilon}(q) \frac{1}{2} \frac{\partial}{\partial q}(\overline{D}(q) \cdot \overline{D}(q)) dq d\tau$$
$$= \int \int \int_{\tau; r > r_q} \frac{1}{2}\underline{\epsilon}(q) \frac{\partial |\overline{D}|^2}{\partial q} dq d\tau = \int \int \int_{\tau; r > r_q} dW_\tau d\tau;$$
$$\overline{\nabla} \cdot d\overline{D} = 0 \text{ in } \tau. \quad (6)$$

We have now established an expression for an incremental energy density dW_τ, which may be integrated over the total charge q to obtain the required expression of the energy density W_τ. The general expression may be verified to be the conventional energy density for a linear medium, when the permittivity is a constant independent of the charge q. The total energy W can then be calculated as the volume integral of the energy density W_τ.

$$dW_\tau = \tfrac{1}{2}\underline{\epsilon}(q)\frac{\partial|\overline{D}|^2}{\partial q}dq,$$

$$W = \int\int\int_\tau W_\tau d\tau = \int\int\int_\tau \left(\int_{q=0}^{q} dW_\tau\right)d\tau = m_0 c^2 \,. \quad (7)$$

In equivalency to a conventional definition of the energy density for a linear medium, it may be useful to define a new variable $\underline{\epsilon}'$ for a non-linear medium. The conventional expression of the energy density for a linear medium, with the inverse-permittivity $\underline{\epsilon}$ for the linear medium simply substituted by the new equivalent variable $\underline{\epsilon}'$, would be valid as well for the non-linear medium.

$$W_\tau = \int_{q=0}^{q} dW_\tau = \int_{q=0}^{q} \tfrac{1}{2}\underline{\epsilon}(q)\frac{\partial|\overline{D}|^2}{\partial q}dq = \tfrac{1}{2}\underline{\epsilon}'|\overline{D}|^2 = \tfrac{1}{2}\underline{\epsilon}_0\underline{\epsilon}'_r|\overline{D}|^2,$$

$$\underline{\epsilon}' = \frac{1}{|\overline{D}|^2}\int_{q=0}^{q}\underline{\epsilon}(q)\frac{\partial|\overline{D}|^2}{\partial q}dq = \frac{1}{q^2}\int_{q=0}^{q}\underline{\epsilon}(q)\frac{\partial q^2}{\partial q}dq$$

$$= \frac{2}{q^2}\int_{q=0}^{q}\underline{\epsilon}(q)q\,dq = \frac{2\underline{\epsilon}_0}{q^2}\int_{q=0}^{q}\underline{\epsilon}_r(q)q\,dq = \underline{\epsilon}_0\underline{\epsilon}'_r. \quad (8)$$

IV. A UNIFIED ELECTRO-GRAVITY MODEL FOR AN ELEMENTARY CHARGE, WITH A NEW DEFINITION OF THE ENERGY DENSITY

For a given total energy W, the energy density W_τ we derived may not be unique. An alternate expression of the energy density W'_τ may be defined by adding a distribution f to the original energy density W_τ, such that the W'_τ would result in the same total energy W when integrated over the total volume τ as that due to the original energy density W_τ. Accordingly, a fixed total energy W is redistributed into the different energy densities W_τ and W'_τ inside the volume τ. This can be accomplished by having the additional distribution f expressed as divergence of a suitable vector distribution $\overline{U}$, which is identically zero everywhere outside the volume τ.

$$W = \int\int\int_\tau W_\tau d\tau = m_0 c^2,$$

$$W_\tau = \frac{\triangle W}{\triangle\tau} = \tfrac{1}{2}\underline{\epsilon}'|\overline{D}|^2 = \frac{1}{16\pi^2 r^4\epsilon_0}\int_0^{q} q\underline{\epsilon}_r(q)dq,$$

$$W'_\tau = W_\tau + f,$$

$$f = \overline{\nabla}\cdot\overline{U} = \overline{\nabla}\cdot(U\hat{u}); \quad \overline{U} = 0 \text{ outside of } \tau, \quad (9)$$

$$W = \int\int\int_\tau W'_\tau d\tau$$

$$= \int\int\int_\tau (W_\tau + f)d\tau = \int\int\int_\tau (W_\tau + \overline{\nabla}\cdot\overline{U})d\tau$$

$$= \int\int\int_\tau W_\tau d\tau + \int\int\int_\tau \overline{\nabla}\cdot\overline{U}d\tau$$

$$= \int\int\int_\tau W_\tau d\tau + \int\int_S \overline{U}\cdot\overline{ds} = \int\int\int_\tau W_\tau d\tau, \quad (10)$$

$$U(W_\tau): \; U(W_\tau = 0) = 0, \; \hat{u} = \hat{r};$$

$$W_\tau = 0 \text{ outside of } \tau, \; \overline{U} = \zeta W_\tau\hat{r}. \quad (11)$$

An alternate expression of the energy density W'_τ, as in (9), would require revision of the Poynting theorem of the electromagnetic theory [27, 28], in order to re-establish proper relationship between different energy and power associated with an electromagnetic field.

Theoretically, there are many possible expressions for the vector function $\overline{U}$. A simple, physically meaningful proposition is to express the function $\overline{U}$ (11), referred to as the UEG function, proportional to the original energy density W_τ, and directed toward the center of mass/gravity of the particle.

Consider the external free-space region of a "neutral" material body, that appears to be charge-less to an external observer, with the electromagnetic field and its associated energy density in the external region equal to zero. With the above choice of the UEG function $\overline{U}$ (11), no new, special treatment would be required to model the gravitational field in the external region, because the original as well as the revised energy densities of (9), W_τ and W'_τ respectively, would be zero in this region. Further, with the choice of the UEG function (11), the total energy W, or its equivalent mass $m = W/c^2$ of the neutral body, as seen by an external observer, would remain the same whether the W is calculated by integrating the original or the revised energy density in the internal region, as per the deduction in (10). Accordingly, Newtonian gravitational field in the external region of such neutral material bodies would remain unaffected by the new UEG theory, which would be consistent with observation.

The selected UEG function $\overline{U}$ (11) could be non-zero in the internal region of a neutral body discussed above, due to non-zero electromagnetic fields associated with any charged sub-structure internal to the body. This would lead to having the revised energy density W'_τ in (9) to be different from the original energy density W_τ in the internal region. Accordingly, it would require a revised treatment for modeling the gravitational field, in the internal charged region of such a neutral material body, or for that matter in any general region in the presence of a non-zero electromagnetic field.

The new alternate expression for the energy density W'_τ of (9), using the new UEG function $\overline{U}$ of (11), may now be substituted for the original energy density $W_{\tau 0} = W_\tau$ in the UEG modeling of the gravitational field in (3).

$$\overline{\nabla}\cdot\overline{E}_g = -c^2\overline{\nabla}\cdot\overline{\nabla}\underline{\epsilon}_r = -4\pi Gm'_\tau = -\frac{4\pi GW'_\tau}{c^2}$$

$$= -\frac{4\pi G}{c^2}(W_\tau + \overline{\nabla}\cdot\overline{U}) = -\frac{4\pi G}{c^2}W_\tau - \overline{\nabla}\cdot(\gamma W_\tau\hat{r}),$$

$$\frac{4\pi G}{c^2}\overline{U} = \frac{4\pi G}{c^2}\zeta W_\tau\hat{r} = \gamma W_\tau\hat{r}\,. \quad (12)$$

It may be observed from the above expression of the gravitational field $\overline{E}_g$, that the new UEG function $\overline{U}$, which was introduced for an alternate definition of the energy density W_τ' in (11), would be equivalent to having an additional gravitational field equal to $-\gamma W_\tau \hat{r}$, referred to as the UEG field. The parameter γ in (12) is a new scalar constant, referred to as the UEG constant, which is related to the constant ζ used in (11).

A. Series Solution for $\underline{\epsilon}_r$, with a Strong UEG Force Assumption

We will solve for the inverse-relative permittivity function $\underline{\epsilon}_r(r)$, by expanding it as power-series of r^{-i} with unknown coefficients b_i, and then solve for the coefficients in order to satisfy the above UEG relation (12). In the limit of large distance r, the $\underline{\epsilon}_r(r)$ needs to satisfy the Newtonian gravitational field (2) due to the particle mass m_0, approaching unity at infinite distance $r \to \infty$. The limiting conditions would fix the first two coefficients b_0 and b_1.

$$\underline{\epsilon}_r(r,q) = \sum_{i=0}^{\infty} b_i r^{-i}, \ b_0 = 1, \ b_1 = -\frac{Gm_0}{c^2}. \quad (13)$$

This assumes that the surrounding medium at infinite distance from the particle is a free-space with $\epsilon = \epsilon_0$, $\epsilon_r = 1 = 1/\epsilon_r = \underline{\epsilon}_r$, and the $m = m_0$ is the mass of the particle when measured in the free-space medium. If the surrounding medium is different from the free-space, with $\epsilon = \epsilon_r \epsilon_0$, $1/\epsilon_r = \underline{\epsilon}_r \neq 1$, then the above solution (13) needs to be scaled with $b_0 = \underline{\epsilon}_r$ and $b_1 = \frac{Gm_0 \underline{\epsilon}_r}{c^2}$. It may be shown from the following iterative solution for the $\underline{\epsilon}_r(r)$, that each term in the series expression of (13), and therefore the entire expression of (13), would be multiplied by the $\underline{\epsilon}_r(r \to \infty)$ of the surrounding medium, in order to obtain the $\underline{\epsilon}_r(r)$ for the particle in the given surrounding medium. Further, the mass function $m = m(r = r_q)$ for the particle measured in the given surrounding medium, as derived in section IV B using the above scaled $\underline{\epsilon}_r(r)$, may be shown to be equal to $m = m_0 \underline{\epsilon}_r(r \to \infty)$, as expected in section II. For simplicity, in the following derivations we will assume the surrounding medium to be free-space, the results from which may be properly scaled as needed for any other surrounding medium.

We may assume that the new UEG field $-\gamma W_\tau \hat{r}$ is much stronger than the conventional Newtonian gravitational field of the charge particle, contributed due to the original energy density W_τ. This is because the conventional Newtonian gravitational field of an elementary charge is known to be very week, having a negligible (essentially no) effect on the permittivity function. It may be shown, that this assumption would be valid given the radius r of the charge particle is much larger than the radius r_0 of a black-hole produced by an elementary charge q, with a mass equal to the classical mass $q^2/(8\pi\epsilon_0 r_0 c^2)$ of the charge with the radius r_0.

$$\overline{\nabla} \cdot \overline{E}_g = -c^2 \overline{\nabla} \cdot \overline{\nabla}_{\underline{\epsilon}_r} \simeq -\overline{\nabla} \cdot (\gamma W_\tau \hat{r})$$

$$= -\overline{\nabla} \cdot (\frac{\gamma \hat{r}}{16\pi^2 r^4 \epsilon_0} \int_0^q q \underline{\epsilon}_r(q,r)dq)$$

$$= -\overline{\nabla} \cdot (\frac{\gamma q^2 \underline{\epsilon}_r'(r)\hat{r}}{32\pi^2 r^4 \epsilon_0}), \ r >> r_0 = \sqrt{\frac{Gq^2}{8\pi\epsilon_0 c^4}},$$

$$\overline{E}_g \simeq -\gamma W_\tau \hat{r} = -\frac{\gamma \hat{r}}{16\pi^2 r^4 \epsilon_0} \int_0^q q \underline{\epsilon}_r(q,r)dq$$

$$= -\frac{\gamma q^2 \underline{\epsilon}_r'(r)\hat{r}}{32\pi^2 r^4 \epsilon_0}, \ r >> r_0 = \sqrt{\frac{Gq^2}{8\pi\epsilon_0 c^4}}. \quad (14)$$

The expression (8) for the energy density W_τ in a non-linear medium is used in the above derivation. Assuming that the charge distribution and the UEG solution are spherically symmetric, the differential operators in the above expression can be expressed in terms of derivatives with respect to the radius. Substituting the series expression of (13) in (14) we get,

$$\frac{\partial}{\partial r}\underline{\epsilon}_r \simeq \frac{1}{c^2}(\gamma W_\tau) = \frac{\gamma}{16\pi^2 r^4 c^2 \epsilon_0} \int_0^q q \underline{\epsilon}_r(r,q)dq$$

$$= \frac{3r_\mu^3}{2q^2 r^4} \int_0^q q \underline{\epsilon}_r(r,q)dq, \ r_\mu^3 = \frac{\gamma q^2}{24\pi^2 c^2 \epsilon_0} \propto q^2,$$

$$r_\mu = (\frac{\gamma q^2}{24\pi^2 c^2 \epsilon_0})^{1/3} = 5.14 \times 10^{-16}\gamma^{1/3},$$

$$\frac{\partial^2 \underline{\epsilon}_r(r,q)}{\partial(r^{-3})\partial(q^2)} \simeq -\frac{r_\mu^3}{4q^2}\underline{\epsilon}_r(r,q). \quad (15)$$

$$\sum_{i=0}^{\infty} b_i(-i)r^{-(i+1)} \simeq \frac{3r_\mu^3}{2q^2} \sum_{i=0}^{\infty} (\int_0^q q b_i(q)dq)r^{-(i+4)}$$

$$= \frac{3r_\mu^3}{2q^2} \sum_{i=3}^{\infty} (\int_0^q q b_{i-3}(q)dq)r^{-(i+1)}. \quad (16)$$

The above relation provides an iterative solution for the coefficients b_i.

$$b_i \simeq -\frac{3r_\mu^3}{2q^2(i)} (\int_0^q q b_{i-3}(q)dq),$$

$$b_0 = 1, \ b_i = 0; \ i \neq 3k = 0, 3, 6, 9\cdots. \quad (17)$$

The series may be re-sequenced with $a_k = b_{3k}$, because all coefficients b_i for i other than $i = 3k = 0, 3, 6, 9\cdots$ are zero.

$$a_k = b_{3k} \simeq -\frac{r_\mu^3}{q^2(2k)} (\int_0^q q b_{3k-3}(q)dq)$$

$$= -\frac{r_\mu^3}{q^2(2k)} (\int_0^q q a_{k-1}(q)dq). \quad (18)$$

From the above iterative relation it may be recognized that a_k would be proportional to q^{2k}. This condition may be used to simplify the iterative relation for a_k and then solve for all the coefficients a_k starting with the known coefficient $a_0 = 1$.

$$a_k(q) \propto q^{2k}, \ a_0 = 1, \ a_1 = -\frac{r_\mu^3}{2\times 2},$$

$$a_2 = \frac{r_\mu^6}{2\times 2\times 4\times 4}; \ a_k = -a_{k-1}\frac{r_\mu^3}{(2k)(2k)} \ . \quad (19)$$

The series expression for the inverse-relative-permittivity function $\underline{\epsilon}_r(r)$ may be re-formatted as a power series of t^{2k}, where t is a normalized variable $t = (r_\mu/r)^{1.5}$, with corresponding normalized coefficients a_k'.

$$\underline{\epsilon}_r(r) = \sum_{i=0}^{\infty} b_i r^{-i} \simeq \sum_{k=0}^{\infty} a_k r^{-3k}$$

$$= \sum_{k=0}^{\infty} a_k'(\tfrac{r_\mu}{r})^{3k} = \sum_{k=0}^{\infty} a_k' t^{2k},$$

$$a_k' r_\mu^{3k} = a_k, \ t = (\tfrac{r_\mu}{r})^{1.5}, \ a_k' = -a_{k-1}'\frac{1}{(2k)(2k)}, \quad (20)$$

$$a_k' = \frac{(-1)^k}{2^{2k}(k!)^2}, \ k! = (k)(k-1)(k-2)\cdots(1), \quad (21)$$

$$\underline{\epsilon}_r(r) \simeq 1 - \frac{t^2}{2^2[1!]^2} + \frac{t^4}{2^4[2!]^2} - \frac{t^6}{2^6[3!]^2} + \cdots$$

$$= J_0(t). \quad (22)$$

The above series is recognized as as the zeroth-order Bessel function $J_0(t)$ [29]. The corresponding effective function $\underline{\epsilon}_r' = 1/\epsilon_r'$ may be deduced from (22) using the definition (8), and similarly recognized in relation to the first-order Bessel function $J_1(t)$ [29].

$$\underline{\epsilon}_r'(r) = \frac{2}{q^2}\int_0^q q\underline{\epsilon}_r(q,r)dq$$

$$\simeq 1 - \frac{t^2}{2^2[1!]^2\times 2} + \frac{t^4}{2^4[2!]^2\times 3} - \frac{t^6}{2^6[3!]^2\times 4} + \cdots$$

$$= (2/t)J_1(t). \quad (23)$$

The inverse-relative permittivity function $\underline{\epsilon}_r = 1/\epsilon_r$ of (22), as well as the corresponding effective function $\underline{\epsilon}_r' = 1/\epsilon_r'$ of (23) are plotted in Fig.3 as a function of the normalized radius $r_\mu/r = t^{2/3}$.

The function $\underline{\epsilon}_r = 1/\epsilon_r$ that would have resulted if a conventional energy density for a linear medium (see (14,8)) were used (incorrectly) in the above derivation of section IV A, where the effective function $\underline{\epsilon}_r' = 1/\epsilon_r'$ from (8) that defines the energy density would be equal to the function $\underline{\epsilon}_r = 1/\epsilon_r$, is expressed in (24), and is also plotted in Fig.3 for reference.

$$\underline{\epsilon}_r(r) = \underline{\epsilon}_r'(r) \simeq 1 - \frac{t^2}{2^2 1!} + \frac{t^4}{2^4 2!} - \frac{t^6}{2^6 3!} + \cdots$$

$$= e^{-t^2/2}. \quad (24)$$

Notice in the Fig.3 that the function $\underline{\epsilon}_r$ of (22) (and the corresponding effective function $\underline{\epsilon}_r'$ of (23)), derived using the rigorous definition of the energy density (8) for a non-linear medium, exhibits an oscillatory behavior changing its sign from positive to negative values and vice versa. This is in contrast with the result for $\underline{\epsilon}_r = 1/\epsilon_r = \underline{\epsilon}_r' = 1/\epsilon_r'$ from (24) (using a simplistic (incorrect) UEG model), which monotonically approaches zero with no oscillatory behavior. The rigorously derived, oscillatory behavior of the $\underline{\epsilon}_r = 1/\epsilon_r$ and $\underline{\epsilon}_r' = 1/\epsilon_r'$ functions is a key development, which would lead also to an oscillatory behavior of the total energy/mass of the charge particle as a function of radius, to be established in the following section. This would allow the charge particle to maintain a stable structure at discrete values of radius, where the total energy/mass of the particle would be locally minimum.

From Fig.3, it may be noted that at discrete locations where $\underline{\epsilon}_r$ of (22) is zero, the corresponding $\underline{\epsilon}_r'$ of (23) is non-zero, and vice versa. Accordingly, the energy density W_τ of (8) would be non-zero, at the discrete locations where the field $\overline{E}$ of (4) is zero, and vice versa. This is unlike a conventional field in a "free-space" medium having a fixed relative permittivity $\epsilon_r = 1$, in which case a non-zero or zero electric field is respectively associated with a non-zero or zero energy density. The above non-conventional behavior is a result of the non-conventional nature of the "free-space" medium, as per the UEG theory, which is no longer a fixed but is a "flexible" or variable medium with a non-linear behavior. The electric field in such a flexible medium would be a non-linear function of the source charge, and the equivalent permittivity is a function of the source charge and location. The energy density in such a non-linear medium needs to be properly re-defined as in (8), resulting in the effective inverse relative-permittivity $\underline{\epsilon}_r'$ of (23), which leads to the non-conventional disconnect between the energy density and the electric field, discussed above.

Further, the relativity permittivity ϵ_r from (22) in Fig.3 is allowed to be negative, which may be theoretically associated with a negative speed of light. The effective permittivity ϵ_r' from (23) in Fig.3 is also allowed to be negative, which as per its definition in (8) would allow the energy density to be negative. These possibilities of negative light speed and negative energy density are remarkable new developments, not encountered in conventional physical problems, which may carry far-reaching physical and philosophical implications.

B.   Particle Energy and Mass, as a Function of the Charge Radius

Once the inverse-relative permittivity function $\underline{\epsilon}_r(r)$ is solved, the energy density can be expressed in terms of the $\underline{\epsilon}_r(r)$ using (8), which can then be integrated over the total volume in the external region of a spherical surface-charge distribution (there is no field or energy in

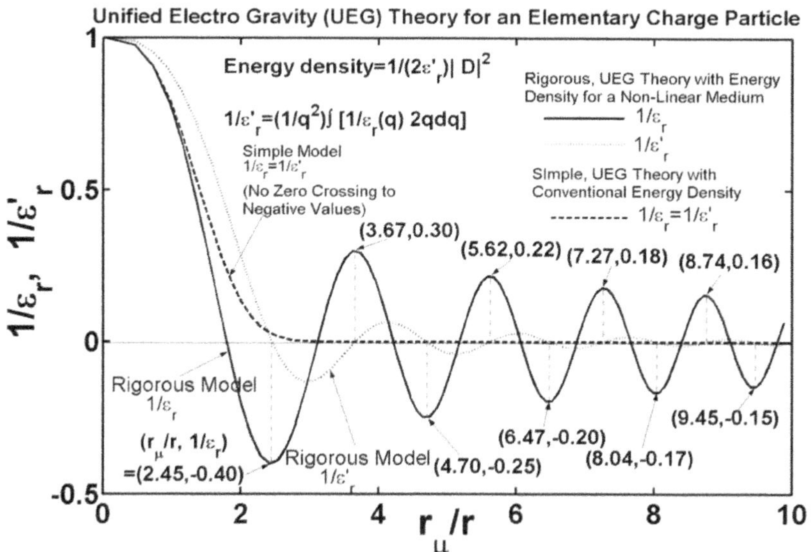

FIG. 3.

the internal region), to obtain the total energy or the equivalent mass m $(=m_0$ in (13)) of the particle.

$$W = \int \int \int_\tau W_\tau d\tau = m_0 c^2$$

$$= \int \int \int_\tau [\frac{1}{16\pi^2 r^4 \epsilon_0} \int_0^q q\epsilon_r(q,r)dq]d\tau,$$

$$m = m_0 = \frac{W}{c^2} = \frac{1}{4\pi c^2 \epsilon_0} \int_r^\infty \frac{1}{r^2} \int_0^q q\epsilon_r(q,r)dqdr$$

$$= m_\mu \sum_{k=0}^\infty \frac{(-1)^k t^{(2k+\frac{2}{3})}}{2^{2k}(k!)^2(k+1)(3k+1)}, \quad t = (\frac{r_\mu}{r})^{1.5},$$

$$m_\mu = \frac{q^2}{8\pi c^2 \epsilon_0 r_\mu} = 2.49 \times 10^{-30}\gamma^{-1/3},$$

$$r_\mu = (\frac{\gamma q^2}{24\pi^2 c^2 \epsilon_0})^{1/3} = 5.14 \times 10^{-16}\gamma^{1/3} . \quad (25)$$

The charge radius in (25) is maintained as a general variable $(=r)$. The general mass function $m(r)$ in (25) would also represent the equivalent energy $(=c^2 m(r))$ contained in the field external to a sphere of radius r, produced due to the charge placed at any radius less than r.

Fig.4 and Fig.5 (with different mass scales/resolutions) plot the normalized mass m/m_μ of (25) as a function of the normalized radius r_μ/r, showing the oscillatory behavior of the mass function, as we anticipated earlier. Any of the minimum points of the mass function would correspond to a possible stable particle with the particular charge radius, as we also anticipated. The mass $m = m_0$ that would have resulted, if the inverse-relative permittivity function of (24) were used in the derivation of (25,8), based on a simplistic (incorrect) UEG model

assuming a linear medium, is expressed in (26). This mass (26) normalized with respect to m_μ is also plotted in Figs.4,5 for reference, showing no stable radius. Also plotted in Figs.4,5 for reference is the normalized mass $(m/m_\mu) = (r_\mu/r)$, based on a simple Coulomb's field, which asymptotically approaches the normalized masses of (25) and (26) for $r \to \infty$, as should be expected. Clearly, the Coulomb mass does not allow any stable radius.

$$m = m_0 = \frac{W}{c^2} = \frac{q^2}{8\pi c^2 \epsilon_0} \int_r^\infty \frac{\epsilon_r(r)}{r^2} dr$$

$$= m_\mu \sum_{k=0}^\infty \frac{(-1)^k t^{(2k+\frac{2}{3})}}{2^{2k} k!(3k+1)}. \quad (26)$$

The smallest possible stable mass deduced from the oscillatory mass of (25) (Figs.4,5) is expected to be the mass of an electron (or a positron) without any spin. This is referred to as the static UEG mass m'_e of an electron. We will assume that the static UEG mass m'_e of an electron is about half of the total electron mass m_e, that includes additional mass/energy due to the electron's spin. This factor of about 2 between the m'_e and m_e is suggested by recognizing that the electron's spin g-factor, as defined below in (27), is approximately equal to 2. The bare static UEG mass m'_e of an electron spins effectively at the same speed and at the same radial distance as the electron's charge q. This would result in having the ratio of the spin magnetic moment M and the spin angular momentum p equal to $q/(2m'_e)$. This is equivalent to having a total electron mass $m_e = gm'_e \simeq 2m'_e$ spinning at about half of a given speed or about half of a given

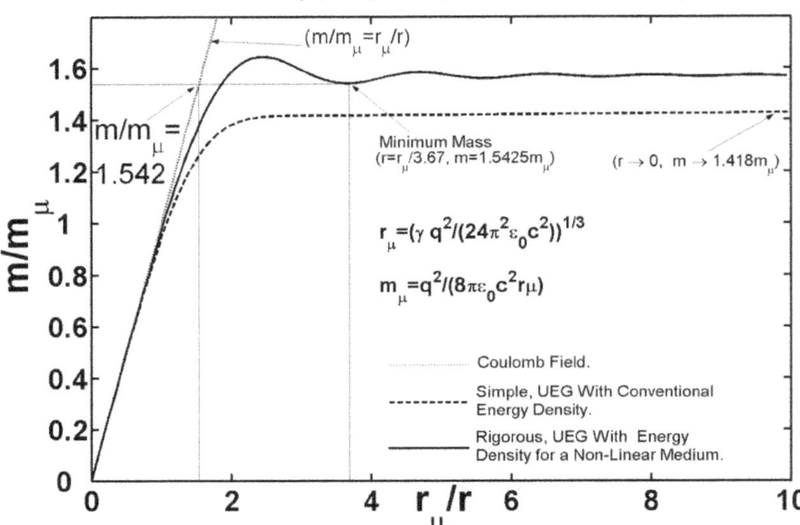

FIG. 4.

radius (or at about half of a given speed-radius product), in order to produce the same given angular momentum p. This factor of about 2 is represented by the electron's spin g-factor.

$$\frac{M}{p} = \frac{q}{2m'_e} = \frac{gq}{2m_e},$$

$$g \simeq 2, \quad m'_e = \frac{m_e}{g} \simeq \frac{m_e}{2}. \tag{27}$$

The same conclusion may also be suggested by observing that the orbital magnetic moment of an atomic electron with an orbital angular momentum $\hbar$ is approximately equal to the magnetic moment of a spinning electron with spin angular momentum $\hbar/2$. The approximately same magnetic moments in the two cases means the velocity-radius product of the orbital and the spinning electrons are about the same. With about the same speed-radius product, having the spin angular moment $(= \hbar/2)$ half of the orbital angular moment $(= \hbar)$ suggests that the bare UEG static mass m'_e of the spinning electron is about half of the total mass $m_e = 9.109 \times 10^{-31} kg$ of the orbiting electron.

$$m'_e \times (vr)_{\text{spin}} = \frac{\hbar}{2}, \ m_e \times (vr)_{\text{orbital}} = \hbar,$$

$$(vr)_{\text{spin}} = \frac{g}{2} \times (vr)_{\text{orbital}} \simeq (vr)_{\text{orbital}},$$

$$m'_e = \frac{m_e}{g} \simeq \frac{m_e}{2}. \tag{28}$$

With the assumption of $m'_e = m_e/2$ for the minimum stable mass in Figs.4,5, the value of the normalization constant m_μ can be calculated, from which the value of the UEG constant γ is estimated.

$$\frac{m'_e}{m_\mu} = \frac{m_e}{2m_\mu} = 1.5425,$$

$$m_\mu = \frac{m_e}{3.085} = 2.49 \times 10^{-30}\gamma^{-1/3},$$

$$\gamma^{1/3} = 3.085 \times 2.49 \times 10^{-30}/m_e,$$

$$\gamma = 5.997 \times 10^2 (m/s^2)/(J/m^3). \tag{29}$$

As per the UEG theory of the electron, the constant γ is declared to be a new natural constant, which is equal to a new gravitational acceleration in m/s^2 toward the center of gravity, produced due to one J/m^3 of energy density.

C. General Relationship Between the UEG Constant γ, the Particle Mass and Classical Radius.

The above estimate of the value of the UEG constant requires the actual UEG static mass m'_e of the electron. However, a general relationship between the smallest stable UEG static mass m'_e of an elementary particle, the corresponding classical radius r'_e, and the UEG constant γ required to produce the mass m'_e, can be derived based on the expressions for the reference mass m_μ (25) and reference radius r_μ (15) used in the above analysis.

$$\left(\frac{m_\mu}{m'_e}\right)^3 = \frac{3q^4}{64\pi c^4 \epsilon_0^2 \gamma m_e'^3} = \frac{3r_e'^2\pi}{\gamma m'_e},$$

$$\frac{\gamma m'_e}{r_e'^2} = 3\pi\left(\frac{m'_e}{m_\mu}\right)^3, \quad m'_e = \frac{q^2}{8\pi\epsilon_0 r'_e c^2}. \tag{30}$$

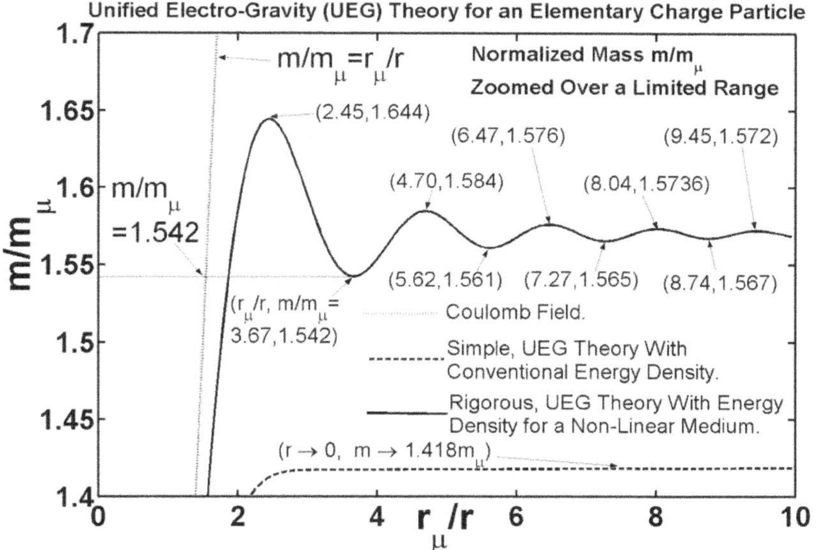

FIG. 5.

The value of the ratio $m/m_\mu = 1.5425$ from the Figs.4,5, for the smallest possible stable mass $m = m'_e$. Using this value, the γ, m'_e and r'_e may be related in term of a dimensionless constant.

$$\frac{\gamma m'_e}{r'^2_e} = 3\pi(\frac{m'_e}{m_\mu})^3 = 34.590 \quad . \tag{31}$$

If we simply assume the total mass m_e of the elementary particle with spin to be twice the UEG mass m'_e, and the classical radius r_e associated with m_e half of that ($= r'_e$) with m'_e, the γ, m_e and r_e may be related using a new dimensionless constant, which would be eight times the above constant.

$$\frac{\gamma m_e}{r^2_e} = 24\pi(\frac{m'_e}{m_\mu})^3 = 8 \times 34.590 = 276.720 \quad . \tag{32}$$

Notice that the above constant is close to twice the inverse-fine structure constant $1/\alpha = 137.036$, and the earlier constant in (31) is one fourth of the $1/\alpha$, with less than one percent of difference. It may be possible that the normalized stable mass in Figs.4,5 is not accurate. This may reflect possible inaccuracy in computation due to poor convergence of the power series in (25), when the normalized parameter t is sufficiently greater than unity (t is close to 7 at the smallest stable mass of Figs.4,5). More significantly, the small difference may also be due to lack of generality or rigor of the basic UEG static theory for the particle, presented in this paper with assumption of a simple UEG function in (11), and without including the particle's spin. The small difference may perhaps be related to the small difference between the actual value of the g-factor and its ideal value of 2 suggested in (27). This may point to possible physical origin of the g-factor associated with the spin, governed by a more rigorous version of the new UEG theory.

Leaving aside any small computational inaccuracy, or any small difference due to lack of generality or rigor of the basic UEG model, the close relations of the above dimensionless constant (31 or 32) to the fine-structure constant is intriguing. First, the very existence of a dimensionless constant based on the UEG theory, and its intriguing close numerological relationship with the known fine-structure constant α, may strongly suggest certain fundamental basis and significance of the new UEG theory. The close numerological relationship may also strongly suggest an explicit close relationship between the UEG constant γ associated with the dimensionless constant (31 or 32) from the UEG theory, and the particle's quantum-theoretical spin angular momentum $\hbar/2$ (consequently, the Planck's constant $\hbar$) associated with the fine-structure constant α. However, any modeling of a physically spinning particle is beyond the scope of the present UEG theory, which is valid only for a static charge. A more advanced modeling, extending the static UEG theory to model an electrodynamic problem of a physically spinning charge, would be needed in order to study any direct physical relationship between the UEG theory and the quantum spin theory (and quantum theory in general), and consequently between the associated dimensionless constant (31 or 32) and the fine-structure constant α, respectively.

V. SUMMARY AND FUTURE SCOPE.

A new unified electro-gravity (UEG) theory is presented to model an elementary charge particle, based on a non-linear permittivity function of the empty space around the charge, which is dependent on distribution of the energy density. A new fundamental physical constant γ, referred to as the UEG constant, is introduced in order to redefine the energy density around the charge, leading to a new gravitational field. The value of the constant γ is estimated to be about 600 $(m/s^2)/(J/m^3)$, by recognizing that the lightest possible elementary charge particle is an electron (or a positron). A fundamental dimensionless constant exists, relating the mass of an elementary charge particle, its classical radius, and the UEG constant γ required to produce the particle as the lightest possible stable particle based on the UEG theory. This dimensionless constant is shown to be closely related to the fine-structure constant α used in quantum electrodynamics [20, 23], with less than one percent of difference. This would strongly suggest a deeper fundamental basis of the UEG theory, with fundamental relationship with the quantum-mechanical concepts, that could possibly be extended to model any other elementary particles.

The basic UEG theory models only a static elementary charge without spin. Further, the energy density associated with the electric field around a charge, which is revised in this paper in terms of a new UEG function, is still not a uniquely-defined concept. The simple UEG theory used in this work may need to to be extended to model the electrodynamic problem of a spinning electron [11]. The theory may be further refined and extended using higher-order UEG functions to model other elementary charge particles [3, 21, 22], such as a proton, in the standard model of particle physics [2, 30]. The basic theory for a charged particle could also be extended for neutral particles composed of concentric layers of opposite charges, and similarly for other possible composite charged or neutral particles consisting of many layers of charge particles in definite concentric patterns. Accordingly, the fundamental basis of the new UEG theory may open research avenues, providing an alternate paradigm to the existing standard model of the particle physics. This could succeed in achieving the long-pending unification of the electromagnetism and gravity into one complete theory, which would allow modeling of all charged and neutral particles of the standard model without need for any other additional force, possibly making the weak and strong forces currently used in the standard model redundant.

[1] J. J. Thomson, Philosophical Magazine Series 5 **44**, 293 (1897).

[2] N. Cottingham and D. Greenwood, *An Introduction to the Standard Model of Particle Physics (2Ed)* (Cambridge University Press, 2007).

[3] Wikipedia, "Leptons, Table of Leptons," `http://en.wikipedia.org/wiki/Lepton`, Retrieved (2013).

[4] E. Rotherford, Philosophical Magazine, Series 6 **21**, 669 (1911).

[5] N. Bohr, "Nobel Lecture: The Structure of the Atom," Nobel Foundation: (Retrieved August 2017) `http://www.nobelprize.org/nobel_prizes/physics/laureates/1922/bohr-lecture.html` (1922).

[6] P. J. Mohr, B. N. Taylor, and D. B. Newell, Review of Modern Physics **88**, 1 (2016).

[7] R. A. Millikan, Physical Review (Series I) **32**, 349 (1911).

[8] G. Gabrielse and D. Hanneke, CERN Courier **46**, 35 (2006).

[9] E. Schrodinger, Annalen der Physik **384**, 361 (1926).

[10] R. de L. Kronig and W. G. Penney, Proceedings of the Royal Society A **130**, 499 (1931).

[11] P. A. M. Dirac, Proceedings of the Royal Society A: Mathematical, Physical and Engineering Sciences **117**, 610 (1928).

[12] R. P. Feynman, Physical Review **80**, 440 (1950).

[13] E. J. Eichten, M. E. Peskin, and M. Peskin, Physical Review Letters **50**, 811 (1983).

[14] R. P. Feynman, R. B. Leighton, and M. Sands, *Lectures on Physics, Vol.II, Ch.28* (Addision Wesley, 1964).

[15] S. Ramo, J. R. Whinnery, and T. V. Duzer, *Fields and Waves in Communication Electronics, 3rd Edition* (John Wiley and Sons, 1993).

[16] C. A. de Coulomb, Histoire de l'Acadimie Royale des Sciences , 569 (1785).

[17] C. A. de Coulomb, Histoire de l'Acadimie Royale des Sciences , 578 (1785).

[18] S. I. Newton, *Principia: Mathematical Principles of Natural Philosophy. I. B. Cohen, A. Whitman and J. Budenz, English Translators from 1726 Original* (University of California Press, 1999).

[19] S. I. Newton and S. Hawking, *Principia* (Running Press, 2005).

[20] A. Sommerfeld, *Atomic Structure and Spectral Lines. (Translated by H. L. Brose)* (Methuen, 1923).

[21] Wikipedia, "List of Baryons," `http://en.wikipedia.org/wiki/List_of_baryons`, Retrieved (2013).

[22] Wikipedia, "List of Mesons," `http://en.wikipedia.org/wiki/List_of_mesons`, Retrieved (2013).

[23] R. P. Feynman, *QED: The Strange Theory of Light and Matter (p. 129)* (Princeton University Press, 1985).

[24] M. H. McGregor, *The Power of Alpha (p. 69)* (World Scientific, 2007).

[25] A. Einstein, Annalen der Physik **354**, 769 (1916).

[26] H. A. Wilson, Physical Review **17**, 54 (1921).

[27] R. F. Harrington, *Time Harmonic Electromagnetic Fields* (McGraw-Hill Co., 1984).

[28] J. D. Jackson, *Classical Electrodynamics, 2 Ed.* (John Wiley and Sons, New York, 1975).

[29] M. Abramowitz and I. Stegun (Editors), *Handbook of Mathematical Functions: Bessel Functions of Integer Order* (Cambridge University Press, 1964).

[30] M. D. Schwartz, *Quantun Field Theory and the Standard Model* (Cambridge University Press, 2013).

A Generalized Unified Electro-Gravity (UEG) Model Applicable to All Elementary Particles

Nirod K. Das

Department of Electrical and Computer Engineering, Tandon School of Engineering,
New York University, 5 Metrotech Center, Brooklyn, NY 11201

(Dated: May 9, 2018; Revised December 20, 2018)

The Unified Electro-Gravity (UEG) theory, originally developed to model an electron, is generalized to model a variety of composite charged as well as neutral particles, which may constitute all known elementary particles of particle physics. A direct extension of the UEG theory for the electron is possible by modifying the functional dependence between the electro-gravitational field and the energy density, which would lead to a general class of basic charged particles carrying different levels of mass/energy, with the electron mass at the lowest level. The basic theory may also be extended to model simple composite neutral particles, consisting of two layers of surface charges of equal magnitudes but opposite signs. The model may be similarly generalized to synthesize more complex structures of composite charged or neutral particles, consisting of increasing levels of charged layers. Depending upon its specific basic or composite structure, a particle could be highly stable like an electron or a proton, or relatively unstable in different degrees, which may be identified with other known particles of the standard model of particle physics. The generalized UEG model may provide a new unified paradigm for particle physics, as a substitute for the standard model currently used, making the weak and strong forces of the standard model redundant.

I. INTRODUCTION

The Unified Electro-Gravity (UEG) theory was successfully established in [1] to model an ideal "static electron," without spin. In this theory, the electro-gravitational field, referred to as the UEG field, is assumed to be proportional to the energy density, with the constant of proportionality referred to as the UEG constant. Stable solutions in this model include discrete levels of mass/energy, where the lowest possible mass/energy state is recognized as a static electron, and differences between the energy levels are found to be small as compared to the energy of the electron. From the solutions, it is clear that the basic form of the theory [1] can neither model a proton, which is another stable charged particle in common occurrence, with significantly larger mass than electron, nor a neutron, which is also in common occurrence but carries a zero total charge, nor many other known charged or neutral particles in the standard model of particle physics. In order that the UEG theory can be established as a truly unified theory, it needs to generalized for application to all known charged or neutral particles.

The UEG theory may be extended by having the UEG field to be dependent on higher powers of the energy density, expressed in terms of a general function of the energy density, referred to as a UEG function. With a suitable form of the UEG function, stable solutions for a charged particle with higher levels of mass/energy would be possible, where a stable solution in the next higher level following the electron maybe identified as a proton. The general UEG function may be properly approximated, with discrete values of the UEG function for the different levels of the stable solutions. A general UEG model with such a discretized approximation of the general UEG function maybe treated analytically equivalent

to a basic UEG model of [1] with a fixed UEG constant, by associating different discrete values of the UEG constant to the different levels of stable mass. Accordingly, the derivations and results in the basic UEG model of the electron [1] maybe directly applicable to model the higher levels of stable particles, by simply substituting the UEG constant with a specific different value for a different level of stable mass. Consequently, a fundamental dimensionless constant, which relates the UEG constant, the stable mass and the associated classical radius, as established in [1] in relation to the fine structure constant, would in principle remain valid for all levels of the stable solutions. This would be a significant development, which would indicate that the UEG theory, to which the dimensionless fine-structure constant may trace its fundamental origin, can be much general in its scope of application to a broad class of - possibly all - charged particles, independent of any specific configuration or mass of the particle.

The derivations of the UEG theory of [1] may also be extended, with reasonable additional effort, to model a general class of composite neutral particles, consisting of a general internal charge structure which is enclosed by an external layer of charge of equal magnitude but opposite in sign, as compared to the total internal charge. A special class of such neutral particles (the zeroth kind) may be identified as neutrinos, when two oppositely charged layers are very closely spaced, resulting in significantly lower mass of the neutral particles than those associated with their internal charge structure without the external charge layer. A composite neutral particle, made of a negative charge layer that encloses a positively-charged layer of a proton, having the total mass close to that of the proton, maybe identified as a neutron. The mass/energy of any general composite neutral particle may be related to that of the internal charge structure, and values of different critical energies, using simple formulations, based on the results of [1]. For a special configuration of the neutral particles (the first kind), the above formulations may need to be numerically solved. In this case, the factor (meson factor) relating the mass of a synthesized neutral particle and that associated with its internal charge structure maybe numerically calculated, that can be tabulated or plotted in a general normalized form for convenient use to model any neutral particle of the special kind.

The above modelings may be extended, formulated in the most general form, to model increasingly complex structures of composite charged or neutral particles. They can be synthesized using multiple charge layers, arranged in multiple levels and sub-levels (shells), and be associated with different orders of stability depending on the specific structure. Such a large class of general particles maybe identified with all known particles in the standard model of particle physics. Depending on the specific charge structure and associated stability, a particle may be identified as a baryon, meson, lepton, or a basic boson, representing all observed particles covered by the standard model of particle physics [2–4]. Such a generalized UEG model would provide a new paradigm that may completely replace the standard model, making the basic weak and strong forces of the standard model [5, 6] redundant. In other words, the electromagnetic and gravitational forces, which were successfully unified through the basic UEG theory of [1], could be effectively unified as well with the hypothetical weak and strong forces of particle physics, through the generalization established in the present work. That would be a remarkable development in modern physics.

All the models presented in the paper are explicitly valid for ideal static particles, that do not include spin. The Planck's constant, which is twice the spin angular momentum of a fermionic (baryon and lepton) particle, should be indirectly related to the UEG constant through their shared relationship with the fine-structure constant, discussed earlier. This may suggest that spin dynamics, described by the Planck's constant, could be closely related to the UEG theory. Accordingly, the UEG theory could conceivably be extended to dynamic modeling of a spinning particle at any general level, where the central acceleration of the spinning particle would be supported by the UEG effects of the particle's own electric and magnetic fields. Such an extended dynamic UEG model maybe separately explored [7], beyond the scope of the present paper. However, for useful mass estimations in this paper, we may simply assume that the total mass/energy of an elementary spinning charge at any given level is about twice that of a static charge at the level without the spin [1, 7]. Accordingly, for all calculations in this paper, the mass in a given level maybe assumed to be twice or equal to the UEG static mass [1] in the particular level, depending on if the spin contribution in the level is included or not, respectively.

II. A GENERAL UEG THEORY, WITH HIGHER ORDER FUNCTIONAL DEPENDENCE OF THE UEG ACCELERATION ON ENERGY DENSITY

In the basic UEG theory of [1], the UEG acceleration $\overline{E}_g = -\frac{4\pi G}{c^2}\overline{U} = -\frac{4\pi G}{c^2}\zeta W_\tau \hat{r}$ was expressed in the simplest form, proportional to the energy density W_τ, with the proportionality constant $\gamma = \frac{4\pi G}{c^2}\zeta$. The basic UEG theory of [1] may be extended using a general functional form of the function $\overline{U} = \hat{r}U(W_\tau)$, dependent on the energy density W_τ. This may be treated as equivalent to substituting the UEG constant parameter γ used in [1] with a general UEG function $\gamma(W_\tau)$. For analytical simplicity, the UEG function $\gamma(W_\tau)$ maybe treated with a "stair-case" approximation, having different discrete values of γ for different ranges of the flux density D, or for the corresponding ranges of the radial distance r, as shown in Fig.1.

$$\overline{U} = \hat{r}U(W_\tau) = \hat{r}\zeta(W_\tau)W_\tau,$$

$$\overline{\nabla} \cdot \overline{E}_g = -\frac{4\pi G}{c^2}(W_\tau + \overline{\nabla} \cdot \overline{U}) \simeq -\frac{4\pi G}{c^2}\overline{\nabla} \cdot \overline{U}$$

$$= -\frac{4\pi G}{c^2}\overline{\nabla} \cdot (\hat{r}\zeta(W_\tau)W_\tau) = -\overline{\nabla} \cdot (\gamma(W_\tau)W_\tau\hat{r}) \quad . \quad (1)$$

$$\gamma(W_\tau) = \frac{4\pi G}{c^2}\zeta(W_\tau) = \gamma_1 \frac{1+\alpha_1' W_\tau^2 + \alpha_2' W_\tau^4 + \alpha_3' W_\tau^6 + \cdots}{1+\alpha_1 W_\tau^2 + \alpha_2 W_\tau^4 + \alpha_3 W_\tau^6 + \cdots}$$

$$= \gamma_1 \frac{(1+(\frac{W_\tau}{W_{\tau 10}'})^2)(1+(\frac{W_\tau}{W_{\tau 20}'})^2)(1+(\frac{W_\tau}{W_{\tau 30}'})^2)\cdots}{(1+(\frac{W_\tau}{W_{\tau 10}})^2)(1+(\frac{W_\tau}{W_{\tau 20}})^2)(1+(\frac{W_\tau}{W_{\tau 30}})^2)\cdots}$$

$$\cong \gamma_1 \frac{(1+(\frac{D}{D_{10}'})^4)(1+(\frac{D}{D_{20}'})^4)(1+(\frac{D}{D_{30}'})^4)\cdots}{(1+(\frac{D}{D_{10}})^4)(1+(\frac{D}{D_{20}})^4)(1+(\frac{D}{D_{30}})^4)\cdots}$$

$$= \gamma_1 \frac{(1+(\frac{r_{10}'}{r})^8)(1+(\frac{r_{20}'}{r})^8)(1+(\frac{r_{30}'}{r})^8)\cdots}{(1+(\frac{r_{10}}{r})^8)(1+(\frac{r_{20}}{r})^8)(1+(\frac{r_{30}}{r})^8)\cdots}, \quad (2)$$

$$\gamma \simeq \gamma_1,\ r > r_{10};\ \gamma \simeq \gamma_2 = \gamma_1(\frac{r_{10}'}{r_{10}})^8,\ r_{10} > r > r_{20};$$

$$\gamma \simeq \gamma_3 = \gamma_1(\frac{r_{10}'}{r_{10}})^8(\frac{r_{20}'}{r_{20}})^8,\ r_{20} > r > r_{30}; \quad (3)$$

$$\gamma \simeq \gamma_i = \gamma_1(\frac{r_{10}'}{r_{10}})^8(\frac{r_{20}'}{r_{20}})^8 \cdots (\frac{r_{(i-1)0}'}{r_{(i-1)0}})^8,\ r_{(i-1)0} > r > r_{i0}.$$

The basic mass (energy) function $m(r)$ ($W(r) = m(r)c^2$), which is the total mass (energy) of an elementary spherical charge layer placed at radius r, and the inverse relative-permittivity function $\epsilon_r(r)$ which is the inverse of the relative permittivity seen at the charge layer at radius r, maybe derived (see the sketches in Figs.2, 3) using the basic UEG theory of [1], based on the stair-case approximation of (3) for the γ. The radii where the mass function is stable would represent stable elementary charge particles. The mass and radii of such stable

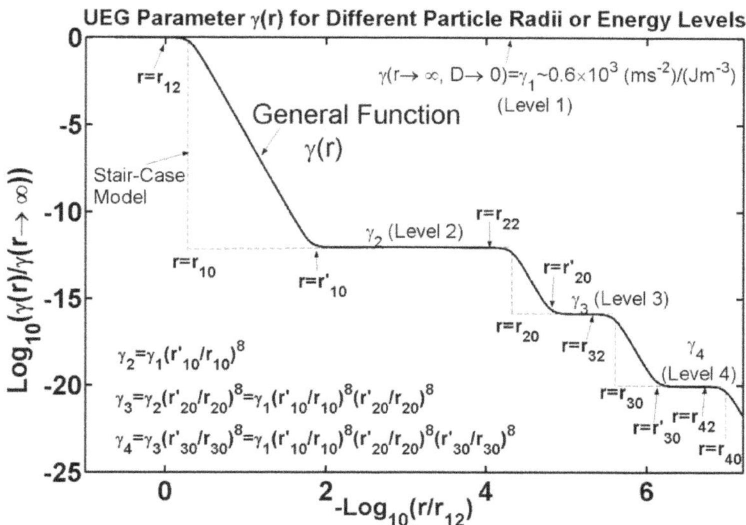

FIG. 1.

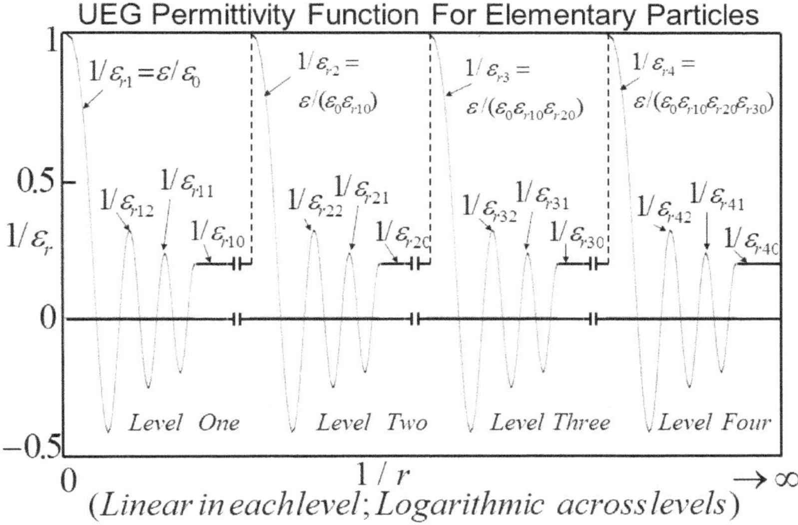

FIG. 2.

charged particles may be indexed as m_{ij} and r_{ij}, respectively, in reference to a particular level i of the general UEG theory, and a particular shell j ($= 1, 2$) in the given level (see Figs.4, 5).

Note that the mass profile $m(r)$ in a given level i refers to an ideal derivation in the absence of all levels lower than i, with a fixed UEG constant γ for the given level that is valid for all r to infinite distance. However, in the presence of a neighboring lower level $(i-1)$, the mass $m(r)$ associated with the level i needs to be properly truncated at the boundary of the level $(i-1)$ at $r = r_{(i-1)0}$, resulting in the effective truncated mass $m_t(r)$ to be valid only for $r < r_{(i-1)0}$, with an initial condition $m_t(r = r_{(i-1)0}) = 0$, and $m_t(r < r_{(i-1)0})$ equal to $m(r) - m(r = r_{(i-1)0})$. Therefore, to be particular, any mass $m_{ij} = m(r = r_{ij})$ listed in Table V actually refers to the respective truncated value $m_t(r = r_{ij})$, which would be exactly and approximately equal to its ideal non-truncated value, respectively for levels 1 and 2, but be somewhat lower than the ideal value for levels 3 and 4.

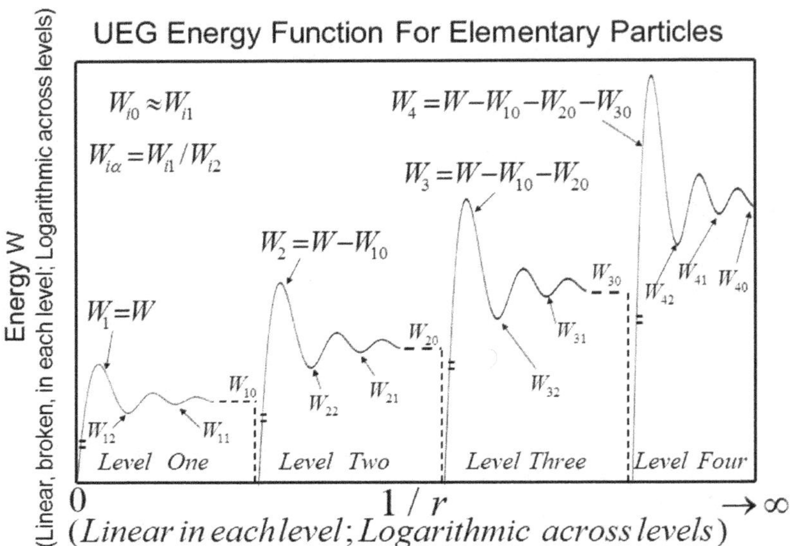

FIG. 3.

In addition to the stable elementary charge particles, various kinds of neutral particles that carry zero total charge, as well as various composite charge particles combining the neutral and the stable elementary particles, can be synthesized based on certain basic principles of the UEG theory [1]. A basic neutral particle may consist of two elementary charges of opposite signs, placed at two different radii. Alternatively, a neutral particle may consist of an internal composite charge ($\pm q$) structure surrounded by an external elementary charge ($\mp q$) layer, with zero total charge. This way a large number of particles could be synthesized from the UEG theory, consisting of all particles (leptons, baryons and mesons) as well as different force carriers (bosons), and possibly even other particles that have not yet been discovered or are not practically realized because suitable decay paths might not be realized in particle-collision experiments. Such particle synthesis using the UEG theory would provide a complete, alternate model to the existing standard model of the particle physics [5, 6].

The stability of a neutral or a composite charge particles is determined by the stability of the individual parts of its total structure. Accordingly, such particles may be stable or "quasi-stable" depending on if all or most parts are definitively stable, while any remaining parts are only quasi-stable. The two different kinds of stability of the parts, referred to here, are analogous to having a massive particle on earth placed inside a bowl, or on top of an inverted bowl, where the first kind is definitively stable and the second kind is conditionally stable or quasi-stable. A quasi-stable state would represent a transient state that would decay into stable particles, or other quasi-stable particles that are relatively more stable, having lower total mass/energy. Even a definitively stable particles, with availability of enough energy to overcome its local "en-

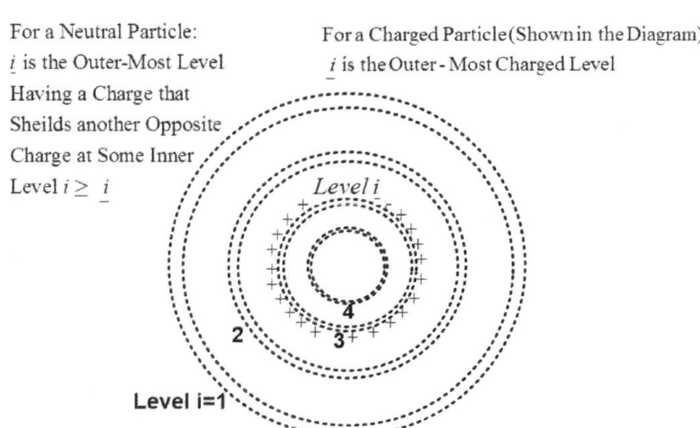

Energy Levels of Particles Associated With Distinct Levels of Radial Regions

FIG. 4.

ergy valley", may decay into other stable or quasi-stable particles of lower mass/energy. This will determine possible decay paths and associated transient times for the different particles.

In the following we will separately discuss the individual types of neutral or composite charge particles.

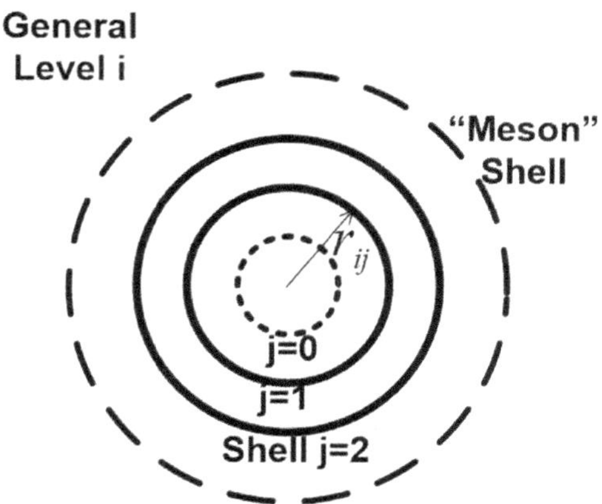

Details of the Radial Region for One Energy Level (i), Having Shells (j)

of Finer Structures with Critical Radii r_{ij} and Associated Mass/Energy Sub-

Levels m_{ij}

FIG. 5.

III. NEUTRINO: A NEUTRAL PARTICLE OF THE ZEROTH KIND, WITH OPPOSITELY CHARGED LAYERS CLOSE TO EACH OTHER.

A. Neutrino for the First Level, Based on the Basic UEG Model

We will first consider the basic UEG model, which is applicable to the level one. Similar results can then be extended to the general UEG model as applicable to any higher level.

The inverse-permittivity function $\epsilon_r(r)$ (see Fig.2) of the basic UEG theory [1] (or a general UEG theory for any higher level) oscillates around $\epsilon_r = 0$. Given $\epsilon_r(r = r_{n0}) = 0$, two layers of opposite charges at radii close to but slightly (infinitesimally) larger than r_{n0}, $r_2 > r_1 > r_{n0}$, would produce a stable synthesized neutral particle having a relatively small, non-zero mass. Such a particle is recognized as an electron neutrino [8–10]. The oppositely charge layers in the above configuration, when they are closely spaced around any other radii where $\epsilon_r \neq 0$ would result in a theoretically stable body but with a zero mass/energy. It may be noted, if the two radii r_1 and r_2, $r_2 > r_1$, are close to each other but both are smaller than r_{n0}, it can be shown to result in a negative, unstable energy. This case is not considered in the following detailed analyses because the resulting negative, unstable energy would not represent any physical particle.

Based on the UEG theory [1], given the mass $m(r)$ and the inverse relative-permittivity $\epsilon_r(r)$ profiles of an elementary charge particle, the mass $m_{sn}(r_1, r_2)$ of a composite neutral body, synthesized with two elementary charges ($\pm q$) of opposite signs, placed at radii r_2 and r_1, $r_2 > r_1$, can be expressed as:

$$m_{sn}(r_1, r_2) = [m(r_1) - m(r_2)]/\epsilon_r(r_2), \quad r_1 < r_2. \quad (4)$$

The electric fields due to the two layers of charges of equal magnitude but opposite signs would cancel with each other, resulting in zero total field and its associated energy density, in the external region ($r > r_2$). Accordingly, the equivalent mass $m(r_2)$ associated with the energy in the external region, produced due the inner charge layer ($+q$) placed at $r = r_1$ (without presence of the outer charge ($-q$) layer at $r = r_2$), is first subtracted in (4) from the total mass/energy $m(r_1)$. Further, the inverse relative-permittivity ϵ_r in the external region ($r > r_2$) of the composite neutral body is assumed to be unity, which needs to be continuous with that in the region between the two charge layers across the external boundary at $r = r_2$. Therefore, the original $\epsilon_r(r)$ function due to the the inner charge ($+q$) (without presence of the external charge ($-q$)) needs to be scaled by multiplying it with the factor $1/\epsilon_r(r = r_2)$, in order to obtain the new inverse relative-permittivity function of the composite neutral particle that would be valid in the region between its two charge layers $r_1 < r < r_2$. Consequently, the original energy content ($m(r_1) - m(r_2)$) between the two charge layers, as discussed above, also needs to be multiplied by the same factor ($1/\epsilon_r(r = r_2)$) in order to find the actual new mass of the composite neutral particle. This is because the mass/energy scales in proportion to the inverse relative permittivity [1].

Now, based on (4), the m_{sn} would be zero as $r_1 \to r_2$, except when $\epsilon_r(r_2)$ is zero.

$$r_1 \to r_2, \quad m_{sn} \to 0, \quad \epsilon_r(r_2) \neq 0;$$
$$m_{sn} \neq 0, \quad \epsilon_r(r_2) \to \epsilon_r(r_{n0}) = 0. \quad (5)$$

An approximate model for the $m(r)$ and $\epsilon_r(r)$ near $r = r_{n0}$ may be used, in order to simplify the model for the resulting mass m_{sn} of the synthesized neutral particle, and its derivative with respect to r, from which specific conclusions may be conveniently established. Note that the derivatives of $m(r)$ and $\epsilon_r(r)$ with radius r, at $r = r_{n0}$, are of opposite signs (see Figs.2, 3 and [1]), represented by the variables $\pm\alpha$ and $\mp\beta$; $\alpha, \beta > 0$, respectively.

$$r = r_{n0} + \delta r, \quad r_2 = r_{n0} + \delta r_2, \quad r_1 = r_{n0} + \delta r_1,$$
$$m(r) \simeq m(r_{n0}) \pm \alpha(\delta r) = m_0 \pm \alpha(\delta r), \quad \alpha > 0,$$
$$\epsilon_r(r) = \epsilon_r(r_{n0}) \mp \beta(\delta r) = \mp\beta(\delta r), \quad \epsilon_r(r_{n0}) = 0, \quad \beta > 0,$$
$$m_{sn}(\delta r_1, \delta r_2) = [m(r_1) - m(r_2)]/\epsilon_r(r_2)$$
$$= [\pm\alpha(\delta r_1) \mp \alpha(\delta r_2)]/(\mp\beta(\delta r_2)) = \frac{\alpha}{\beta}[1 - \frac{\delta r_1}{\delta r_2}];$$
$$\frac{\partial m_{sn}}{\partial(\delta r_2)} > 0, \quad \delta r_1 > 0; \quad \frac{\partial m_{sn}}{\partial(\delta r_1)} < 0; \quad \delta r_2 > 0. \quad (6)$$

As mentioned earlier, we assume $r_2 \geq r_1$ as required or assumed in the above mass formula.

$$r_2 \geq r_1; \ r_2 = r_{n0} + \delta r_2,$$
$$r_1 = r_{n0} + \delta r_1, \ \delta r_2 \geq \delta r_1. \tag{7}$$

When $r_2 = r_1 = r_{sn}$, the resulting m_{sn} of (6) can be shown to be zero, as anticipated earlier, for all r_{sn} other than $r_{sn} = r_{n0}$, or for all $\delta rn \neq 0$.

$$\delta r_2 = \delta r_{2n}, \ \delta r_1 = \delta r_{1n}; \ r_1 = r_{sn1}, \ r_2 = r_{sn2};$$
$$r_{sn1} \leq r_{sn2}, \ \delta r_{1n} \leq \delta r_{2n};$$
$$r_{sn1} = r_{sn2} = r_{sn}; \ \delta r_{2n} = \delta r_{1n} = \delta rn, \ r_{sn} = r_{n0} + \delta rn;$$
$$m_{sn}(\delta r_1 = \delta r_{1n} = \delta rn, \delta r_2 = \delta r_{2n} = \delta rn)$$
$$= \frac{\alpha}{\beta}[1 - \frac{\delta r_{1n}}{\delta r_{2n}}] = 0, \ \delta rn \neq 0. \tag{8}$$

Following the above case with $r_1 = r_2 = r_{sn}$, only when $r_{sn} > r_{n0}$, $\delta rn > 0$, it is a stable point as can be shown from the derivative of the approximate mass expression (6) . Note that when $r_1 = r_2$, the stability condition is different from a standard stability condition (having the first derivative of the energy/mass function with respect to the radius equal to zero and the second derivative negative for both the radius variables r_1 and r_2) used elsewhere when $r_1 \neq r_2$. In this case with $r_1 = r_2 = r_{sn}$, we need a positive energy derivative with respect to r_2 for r_2 larger than the stable point, and a negative derivative with r_1, for r_1 less than the stable point (so called, a "V" type of stability).

$$r_{sn} = r_{n0} + \delta rn > r_{n0}; \ \delta r_{2n} = \delta r_{1n} = \delta rn > 0,$$
$$\frac{\partial m_{sn}}{\partial(\delta r_2)} > 0, \ \delta r_1 = \delta rn > 0;$$
$$\frac{\partial m_{sn}}{\partial(\delta r_1)} < 0, \ \delta r_2 = \delta rn > 0. \tag{9}$$

Consider the limiting case, when the above stable point r_{sn} approaches r_{n0} from the larger side, which is equivalent to having δrn positively approaching zero ($\delta rn \to 0_+$). More specifically, we have $\delta r_{2n} \geq \delta r_{1n} \geq 0$, and they both approach the same value $\delta rn = 0$, but the δr_{1n} is closer to zero than the δr_{2n}. The limiting stable mass in this case is not necessarily zero, having a range of possible positive values between zero and (α/β).

$$m_{sn}(\delta r_{1n}, \delta r_{2n}) = \frac{\alpha}{\beta}[1 - \frac{\delta r_{1n}}{\delta r_{2n}}], \ \delta r_{1n} \leq \delta r_{2n};$$
$$\frac{\alpha}{\beta} \geq m_{sn}((\delta r_{1n} \to 0) \leq \delta r_{2n}, \delta r_{2n} \to 0) \geq 0. \tag{10}$$

It may also be noted, that the original inverse relative-permittivity $\epsilon_r(r)$, which is unity at $r \to \infty$, corresponds to a standard light speed $c(r \to \infty) = c_0$. In contrast, the scaled inverse relative-permittivity $\epsilon_r(r)/\epsilon_r(r = r_2)$, valid for $r_1 \leq r \leq r_2$ between the charges at radii $r = r_1, r_2$ (discussed earlier), is equal to $1/\epsilon_r(r = r_2)$ at $r \to \infty$, which is greater than unity in magnitude, approaching infinity for $r_2 \to r_{n0}$. The corresponding light speed in this case

$c(r \to \infty)$ is larger than the standard light speed c_0, approaching infinity for $r_2 \to r_{n0}$. Accordingly, the speed limit in the medium between the charges $r_1 \leq r \leq r_2$ is no longer governed by the standard light speed c_0, but by the new light speed $c(r \to \infty)$ which could approach infinity for $r_2 \to r_{n0}$. This would allow the charges to spin at speeds greater than c_0, even approaching infinite speed for $r_2 \to r_{n0}$. This is a remarkable new understanding, which would allow the neutral particle to have a significant, non-zero spin angular momentum (as expected from a fermion), even though the total mass is expected to be relatively small or negligible. Such a particle with a small mass, which could even approach zero, but with a non-zero spin angular momentum ($= \hbar/2$), may clearly be identified as an electron neutrino [8–10], which is a spin-half particle grouped under leptons in the standard model of particle physics [4, 6].

The ratio (α/β) in (10) maybe estimated based on the $m(r)$ and $\epsilon_r(r)$ profiles for the level 1 ([1], Figs.2, 3), to be of the order of 5000 eV or so. As per (10), this places only an upper limit, predicting the mass of an electron neutrino to be actually any value between zero and about 5000 eV, likely much smaller than the 5000eV limit, as per measured estimates [8]. The upper limit could also be significantly reduced by a more rigorous UEG model. A reference (data-fit) value of 50 eV ($= 0.5$Mev (electron mass) x 0.0001 (neutron factor)) for this upper limit is adopted in Table III, such that an extension of the UEG theory of the electron neutron to predict similar upper limits for the masses of the muon- and tauon- neutrinos, as presented in the following, would also be consistent with respective measured estimates (see Table III) [8].

B.   Neutrino at Higher Levels, Based on a General UEG Model

The above neutrino analysis using the basic UEG theory for the level 1, may be similarly extended to a general model applicable to any level. The resulting neutrino in the second and third levels may be identified as the muon and tau neutrinos, respectively [8, 11, 12]. For such a general model, the basic mass function $m(r)$ and inverse-permittivity function $\epsilon_r(r)$ in the above analysis maybe substituted by the respective functions $m_i(r)$ and $\epsilon_{ri}(r)$ for a particular level i. Accordingly, the final neutrino mass m_{sni} for the level i can be obtained from the mass m_{sn1} for the level 1 by simply multiplying m_{sn1} by a normalization factor m_{i2}/m_{12}.

$$m_{sni} = m_{sn1} m_{i2}/m_{12} = (m_{sn1}/m_{12}) \times m_{i2}. \tag{11}$$

(m_{sn1}/m_{12}) is a useful factor, referred as the neutrino factor, which describes the neutrino mass m_{sni} at a given level as a fraction of the mass m_{i2} of an elementary charge at the respective level.

It may also be noted that in the general higher-order UEG model, for notational and formulational convenience a synthesized neutral mass m_{sni} at any given level i is a standard theoretical mass which assumes that the surrounding external medium has a reference relative permittivity equal to that $(=(\epsilon_{r(i-1)0}\epsilon_{r(i-2)0}\cdots(\epsilon_{r00}=1)))$ seen by an elementary charge particle in the level i. This is a hypothetical situation. The actual mass in a practical case, when the external medium is the free space with $\epsilon_{r00}=1$, would be equal to the standard mass m_{sni} multiplied by the above reference relative permittivity.

$$m_{sni}(\text{actual}) = m_{sni}/$$
$$(\underline{\epsilon}_{r(i-1)0}\underline{\epsilon}_{r(i-2)0}\cdots\underline{\epsilon}_{r10}(\underline{\epsilon}_{r00}=1)). \qquad (12)$$

Such a relationship between an $m_{sni}(\text{actual})$ and its theoretical value m_{sni} would apply as well for any other kind of synthesized neutral particle, covered in the following sections IV and V.

IV. NEUTRAL PARTICLE OF THE FIRST KIND, WITH AN EXTERNAL CHARGE IN A "MESON SHELL", AND AN INTERNAL OPPOSITELY CHARGED BODY PLACED AT THE SAME OR A DIFFERENT LEVEL

A neutral particle may be synthesized with opposite charges placed at the same or different levels i and i'; $i' \geq i$. The charge at the inner level i' may be placed at a shell $j' = 1,2$ at a radius $r_{i'j'}$, and the opposite charge of the outer level i is placed at a special shell n referred to as the "neutral shell" or "meson shell", which is different from a regular shell $j = 1,2$. The name of this special shell is in reference to synthesis of mesons, which often uses this cell to produce relatively lower-mass particles (compared to baryons). Unlike the regular shells $j = 1,2$ that are defined with fixed radii r_{ij} pre-determined as per the basic UEG model, the meson shell radius r_{sni} for the synthesized neutral particle at the level i is a variable determined by the mass $m_{i'}$ of the internal charge particle and masses m_{k0} of all levels $i \leq k < i'$. The mass m_{sni} is stable at the radius r_{sni}, determined by having the first derivative of the mass with respect to the radius to be zero and the second derivative positive.

$$m_{sn}(r_{i'}, r_i) = (m_{i'}(r_{i'}) + m_{(i'-1)0} + m_{(i'-2)0}$$
$$+ \cdots + m_{i0} - m_i(r_i))/\underline{\epsilon}_{ri}(r_i), \; i' > i,$$
$$m_{sn}(r_{i'}, r_i) = (m_{i'}(r_{i'}) - m_i(r_i))/\underline{\epsilon}_{ri}(r_i), \; i' = i,$$
$$\frac{\partial m_{sn}}{\partial r_i} = \frac{\partial m_{sn}}{\partial r_{i'}} = 0, \; \frac{\partial^2 m_{sn}}{\partial r_i^2} > 0, \; \frac{\partial^2 m_{sn}}{\partial r_{i'}^2} > 0, \qquad (13)$$

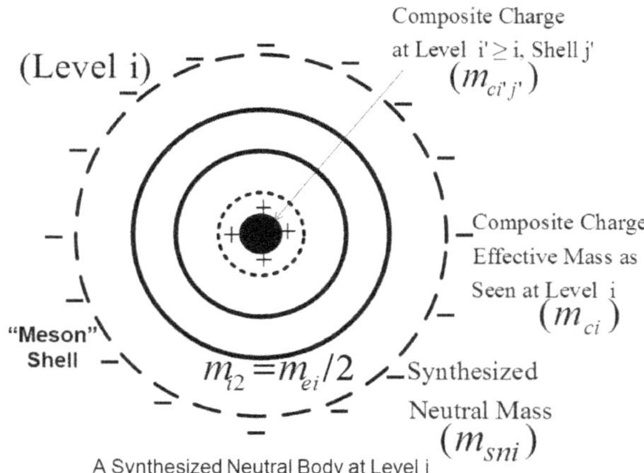

FIG. 6.

$$r_{i'} = r_{i'j'}, \; r_i = r_{sni}, \; i' \geq i, \; j' = 1,2,$$
$$m_{sni} = \text{Min}[(m_{i'j'} + m_{(i'-1)0} + m_{(i'-2)0}$$
$$+ \cdots + m_{i0} - m_i(r_i))/\underline{\epsilon}_{ri}(r_i)]r_i = r_{sni}$$
$$= (m_{i'j'} + m_{(i'-1)0} + m_{(i'-2)0}$$
$$+ \cdots + m_{i0} - m_i(r_{sni}))/\underline{\epsilon}_{ri}(r_{sni}), \; i' > i,$$
$$m_{sni} = \text{Min}[(m_{i'j'} - m_i(r_i))/\underline{\epsilon}_{ri}(r_i)]r_i = r_{sni}$$
$$= (m_{i'j'} - m_i(r_{sni}))/\underline{\epsilon}_{ri}(r_{sni}), \; i' = i. \qquad (14)$$

The expression of $m_{sn}(r_{i'}, r_i)$ in (13) is similar in principle to that of $m_{sn}(r_1, r_2)$ in (4), sharing the same basic concepts of the UEG theory [1]. With reference to (13), and Figs.2, 3 [1], for a given $r_{i'}$ the $m_i(r_i)$ increases, and therefore the numerator of m_{sn} reduces, whereas the factor $1/\underline{\epsilon}_{ri}(r_i)$ first remains relatively unchanged but then rapidly increases, as the radius r_i is reduced from $r_i \to \infty$ closer to the central core of the level i ($r_i > r_{i2}$). As we expected, a minimum (stable) value of the $m_{sn} = m_{sni}$ can be clearly established by balancing the two opposing trends indicated above, at a suitable location with $r_i = r_{sni}$ outside of the core region, referred to as the "meson shell".

Note that the standard theoretical value of m_{sni} in (14) needs to be properly scaled using (12), in order to obtain its actual value realized when the external medium is the free space with relative permittivity $\epsilon_{r00} = 1$.

General Neutral Particle of the First Kind, with a Regular or a Composite Charge at an Inner Level:

This is a general treatment for the primary kind of neutral particle discussed above. In this case, the inner level charge in the above model maybe substituted by a general charge with effective mass m_{ci} seen at the level i (see Fig.6), which may be a regular charge, or a general composite charge, in the same or different level. If the inner regular or composite charge is stable or quasi-stable without the external opposite charge, it would also be stable/quasi-stable with the external opposite charge. This should be evident from the formula for the synthesized neutral mass m_{sni}.

$$m_{sn}(r_i) = (m_{ci} - m_i(r_i))/\underline{\epsilon}_{ri}(r_i), \quad \frac{\partial m_{sn}}{\partial r_i} = 0, \quad \frac{\partial^2 m_{sn}}{\partial r_i^2} > 0,$$

$$r_i = r_{sni}, \quad m_{sni} = \mathrm{Min}[(m_{ci} - m_i(r_i))/\underline{\epsilon}_{ri}(r_i)]_{r_i=r_{sni}}$$

$$= (m_{ci} - m_i(r_{sni}))/\underline{\epsilon}_r(r_{sni}), \tag{15}$$

$$m_{sni}(\text{actual}) = m_{sni}/(\underline{\epsilon}_{r(i-1)0}\underline{\epsilon}_{r(i-2)0}\cdots\underline{\epsilon}_{r10}(\underline{\epsilon}_{r00}=1)),$$

$$m_{ci} = m_{ci'j'} + m_{(i'-1)0} + m_{(i'-2)0}\cdots + m_{i0}, \quad i' > i;$$

$$m_{ci} = m_{ci'j'}, \quad i' = i; \quad j' = 1, 2,$$

$$m_{ci} \geq m_{i2} = m_{ei}/2; \quad m_{sni} \simeq m_{ci}, \quad m_{ci} >> m_{ei}. \tag{16}$$

Normalized values for (m_{sni}/m_{ci}) versus $(2m_{ci}/m_{ei}) = (m_{ci}/m_{i2}) \geq 1$ are plotted in Fig.7, that maybe applicable for general use at all levels i. These plots are derived using the normalized functions $m_i(r_i/r_{i2})/m_{i2} = m(r/r_e)/m_e$ and $\underline{\epsilon}_{ri}(r_i/r_{i2}) = \underline{\epsilon}_r(r/r_e)$, which were originally derived from the UEG analysis [1] for the first level $i = 1$, but are assumed to be approximately valid as well for all levels. This is due to primary similarity of the basic UEG model in all levels. In principle, however, the chart in Fig.7 should be separately established with different best-fit data for each different level. This would accommodate secondary differences in the UEG function $\gamma(W_\tau)$, and in the associated mass $m_i(r_i/r_{i2})$ and inverse-permittivity $\underline{\epsilon}_{ri}(r_i/r_{i2})$ profiles, in the different levels, as well as differences in any inter-level interactions.

However, we will ignore the secondary deviations between the levels, and instead propose to use the same chart of Fig.7 for all levels. This would be accomplished by simply substituting the ideal non-truncated mass m_e in Fig.7 with the effective truncated mass $m_{i2} = W_{i2}/c^2$ from Table V (see section II, Fig.3), without having to introduce additional truncation parameters for each level. Any resulting deficiency in using the common chart of Fig.7, due to the above non-ideal substitution, appears to be approximately compensated by all the different secondary effects in the given level. This would allow uniform use of Fig.7 for all levels, maintaining the same required trend across the levels, resulting in a simplified mass estimation of any synthesized neutral body of the first kind.

V. NEUTRAL PARTICLE OF THE SECOND KIND, WITH THE EXTERNAL CHARGE PLACED IN A SHELL $j = 1, 2$

A second kind of a neutral charge may be synthesized with oppositely charged bodies placed in different levels i and i'; $i' \geq i$. The charged body in the internal level i' is associated with a shell $j' = 1, 2$, as in the first kind of neutral particle (meson, Fig.6) discussed above. However, unlike the first kind of neutral particle, in this case the charge layer in the external level is placed in a conventional shell $j = 1, 2$, not in the "meson shell". For a special case, if i' and i maybe the same level, then $j' < j$, which means that the j' is the internal shell whereas j is the external shell of the common level $i' = i$.

The charged body in the internal level i' has two possibilities. In the first group, it is a layer of a standard elementary charge of mass $m_{i'j'}$, located at radius $r_{i'j'}$, with $i' > i$.

$$m_{sn}(r_{i'}, r_i) = [m_{i'}(r_{i'}) + m_{(i'-1)0} + m_{(i'-2)0}$$

$$+ \cdots + m_{i0} - m_i(r_i)]/\underline{\epsilon}_{ri}(r_i), \quad i' > i \ ,$$

$$\frac{\partial m_{sn}}{\partial r_{i'}} = \frac{\partial m_{sn}}{\partial r_i} = 0, \quad \frac{\partial^2 m_{sn}}{\partial r_{i'}^2} > 0, \quad \frac{\partial^2 m_{sn}}{\partial r_i^2} > 0,$$

$$r_{i'} = r_{i'j'}, \quad r_i = r_{ij}, \quad i' > i; \quad j, j' = 1, 2,$$

$$m_{sni} = (m_{i'j'} + m_{(i'-1)0} + m_{(i'-2)0}$$

$$+ \cdots + m_{i0} - m_{ij})/\underline{\epsilon}_{rij}, \tag{17}$$

$$m_{sni}(\text{actual}) = m_{sni}/(\underline{\epsilon}_{r(i-1)0}\underline{\epsilon}_{r(i-2)0}\cdots\underline{\epsilon}_{r10}(\underline{\epsilon}_{r00}=1)).$$

The expression of $m_{sn}(r_{i'}, r_i)$ in (17) is similar in principle to that of $m_{sn}(r_{i'}, r_i)$ in (13), and of $m_{sn}(r_1, r_2)$ in (4), sharing the same basic concepts of the UEG theory [1].

General Neutral Particle of the Second Kind, with the External Charge Placed in a Shell $j = 1, 2$:

This is the second group of neutral particles of the second kind, following the first group discussed above. This second group is essentially a general treatment of the first group of particles, by replacing the inner charge layer by a composite charge particle of mass $m_{ci'j'}$. If the composite charge is stable/quasi-stable without the external opposite charge, the total neutral charge including the external opposite charge would also be stable/quasi-stable.

$$m_{sn}(r_i) = [m_{ci} - m_i(r_i)]/\underline{\epsilon}_{ri}(r_i),$$

$$m_{ci} = m_{ci'j'}, \quad i' = i;$$

$$m_{ci} = m_{ci'j'} + m_{(i'-1)0} + m_{(i'-2)0}$$

$$+ \cdots + m_{i0}, \quad i' > i; \quad j' = 1, 2,$$

$$\frac{\partial m_{sn}}{\partial r_i} = 0, \quad \frac{\partial^2 m_{sn}}{\partial r_i^2} > 0; \quad r_i = r_{ij}, \quad j = 1, 2;$$

$$m_{sni} = (m_{ci} - m_{ij})/\underline{\epsilon}_{rij}, \tag{18}$$

$$m_{sni}(\text{actual}) = m_{sni}/(\underline{\epsilon}_{r(i-1)0}\underline{\epsilon}_{r(i-2)0}\cdots\underline{\epsilon}_{r10}(\underline{\epsilon}_{r00}=1)).$$

VI. COMPOSITE CHARGED PARTICLES

A composite charged particle consists of an elementary charge layer at a radius $r = r_{ij}$, at a particular level i

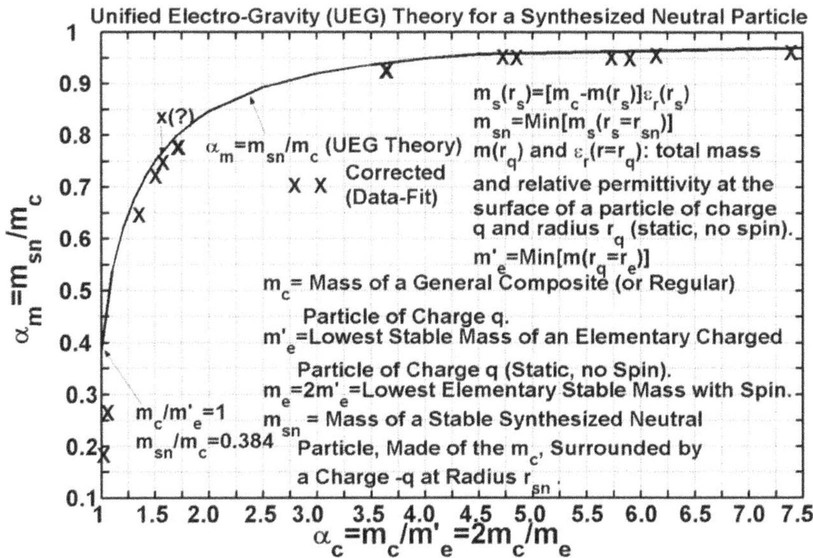

FIG. 7.

and shell j, together with a synthesized neutral particle placed internal to this charged layer at level i'. The mass or energy of the total particle is quasi-stable at the radius r, defined by the derivative of the mass with the r to be zero, whereas the second derivative may be positive or negative for the part of the mass contributed by the external charge layer or the internal synthesized neutral body, respectively. Due to the quasi-stable nature of the particle, the particle is associated with a transient state that would naturally decay to other particles of lower mass. The mass m_{cij} of such a composite particle may be expressed in terms of the mass m_{ij} of an elementary charge particle at the particular level and shell (ij), with radius r_{ij}, and the mass $m_{sni'}$ of the synthesized neutral particle at the level i' (see Fig.8). The level i' is normally greater than the level i, but it maybe at the same level as i if the synthesized neutral particle is of the second kind (see section V), and the shell j' of the outermost charge layer of the synthesized neutral particle is internal to the shell j ($j' < j$).

$$m_{ci}(r) = m_i(r) + m_{sni'}\varepsilon_{ri}(r),\ i' = i;$$
$$m_{ci}(r) = m_i(r) +$$
$$m_{sni'}\varepsilon_{ri}(r)/(\varepsilon_{r(i'-1)0}\varepsilon_{r(i'-2)0}\cdots\varepsilon_{ri0}),\ i' > i;$$
$$\frac{\partial m_{ci}}{\partial r} = 0,\ \frac{\partial m_i}{\partial r} = 0,\ \frac{\partial^2 m_i}{\partial r^2} > 0,$$
$$\frac{\partial \varepsilon_{ri}}{\partial r} = 0,\ \frac{\partial^2 \varepsilon_{ri}}{\partial r^2} < 0, \tag{19}$$

$$r = r_{ij},\ m_{cij} = m_{ij} + m_{sni'}\varepsilon_{rij},\ i' = i;$$
$$m_{cij} = m_{ij} + \tag{20}$$
$$m_{sni'}\varepsilon_{rij}/(\varepsilon_{r(i'-1)0}\varepsilon_{r(i'-2)0}\cdots\varepsilon_{ri0}),\ i' > i.$$

It may be noted that, for notational and formulational convenience, the mass m_{ij} or m_{cij}, respectively of an elementary or a composite charged particle at a given level i, refers to only a theoretical number which is the contribution of mass at the given level i and internal to the level. The actual mass, if there is no other charge layer external to the level i, would be equal to this reference theoretical mass plus sum of masses m_{k0} associated with all levels $k < i$.

$$m_{cij}(\text{actual}) = m_{cij},\ i = 1;$$
$$m_{cij}(\text{actual}) = m_{cij} +$$
$$m_{(i-1)0} + m_{(i-2)0} + \cdots + m_{10},\ i > 1. \tag{21}$$

VII. CALCULATIONS FOR KNOWN PARTICLES USING THE GENERALIZED UEG THEORY

We will apply the generalized UEG theory that we have developed to known particles (leptons, baryons and mesons), and compare the resulting mass/energy estimates from the UEG theory to best available measured values [2–4]. The generalized UEG models in sections III–VI are based on a stair-case approximation of the UEG constant γ in section II for different regions of energy density (see Fig.1), and also assume that the total mass including spin is twice that of the static UEG mass. This ignores any higher-order effects in a rigorous UEG theory, that would require a variable γ having a smooth functional dependence on the energy density, as well as in a rigorous spin model based on a dynamic UEGM (Unified Electro-Gravito-Magnetic) theory that would be valid for simple as well as composite particles. The rigorous models can be significantly more complicated to compute, and may at this point be pre-mature to establish accurately.

However, the effects of the rigorous models, presumably small over a simplified (first order) general UEG model, may be accounted for by introducing reasonable corrections to various key parameters obtained from the simple UEG theory. The corrected parameters are listed in Table V, and are estimated by fitting the simple UEG theory for selected particles to match their measured mass/energy, as shown in Appendix. The corresponding parameters obtained from a simple UEG theory are also listed alongside the corrected values in Table V for comparison. The simple and the corrected parameters are seen to maintain certain relative trends from shell to shell in a given particle level, which may imply that the same general foundation is shared by the simple and the rigorous models, except with reasonable numerical adjustments in the parameter values due to higher-order effects.

These adjusted parameters from Table V are then used in a simple UEG theory, by employing the synthesis rules of sections II-VI, to estimate the mass of all leptons (Table I), and all principal baryons (Table II) and mesons (Table III), and the resulting mass estimates are compared to available measured data [2–4]. Possible UEG configurations that may emulate other basic particles (Higgs Boson [13–15], W and Z bosons [16, 17], Top [18–20] and Bottom [21, 22] quarks) that have been experimentally observed are also listed in Table IV. Note that the Top and Bottom quarks are modeled in the Table IV as equivalent neutral, boson-like particles, which might be detected in pairs that transitionally represent the respective quark-antiquark combinations. Close agreements between the masses estimated using the UEG theory and available measured data in Tables I-IV for such a large class of basic and composite particles clearly suggests the power of the new UEG theory as a potential substitute for the Standard Model of particle physics.

VIII. CONCLUSION

The basic UEG theory, first developed to model an electron [1] and then separately validated through quantum mechanics [7], is proposed to be generalized in this paper to model all basic and composite particles [2–4] covered by the standard model of particle physics. A general structural configuration for a particle, and the associated theoretical and calculation rules to synthesize any such general particle, are proposed and successfully applied to model and predict the masses of a large class of basic and composite particles, including some "force carriers".

The purpose of the proposed particle configurations and the resulting mass estimates based on the new UEG theory, for such a large class of known particles, is not to focus on any definite study of the individual particles. In fact, it should be reasonable to expect that the actual configurations and mass estimates may deviate somewhat or significantly from those proposed here, almost certainly for a handful of the large number of particles studied. The real purpose is to provide a new theoretical paradigm for particle physics, that is convincingly shown here to have the capacity to model a large class of, possibly all, known basic and composite particles. The clear success of this exercise is a remarkable scientific development. It establishes that the new UEG theory, which obviously unifies the electromagnetic and gravitational theories in explicit terms, could also unify the entire standard model of particle physics [5, 6] under its general scope, thus making the strong and weak forces, as well as all classification schemes of elementary particles (leptons, quarks and force carriers), of the standard model physically redundant. Accordingly, a rigorous version of the new UEG theory may provide a definite physical basis for a grand-unified theory (GUT) [23, 24] and a theory of everything (ToE) [25], which have been the grand aspiration of modern physics in recent decades.

Appendix: Estimation of Parameters of the Unified Electro-Gravity (UEG) Theory, Using Available Energy Data of Known Particles

Refer to the UEG synthesis rules for different particles (see sections II-VI). Tables I-IV show the charge structures for all basic and composite particles, synthesized using the UEG theory. The mass/energy formulas associated in the synthesis of the different particles are not explicitly shown, but should be self-evident in the following calculations. For reference, see Table-I for an example calculation of such synthesis.

(1) Electron (e), Proton (p) and Neutron (n), masses determine the energies for levels 1 and 2 :

$$m_e = W_{12} \approx W_{11} \approx W_{10} = 0.5 MeV$$
$$m_p = W_{22} = 938.3 MeV$$
$$m_n = W_{21} \approx W_{20} = 939.6 MeV$$

(2) Use m_μ, $m_{\pi\pm}$, m_η data to calculate $\underline{\varepsilon}_{r12}$ and $\underline{\varepsilon}_{r11}$:

$$\underline{\varepsilon}_{r11} = m_\mu/m_\eta = 105.7/547.8 = 0.193$$
$$\underline{\varepsilon}_{r12}/\underline{\varepsilon}_{r11} = m_{\pi\pm}/m_\mu = 139.6/105.7 = 1.32$$
$$\underline{\varepsilon}_{r12} = 0.193 \times 1.32 = 0.255$$

(3) Use $m_{\Lambda+}$, $m_{\Xi'c+}$, ε_{r11} to calculate ε_{r10} :

$$\varepsilon_{r11}/\varepsilon_{r10} > m_{\Xi'c+}/m_{\Lambda+} = 2576/2286 = 1.127$$

$$\varepsilon_{r10} < \varepsilon_{r11}/1.127 = 0.193/1.127 = 0.171$$

$$m_{c2} = m_{\Lambda+} = 2286, \ m'_{e2} = m_p/2$$

$$\alpha_{c2} = m_{c2}/m'_{e2} = m_{\Lambda+}/(m_p/2)$$

$$= 2286/(938.3/2) = 4.87$$

$$\alpha_{m2} = 0.95 \ (\text{from chart})$$

$$m_{sn2} = m_{c2} \times \alpha_{m2} = 2286 \times 0.95 = 2171.7$$

$$\varepsilon_{r11}/\varepsilon_{r10} = m_{\Xi'c+}/m_{sn2} = 2576/2171.7 = 1.186$$

$$\varepsilon_{r10} = \varepsilon_{r11}/1.186 = 0.193/1.186 = 0.162$$

(4) $\Lambda+$ and $W_{20} = m_n$ energies determine W_{31} :

$$W_{31} = m_{\Lambda+} - W_{20}/2 = 2286 - 939.6/2 = 1816.2$$

(5) $\Xi'c+$, $\Xi c+$ and W_{31} energies determine W_{32}. This assumes that the meson factors α_{m2} for both $\Xi'c+$, $\Xi c+$ are approximately the same, because the respective meson mass coefficients α_{c2} are expected to be very close:

$$m_{\Xi'c+}/m_{\Xi c+} = W_{31}/W_{32} = 2576/2467 = 1.044$$

$$W_{32} = W_{31}/1.044 = 1816.2/1.044 = 1739.7$$

(6) Muon mass determines the meson factor $\alpha_{m2} = m_{sn2}/m_{c2}$ for $\alpha_{c2} = m_{c2}/m'_{e2} = m_{c2}/(W_{22}/2) = 1$, $m_{c2} = W_{22}/2$, in level $i = 2$. The result would be valid for all levels i :

$$\alpha_{m2} = m_{sn2}/m_{c2} = W_{sn22}/(W_{22}/2)$$

$$= 105.7 \times (\varepsilon_{r10}/\varepsilon_{r11})/(938.3/2)$$

$$= 105.7 \times 0.162/0.193/(938.3/2) = 0.189$$

$$= W_{sni2}/(W_{i2}/2) = \alpha_{mi2}, \ \text{for all i.}$$

(7) Use Ξ_- energy, and W_{31} from result (4), ε_{r20} from result (8b) below, and the factor α_{m31} (see the end note), to get ε_{r22} :

$$m_{\Xi-} - m_{e2} = 1321 - 938.3 = 382.7 = W_{sn31} \times (\varepsilon_{r22}/\varepsilon_{r20})$$

$$= \alpha_{m31} \times (W_{31}/2) \times (\varepsilon_{r22}/\varepsilon_{r20})$$

$$= 0.269 \times 1816.2/2 \times (\varepsilon_{r22}/0.110)$$

$$\varepsilon_{r22} = 382.7 \times 0.11 \times 2/0.269/1816.2 = 0.172$$

(8a) Use $\Lambda 0$, W_{32} energies and the ratio $\alpha_{m3} = W_{sn32}/W_{32} = 0.189/2 = 0.0945$ from result (6) to get the ratio $\varepsilon_{21}/\varepsilon_{20}$:

$$m_{\Lambda 0} - m_n = 1115 - 939.6 = 175.4 = W_{sn32} \times (\varepsilon_{r21}/\varepsilon_{r20})$$

$$= 0.0945 \times W_{32} \times (\varepsilon_{r21}/\varepsilon_{r20}) = 0.0945 \times 1740 \times (\varepsilon_{r21}/\varepsilon_{r20})$$

$$\varepsilon_{r20}/\varepsilon_{r21} = 1740 \times 0.0945/175.4 = 0.937$$

(8b) Use Tauon energy, and results from (2), (3) and (8a) to calculate ε_{r21} and ε_{r20} :

$$m_\tau \times (\varepsilon_{r10}/\varepsilon_{r11}) = 1776 \times 0.162/0.193 = 1490.74$$

$$= W_{sn32}/\varepsilon_{r20} = 0.0945 \times 1740/\varepsilon_{r20}$$

$$\varepsilon_{r20} = 0.0945 \times 1740/1490.74 = 0.110$$

$$\varepsilon_{r21} = \varepsilon_{r20}/(\varepsilon_{r20}/\varepsilon_{r21}) = 0.110/0.937 = 0.117$$

(9) $\Lambda 0b$, $\Sigma b+$, W_{21}, and W_{31} energies determine the energies of level $i = 4$:

$$W_{42} = m_{\Lambda 0b} - (W_{20}/2) - (W_{30}/2)$$

$$= 5620 - (939.6/2) - (1816/2) = 4242.1$$

$$W_{41} \approx W_{40} = m_{\Sigma b+} - (W_{20}/2) - (W_{30}/2)$$

$$= 5807 - (939.6/2) - (1816/2) = 4429.1$$

(10) Use Ξb, W_{20}, W_{42} energies and results from (2), (3), (6) and (8) to get ε_{r30} :

$$[m_{\Xi b-} \times (\varepsilon_{r10}/\varepsilon_{r11}) - (W_{20}/2)] \times (\varepsilon_{r20}/\varepsilon_{r21})$$

$$= [5790 \times (0.162/0.193) - (939.8/2)] \times (0.11/0.117)$$

$$= 4390.2 \times 0.937 = 4113.6 = W_{sn42}/\varepsilon_{r30}$$

$$= (W_{42}/2) \times 0.189/\varepsilon_{r30} = 4242 \times 0.0945/\varepsilon_{r30}$$

$$\varepsilon_{r30} = 4242 \times 0.0945/4113.6 = 0.097$$

The above result assumes $\alpha_{m2} \approx 1$. This can now be verified to be correct, because in this case we have $\alpha_{c2} = (4390.2 + (939.6/2))/(938.3/2) = 10.4 >> 1$.

(11) Use ηc, W_{21}, W_{22}, W_{31}, W_{42} energies and results from (2), (3), (6), (8) and (10) to estimate ε_{r31}, which would best-fit with the $(\alpha_m \sim \alpha_c)$ meson-factor chart (Fig.7):

Increasing ε_{r31} would increase meson coefficient α_c and meson factor α_m, and accordingly the particle mass. We assume that $\varepsilon_{r31} \geq \varepsilon_{r30} = 0.097$. Try first the lowest value for $\varepsilon_{r31} = \varepsilon_{r30} = 0.097$:

$$m_{\eta c} = (W_{42}/2 \times \alpha_{m4} \times (\varepsilon_{r31}/\varepsilon_{r30}) + W_{31} + W_{21}/2)$$

$$\times \alpha_{m2} \times (\varepsilon_{r11}/\varepsilon_{r10}) = (4242/2 \times 0.189 \times (0.097/0.097)$$

$$+ 1816 + 939.6/2) \times 0.95 \times (0.193/0.162) = 3041\text{MeV};$$

$$\alpha_{c2} = ((4242/2 \times 0.189 \times (0.097/0.097) + 1816$$

$$+ 939.6/2)/(W_{22}/2) = 5.73, \ \alpha_{m2} = 0.95 \ (\text{from chart}).$$

The above calculated mass is reasonably close to the available data for the particle mass $m_{\eta c}$=2980MeV, within about a few percent accuracy. Note that the calculation is already larger than the available mass data. Any increase of ε_{r31} would increase the particle mass and increase the deviation from the mass data. Therefore, the best estimate for ε_{r31} is equal to $\varepsilon_{r30} = 0.097$.

(12) Use $B\pm$, W_{21}, W_{22}, W_{32}, W_{41}, W_{42} energies and results from (2), (3) and (10) to estimate ε_{r32}, which would best fit with the $(\alpha_m \sim \alpha_c)$ meson-factor chart (Fig.7):

$$m_{B\pm} = (W_{41}/2 \times \alpha_{m4} \times (\varepsilon_{r32}/\varepsilon_{r30}) + W_{32} + W_{21}/2)$$

$$\times \alpha_{m2} \times (\varepsilon_{r21}/\varepsilon_{r10}) = (4429/2 \times 0.269 \times (\varepsilon_{r32}/0.097)$$

$$+ 1740 + 939.6/2) \times \alpha_{m2} \times (0.255/0.162) = 5279\text{MeV};$$

$$\alpha_{c4} = (4429/2)/(W_{42}/2) = (4429/2)/(4242/2) = 1.044,$$

$$\alpha_{m4} = 0.269 \, (\text{from chart})$$

$$\alpha_{c2} = (4429/2 \times 0.269 \times (\varepsilon_{r32}/0.097) + 1740 + 939.6/2)$$

$$/(W_{22}/2) = (6141.24 \times \varepsilon_{r32} + 2209.8)/(938.3/2)$$

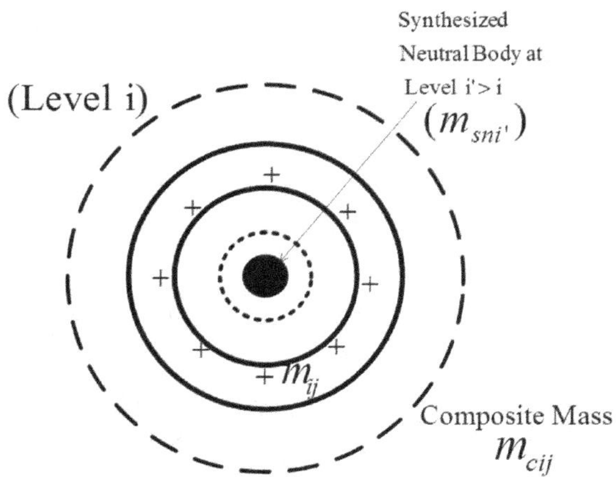

A General "Composite" Positive Charged Body Seen at
Level i, Shell (j=1,2)

FIG. 8.

A bit of trial iterations would be needed in the above calculations to get solution for ε_{r32}=0.206, $\alpha_{c2} = 7.407$, $\alpha_{m2} = 0.965$ (from the chart, Fig.7).

Note: $\alpha_{ci} = m_{ci}/m'_{ei} = m_{ci}/(W_{i2}/2) \approx 1.044$ for $m_{ci} = W_{i1}/2$, for $i = 3$ and 4. That is, $W_{31}/W_{32} = 1740/1816 \approx W_{41}/W_{42} = 4429/4242 = 1.044$. Therefore, the corresponding $\alpha_{mi} = m_{sni}/m_{ci} = W_{sni1}/(W_{i2}/2)$ would be same. For this value of $\alpha_{ci} = 1.044$, α_{mi} is estimated to be 0.269, which best fit all particle data consistent with the UEG theory. Accordingly, we will use $W_{sni1}/(W_{i2}/2) = 0.269 = \alpha_{mi1}$ for $i = 3$, 4, for all calculations.

[1] N. Das, "A New Unified Electro-Gravity (UEG) Theory of the Electron," Paper #1, pp.4-13, in "A Unified Electro-Gravity (UEG) Theory of Nature," (2018).

[2] Wikipedia, "List of Baryons," http://en.wikipedia.org/wiki/List_of_baryons, Retrieved (2013).

[3] Wikipedia, "List of Mesons," http://en.wikipedia.org/wiki/List_of_mesons, Retrieved (2013).

[4] Wikipedia, "Leptons, Table of Leptons," http://en.wikipedia.org/wiki/Lepton, Retrieved (2013).

[5] M. D. Schwartz, *Quantun Field Theory and the Standard Model* (Cambridge University Press, 2013).

[6] N. Cottingham and D. Greenwood, *An Introduction to the Standard Model of Particle Physics (2Ed)* (Cambridge University Press, 2007).

[7] N. Das, "Unified ElectroGravity (UEG) Theory and Quantum Electrodynamics," Paper #3, pp.31-42, in "A Unified Electro-Gravity (UEG) Theory of Nature," (2018).

[8] Wikipedia, "Neutrino," http://en.wikipedia.org/wiki/Neutrino, Retrieved (2017).

[9] F. Reines, "Nobel Lecture: The Neutrino - From Poltergeist to Particle," Nobel Foundation: (Retrieved August 2017) http://www.nobelprize.org/nobel_prizes/physics/laureates/1995/reines-lecture.html (1995).

[10] C. L. Cowan Jr., F. Reines, F. B. Harrison, and H. W. Kruse, Science **124**, 103 (1956).

[11] L. M. Lederman, "Nobel Lecture: The Neutrino: Observations in Particle Physics from Two Neutrinos to the Standard Model," Nobel Foundation: (Retrieved August 2017) http://www.nobelprize.org/nobel_prizes/physics/laureates/1988/lederman-lecture.html (1988).

[12] Fermilab, "Physicists Find First Direct Evidence of Tau Neutrino at Femilab," (Retrieved August 2017) http://www.fnal.gov/pub/inquiring/physics/neutrino/discovery/index.html (2000).

[13] Wikipedia, "Higgs Boson," http://en.wikipedia.org/wiki/Higgs_boson, Retrieved (2017).

[14] ATLAS Collaboration, Physics Letters B **716**, 1 (2012).

[15] CMS Collaboration, Physics Letters B **716**, 30 (2012).

[16] Wikipedia, "W and Z Bosons," http://en.wikipedia.org/wiki/W_and_Z_bosons, Retrieved (2017).

[17] CERN Courier, "CERN Discoveries: Heavylight," (Retrieved August 2017) http://cern-discoveries.web.cern.ch/cern-discoveries/Courier/Heavylight/Heavylight.html (1983).

[18] Wikipedia, "Top Quark," http://en.wikipedia.org/wiki/Top_quark, Retrieved (2017).

[19] CDF Collaboration, Physical Review Letters **74**, 2626 (1995).

[20] D0 Collaboration, Physical Review Letters **74**, 2422 (1995).

[21] Wikipedia, "Bottom Quark," http://en.wikipedia.org/wiki/Bottom_quark, Retrieved (2017).

[22] Fermilab, "Discoveries at Fermilab: Discovery of the Bottom Quark," (Retrieved August 2017) http://www.fnal.gov/pub/inquiring/physics/discoveries/bottom_quark_pr.html (1977).

[23] H. Georgi and S. Glashow, Physical Review Letters **32**, 438 (1974).

[24] J. Pati and A. Salam, Physical Review D **10**, 275 (1974).

[25] J. Ellis, Nature **323**, 595 (1986).

Table I

UEG Shell Model of Baryons

Name	Energy	Energy (Est)	Level One Configuration			Level Two Configuration			Level Three Configuration			Level Four Configuration		
	(MeV)	(MeV)	Meson Shell	Shell 2	Shell 1	Meson Shell	Shell 2	Shell 1	Meson Shell	Shell 2	Shell 1	Meson Shell	Shell 2	Shell 1
p	938.3	938.3					+							
n	939.6	939.6	—					+						
Λ 0	1115	1114.5	—					+	—	+				
Λ +	2286	2285.8									+			
Λ 0b	5620	5619.8	—										+	
Σ +	1189	1199.4						+	—		+			
Σ 0	1192	1199.4	—					+	—		+			
Σ −	1197	1199.4						—	+		—			
Σc++(?)	2454													
Σc +	2453	2353		+					—	+				
Σc 0	2454	2353	—	+					—	+				
Σb +	5807	5806.8												+
Σb 0		5806.8	—											+
Σb −	5815	5806.8												—
Ξ 0	1314	1320.2	—				+		—		+			
Ξ −	1321	1320.2					—		+		—			
Ξc +	2467	2501			+	—				+				
Ξc 0	2470	2501	—		+	—				+				
Ξc +'	2576	2587			+	—					+			
Ξc 0'	2578	2587	—		+	—					+			
Ξcc++(?)														
Ξcc +	3518	3495.2		+					—		+			
Ξb 0		5796.5	—				+	—	+			—	+	
Ξb −	5790	5796.5					—	+	—			+	—	
Ωc 0	2695	2645.4	—		+				—		+			
Ωb −	6165	6143							—	+		—		
Λ +	1232							+	+	—				
Σ +	1383						+		+		—			
Σ 0	1384		—				+		+		—			
Σ −	1387							—	—		+			
Σc +	2517			+					+	—				
Σc 0	2518		—	+					+	—				
Ξ 0	1531		—				+		+		—			
Ξ −	1535						—		—		+			

Lower block for selected J=3/2 baryons as examples. Top block for regular J=1/2 baryons.

Compare J=3/2 baryons with corresponding J=1/2 baryons, in terms of their relative charge structure.

They are different equivalent charge states of the same composite structure. Although the two charge states are equivalent electrically, but with spinning they lead to different (magnetically) dynamic states, having somewhat diffeerent energy/mass.

Name	Energy (MeV)	Energy (Est) (MeV)	Calculations
P	938.3	938.3	
n	939.6	939.6	
$\Lambda\,0$	1115	1114.5	1740/2*0.189*0.117/0.11+939.6=1114.5. Meson factor: 0.189, Level 3.
$\Lambda\,+$	2286	2285.8	1816+939.6/2=2285.8
$\Lambda 0 b$	5620	5619.8	4242+1816/2+939.8/2=5619.8
$\Sigma\,+$	1189	1199.4	1816/2*0.269*0.117/0.11+939.6=1199.4. Meson factor: 0.269, Level 3.
$\Sigma\,0$	1192	1199.4	
$\Sigma\,-$	1197	1199.4	
$\Sigma c++(?)$	2454		
$\Sigma c\,+$	2453	2353	1740/2*0.189/0.11*0.255/0.162=2353. Meson factor: 0.189, Level 3.
$\Sigma c\,0$	2454	2353	
$\Sigma b\,+$	5807	5806.8	4429+1816/2+939.6/2=5806.8
$\Sigma b\,0$		5806.8	
$\Sigma b\,-$	5815	5806.8	
$\Xi\,0$	1314	1320.2	1816/2*0.269*0.172/0.11+938.3=1320.2. Meson factor: 0.269, Level 3.
$\Xi\,-$	1321	1320.2	
$\Xi c\,+$	2467	2501	(1740+939.6/2)*0.95*0.193/0.162=2501. Meson factor: 0.95 (alpha_c=4.71), Level 2.
$\Xi c\,0$	2470	2501	
$\Xi c+'$	2576	2587	(1816+939.6/2)*0.95*0.193/0.162=2587. Meson factor: 0.95 (alpha_c=4.87), Level 2.
$\Xi c 0'$	2578	2587	
$\Xi cc++(?)$			
$\Xi cc+$	3518	3495.2	1816/2*0.269/0.11*0.255/0.162=3495.2. Meson factor: 0.269, Level 3.
$\Xi b 0$		5796.5	(4242/2*0.189/0.097*0.117/0.11+939.6/2)*(1.0)*0.193/0.162=5796.5. Meson factors: 1.0 (alpha_c=10.37), Level 2; 0.189, Level 4.
$\Xi b\,-$	5790	5796.5	
$\Omega c 0$	2695	2645.4	1816/2*0.269/0.11*0.193/0.162=2645.4. Meson factor: 0.269, Level 3.
$\Omega b\,-$	6165	6143	(4242+1816/2)*0.95*0.117/0.11+939.6=. Meson factor: 0.95 (alpha_c=5.92), Level 3.
$\Lambda\,+$	1232		
$\Sigma\,+$	1383		
$\Sigma\,0$	1384		
$\Sigma\,-$	1387		
$\Sigma c\,+$	2517		
$\Sigma c\,0$	2518		
$\Xi\,0$	1531		
$\Xi\,-$	1535		

Refer to the UEG synthesis rules for different particles (sections II-VI). The mass/energy formula associated in the synthesis of a particular particle maybe evident from its calculation shown above. For example, the specific calculations for the particle $(\Xi 0)$ are explained in the following:

Step 1: Neutral Particle of Kind 1, at level 3 (see section IV):

$m_{31} = W_{31}/2 = 1816/2$ MeV (Table V), $m'_{e3} = W_{32}/2 = 1740/2$ MeV (Table V),

$\alpha_c = m_{31}/m'_{e3} = m_c/m'_{e3} = 1.044$, $\alpha_m = 0.269 = \alpha_{mi1}$ (Table V, Fig.7),

$m_{sn3} = \alpha_m m_c = \alpha_{mi1} m_{31} = 1816/2*0.269$ MeV

Step 2: Composite Charge Particle, at level 2 (see section VI):

$m_{22} = W_{22} = 938.3$ MeV (Table V, assume full mass with spin for the level 2),

$\varepsilon_{r22} = 0.172$, $\varepsilon_{r20} = 0.11$ (Table V),

$m_{c2} = m_{22} + [m_{sn3}/\varepsilon_{r20}]\varepsilon_{r22} = 1816/2*0.269*0.172/0.11$ MeV.

Step 3: Neutral Particle of Kind 1, at level 1 (see section IV):

$m_c = m_{c2}$, $m'_{e1} = W_{12}/2 = 0.5/2$ MeV (Table V),

$\alpha_c = m_c/m'_{e1} >> 1$, $\alpha_m \simeq 1$ (Fig.7),

$m_{sn1} = \alpha_m m_c \simeq m_c = m_{c2} = 1816/2*0.269*0.172/0.11$ MeV=1320.2 MeV=mass of the particle Ξ_0.
(Notice that this last step is a trivial approximation. Such a trivial approximate step
for synthesis of a neutral particle at the level 1 may not be explicitly shown in the
above calculations table.)

Table II
UEG Shell Model of Mesons

Name	Energy (MeV)	Energy (Est.) (MeV)	Level One Configuration			Level Two Configuration			Level Three Configuration			Level Four Configuration		
			Meson Shell	Shell 2	Shell 1	Meson Shell	Shell 2	Shell 1	Meson Shell	Shell 2	Shell 1	Meson Shell	Shell 2	Shell 1
$\pi +$	139.6	139.6		+		−	+							
$\pi -$	139.6	139.6		−		+	−							
$\pi\,0$	135	139.6	−	+		−	+							
η	547.8	547.3				−	+							
$\eta\,'$	957.8	937	−	+		−	+		−	+				
$\eta\,c$	2980	3041	−		+	−					+	−	+	
$\eta\,b$	9390	9227							−	+				
$K +$	493.7	495.4			+	−		+	−	+				
$K -$	493.7	495.4			−	+		−	+	−				
$K\,0$	497.6	495.4	−		+	−		+	−	+				
$D +$	1869	1883			+	−		+	−		+	−		+
$D -$	1869	1883			−	+		−	+		−	+		−
$D\,0$	1864	1883	−		+	−		+	−		+	−		+
$Ds +$	1968	1942						+	−		+	−	+	
$Ds -$	1968	1942						−	+		−	+	−	
$B +$	5279	5278		+		−		+				−		+
$B -$	5279	5278		−		+		−				+		−
$B\,0$	5279	5278	−	+		−		+				−		+
$B\,0s$	5366	5335	−					+				−	+	
$Bc +$	6277	6349						+	−					+
$Bc -$	6277	6349						−	+					−
$\rho +$	775			+		−	+							
$\rho -$	775			−		+	−							
$\rho\,0$	775		−	+		−	+							

$\rho +/-/0$ are shown as examples of vector mesons, all others are pseudo-scalar mesons.

Compare $\rho +/-/0$ mesons with corresponding scalar mesons $\pi +/-/0$ in terms of their relative charge structure.

Vector mesons are equivalent composite charge states of the corresponding pseudo-scalar mesons. Although the two charge states look identical electrically, with difference in the spin state of level 2 they lead to somewhat different (magnetically) mass/energy.

Name	Energy (MeV)	Energy (Est.) (MeV)	Calculations
$\pi +$	139.6	139.6	938.3/2*0.189*0.255/0.162=139.6MeV. Meson factor: 0.189, Level 2.
$\pi -$	139.6	139.6	
$\pi\,0$	135	<139.6	Meson factors: <1, Level 1; 0.189, Level 2.
η	547.8	547.3	938.3/2*0.189/0.162=547.3MeV. Meson factor: 0.189, Level 2.
$\eta\,'$	957.8	937	(1740/2*0.189*0.172/0.11+(938.3/2.0))*0.82*0.255/0.162=937. Meson factors: 0.837 (alpha_c=1.547), Level 2; 0.189, Level 3.
$\eta\,c$	2980	3041	(4242/2*0.189*0.097/0.097+1816+939.6/2)*0.95*0.193/0.162=3041MeV. Meson facors: 0.95 (alpha_c=5.73), Level 2; 0.189, Level 4.
$\eta\,b$	9390	9227	1740/2*0.189/0.11/0.162=9227MeV. Meson factor: 0.189, Level 3.
$K +$	493.7	495.4	(1740/2*0.189*0.117/0.11+939.6/2)*0.645*0.193/0.162=495.4. Meson factors: 0.645 (alpha_c=1.374), Level 2; 0.189, Level 3.
$K -$	493.7	495.4	
$K\,0$	497.6	495.4	
$D +$	1869	1883	((4429/2*0.269*0.097/0.097+1816/2)*(0.775)*0.117/0.11+939.6)*(0.925)*0.193/0.162=1883MeV.
$D -$	1869	1883	Meson factors: 0.925 (alpha_c=3.64), Level 2; 0.775 (alpha_c=1.728), Level 3; 0.269, Level 4.
$D\,0$	1864	1883	
$Ds +$	1968	1942	((4242/2*0.189*0.097/0.097+1816/2)*0.72)*0.117/0.11+939.6=1942MeV. Meson factors: 0.72 (alpha_c=1.504), Level 3;
$Ds -$	1968	1942	0.189, Level 4.
$B +$	5279	5278	(4429/2*0.269*0.206/0.097+1740+939.6/2)*(0.965)*0.255/0.162=5278MeV; Meson factors: 0.965 (alpha_c=7.407), Level 2;
$B -$	5279	5278	0.269, Level 4.
$B\,0$	5279	5278	
$B\,0s$	5366	5335	4242/2*0.189*0.097*0.117/0.11+939.6=5335MeV. Meson factor: 0.189, Level 4.
$Bc +$	6277	6349	(4429+1816/2)*0.953*0.117/0.11+939.6=6349 Meson factor: 0.953 (alpha_c=6.13), Level 3.
$Bc -$	6277	6349	
$\rho +$	775		
$\rho -$	775		
$\rho\,0$	775		

Refer to the UEG synthesis rules for different particles (sections II-VI). The mass/energy formula associated in the synthesis of a particular particle maybe evident from its calculation shown above. See Table-I for an example of such synthesis.

Table III
UEG Shell Model of Leptons

Name	Energy (MeV)	Energy(Est.) (MeV)	Level One Configuration			Level Two Configuration			Level Three Configuration			Level Four Configuration		
			Meson Shell	Shell 2	Shell 1	Meson Shell	Shell 2	Shell 1	Meson Shell	Shell 2	Shell 1	Meson Shell	Shell 2	Shell 1
$e\ +$	0.5	0.5		+										
$e\ -$	0.5	0.5		−										
$e\ /\ \nu$	<0.000005	<0.00005		− +										
$\mu\ +$	105.7	105.6			+	−	+							
$\mu\ -$	105.7	105.6			−	+	−							
$\mu\ /\ \nu$	<0.17	<0.57					− +							
		0.0473	−	+										
$\tau\ +$	1776	1780			+				−	+				
$\tau\ -$	1776	1780			−				+	−				
$\tau\ /\ \nu$	<15.5	<9.8								− +				

Note: For neutrinos, both charges are close to each other in the same shell, either shell #1 or #2, placed near one of the locations where permittivity is infinity

Name	Energy (MeV)	Energy (Est.) (MeV)	Calculations
$e\ +$	0.5	0.5	UEG parameter γ_1 for level 1 determines the electron/positron energy.
$e\ -$	0.5	0.5	
$e\ /\ \nu$	<0.000005	<0.00005	< 0.5*0.0001=0.00005MeV; Assume neutrino factor <0.0001.
$\mu\ +$	105.7	105.6	938.3/2*0.189*0.193/0.162=105.6MeV. Meson Factor: 0.189, Level 2.
$\mu\ -$	105.7	105.6	
$\mu\ /\ \nu$	<0.17	<0.57	<938.3*0.0001/0.162=0.57MeV; Neutrino factor < 0.0001.
		0.0473	0.5/2*0.189=0.0473MeV; Meson Factor: 0.189, Levcel 1.
$\tau\ +$	1776	1780	1740/2*0.189/0.11*0.193/0.162=1780MeV. Meson factor: 0.189, Level 3.
$\tau\ -$	1776	1780	
$\tau\ /\ \nu$	<15.5	<9.8	<1740*0.0001/0.11/0.162=9.8MeV; Neutrino factor<0.0001.

Refer to the UEG synthesis rules for different particles (sections II-VI). The mass/energy formula associated in the synthesis of a particular particle maybe evident from its calculation shown above. See Table-I for an example of such synthesis.

Table IV
UEG Shell Model of Special Particles
(W, Z and H Bosons, Top (t) and Bottom (b) Quarks)

Name	Energy (GeV)	Energy(Est.) (GeV)	Level One Configuration			Level Two Configuration			Level Three Configuration			Level Four Configuration		
			Meson Shell	Shell 2	Shell 1	Meson Shell	Shell 2	Shell 1	Meson Shell	Shell 2	Shell 1	Meson Shell	Shell 2	Shell 1
$W\ +$	80.39	75.3			+		−			+	−			+
		87.9		+								−		+
		82.6		+				− +				−		+
$W\ -$	80.39	82.6(81.9)		−				− +				−		+
Z	91.19	92.1					−			+		−	+	
H	125.09	127.2					−				+	−		+
$(t^+ + t^-)/2$	173.21	175.5		−	+				−	+		−	+	
$(b^+ + b^-)/2$	4.18	4.51		−				+	−	+				

Name	Energy (GeV)	Energy (Est.) (GeV)	Calculations
$W\ +$	80.39	75.3	(4.429/0.097*0.2+1.740)/0.172/0.162*0.193=75.3GeV
		87.9	(4.429/2*0.269)/(0.162*0.11*0.097)*0.255=87.9GeV. Meson factor: 0.269, Level 4.
		82.6	(4.429/2*0.269)/0.097/0.11*(0.11/0.117)/0.162*0.255=82.6GeV. Similar to above. Level 2 (special 0th shell and shell 1 used).
$W\ -$	80.39	82.6(81.9)	(75.3+87.9+82.6)/3=81.9GeV. W+, but level 1 charge negative. One state shown, average of three states (=81.9GeV) listed.
Z	91.19	92.1	(1.740+(4.242/2*0.189)*0.2/0.097)/.172/.162=92.1GeV. Meson factor: 0.189, Level 4.
H	125.09	127	(4.429/2.0*0.269/0.097*0.097+1.816+0.9396-0.9396)/0.117/0.162=127.2GeV. Meson factor: 0.269, Level 4.
$(t^+ + t^-)/2$	173.21	175.5	4.242/2.0*0.189/0.097/0.11/0.162*0.193*0.255=175.5GeV. Meson factor: 0.189, Level 4.
$(b^+ + b^-)/2$	4.18	4.37	(1.740/2.0*0.189*0.117/0.11+0.9396)*0.255=4.37GeV. Meson factor: 0.189, Level 3.

Refer to the UEG synthesis rules for different particles (sections II-VI). The mass/energy formula associated in the synthesis of a particular particle maybe evident from its calculation shown above. See Table-I for an example of such synthesis.

Table V

UEG Parameters For Particle Modeling

	Level One Parameters			Level Two Parameters			Level Three Parameters			Level Four Parameters		
	$1/\varepsilon_{r12}$	$1/\varepsilon_{r11}$	$1/\varepsilon_{r10}$	$1/\varepsilon_{r22}$	$1/\varepsilon_{r21}$	$1/\varepsilon_{r20}$	$1/\varepsilon_{r32}$	$1/\varepsilon_{r31}$	$1/\varepsilon_{r30}$	$1/\varepsilon_{r42}$	$1/\varepsilon_{r41}$	$1/\varepsilon_{r40}$
Simple UEG Theory	0.3	0.22	0.18	0.3	0.22	0.18	0.3	0.22	0.18	0.3	0.22	0.18
Data Fit	0.255	0.193	0.162	0.172	0.117	0.11	0.2	0.097	0.097			
(MeV)	W_{12}	W_{11}	W_{10}	W_{22}	W_{21}	W_{20}	W_{32}	W_{31}	W_{30}	W_{42}	W_{41}	W_{40}
Simple UEG Theory	0.5	0.51	0.51	938.3	950.5	950.5	1740	1763	1763	4242	4297	4297
Data Fit	0.5			938.3	939.6	939.6	1740	1816	1816	4242	4429	4429

Meson Factors:

$$\alpha'_{mi2} = W_{sni2} / W_{i2}; \qquad \alpha'_{mi2} = 0.0945\,(Data\,Fit); \qquad \alpha'_{mi2} = 0.192\,(UEG\,Theory)$$

$$\alpha_{mi2} = W_{sni2} / (W_{i2} / 2); \qquad \alpha_{mi2} = 0.189\,(Data\,Fit); \qquad \alpha_{mi2} = 0.384\,(UEG\,Theory)$$

$$\alpha'_{mi1} = W_{sni1} / W_{i1}; \qquad \alpha'_{mi1} = 0.1345\,(Data\,Fit); \qquad \alpha'_{mi1} = 0.226\,(UEG\,Theory)$$

$$\alpha_{mi1} = W_{sni1} / (W_{i1} / 2); \qquad \alpha_{mi1} = 0.269\,(Data\,Fit); \qquad \alpha_{mi1} = 0.452\,(UEG\,Theory)$$

Notes:

- Data-fit and UEG theoretical values for the meson factor for any general energy W, or its equivalent mass m, is provided separately in a graphical plot (see Fig.7).
- Energy W, or its equivalent mass m, of a particular level and shell listed above is twice the associated UEG static (without spin) energy/mass. The listed energy/mass is the total energy/mass of the particular level and shell if there is a spinning charge layer at the particular shell and level.

Unified Electro-Gravity (UEG) Theory and Quantum Electrodynamics

Nirod K. Das

Department of Electrical and Computer Engineering, Tandon School of Engineering,
New York University, 5 Metrotech Center, Brooklyn, NY 11201

(Dated: May 9, 2018; Revised December 20, 2018)

The Unified Electro-Gravity (UEG) theory, originally developed to model a stable static charge, is extended to a spinning charge using a "quasi-static" UEG model. The results from the new theory, evaluated in comparison with concepts and parameters from basic quantum mechanics (QM) and quantum electrodynamics (QED), show that the QM and the QED trace their fundamental origins to the UEG theory. The fine structure constant and the electron g-factor, which are key QED parameters, can be directly related to the proportionality constant (referred to as the UEG constant) used in the UEG theory. A QM wave function is shown to be equivalent to a space-time ripple in the permittivity function of the free space, produced by the UEG fields surrounding a spinning charge, and the basic QM relationships between energy and frequency naturally emerge from the UEG model. Further extension and generalization of the theory may also explain all other quantum mechanical concepts including particle-wave duality, frequency shift in electrodynamic scattering, and charge quantization, leading to full unification of the electromagnetics and gravity with the quantum mechanics.

I. INTRODUCTION

A new theory unifying the electromagnetic and gravitational concepts, referred to as the Unifed Electro-Gravity (UEG) theory, was proposed in [1] to model a stable, static electronic charge, referred to as a static UEG electron. In its most basic form, the UEG theory introduces a gravitational field proportional to the energy density surrounding the charge, with the constant of proportionality γ, referred to as the UEG constant, which results in a strong gradient of the the permittivity function $\epsilon_r(r)$ around the charge. With the success of the static UEG theory, an electron with a spin angular momentum $\hbar/2$ may be conceived in terms of the static UEG electron, that physically spins at a certain radial distance r_0 to produce the given angular momentum. The central acceleration of the spinning electron would be supported by suitable UEG forces produced by the surrounding electric and magnetic fields. The spinning electron would be self-supported by the radial forces due to the electron's own UEG fields, in distinct contrast with orbiting of an electron around the nucleus of an atom, which instead is externally supported by the radial forces due the electric field of the central nucleus. The permittivity function $\epsilon_r(r)$ of the static UEG electron, would transform into a space-time-dependent permittivity function $\epsilon_r(r,t)$ for the spinning electron, which would be equivalent to having a space-time ripple, representing a quantum mechanical wave function. The spinning radius, speed, associated wave frequency, angular momentum, energy/mass may be modeled by extending the static UEG theory of [1], by including additional dynamic UEG effects due to the magnetic field and field momentum-distribution of the spinning electron.

A rigorous, dynamic version of the static UEG theory of [1] would be needed to fully model the spinning electron, which is premature at this point. In the absence of the rigorous dynamic UEG theory, we will use suit-able extension of the basic static UEG theory of [1]. The extended model, referred to as the "quasi-static" UEG model, will be guided by existing concepts from Newtonian mechanics and gravity [2], relativistic mechanics [3], electromagnetics [4] and general relativity [5], and build upon the basic principles of the static UEG theory of [1]. The objective is to explain different quantum-mechanical and quantum-electrodynamic concepts and parameters, such as the wave function [6], Planck's constant [7] and angular momentum [8], fine structure constant [9, 10] and g-factor [11], in terms of UEG concepts and parameters such as the permittivity function, the UEG constant(s) and different UEG forces [1]. Further extension of the principles of the quasi-static UEG model of the spinning electron may physically explain energy and frequency shift in an electrodynamic scattering process, charge quantization linked to quantization of the angular momentum, and wave-particle duality based on a pilot-wave concept. In any event, development of the UEG theory would open a wider unified theoretical framework, combining electromagnetic, gravitational, together with the quantum mechanical and electrodynamic concepts, that would be applicable to all elementary particles. This would provide a unified alternative to the standard model of particle physics [12], without need for additional strong and weak nuclear forces.

The sequence of presentation in different sections maybe outlined as follows:

Section II presents the basic model of a spinning electron, in equivalence to an orbiting electron, and extracts basic relations between the mass of the static UEG electron, the total mass of the spinning electron, the electron g-factor and the spin angular momentum.

This is followed in section III by identifying different UEG forces in a spinning electron, and formulating the total UEG acceleration that would support the spinning motion, based on first-order estimates. This would allow relating the fine structure constant from quantum electrodynamics to the UEG constant in section IV, in an approximate form, that can be verified with the UEG constant available from the static UEG model of electron in [1]. A much closer evaluation is explored in subsection IV A, with deeper insights into the UEG spin model, which may assist in future development of a rigorous UEG theory.

Section V models the UEGravito-Magnetic effect due to field momentum associated with the spinning motion, which is shown to cancel with the basic UEG effect due to the magnetic energy density of the spinning charge. This allowed the formulations presented in the sections II, III and IV using only the UEG acceleration due to the electric energy density, in order to support the spinning motion.

Section VI relates the quantum-mechanical wave frequency to the spinning frequency in terms of the spin velocity and the g-factor. This is based on relativistic transformation between the spinning frame and a stationary external frame. The value of the g-factor is shown to be estimated from the UEG spin model in different degrees of accuracy, as compared with its known measured value. This is to reinforce validity of the spin UEG model, and illustrate finer predictive power of the model.

Fundamental significance of the spin UEG model, and potential implications of the UEG theory in general, are discussed in section VII, outlining concepts for full unification of electromagnetics and gravity, together with the physics of quantum mechanics and elementary particles.

II.   ELECTRON SPIN MODELED AS ORBITING OF A STATIC UEG ELECTRON, AROUND ITS OWN FIELDS

Consider a static UEG electron, which is originally modeled as a stable charge body using the basic, static UEG theory of [1]. Then, consider the static UEG electron to spin at radius r_0 at a speed v_0, close to the speed of light c, the central acceleration of which could be sustained by suitable UEG force(s). Clearly, the basic UEG theory of [1] which rigorously models the static UEG charge without spin, may no longer be rigorously valid for the spinning charge. A dynamic UEG theory for a moving charge would be required, that would include additional UEG forces due to energy density of the magnetic field, as well as UEGravito-magnetic effects due to the field momentum associated with the electromagnetic fields. The development of a such a complete dynamic theory, referred to as a Unified Electro-Gravito-Magnetic (UEGM) theory, is premature at this point, beyond the scope of the present work. However, in absence of such a full dynamic theory, we will model the spin behavior using a quasi-static UEG model, complemented by established results and insights from quantum electrodynamics.

A static UEG electron (modeled by a static UEG theory) may spin at a specific radial distance and velocity, that could be sustained by the UEG forces due to its own fields. The spinning of the static UEG electron maybe considered equivalent to orbiting of a complete electron structure (that already spins) around a central nucleus at a suitable orbital radius. Except, the complete-electron orbiting is sustained by the electric fields of an external body, the nucleus, whereas the spinning of the electron is sustained by the UEG forces due to the fields produced by the electron itself. The spinning electron may be treated similar to an orbiting electron with orbital quantum number equal to one, where the complete electron mass m_e (already including the spin effects) for the orbiting electron is substituted by the static UEG mass m_e' of the "bare" (without the spin) electron. We know from quantum electrodynamics, that the magnetic moment μ_J due to an orbiting electron with orbital quantum number equal to one, is about the same as that due to a spinning electron, different by a factor $g = g/2$ [13] close to unity. This means the velocity-radius products of the orbiting and the spinning electrons are also close to each other, different with the same above factor g. In addition, we also know from quantum electrodynamics, that the angular momentum J of the orbiting and spinning states are $\hbar$ and $\hbar/2$, respectively, different exactly by a factor of two. Based on the above information we already have, it can be deduced that the total mass m_e (with spin) of the orbiting electron is $g(= 2g)$ times, or about twice, the mass m_e' of a static UEG electron (without spin, modeled by a static UEG theory). Also can be deduced, that the angular momentum of the spinning electron is exactly equal to the above mass m_e' of the bare static UEG electron, multiplied by the velocity-radius product, $(v_0 r_0)$ of the spinning electron.

$$\mu_J = \tfrac{q}{2} \times (vr),$$
$$\mu_J(\text{spin}) \simeq \mu_J(\text{orbital}) = \tfrac{\hbar q}{2m_e} = \tfrac{1}{g}\mu_J(\text{spin}),$$
$$(vr)_{\text{spin}} \simeq (vr)_{\text{orbital}} = \tfrac{\hbar}{m_e} = \tfrac{1}{g}(vr)_{\text{spin}},$$
$$g = \tfrac{g}{2} = 1.00115965218091,$$

$$J = m \times (vr), \quad J(\text{spin}) = \tfrac{1}{2}J(\text{orbital}) = \tfrac{\hbar}{2},$$
$$m_e'(vr)_{\text{spin}} = \tfrac{1}{2}m_e(vr)_{\text{orbital}} = \tfrac{\hbar}{2}$$

$$m_e' \simeq \tfrac{1}{2}m_e = g m_e', \quad m_e = g m_e',$$
$$J(\text{spin}) = \tfrac{\hbar}{2} = \tfrac{J(\text{orbital})}{2} = \tfrac{m_e}{2}(vr)_{\text{orbital}}$$
$$= (g m_e')\tfrac{1}{g}(vr)_{\text{spin}} = m_e'(vr)_{\text{spin}} = m_e' v_0 r_0. \tag{1}$$

As we deduced, the ratio between the spinning and the static electron masses is approximately equal to two. One might casually expect the ratio to be equal to the relativistic boost factor, which is dependent on the spin speed, as per special relativity. However, as mentioned before, we anticipate the spinning speed v_0 to be close to the speed of light c, in which case the relativistic boost factor would be much larger than the above ratio close to two. Accordingly, this might appear, at first, to be a contradiction to the casual expectation, but that may not be a valid observation. The mass transformation relation of special relativity is applicable only to a complete, stable massive particle in motion, but not for transformation of mass of the static UEG electron as it spins. This is because, the static UEG electron is an ideal state that is not dynamically stable in motion, and therefore does not constitute a complete, valid particle by itself to which special relativity can be independently applied. The static UEG electron is only a part of the internal formation of the complete electron structure, and the special relativity can only be applied to the complete structure. Further, the environment around a spinning electron, which is governed by the UEG theory involving non-linear deformation of the free-space structure around the electron, is significantly different from a simple free-space medium assumed in the special relativity. Accordingly, the principles of special relativity may not apply strictly in their conventional forms, in this spinning environment, particularly for transformation of mass.

The angular momentum relation of (1) may now be used to express the ratio of the spin radius r_0 and an equivalent radius r'_e of the static UEG electron, in terms of the fine structure constant α [9, 14]. The ratio is approximately equal to $1/\alpha$, assuming that the spin velocity v_0 is close to the speed of light c.

$$m'_e r_0 v_0 = \frac{q^2 r_0 v_0}{8\pi\epsilon_0 r'_e c^2} = \frac{\hbar}{2}, \; m'_e = \frac{q^2}{8\pi\epsilon_0 r'_e c^2},$$

$$\frac{r_0}{r'_e} = \frac{4\pi\epsilon_0 \hbar c}{q^2}(\frac{c}{v_0}) = \frac{1}{\alpha}(\frac{c}{v_0}) \simeq \frac{1}{\alpha}, \; v_0 \simeq c. \tag{2}$$

III.   UEG ACCELERATION COMPONENTS THAT SUPPORT THE SPINNING CENTRAL MOTION)

The fields and dynamics of a moving charged body with an expected speed close to the speed of light would need special modeling and interpretation. We would show in the following section V that the UEG acceleration due to the energy density of the magnetic field of the spinning charge would cancel with the UEGravito-Magnetic acceleration produced by the momentum distribution associated with the equivalent UEG mass/energy distribution. Therefore, the central acceleration of the spinning charge would be sustained only by the remaining UEG acceleration due to energy density of the electric field. The central spinning motion of the electron, thus balanced by all the UEG and the UEG-Magnetic effects, may all be viewed as gravitational in nature in the fundamental sense. Accordingly, consistent with general relativity, a moving frame attached to the spinning orbit may be interpreted as an orbiting inertial frame (primed frame), moving along with the charge body, and the orbiting frame would be inertially equivalent to an external stationary frame (unprimed frame) far from the spinning center. We would estimate the electric field, electric energy density, and the associated UEG acceleration in the external stationary frame. This UEG-acceleration due to the electric energy density of the spinning electron, as seen in the external unprimed frame, would support the central acceleration of the spinning body. Space-time relations of special relativity may be used, for relativistic transformation between the external unprimed frame and the spinning primed frame.

A length parameter, radius r'_e of the charge, along the orbital motion, as seen at a given instant in the orbiting primed frame, would be multiplied by the relativistic boost factor $(= N)$ as seen in the external unprimed frame. Accordingly, one may interpret that the electronic charge would "look stretched" along the orbit by the boost factor (N). If $N = 2\pi r_0/r'_e$, the charge may appear wrapped around the spinning orbit, satisfying a suitable periodic physical condition. The periodic condition may be assumed to be a required "resonant" condition in a dynamic UEG theory, yet to be rigorously developed, in order to maintain a stable spin structure. Under this resonant condition, the stretched charge may be viewed in the form of N number of virtual unit cells, that are periodically arranged with proper overlap (assumed overlap factor 2) between neighboring units, over the entire circumference of the spin orbit (see Fig.1). Accordingly, the spinning charge may be viewed as a ring-charge, as well as a ring-current distribution. In fact, because the spinning orbit is actually in random orientations, with the spin-axis pointing randomly in all possible directions, the charge may be viewed to be wrapped around the entire surface of a sphere of radius equal to the spin radius r_0. Accordingly, the structure may be approximately modeled as a spinning surface-charge distribution, uniformly distributed over the sphere of radius r_0, with axis of the spinning randomly changing in time.

As per the above model, we would derive the average electric energy density at radial distance r_0, as seen by the external unprimed frame, by assuming a spherically symmetric electric field. The average electric energy density may first be expressed assuming that the uniform charge distribution on the sphere of radius r_0 is stationary with respect to the unprimed frame, having only radial electric field. When the charge spins, the radial electric field at a given point, which is directed orthogonal to the spinning velocity at the point, is expected to be increased by the relativistic boost factor N, as per special relativity. Consequently, the average electric energy density that we derived first, assuming the stationary charge distribution, may now be multiplied by the square of the boost factor, in order to find the average electric energy density of the spinning electron. This average electric energy density would be used to calculate the UEG acceleration to support the central acceleration of the spinning charge.

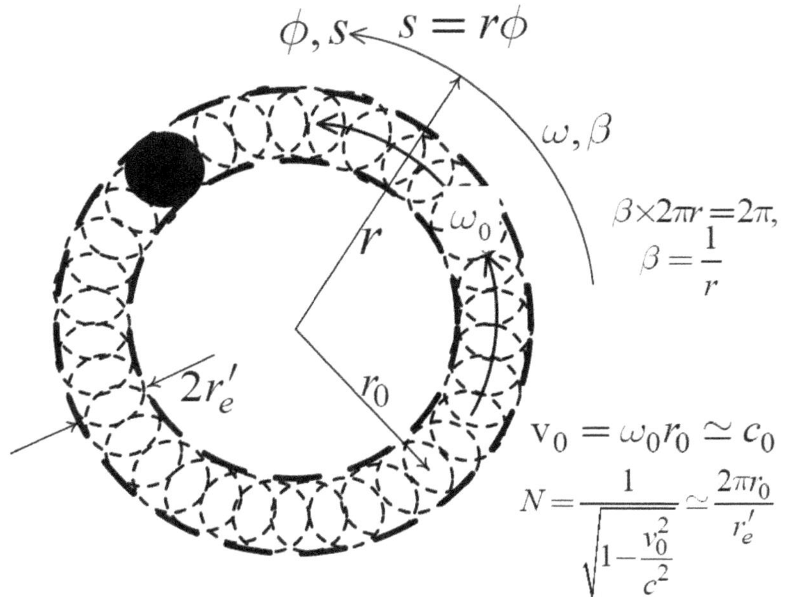

A Spinning Electron Shown on the X-Y (Azimuth) Plane

FIG. 1.

$$E = \frac{q}{4\pi\epsilon_0 r_0^2} \frac{1}{\sqrt{1 - \frac{v_0^2}{c^2}}} = \frac{qN}{4\pi\epsilon_0 r_0^2},$$

$$N = \sqrt{1 - \frac{v_0^2}{c^2}} = a \times (\frac{2\pi r_0}{r_e'}) \simeq (\frac{2\pi r_0}{r_e'}), \ a \simeq 1. \quad (3)$$

IV. PLANCK'S AND FINE STRUCTURE CONSTANTS RELATED TO THE UEG CONSTANT USING THE SPIN MODEL

As discussed earlier, the central acceleration of the spin is to be sustained only by the UEG force due to the average electric energy density at the radius r_0. The UEG force due to magnetic energy density is assumed to be balanced by the UEGravito magnetic force, as shown in section V.

As per the charge model discussed above, the charge structure of Fig.1 maybe effectively interpreted in the form of overlapping (overlapping factor 2) square grids of $2r_e'$ x $2r_e'$ size each, wrapped in a ring configuration around the sphere of radius r_0. Further, because the axis of the ring structure of Fig.1 is randomly changing in time, the $2r_e'$ x $2r_e'$ sized grid structure would be effectively overlapping in two dimensions, wrapped over the surface of the sphere. Therefore, the UEG force at the center of the grid may be calculated by multiplying the average energy density on the spherical surface by a factor $(4/\pi)$. The factor is equal to the ratio of the area of a r_e' x r_e' (excluding overlap region) square grid to that of an enclosed circle of radius r_e'. This geometric factor may

be considered an empirical "filling factor," necessary for proper estimation of the effective UEG force seen at the center of the spinning electron.

$$W_\tau = \frac{\epsilon_0}{2} E^2 = \frac{\epsilon_0}{2} (\frac{q}{4\pi\epsilon_0 r_0^2})^2 (N)^2 \simeq \frac{\epsilon_0}{2} (\frac{q}{4\pi\epsilon_0 r_0^2})^2 (\frac{2\pi r_0}{r_e'})^2,$$

$$Eg \simeq \gamma W_\tau (\frac{4r_e'^2}{\pi r'^2}) \simeq \gamma \frac{\epsilon_0}{2} (\frac{q}{4\pi\epsilon_0 r_0^2})^2 (\frac{2\pi r_0}{r_e'})^2 (\frac{4}{\pi}) = \frac{v_0^2}{r_0} \simeq \frac{c^2}{r_0},$$

$$\frac{\gamma m_e'}{r_e'^2} = \gamma \frac{q^2}{8\pi\epsilon_0 r_e'^3 c^2} \simeq \frac{r_0}{4r_e'},$$

$$\frac{r_0}{r_e'} \simeq 4\frac{\gamma m_e'}{r_e'^2} = 138.359 \,(\text{UEG Theory}),$$

$$\frac{r_0}{r_e'} = \frac{1}{\alpha}(\frac{c}{v_0}) = \frac{1}{\alpha}(\frac{1}{\sqrt{1 - \frac{1}{N^2}}})$$

$$\simeq \frac{1}{\alpha} = \frac{4\pi\epsilon_0 \hbar c}{q^2} \simeq 137.036 \,(\text{QED}). \quad (4)$$

The angular momentum associated with the above spinning would be equal to $\hbar/2$, as expected from quantum electrodynamics. The required ratio of the spin-radius r_0 and the charge-radius r_e', as derived in (2) from quantum electrodynamics, is approximately equal to the inverse of the fine structure constant α [14]. This ratio r_0/r_e' is shown above in (4) to approximately compare to that $r_0/r_e' = 4\gamma m_e'/(r_e'^2)$ independently estimated from the UEG theory, based on the spinning model of Fig.1, using the UEG constant γ derived in [1] from a static UEG model of an electron. The small fractional difference between the above two results for the ratio r_0/r_e' is calculated to be of the order of the fine structure constant. Conversely, if one would estimate the UEG constant $\gamma = r_e'^2/(4\alpha m_e')$ from the above UEG theory and spin model, using the ratio $1/\alpha = r_0/r_e'$ (2) from quantum electrodynamics, and known values of the electron mass $m_e' = m_e/g$ from (1) and corresponding electron radius r_e' from (3), the value of γ would be different from that in [1] derived from a static UEG electron model. The two different independent values of γ would introduce a fractional ambiguity close to the fine structure constant, which we will address shortly in the following section IV A.

$$\gamma(\text{UEG}) = 138.359 \times \frac{r_e'^2}{4m_e'}$$

$$= 138.359 \times \frac{r_e^2 g^3}{4me} \simeq 6.017 \times 10^2 (\text{ms}^{-2})/(\text{Jm}^{-3}),$$

$$\gamma(\text{QED}) = 137.036 \times \frac{r_e'^2}{4m_e'}$$

$$= 137.036 \times \frac{r_e^2 g^3}{4me} \simeq 5.96 \times 10^2 (\text{ms}^{-2})/(\text{Jm}^{-3}),$$

$$\gamma(\text{UEG}) - \gamma(\text{QED})$$

$$\simeq \gamma(\text{QED}) \times 1.32\alpha \sim \gamma(\text{QED}) \times \alpha. \qquad (5)$$

Leaving aside the small fractional ambiguity, discussed above, the close results from the UEG theory and quantum electrodynamics point to a definite fundamental connection between the two theories, relating the UEG constant γ to the fine structure constant α. This is a significant development, also providing a direct physical relation between the UEG constant γ and the Plancks constant $\hbar$, via the fine structure constant α to which both the γ and $\hbar$ are related to, founded on the dynamic modeling of the spin, sustained by the UEG forces. In other words, the Planck's constant $\hbar$, with its origin in quantum mechanics, may no longer be considered a fully independent natural constant, but is rather unified together with the UEG constant γ. Accordingly, the UEG theory, which already unifies the electric and gravitational principles, is now positioned to be fully unified with quantum mechanics as well.

A. Closer Relationship Between the UEG and Quantum Electrodynamics

It may be noted that the UEG theory from which the constant γ was estimated in (4) is only a basic theory, where the UEG acceleration is assumed to be proportional to the energy density, with γ as the constant of the proportionality. A rigorous UEG theory would include higher-order acceleration proportional to higher powers of the energy density, which is expected to reduce the value of the stable mass m_e', as compared to that from the basic theory with a given γ without the higher-order terms [1]. Conversely, in order to have the same final stable mass m_e', one may need to start with a basic UEG theory producing a higher stable mass, or equivalently with a lower γ, before introducing higher-order UEG terms. In other words, the actual value of γ in the dominant acceleration in a rigorous UEG theory, which is the the constant of proportionality between the UEG acceleration and the energy density, in the low energy-density range, is expected to be lower than than the value of γ in [1] obtained from a basic UEG theory without any higher-order effects. This is under the condition that the rigorous and the basic UEG theories produce the same static electron mass m_e'. The lower value of γ in the rigorous theory would be associated with a reduction of the effective radius r_e', in proportion to the cube-root of γ [1].

Based on the above discussion, we may recognize that in principle there are three theoretical values for the constant γ. (I) The value of γ obtained from a basic UEG theory [1], that produces a stable electron mass equal to $m_e' = m_e/g$. (II) The actual value of the γ, which is the constant of proportionality between the UEG acceleration and the energy density, valid when the energy density is sufficiently small. This would be the dominant term, or the first order approximation, in a fully rigorous UEG theory. And, (III) the value of the $\gamma = r_e'^2/(4\alpha m_e')$ that is indirectly estimated from an ideal spin model of the electron, as derived in section IV, which expects the known fine structure constant from quantum electrodynamics to be related to the γ, and the known values of the electron mass m_e' and the electron radius r_e'. A higher-order UEG theory for a bare, static electron, combined with a rigorous, dynamic UEG model for a spinning electron would be needed to explain any differences or specific relationship between the three parameters, which is beyond any scope of the present work. The parameters (I) and (III) are shown in (5) to be close to each other with a fractional difference of the order of the fine structure constant, and we may suspect similar closeness of the parameter (II) to the other two values. Additional insight may assist in more accurate evaluation for the parameter (II), which is the actual constant of proportionality between UEG acceleration and energy density, in an environment with low energy density.

The effective radius used in an ideal spin model of section II, Fig.1, is assumed to be the classical radius r_e' of the bare electron, which determines the required relativistic boost factor to be ideally equal to $N = 2\pi r_0/r_e'$. The actual value of the boost factor is slightly larger than this ideal value, represented by the factor a, the value of which can be estimated as shown in (7), from the known values of the fine structure constant α and electron g-factor. This increase is equivalent to having an effective radius r_e' to be smaller than the ideal value by the same factor a. It may be reasonable to estimate that the actual increased value of the boost factor $N = 2\pi r_0 a/r_e'$, and the corresponding reduced effective radius r_e'/a, is associated with the average between the two values of γ (I) and (II), that is the average between the values needed in a basic UEG model and in a rigorous UEG model to produce the same stable mass m_e'. Whereas, the ideal value of the boost factor $N = 2\pi r_0/r_e'$, and the corresponding effective radius r'_e, is associated with the first value of γ (*I*), that is the value needed in a basic UEG model to produce the stable mass m'_e. As per the earlier discussion on the effect of the higher-order UEG theory, the reduction in the effective radius would mean that the average of the two values of γ (*I*) and (*II*) would be lower than the first value of γ (*I*), by a factor equal to $a^3 \simeq 1.0045 \simeq 1 + 0.62\alpha$ (see (7)). This would place the estimate for the actual value of γ (*II*), fractionally about $(1 + 1.24\alpha)$ lower than the estimate of γ (*I*) from the basic UEG theory. This estimate for the actual value of the γ (*II*) is fairly close to the estimate (*III*) from quantum electrodynamics, which we know from (5) to be fractionally about $(1 + 1.32\alpha)$ lower than the estimate (*I*). In other words, the estimates of γ (*II*) and (*III*) would be essentially equal to each other with a fractional difference of less than 0.1α, or within 0.1%.

$$\gamma(\text{actual}) \simeq \frac{\gamma(\text{Basic UEG})}{(1+2a^3)}$$

$$= \frac{\gamma(\text{Basic UEG})}{(1+1.24\alpha)} = 5.963 \times 10^2 (\text{ms}^{-2})/(\text{Jm}^{-3}),$$

$$\gamma(\text{QED}) \simeq \frac{\gamma(\text{Basic UEG})}{(1+1.32\alpha)} = 5.96 \times 10^2 (\text{ms}^{-2})/(\text{Jm}^{-3}),$$

$$\gamma(\text{actual}) \simeq \gamma(\text{QED}), \quad \frac{\gamma(\text{actual})}{\gamma(\text{QED})} < 1.001 \quad . \tag{6}$$

The parameter a, used in the above discussion and deduction, is expressed as follows, using (2) for the ratio r_0/r'_e, and (15) to relate the boost factor N to the factor g. The value of a may be calculated using known measured values of the fine structure constant α and the electron g-factor $g = 2\underline{g}$.

$$\frac{r_0}{r'_e} = \frac{4\pi\epsilon_0 \hbar c}{q^2}\left(\frac{c}{v_0}\right) = \frac{1}{\alpha}\left(\frac{c}{v_0}\right) = \frac{1}{\alpha}\left(\frac{1}{\sqrt{1-\frac{1}{N^2}}}\right),$$

$$N = a \times \left(\frac{2\pi r_0}{r'_e}\right) = \frac{2\pi a}{\alpha}\left(\frac{1}{\sqrt{1-\frac{1}{N^2}}}\right),$$

$$\frac{1}{a} = \frac{2\pi/\alpha}{N\sqrt{1-\frac{1}{N^2}}} = \frac{(2\pi/\alpha)(\underline{g}-1)}{\sqrt{1-(\underline{g}-1)^2}}$$

$$= (2\pi/\alpha) \times 0.0011596529 = 1 - 0.0015126724 \quad . \tag{7}$$

Based on the close estimated values (*II*) and (*III*) of γ, as discussed above, it may be suggested that the two values (*II*) and (*III*), namely, the value of γ from a rigorous UEG model of electron, and the value $\gamma = r_e'^2/(4\alpha m'_e)$ derived from quantum electrodynamics, could be, after all, equal to each other, or close to each other with relatively higher precision. This proposition may be supported by further insights and more accurate modeling of the central acceleration of the spinning electron.

The above modeling in (4) of the spinning electron using the UEG theory was established in an approximate form, in the absence of a rigorous dynamic UEG theory, as an initial estimate in order to illustrate fundamental relations between the UEG and the fine structure constants. Conversely, when a rigorous dynamic UEG theory would be established and it validates the basic principles of the modeling (4), the fine structure and the Planck's constants could in principle be derived and predicted exactly from the UEG theory. For now, we may evaluate the fine structure constant α, which is the inverse of ratio of the spin radius and the electron radius, more accurately from the modeling of (4), guided by the following insight.

We know from (7) that the boost factor N is slightly larger than the ratio $(2\pi r_0/r'_e)$ obtained from the angular momentum in (2), by the factor a. This is equivalent to having increased overlap between the neighboring particles in the ring model of section II, Fig.1. The average energy density in (4) maybe properly redistributed over the surface of the spin sphere, weighted in proportion to the actual energy/mass distribution. Accordingly, the redistributed energy density at the particle center would be inversely proportional to the square of the overlap factor a, considering overlap of the spinning particle in two dimensions over the surface of the spin sphere. More is the overlap, which is on the outer edges of the particle, more energy density needs to be redistributed away from the center, leaving less energy density at the particle center. This redistributed energy density, evaluated at the center of the particle, would be multiplied with the UEG constant γ, in order to obtain the UEG acceleration that supports the central acceleration. Accordingly, the UEG acceleration would be reduced by a factor a^2. This may be introduced as an multiplying factor $1/a^2$, in addition to the ideal redistribution factor $4/\pi$ that we already have in our model of (4).

$$\underline{W}_\tau = \frac{\epsilon_0}{2}\underline{E}^2 = \frac{\epsilon_0}{2}\left(\frac{q}{4\pi\epsilon_0 r_0^2}\right)^2 (N)^2 = \frac{\epsilon_0}{2}\left(\frac{q}{4\pi\epsilon_0 r_0^2}\right)^2\left(\frac{2\pi r_0}{r'_e}\right)^2 (a)^2,$$

$$E_g = \gamma W_\tau \left(\frac{4r_e'^2}{\pi r_e'^2}\right)\left(\frac{1}{a}\right)^2 = \gamma\frac{\epsilon_0}{2}\left(\frac{q}{4\pi\epsilon_0 r_0^2}\right)^2\left(\frac{2\pi r_0}{r'_e}\right)^2\left(\frac{4}{\pi}\right) = \frac{v_0^2}{r_0},$$

$$\frac{\gamma m'_e}{r_e'^2} = \gamma\frac{q^2}{8\pi\epsilon_0 r_e'^3 c^2} = \left(\frac{r_0}{4r'_e}\right)\left(\frac{v_0}{c}\right)^2$$

$$= \left(\frac{r_0}{4r'_e}\right)\left(1 - \frac{1}{N^2}\right) = \left(\frac{r_0}{4r'_e}\right)(1 - (1 - \underline{g})^2). \tag{8}$$

The expression for the ratio of the spin and classical static electron radii, derived from spin angular momentum relation (2), may now be used for a closer relationship between the rigorous UEG constant γ to the fine structure constant α.

$$\frac{r_0}{r'_e} = \frac{4\pi\epsilon_0 \hbar c}{q^2}\left(\frac{c}{v_0}\right) = \frac{1}{\alpha}\left(\frac{c}{v_0}\right) = \frac{1}{\alpha}\left(\frac{1}{\sqrt{1-\frac{1}{N^2}}}\right) = \frac{1}{\alpha}\left(\frac{1}{\sqrt{1-(1-\underline{g})^2}}\right),$$

$$\frac{4\gamma m'_e}{r_e'^2} = \left(\frac{r_0}{r'_e}\right)(1 - (1 - \underline{g}^2)) = \frac{1}{\alpha}\sqrt{1 - (1 - \underline{g}^2)} = \frac{1}{\alpha}\sqrt{1 - \frac{1}{N^2}},$$

$$\left(\frac{4\gamma m'_e}{r_e'^2}\right)\left(\frac{r_0}{r'_e}\right) = \left(\frac{1}{\alpha}\right)^2. \tag{9}$$

The dimensionless constant $4\gamma m'_e/r_e'^2$, where γ is the rigorous UEG constant, and the other dimensional constant $1/\alpha$, which is the inverse of fine structure constant, are now shown in (9) to be close to each other with fractional difference of approximately $1/(2N^2)$. This fractional difference is of the order of the square of $\alpha/(2\pi)$, which would amount to having the above two dimensionless constants essentially equal to each other, with their ratio different from unity only in the sixth or higher decimal places. This is a significant development, which, in addition to reinforcing unmistakable unified connection between the UEG theory and quantum electrodynamics, opens valuable insights for any future development of a fully rigorous UEG theory. The effective γ for a rigorous UEG theory is now very accurately estimated from a basic UEG theory and available information from quantum electrodynamics. Additional details for a rigorous UEG theory could also be extracted from the g-factor, the measured value of which is available with very high precision. This would be possible through the parameter a in (7), which is the change of the effective radius of the particle as compared to its ideal classical value r'_e, carrying information that would constrain any variation of a general UEG function $\gamma(W_\tau)$ in a rigorous UEG theory. This is in addition to the effective γ deduced above, which would be the first-order constant coefficient of the general UEG function, which is only an approximation of the general UEG function for low energy density W_τ.

V. THE UEG ACCELERATION DUE TO THE MAGNETIC FIELD, AND THE UEGM (UEGRAVITO-MAGNETIC) ACCELERATION DUE TO THE FIELD MOMENTUM

We will find the expression of the velocity due to spinning at a given radius r. This may be derived from the electromagnetic field momentum, using the Coulomb electric field due to the electron charge and the magnetic field produced due to spin magnetic moment μ_S. The velocity may also be estimated from a quantum-mechanical model where the spinning of the static mass m'_e is treated similar to the orbital motion of the total electron mass m_e. The two velocity expressions from the electromagnetic and the quantum models are similar except the $\sin\theta$ factors.

$$\bar{\mu}_S = \frac{\hbar q}{2m e}\hat{z}, \ \ \bar{H} = \hat{\theta}\frac{\mu_S}{4\pi r^3}\sin\theta + \hat{r}\frac{\mu_S}{2\pi r^3}\cos\theta,$$

$$\bar{E} = \hat{r}\frac{q}{4\pi\varepsilon r^2}, \ \ \bar{v}(EM) = \frac{\bar{E}\times\bar{H}}{(\frac{\varepsilon}{2}E^2)} = \hat{\phi}\frac{2\mu_S\sin\theta}{qr} = \hat{\phi}\frac{\hbar\sin\theta}{m_e r},$$

$$\bar{S} = m'_e\bar{r}_0 \times \bar{v}_0 = \tfrac{1}{2}m_e\bar{r}\times\bar{v}$$

$$= \hat{z}\tfrac{1}{2}m e v_\phi r\sin\theta = \hat{z}\frac{\hbar}{2}, \ \ \bar{v}(QM) = \hat{\phi}\frac{\hbar}{m_e r\sin\theta}. \quad (10)$$

The energy density in the magnetic field would produce an UEG acceleration E_{gum}, which may be expressed by multiplying the average energy density in the magnetic field with the UEG constant γ.

$$\bar{E}_{gum} = -\hat{r} < \gamma(\tfrac{\mu}{2}H^2) > = -\hat{r}\frac{\gamma\mu\mu_S^2}{32\pi^2 r^6} < (\sin^2\theta + 4\cos^2\theta) >$$

$$= -\hat{r}\frac{\gamma\mu\mu_S^2}{32\pi^2 r^6}\frac{\int_0^\pi (\sin^2\theta + 4\cos^2\theta)\sin\theta\, d\theta}{\int_0^\pi \sin\theta\, d\theta}$$

$$= -\hat{r}\frac{\gamma\mu\mu_S^2}{16\pi^2 r^6} = -\hat{r}\frac{\gamma\mu q^2\hbar^2}{64\pi^2 m_e^2 r^6}. \quad (11)$$

Unlike a static electron without any spin, which produces a UEG force field and is associated with a gravitational mass distribution (mass-density) as per Gauss' Law, a spinning electron would in addition be associated with an effective UEG momentum distribution (momentum-density) that may be expressed by multiplying the UEG mass density and the velocity derived above. This momentum-density due to the moving UEG mass-density is expected to produce a gravito-magnetic field, in a very similar way as an electric current distribution due to a moving electric charge distribution produces a magnetic field as per the Ampere's Law of the electromagnetic theory. Accordingly, the gravito-magnetic field may also be derived from the UEG momentum density using an equivalent version of the Ampere's Law.

The acceleration due to the gravito-magnetic field may be expressed as the cross-product of gravito-magnetic field and the velocity. Note that there are two velocity terms in the above derivation: (I) the velocity used in derivation of the gravito-magnetic field to begin with, and then (II) the velocity that multiplies with the gravito-magnetic field to find the gravito-magnetic acceleration. As a reasonable approach to estimate the average gravito-magnetic acceleration, we choose the two velocity terms to be expressed differently as in (10) - the former derived electromagnetically ($\bar{v}(EM)$) and the later quantum-mechanically ($\bar{v}(QM)$). Also note that we treat the gravito-magnetic acceleration $\bar{E}_{gm}$ in (12) just like an equivalent acceleration in an electromagnetic modeling, without any adjustment factor. This is unlike conventional gravito-magnetic modeling [15] where an additional factor of $1/4$ might be needed. This is because, in conventional gravito-magnetic modeling [15] the mass, which is the source of gravitation, relativistically varies with velocity. Whereas, the average mass density ρ_{vu} in the present modeling, associated with the azimuthal ($\hat{\phi}$-directed) is assumed to be independent of the velocity $\bar{v}$, just like the electric charge density, which is the source of an electromagnetic field, would be in an equivalent electromagnetic modeling.

$$\bar{E}_{gue} = -\hat{r}\gamma(\tfrac{\varepsilon}{2}E^2) = -\hat{r}\frac{\gamma q^2}{32\pi^2\varepsilon r^4},$$

$$\rho_{vu} = -\varepsilon\bar{\nabla}\cdot\bar{E}_{gue} = -\frac{\gamma q^2}{16\pi^2 r^5},$$

$$\bar{\nabla}\times\bar{H}_{gu} = \bar{J}_{gu} = \rho_{vu}\bar{v}(EM), \quad \bar{H}_{gu} = \hat{\theta}H_{gu\theta},$$

$$\frac{1}{r}\frac{\partial(rH_{gu\theta})}{\partial r} = \rho_{vu}v_\phi(EM) = -\frac{\gamma q^2\hbar\sin\theta}{16\pi^2 m_e r^6},$$

$$H_{gu\theta} = \frac{\gamma q^2\hbar\sin\theta}{64\pi^2 m_e r^5},$$

$$\bar{E}_{gm} = -\mu < \bar{v}\times\bar{H}_{gu} >= -\mu\bar{v}(QM)\times\bar{H}_{gu}$$

$$= \hat{r}\mu v_\phi(QM)H_{gu\theta} = \hat{r}\mu(\frac{\hbar}{m_e r\sin\theta})(\frac{\gamma q^2\hbar\sin\theta}{64\pi^2 m_e r^5})$$

$$= \hat{r}\frac{\gamma\mu q^2\hbar^2}{64\pi^2 m_e^2 r^6}. \tag{12}$$

It is shown that the gravito-magnetic acceleration (12) due to UEG momentum density is negative of the UEG acceleration (11) due to the energy density in the magnetic field. Therefore, the total UEG force is simply the UEG force due to the energy density in the electric field, independent of the magnetic field generated due to the spin.

$$\bar{E}_{gm} + \bar{E}_{gum} = 0,$$

$$\bar{E}_g = \bar{E}_{gue} + \bar{E}_{gm} + \bar{E}_{gum}$$

$$= \bar{E}_{gue} = -\hat{r}\gamma(\tfrac{\varepsilon}{2}E^2) = -\hat{r}\frac{\gamma q^2}{32\pi^2\varepsilon r^4}. \tag{13}$$

The theory developed in this section is an important recognition of the existence and significance of the gravito-magnetic effect surrounding the electron, produced as per the new UEG theory. The gravito-magnetic effect constitutes a critical physical mechanism of the complete internal structure of the electron.

VI. QUANTUM MECHANICAL WAVE IS A RIPPLE IN THE "NON-LINEAR" FREE-SPACE MEDIUM, WITH THE QUANTUM FREQUENCY CLOSE TO THE SPIN FREQUENCY

The quantum mechanical (QM) wave of frequency ω may be viewed as a ripple in the free space produced due to the spinning of the electron, as a result of the strong UEG force. The non-linear permittivity function of the free-space in the UEG (static) theory would transform into the QM wave function of the "free-space" as a result of the spinning. It was discussed in sections III, V, that the strong UEG field around the spinning charge would produce an equivalent rotating inertial frame, dragged along with the moving charge due to the UEGravito-Magnetic (UEGM) effect. The frequency ω of the QM wave maybe intuitively "seen" as a difference-frequency $\omega - \omega_0$ relative to the rotating frame spinning with the frequency ω_0. The difference frequency $\omega - \omega_0$, and the actual QM frequency ω may be related with each other

by the relativistic boost factor N between the rotating frame (primed frame) and a stationary frame (unprimed frame) far from the spin center. Accordingly, the QM frequency ω may be shown to be slightly larger than the spin frequency ω_0, with a small difference of ω/N. The intuitive relationships may also be established using space-time transformation between the primed and unprimed frames, and enforcing a periodic symmetry condition ($\beta \times (2\pi r_0) = 2\pi$) around the circumference $2\pi r_0$ of the rotating frame.

This is a significant development, which provides a direct physical process that represents the QM wave, in the form of ripples produced due to spinning in a a non-linear free-space medium. This may be established by directly relating the QM wave frequency ω to the physical spinning frequency ω_0 of the charge.

$$e^{j\omega t}e^{-j\beta s} = e^{j\omega' t'}e^{-j\beta' s'}, \quad t = \frac{t'+s'v_0/c^2}{\sqrt{1-\frac{v_0^2}{c^2}}}, \quad s = \frac{s'+t'v_0}{\sqrt{1-\frac{v_0^2}{c^2}}},$$

$$\omega' = \frac{\omega-\beta v_0}{\sqrt{1-\frac{v_0^2}{c^2}}}, \quad \beta' = \frac{\beta-\omega v_0/c^2}{\sqrt{1-\frac{v_0^2}{c^2}}},$$

$$\omega' = \omega = \frac{\omega-v_0/r_0}{\sqrt{1-\frac{v_0^2}{c^2}}} = \frac{\omega-\omega_0}{\sqrt{1-\frac{v_0^2}{c^2}}};$$

$$\beta\times(2\pi r_0) = 2\pi, \quad \beta = \frac{1}{r_0}. \tag{14}$$

For a general interpretation of the above concept of the quantum/UEG wave, first consider a "stationary" spinning charged body with a total mass m (including spin and static UEG mass) and linear momentum $p = 0$, with no linear motion of the center of spinning. The region surrounding the charge will be associated with a space-time dependent permittivity function $\epsilon_r(r,t)$ expressed in the harmonic form (14), which would represent the quantum/UEG wave function of the stationary particle. The wave will be seen by a stationary observer to be oscillating as $e^{j\omega t}$ with frequency ω, but having no spatial dependence with wave number $\beta = 1/r = 0$, in the region far from the center ($r = \infty$). We may assume that the wave amplitude in the far region is uniform in space, independent of the spatial variation of the UEG field. This wave function would be consistent with quantum mechanics, with the expected energy-wave frequency relationship $w = mc^2 = \hbar\omega$, and momentum-wave number relationship $p = mv = \hbar\beta = 0$.

Now, the above quantum-mechanical relationships for the "stationary" spinning charge may be extended as well when the charged body undergoes a linear motion of the center of spinning, with velocity v in a given direction s. Applying space-time transformation of special relativity, the above wave function $e^{j\omega t}$ of the stationary charge in the far region, dependent only on time, maybe shown to transform into a wave $e^{j\omega(t-sv/c^2)\eta} = e^{j\omega' t}e^{-j\beta' s}$, with both space and time variation, as seen by a stationary observer. The new frequency $\omega' = \eta\omega = \eta mc^2/\hbar$

$= m'c^2/\hbar$, and the new wave number $\beta' = \omega'v/c^2 = m'v/\hbar = p'/\hbar$, are related to the new mass $m' = \eta m$ and momentum $p' = m'v$, where $\eta = (1 - v^2/c^2)^{-0.5}$ is the relativistic boost factor associated with the velocity v. The basic quantum mechanical energy/momentum and frequency/wave number relationships, $W' = m'c^2 = \omega'\hbar$ and $p' = m'v = \beta'\hbar$, are clearly established between the wave parameters in the region far from the center of the moving charge, and the mass m' and linear momentum p' of the physical charged body moving at the center of wave.

Clearly, the above quantum-mechanical relationships for the quantum/UEG wave would not be valid in the region closer to the central charge. A full dynamic UEG theory may be needed to rigorously model the wave function in the central region, particularly in the immediate vicinity of the charge with strong energy density.

A. Electron g-Factor Related to Relativistic Boost factor, and to the Spin and Quantum Wave Frequencies

Based on the above quantum-mechanical interpretation, the frequency ω in (14) may be related to the total electron mass m_e. On the other hand, the spin frequency ω_0 is related to the static electron mass m'_e through the spin angular momentum $\hbar/2$. Accordingly, given that the two frequencies ω and ω_0 are related to each other in (14) by the boost factor N, the total and the static masses would also be related to each other by the boost factor. Consequently, the electron g-factor, which is the ratio of the total and the static masses, would be directly related to the boost factor.

$$\frac{1}{\sqrt{1-\frac{v_0^2}{c^2}}} = N, \quad \frac{\omega-\omega_0}{\sqrt{1-\frac{v_0^2}{c^2}}} = N(\omega - \omega_0) = \omega,$$

$$\omega(1 - \tfrac{1}{N}) = \omega_0, \quad \hbar\omega = m_e c^2,$$

$$J = m'_e r_0 v_0 = m'_e \frac{v_0^2}{\omega_0} = \frac{\hbar}{2}, \quad v_0 = \omega_0 r_0,$$

$$\frac{m_e c^2}{\hbar}(1 - \tfrac{1}{N}) = \frac{2m'_e v_0^2}{\hbar}, \quad m'_e = \frac{m_e c^2}{2v_0^2}(1 - \tfrac{1}{N})$$

$$= \frac{m_e}{2(1-\frac{1}{N^2})}(1 - \tfrac{1}{N}) = \frac{m_e}{2(1+\frac{1}{N})} = \frac{m_e}{g},$$

$$\tfrac{1}{N} = \tfrac{g}{2} - 1 = 0.001159652 \,(\text{measured}). \tag{15}$$

B. Estimating g-Factor from the Fine Structure and UEG Constants, Based on the Spin Model

The small difference between the quantum wave and the spinning frequencies appears in the form of the g-factor of the electron. The value of the g-factor may be estimated directly from the UEG constant, or equivalently from the fine structure constant, to the first or-

der, consistent with the prediction from quantum electrodynamics (QED). This estimate for the g-factor, when rounded up, is accurate up to the 5th decimal point, as compared to the currently measured value.

$$\mu_J = q f_0 \pi r_0^2 = \tfrac{q}{2}\omega_0 r_0^2 = \tfrac{q}{2}v_0 r_0, \quad J = m'_e v_0 r_0,$$

$$\frac{\mu_J}{J} = \frac{q}{2m'_e} = \frac{q}{2m_e}2(1 + \tfrac{1}{N}) \simeq \frac{q}{2m_e}2(1 + \tfrac{r'_e}{2\pi r_0})$$

$$= \frac{q}{2m_e}2(1 + \tfrac{\alpha}{2\pi}) = \frac{q}{2m_e}g, \quad g = 2(1 + \tfrac{\alpha}{2\pi}),$$

$$\tfrac{g}{2} = (1 + \tfrac{\alpha}{2\pi}) = 1.0011614097; \quad \tfrac{1}{\alpha} = 137.035999139 \,,$$

$$\tfrac{g}{2}(\text{measured}) = 1.0011596521 \,. \tag{16}$$

C. Higher Order Corrections to the g-factor

Higher order correction to the g-factor may also be estimated from the UEG/QM theory. This follows up on the above result that the total electron mass is slightly larger than twice (factor of about $2(1+\alpha/(2\pi))$) the UEG electrostatic mass, which is different from the ideal factor of 2 assumed in a simple spinning model with an ideal relativistic boost factor $N = 2\pi r_0/r'_e = 2\pi/\alpha$ Accordingly, we need the electric and magnetic energies of the spinning electron to be each slightly larger than the static electric energy. This would be accomplished by having a slightly larger relativistic boost factor than the ideal value of $2\pi/\alpha$ (boost factor increased to $(2\pi/\alpha)(1 + \alpha/(2\pi))$). Following the similar derivation for the g-factor presented earlier, this would lead to a smaller g-factor than the first order estimate above, the trend being consistent with the measured g-factor and the theoretical derivation from quantum electrodynamics.

$$g = 2(1 + \tfrac{\alpha}{2\pi}/(1 + \tfrac{\alpha}{2\pi}))$$

$$\simeq 2(1 + \tfrac{\alpha}{2\pi}(1 - \tfrac{\alpha}{2\pi})) = 2(1 + \tfrac{\alpha}{2\pi} - (\tfrac{\alpha}{2\pi})^2),$$

$$\tfrac{g}{2} \simeq (1 + \tfrac{\alpha}{2\pi} - (\tfrac{\alpha}{2\pi})^2) = 1.0011600608 \,,$$

$$\tfrac{g}{2}(\text{measured}) = 1.0011596521 \,. \tag{17}$$

The above estimate for the g-factor, when rounded up, is accurate up to the sixth decimal point, as compared to the currently measured value. This is one order improvement compared to the first order estimation deduced earlier.

This above estimation is based on the assumption that the mass/energy of the spinning electron increases proportional to the boost factor. This trend is consistent with the special relativity, which is expected not to strictly apply in the dynamic UEGM model. Alternate improvement in accuracy of estimation of the g-factor is possible by assuming that the difference between the inverse-fine structure constant and the UEG dimensionless constant $4\gamma m'_e/r'^2_e$ is related to the higher-order correction term of the g-factor (see section IV A).

$$g = 2(1 + \tfrac{1}{N}) = 2(1 + \tfrac{r'_e}{2\pi r_0 a})$$

$$\simeq 2(1 + \tfrac{\alpha}{2\pi} \times (\tfrac{(1/\alpha)}{(4\gamma m'_e / r'^2_e)})^{1/6})$$

$$= 2(1 + \tfrac{\alpha}{2\pi} \times (\tfrac{137.0360}{138.3588})^{1/6}) = 2(1 + \tfrac{\alpha}{2\pi} \times (1 - 0.0016)),$$

$$\tfrac{g}{2} \simeq (1 + \tfrac{\alpha}{2\pi} \times (1 - 0.0016)) = 1.0011595514 ,$$

$$\tfrac{g}{2}(\text{measured}) = 1.0011596521 . \tag{18}$$

This is improvement in the higher-order corrections of the g-factor, compared to the earlier estimation in (17), with improvement showing in the seventh and eighth decimal points. This estimation uses a simple averaging of the two UEG constants γ, one from the basic UEG theory of electron [1] and the other from QED using the fine structure constant, as reasoned in section IV A, in order to deduce an effective γ. This effective γ determines an effective radius ($=r'_e/a$) for estimation of the boost factor N, from which the g-factor is estimated as shown in (18). Accordingly, a more accurate prediction/estimation of the g-factor would be possible by deducing a more accurate effective γ using a higher-order UEG model of [1].

An exact value of the g-factor can be predicted directly from an exact boost factor N, if it could be available, using the exact relationship $g = 2(1+1/N)$ (see 15), (18)). In principle, the $N = 1/\sqrt{1 - (v_0/c)^2}$ could be solved from a fully rigorous (both static and dynamic parts) UEG model, as the required relativistic boost factor for an electron with a static UEG mass m'_e, spinning at a radius $r_0 = \hbar/(2v_0 m'_e)$ and speed v_0, to acquire its total known dynamic mass $m_e = g m'_e = 2m'_e(1+1/N)$ and an angular momentum $\hbar/2$. Such a rigorous and dynamic Unified Electro-Gravito-Magnetic (UEGM) theory maybe at this point premature, and is beyond the scope of the present work.

VII.　DISCUSSION: FUNDAMENTAL IMPLICATIONS FROM THE UEG THEORY OF QUANTUM ELECTRODYNAMICS

The fine structure constant α, first introduced by Sommerfeld [9] as a dimensionless number relating physical constants from quantum mechanics ($\hbar$), electromagnetics (q and ϵ_0) and relativity (c), remained mysterious in its origin [10, 16, 17], even though the constant has been widely used in all quantum field theories [11, 12]. As per the current work, it is now clear that the fine structure constant has its fundamental origin in a new Unified Electro-Gravity (UEG) theory, developed for modeling of elementary particles [1]. A dimensionless constant emerges in the UEG theory, relating a constant used in the theory (the UEG constant γ) with an elementary particle's stable mass and the particle's classical radius, which appeared to be closely related (numerically) to the fine structure constant [1]. In the present work, this dimensionless constant from the UEG theory of [1] is shown

to also govern the spin dynamics of the electron that determines the spin angular momentum, and consequently is shown to be directly related (on physical basis) to the fine structure constant. Interestingly, the dimensionless constant from the UEG theory, which is now related to the fine structure constant, is a normalized-parameter independent of any specific mass or charge of a particle, and therefore is a mathematically-based number, required to maintain a stable static particle (based on the UEG theory, before any spin is introduced) with a given charge q and a given UEG constant γ. Considering that it is a mathematically-based number, independent of any specific particle mass or charge, the dimensionless UEG constant or equivalently the fine structure constant is expected to carry a general scope of application to any elementary particle (electron/positron, proton/anti-proton, for example). By extension, the scope of the constant would cover composite charged as well as neutral particles, consisting of of multiple charge layers. However, in the present work the theory is specifically applied to the spin dynamics of an electron, which is the simplest particle.

A.　Quantization of Charge and Angular Momentum as Complementary, Emergent Concepts

The discovery of the new UEG theory of such significance, to which the fundamental origin of the fine structure constant of quantum electrodynamics could be traced, is bound to open reexamination of many related physical phenomena, that remained mysterious and unsolved to date. Consider an immediate consequence of the discovery. Once the fine structure constant $\alpha = q^2/(4\pi\epsilon_0 \hbar c)$ is independently established as a fundamental dimensionless constant that determines the stable mass and spin dynamics of an elementary particle, then the required constant α, for a given angular-momentum parameter $\hbar$ and a reference value of c, would force the elementary quantity q^2/ϵ_0 (or equivalently $q/\sqrt{\epsilon_0}$) to be a fixed, quantized value. This would be the case, when any new charge is created in the form of a particle-antiparticle pair. The available quantized angular momenta, in integral multiples of $\hbar$ from any transitional "photon packets" (see later discussion on the photon concept), are expected to dynamically force the two charges (positive and negative) in the particle-antiparticle pair, to each acquire a fixed value of magnitude q (given ϵ_0 and c as reference constants). This is a significant new understanding of the elementary charge q as a dynamically emergent, fixed quantity, no longer a pre-assigned parameter as currently understood. The new understanding could solve the current mystery of the natural quantization of all available charges, because they all would consist of an integral number of the elementary charge ($+q$ or $-q$), each having the same magnitude, which is dynamically fixed at the time of their production, enforced by the UEG theory and quantization of the available angular momenta.

Conversely, given the fixed magnitude q of an elementary charge already available, the required (dictated by the UEG theory) constant $\alpha = q^2/(4\pi\epsilon_0 \hbar c)$ would fix the charge's angular momentum $\hbar/2$ (given ϵ_0 and c as reference constants), as well as its energy-frequency relationship $W' = \hbar\omega'$ (section VI). Consequently, all "photon packets" (light radiation), that are naturally produced through a coupling process with the non-linear UEG fields of the elementary charge (see later discussion on the photon concept), would be each associated with a quantized angular momentum $(= \hbar)$ and energy $(= \hbar\omega)$, which are pre-fixed by the angular momentum $\hbar/2$ of the coupling charge. These available transitional "photons," which are assumed to be general exchange media in the charge creation process discussed earlier, would, in turn, determine the magnitude of each new elementary charge $\pm q$ created. Accordingly, the Planck's constant $\hbar$ and the elementary charge magnitude q would constitute a complementary pair of constants, that are naturally emergent, balanced with each other through the dynamics of the UEG theory and the classical electromagnetic theory.

The continual balancing process between the elementary charge q and the Planck's constant $\hbar$, as discussed above, may be traced back to the beginning of the current universe. All naturally-existing elementary charges were created in this beginning phase, possibly through a chained reaction process that was originally balanced by the angular momentum of a transitional photon, which in turn was synchronized with the annihilating elementary charges from a preceding collapsing universe. This may presume a cyclic universe, where the same fixed magnitude of the elementary charge in the current universe would also be maintained through annihilation in a collapsing phase in the future, into re-creation in a new bouncing universe, by repeating the above $q - \hbar$ synchronization process.

B.　Wave-Particle Duality

As the new model of electron spin clearly establishes, the charged center of the electron is surrounded by the "quantum ripples" which are actual ripples or variations in the structure or characteristics (permittivity) of the "free-space" itself. Accordingly, the electron would exhibit particle-like behavior governed by its central core, and as well exhibit its wave-like behavior due to the surrounding ripples. This would explain the wave-particle dual behavior of the electron, which has been experimentally observed, but is considered to be mysterious based on the current quantum-mechanical understanding. The ripples are produced by non-linear spin dynamics of the central electron, based on the UEG theory which is fundamentally non-linear. The central particle and the surrounding quantum ripples can not be de-linked from each other, and are expected to complement each other in all physical processes. Any motion of the electron at the center would also be guided by the surrounding quantum ripples, that are constrained by suitable UEG principles, or equivalently governed by the quantum-mechanical principles [6, 8, 18]. These ripples in the free-space may represent the pilot wave proposed by de Broglie [19, 20], which could be used to physically explain the measured interference pattern of the electron when it passes through a screen with two closely-spaced slits. The central core of the particle could be physically guided by the interference pattern created by its own surrounding pilot wave [21]. This would result in having the physical locations, where the central charged particle is actually detected by a suitable measurement, to be probabilistically distributed by the same pattern as the pilot-wave's interference.

C.　Electrodynamic Scattering, Photoelectric Effect, and the Photon Concept

Further, a non-linear UEG process similar to that responsible for generation of the UEG/quantum-mechanical ripple or wave of a spinning electron, with its energy (momentum) directly related in proportion to the wave frequency (wave number), could also be responsible for non-linear interaction of the UEG/quantum-mechanical wave of an electron with a UEG/field wave of an incident or outgoing light (photon). This would result in dynamic "mixing" between the UEG/quantum-mechanical/field waves of the electron and the photon. The process would be analogous to frequency up- or down-conversion in transistor electronic circuits [22], produced due to non-linear mixing of two time-dependent electrical signals of different frequencies, having the concept extended for both time- and space-dependent signals. Based on a suitable non-linear mixing process, it is conceivable that any change of the light's frequency (wave number) would be negative of that of the electron's UEG/quantum-mechanical frequency (wave number). The change of the electron's frequency (wave number) would be in direct proportion to that of its energy (momentum), with the constant of proportionality equal to $\hbar$, as per the UEG theory of the electron. In addition, the change of the electron's energy (momentum) would be equal to the negative change of the light's energy (momentum), as per the principle of energy (momentum) conservation. Therefore, combining the above three conditions, the change of the light's frequency (wave number) would be in direct proportion to that of its own, or equivalently negative of the electron's, energy (momentum), with the constant of proportionality equal to $\hbar$. This mechanism could physically explain the Compton scattering [23], without having to accept it as some mysterious fundamental "quantum phenomenon".

A similar non-linear, dynamic mixing process could also explain the nature of quantized absorption/radiation of light (photon) energy, by/from a given material, by associating the process with a known quantized energy transition of the material's electrons (due to material's atomic or molecular structure). As per the non-linear mixing process and the principle of energy conservation, the wave frequency and energy quanta of any absorbed/radiated light (photon) could be explained to be equal to positive/negative changes in UEG-quantum-mechanical wave frequency and energy of a transitioning electron of the material, respectively. The changes in the electron's radian frequency and energy are known to be proportional to each other, with the constant of proportionality equal to $\hbar$, as per the UEG theory of the electron. Therefore, combining the above conditions, the absorbed/radiated light's radian frequency and the energy quantum would also be directly related in proportion to each other, with the constant of proportionality $\hbar$. Extending this principle, in case an incident light's frequency exceeds the above threshold frequency of absorption, the process would be associated with a scattered light of a lower frequency. In this process, using a similar explanation as above, the energy quantum of electron transition can be shown to be proportional to the difference in the radian frequencies between the incident and scattered light, with the constant of proportionality $\hbar$. This could physically explain Raman type scattering [24] as well as Einstein's photoelectric effect [25], without invoking any "quantum mystery".

Further, using known relationship between the light's energy and the angular momentum (in a circularly-polarized state), with their ratio equal to the radian frequency ($= \omega$) as per the classical electromagnetic theory [26, 27], the spin-like angular momentum associated with each energy-quantum of light ($= \hbar\omega$), as deduced above, would be equal to $\hbar$. All these combined principles of light would now provide a complete physical explanation, based on the UEG theory and classical electromagnetic theory, for the nature of a "photon packet" in the Einstein's photoelectric effect [25], or the Compton/Raman type scatterings [23, 24], and similarly in the Planck's black-body radiation [7]. Accordingly, Planck's initial suspicion - that the quantum-mechanical "photon packet" might not represent any "mysterious" fundamental nature of the light itself, but could simply be a book-keeping tool that happened to properly model the absorption/radiation of light [28, 29] - may after all be validated by the new UEG theory.

The underlying mechanism of a dynamic, non-linear mixing processes, as discussed above, seem conceptually clear. However, its detailed understanding and modeling may require development of a complete, dynamic Unified Electro-Gravito-Magnetic (UEGM) theory of an elementary charge, interacting or mixing in the presence of an external electromagnetic radiation (light). Such a general theory is at this point premature, beyond the scope of the present work.

---

[1] N. Das, "A New Unified Electro-Gravity (UEG) Theory of the Electron," Paper #1, pp.4-13, in "A Unified Electro-Gravity (UEG) Theory of Nature," (2018).

[2] S. I. Newton, *Principia: Mathematical Principles of Natural Philosophy. I. B. Cohen, A. Whitman and J. Budenz, English Translators from 1726 Original* (University of California Press, 1999).

[3] A. Einstein, Annalen der Physik **322**, 891 (1905).

[4] J. C. Maxwell, *A Treatise on Electricity and Magnetism, Vol. I and II (Reprint from 1873)* (Dover Publications, 2007).

[5] A. Einstein, Annalen der Physik **354**, 769 (1916).

[6] E. Schrodinger, Annalen der Physik **384**, 361 (1926).

[7] M. Planck, Annalen der Physik **309**, 553 (1901).

[8] P. A. M. Dirac, Proceedings of the Royal Society A: Mathematical, Physical and Engineering Sciences **117**, 610 (1928).

[9] A. Sommerfeld, *Atomic Structure and Spectral Lines. (Translated by H. L. Brose)* (Methuen, 1923).

[10] R. P. Feynman, *QED: The Strange Theory of Light and Matter (p. 129)* (Princeton University Press, 1985).

[11] S. Brodsky, V. Franke, J. Hiller, G. McCartor, S. Paston, and E. P. and, Nuclear Physics B **46**, 353 (2004).

[12] N. Cottingham and D. Greenwood, *An Introduction to the Standard Model of Particle Physics (2Ed)* (Cambridge University Press, 2007).

[13] Wikipedia, "g-factor," `http://en.wikipedia.org/wiki/G-factor_(physics)`, Retrieved (2017).

[14] Wikipedia, "Fine-Structure Constant," `http://en.wikipedia.org/wiki/Fine_structure_constant`, Retrieved (2017).

[15] B. Mashhoon, F. Gronwald, and H. I. M. Lichtenegger, Gyros, Clocks, Interferometers ...: Testing Relativistic Gravity in Space **562**, 83 (2001).

[16] M. H. McGregor, *The Power of Alpha (p. 69)* (World Scientific, 2007).

[17] L. M. Lederman and D. Teresi, *The God Particle: If the Universe is the Answer, What is the Question (ch.2)* (Dell Publishing, 1993).

[18] W. Pauli, Journal of Physics **43**, 601 (1927).

[19] L. de Broglie, Journal de Physique et le Radium **8**, 225 (1927).

[20] D. Bohm, Physical Review **85**, 166 (1952).

[21] Y. Couder and E.Fort, Physical Review Letters **97** (2006).

[22] D. M. Pozar, *Microwave Engineering, 2nd Edition* (John Wiley and Sons, 1998).

[23] A. H. Compton, Physical Review **21**, 483 (1923).

[24] C. V. Raman and K. S. Krishnan, Nature **121**, 501 (1928).

[25] A. Einstein, Annalen der Physik **17**, 132 (1905).

[26] Wikipedia, "Angular Momentum of Light," `http://en.wikipedia.org/wiki/Spin_angular_momentum_of_light`, Retrieved (2018).

[27] A. M. Stewart, arXiv:physics. class-ph, physics/0504082v3 (2005).

[28] T. S. Kuhn, *Black-Body Theory and Quantum Discontinuity* (Oxford: Clarendon Press, 1978).

[29] H. Kragh, "Max Planck: The Reluctant Revolutionary 1894-1912," PhysicsWorld.com (2000).

Part-II: Extension of the Unified Electro-Gravity (UEG) Theory
in the Large Scale: Stellar, Galactic and Cosmology Models

Unified Electro-Gravity (UEG) Theory Applied to Stellar Gravitation, and the Mass-Luminosity Relation (MLR)

Nirod K. Das

Department of Electrical and Computer Engineering, Tandon School of Engineering,
New York University, 5 Metrotech Center, Brooklyn, NY 11201
(Dated: May 9, 2018)

The Unified Electro-Gravity (UEG) theory is applied to model gravitational effects of an individual star or a binary-star system, including that of the Sun which is the only star of our solar system. The basic UEG theory was originally developed to model elementary particles, as a substitute for the standard model of particle physics. The UEG theory is extended in this paper (a) to model gravitational force due to light radiation from an individual star, which determines its energy output due to nuclear fusion in the star, as well as (b) to model the gravitational force between two nearby stars, which determines the orbital dynamics in a binary-star system. The mass-luminosity relation (MLR) derived separately from each of the above two models are compared and studied together with the MLR currently available from measured orbital data for binary stars, as well as from an existing energy-source model for stellar nuclear fusion (Eddington's model). The current MLR data uses conventional Newtonian gravity, where the gravitational force is produced due to the "conventional gravitational mass" of a star, which is assumed to be equal to the inertial mass as per the principle of equivalence. This Newtonian gravitational model is modified by including new UEG effect due to the light radiation of a star, in order to establish the actual MLR which can be significantly different from the currently available MLR. The new UEG theory is applied to an individual isolated star (for modeling the force for stellar nuclear fusion), which is spherically symmetric about its own center, in a fundamentally different manner from its application to a binary-star system (for modeling orbital motion of a binary-star), which is not a spherically-symmetric structure.

I. INTRODUCTION

A new Unified Electro-Gravity (UEG) theory was developed in [1, 2], as a substitute for the standard model of particle physics, which successfully modeled elementary particles. The UEG theory introduced a new definition for the energy density in an electromagnetic field, which effectively resulted in having a new gravitational force proportional to the conventional energy density, directed toward the center of gravity of a particle. The center of gravity of the particle is located at its physical center due to spherical symmetry of the structure, because the particle is assumed to be spherically symmetric with respect to itself and it is treated ideally in isolation from any surrounding object. This simplicity of spherical symmetry may not be valid in general situations, for example in modeling gravitation due to light radiation from individual stars in a binary-star system [3], which clearly is not spherically symmetric with respect to the total structure, even though its two individual partner stars may be spherically symmetric with respect to their own physical centers. The basic UEG theory of [1] developed for particle physics, needs to be modified for a general radiating structure with no simple symmetry, particularly to model gravitation in a binary-star system with approximately identical partner stars.

Computation of an equivalent gravitational force due to stellar radiation from a given star, as per the new UEG theory, requires definition of (a) a suitable gravitational center toward which the force is directed at, determined by the gravitational parameters of the particular star as well as of its surrounding objects, and (b) a suitable effective energy density defined at the point of observation of the force, determined by the intensity distribution due to the star's radiation in the vicinity of the observation point. A rigorous UEG model that would be applicable for any stellar or galactic structure, with general distribution of radiation, appear premature at this point. In this paper, we postulate a suitable model for a binary-star structure, applied specifically when its individual partner stars are approximately similar to each other and are positioned relatively close to each other (eclipsing binary), as useful special situations. This would allow us to revisit the mass-luminosity relation (MLR) of [3, 4], deduced from measured observation of mostly closely spaced, eclipsing binaries [5]. Considering the large range of star luminosities in [3], with upper limit as large as 10^5 solar luminosity, we expect the effective gravitational mass of an individual star in a binary system to be in general appreciably different from its inertial mass, due to additional UEG effect from the stellar radiation. In other words, the mass term in the MLR of [3], which should in principle be the gravitational mass of a star but is assumed to be equal to its inertial mass as per the principle of equivalence of general relativity [6], might not be really equal to the inertial mass of a star. The actual inertial mass would be deduced using the proposed model to provide a new stellar MLR ((actual inertial)mass-luminosity relation). This would be a modern advancement in the physics of stellar gravitation, as it relates to the orbital dynamics of binary stars, based on the new UEG theory.

The MLR data from orbital measurement of binary stars were also believed to be confirmed in [4, 7], with sound theoretical results from a stellar energy-source model based on balancing of gravitational pressure with thermal pressure from nuclear fusion (Eddington's Model). Therefore, in order to definitively validate the UEG theory, the energy-source model also needs to be modified based on the UEG theory, and the results for both the models of [3, 7] must be shown to be consistent with each other. Accordingly, the new MLR ((actual inertial) mass-luminosity relation) as derived from a stellar energy-source model should be the same or sufficiently similar to that deduced, as discussed earlier, from binary-star measurements, when the additional gravitation effects of the new UEG theory are included. In equivalent terms, for a given actual mass (inertial) and its associated light output of a star, the presence of the additional gravitational effects due to the new UEG theory in the two MLR models should lead to the same or comparable "equivalent-mass" as the mass-term in the MLR data of [3, 4, 7], which is derived using only conventional Newtonian gravity. The "equivalent-mass" parameter, which is a function of the inertial mass and star light, is defined here such that the expression of the star's luminosity derived using any particular model based on only Newtonian gravity, and that using a rigorous derivation including additional gravitation due to the star light as per the UEG theory, would appear in functionally identical forms. Except, the mass term in the simple Newtonian case is replaced by the equivalent-mass in the rigorous derivation using the UEG theory.

The gravitational forces which determine nuclear fusion in the energy-source model of a star act differently from those in a binary-star system which determine the orbital motion of the partner stars. In the former case, the gravitational forces of a given star act upon the star's own mass (ignoring any small opposing gravitation from nearby star(s)), whereas in the later the gravitational forces from one partner star acts upon the mass of the other of the binary system. The former is a spherically symmetric problem, whereas the later is not. The existing models in [3, 7] are based on conventional Newtonian gravity, where the the same gravitational mass is used when the star is either a source or target of gravitation, which is equal to the inertial mass of the star. Consequently, the same unique mass term, equal to the inertial mass of the star, is used in the two existing MLR models of [3, 7]. However, due to the basic differing natures of gravitation acting in the two MLR models, as explained above, one might be inclined to expect that the presence of any additional gravitational forces due to the new UEG theory would in general result in two different "equivalent-mass" terms for the two models, leading to apparent inconsistency in the UEG theory. However, the "equivalent-mass" terms in the two MLR models, based on the new UEG theory, would be shown in this paper to end up with approximately the same functional trend and magnitude, thus resolving the apparent inconsistency. This would be a significant result, definitively validating the UEG theory, as extended to stellar nuclear

fusion as well as orbital dynamics of binary stars.

It may be noted, that the MLR of [3, 4, 7] for solar-mass stars is implicitly assumed to confirm with the measured luminosity of the Sun and its effective gravitational mass as observed from planetary motions in our solar system. The Sun is the only star in our solar system, with orbiting planets having a fraction of the solar mass [8]. Accordingly, the Sun may be treated essentially as an isolated star, for modeling its gravitation using the UEG theory. Under this condition, the effective gravitational mass m_g of the Sun would be equal to the sum of its inertial mass m and the UEG mass m_u due to its total luminosity L_0. That is, $m_g = m + m_u$. The UEG mass m_u may be calculated using the known value of solar luminosity L_0 [9] and the UEG constant γ deduced in [1, 2] from modeling of elementary particles. As mentioned, the total effective gravitational mass of the Sun is also known [9], based on the observed orbital periods of planets. The inertial mass of the Sun may then be estimated by subtracting the UEG mass from the total effective gravitational mass. Now, in order that the UEG theory confirms with the two models of MLR [3, 4, 7], specifically for the mass parameters of the Sun, we need to show that the mass (actual inertial) term in the "new" MLR derived using the UEG theory is equal to the known inertial mass m of the Sun, whereas the mass (equivalent gravitational) term in the "existing" MLR [3, 4, 7] is equal to the known gravitational mass m_g of the Sun, when the luminosity is equal to the solar luminosity. Conversely, the expressions of the MLRs (new and existing) derived in functional forms, with the additional functional constraint $m_g = m + m_u$ required specifically for the Sun, could allow for an estimate solution of the unknown UEG mass m_u of the Sun, from which the UEG constant γ could be deduced. This would provide a useful estimation for the UEG constant γ, which may be verified with estimation from the particle physics model [1]. This would independently support the UEG theory as well as the value of the UEG constant, for the stellar models.

The expressions of the MLR, currently existing based on the conventional Newtonian gravity, is introduced in section II. This is followed by presentations of the two new models including the UEG effects. The spherically symmetric problem of the stellar energy-source model would be presented first in section III. The relatively simple and definitive results from this study would then be used together with the required constraints for the Sun, in order to analytically estimate the UEG constant γ. This would be followed by modeling of the gravitation in a binary-star system in section IV, based on the UEG theory. A general treatment applicable for any separation between the partner stars, and any level of luminosity and associated UEG mass of each star, would be presented. This would require numerical integration for evaluating the gravitational force between the two stars. In addition, a useful limiting situation when the effective gravitational force of each star is much larger than its inertial mass, will be presented. The gravitational force in the limiting case can be evaluated using simple analytical formulas, which may be compared with the results from the general derivation for validation. The results for new MLR deduced from the energy-source and the binary-star models would be compared with each other, as well cross-checked with the parameters of the Sun in section V, followed by general discussions and conclusions from the study in section V.

II. STELLAR MASS LUMINOSITY RELATION (MLR) BASED ON NEWTONIAN GRAVITATION

The relationship between stellar mass, m, and luminosity, L, as it currently exists to date, is expressed as [4]:

$$
\begin{aligned}
\frac{L}{L_0} &= 0.23(\frac{m}{m_0})^{2.3}, \ m < 0.43m_0, \\
&= (\frac{m}{m_0})^4, \ 0.43m_0 < m < 2m_0, \\
&= 1.5(\frac{m}{m_0})^{3.5}, \ 2m_0 < m < 20m_0, \\
&= 3200(\frac{m}{m_0}), \ m > 20m_0.
\end{aligned}
\tag{1}
$$

where the parameters with a subscript 0 are associated with the Sun, which is the only star in our solar system. This existing MLR was deduced from measurements of binary stars based on stellar dynamics using Newtonian gravitation, and was independently supported by a theoretical model of the stellar energy source based on balancing the pressure of Newtonian gravitation with the thermal pressure due to nuclear fusion. According to the equivalent modelings presented in the following sections, the mass m in (1) would be equal to the equivalent gravitational mass $m_g = m_{ge}$ in the orbital dynamics model of section IV, or the equivalent mass m_e in the energy source model of section III. Therefore, the solar mass m_0 in (1) refers to the equivalent gravitational mass m_{g0} of the Sun, which is also equal to the equivalent solar mass m_{e0} from the energy source model. It may be noted, the $m_0 = m_{g0} = m_{e0}$ may be different from the actual solar mass (inertial) based on the UEG theory, as discussed in the section I.

The m_g and m_e would be functions of both the conventional inertial mass m and the luminosity L of a star. Each of these equivalent masses is expected to be equal to the inertial mass m, when the UEG effects are excluded in the modeling, keeping the existing MLR (1) unchanged in this case. On the other hand, when the UEG effects are included, the luminosity derived from the following new models would be equal to that from the existing MLR (1), if the mass m in the existing MLR is replaced by the equivalent mass, m_g or m_e, of the respective models. The MLR (1) is shown in Fig.6, indicated as the (m_g - L)

or (m_e - L) relationship, according to the above equivalence. The actual mass m (inertial) is expected to be in general different from the m_g or m_e. Therefore, an actual MLR (mass (actual, inertial)-luminosity relation) is also expected to be different from (1), as derived and presented in section V.

III. ENERGY SOURCE MODEL FOR THE MASS LUMINOSITY RELATION, USING CONVENTIONAL GRAVITY AND UEG THEORY

Let us first consider derivation based on a conventional Newtonian model, but keeping in mind distinct contributions that may need be modified when the UEG effects are then included in a new model. Note that there are actually two distinct mass parameters that together would contribute to the energy or light output in a star: one mass parameter is the source of gravity, and the other is the target mass on which gravity is acting upon. However, in the Newtonian gravity model, the two gravitational mass parameters happen to be equal to each other and are equal to the inertial mass. Let us take for granted that the existing Eddington's model [4, 7] (1) for the mass-luminosity relation (MLR), which expresses the luminosity L as a function $L(m)$ of the mass m, is in principle correct, assuming only the Newtonian gravity is applied without any UEG effect. Let us rewrite the function $L(m)$ in the form of its inverse function $m(L)$, the square of which is the mass-square function $m^2(L)$. When the UEG effects are added, let us define an equivalent-mass m_e, such that the new MLR would be equal to the Eddington's MLR when its mass term m is replaced by the m_e. Accordingly, the Eddington's mass-square function $m^2(L)$ is actuality the $m_e^2(L)$ function when the UEG effects are added. Clearly, the m_e^2 is equal to m^2 when only the Newtonian gravitation is included. We assume that the equivalent mass-squared function is a product of two mass terms indicated above. One of the mass terms, corresponding to the target mass of gravitation would remain unchanged equal to the inertial mass m, with or without the UEG effect. This is because the UEG theory only changes the gravitational acceleration, which needs to be multiplied with the same target (inertial) mass to get the gravitational force, just as in the Newtonian case. The source-mass term would be sum of two parts, one of which represents the Newtonian gravitation which remains unchanged as the inertial mass m. Whereas, the second part of the source mass is contributed due to the UEG effect, and is expected to be proportional to the luminosity L or equivalently to its UEG mass m_u.

$$m_e^2(L) = m(L)(m(L) + \alpha m_u(L)), \ m_e = [m(m + \alpha m_u)]^{0.5}.$$

$$m_e^2 = m^2 + \alpha m m_u \simeq (m + \tfrac{\alpha}{2} m_u)^2,$$

$$m_e \simeq (m + \tfrac{\alpha}{2} m_u); m_u << m.$$

$$m_e^2 = m(m + \alpha m_u) = m(m + m_{ue}) = m m_{ge};$$

$$E_{gu}(r = d >> R) = \frac{G m_u}{d^2} = \gamma \frac{L}{4\pi d^2 c}, \ m_u = \frac{\gamma L}{4\pi G c}. \quad (2)$$

The equivalent model proposed above maybe established by deriving the average pressure in a star by including the UEG effects in addition to the conventional Newtonian gravitation, and equating it with that by including only the conventional Newtonian gravitation [7], when mass m in the later result is substituted with the equivalent mass m_e. This equivalent mass parameter associated with the average pressure would substitute for all mass-terms in the Eddington's model [7], in order to properly predict the luminosity, as per the new UEG theory of stellar radiation and thermodynamics.

With this goal, let us first derive the average pressure due to only the UEG effect. For a typical star like the Sun, the volume density ρ_{vL} of luminosity, resulting in the total luminosity L, may be assumed to be uniform. The energy density of radiation produced by a volume element of the energy source located at (r', θ, ϕ), and observed at $(r = z, \theta = 0)$, may be integrated over the entire spherical volume of the star of radius R, to obtain the total energy density $W_\tau(r)$. Due to spherical symmetry, the energy density would be independent of the θ and ϕ coordinates of the observation location, dependent only on its radial distance r.

$$W_\tau(r) = \int_{r'=0}^{R} \int_{\theta=0}^{\pi} \int_{\phi=0}^{2\pi} \frac{\rho_{vL} r'^2 \sin\theta \, d\phi \, d\theta \, dr'}{4\pi c(r^2 + r'^2 - 2rr'\cos\theta)}$$

$$= \frac{\rho_{vL}}{4c} \int_{r'=0}^{R} \int_{t=(r-r')^2}^{(r+r')^2} (\tfrac{r'}{r})(\tfrac{1}{t}) dt \, dr'; (t = r^2 + r'^2 - 2rr'\cos\theta)$$

$$= \frac{\rho_{vL}}{4c} \int_{r'=0}^{R} (\tfrac{r'}{r}) \ln \frac{(r'+r)^2}{(r'-r)^2} dr' = \frac{\rho_{vL}}{4c}[(\tfrac{R^2}{2r}) \ln \frac{(R+r)^2}{(R-r)^2}$$

$$+ \int_{0}^{R} \frac{2r'^2}{(r'^2 - r^2)} dr'] = \frac{\rho_{vL}}{2c}[R + (\frac{R^2 - r^2}{2r}) \ln \frac{R+r}{R-r}];$$

$$W_\tau(r = 0) = \frac{\rho_{vL} R}{c}, \ W_\tau(r = R) = \frac{\rho_{vL} R}{2c}. \quad (3)$$

The UEG acceleration $E_{gu}(r)$, directed towards the center, can now be expressed by multiplying the energy density with the UEG constant γ [1], from which the pressure $P_u(r)$ and average pressure $< P_u >$ may be obtained as follows. For an approximate reference and simplicity of understanding, the energy density function $W_\tau(r)$ may be roughly approximated over the region $r < R$ by linear interpolation of the values at $r = 0$ and $r = R$, which can then be analytically integrated to obtain the pressure function and the average pressure. Numerical integration

would be needed for accurate calculations, which may be verified with the analytical results from the approximate reference.

$$E_{gu}(r) = \gamma W_\tau(r),$$

$$E_{gu}(r = 0) = \gamma W_\tau(r = 0) = \frac{\gamma \rho_{vL} R}{c} = \frac{3 G m_u}{R^2},$$

$$E_{gu}(r = R) = \gamma W_\tau(r = R) = \frac{\gamma \rho_{vL} R}{2c} = \frac{1.5 G m_u}{R^2},$$

$$E_{gu}(r < R) \simeq \frac{G m_u}{R^2}(3 - 1.5(\tfrac{r}{R})), \quad (4)$$

$$P_u(r) = \int_{r}^{R} \rho_{vm} E_{gu}(r) dr$$

$$\simeq \frac{G m_u m}{(4/3\pi R^4)}[3(1 - (\tfrac{r}{R}) - 0.75(1 - (\tfrac{r}{R})^2)],$$

$$< P_u >= \frac{1}{R} \int_{0}^{R} P_u(r) dr = 1.20 \frac{G m_u m}{(4/3)\pi R^4} \sim \frac{G m_u m}{(4/3)\pi R^4};$$

$$\rho_{vm} = \frac{m}{(4/3)\pi R^3}, \ \rho_{vL} = \frac{L}{(4/3)\pi R^3}. \quad (5)$$

Similar steps as above may be used for Newtonian gravitation to obtain the acceleration function $E_{gm}(r)$, pressure function $P_m(r)$, and average pressure $< P_m >$.

$$E_{gm}(r < R) = \frac{G m r}{R^3},$$

$$P_m(r) = \int_{r}^{R} \rho_{vm} E_{gm}(r) dr = \frac{G m^2}{(4/3)\pi R^4}[0.5(1 - (\tfrac{r}{R})^2)],$$

$$< P_m >= \frac{1}{R} \int_{0}^{R} P_u(r) dr = \frac{G m^2}{4\pi R^4}. \quad (6)$$

The average pressure $< P >$ in the presence of both the Newtonian and UEG forces would be the sum of the two terms $< P_u >$ and $< P_m >$. Whereas, the average pressure for conventional Newtonian gravity is $< P_m >$. As prescribed earlier for the equivalent modeling in (2), the equivalent mass m_e may now be expressed in terms of the UEG mass m_u and the inertial mass m. This may be compared with what we expected in (2), from which the equivalent UEG mass $m_{ue} = \alpha m_u$, and consequently the parameter α, may be deduced. The α is roughly estimated to be 3.0 using analytical integration based on the reference approximation of $E_{gu}(r)$ in (4), but is accurately calculated to be 3.60, using numerical integration based on the rigorous expressions of $E_{gu}(r)$ and $W_\tau(r)$ in (3,4).

$$< P_m >_{m=m_e} =< P >=< P_m > + < P_u >,$$

$$\frac{G m_e^2}{4\pi R^4} = \frac{G m^2}{4\pi R^4} + \frac{1.20 G m m_u}{(4/3)\pi R^4} \sim \frac{G m^2}{4\pi R^4} + \frac{G m m_u}{(4/3)\pi R^4},$$

$$m_e^2 = m(m + 3.60 m_u) = m(m + m_{ue}), \ \alpha = 3.60. \quad (7)$$

This calculation for the α is expected to be generally valid for most typical stars, similar to our Sun. For very high luminosity stars, as compared to the Sun, the source distribution of the luminosity may not be uniform as assumed in the above analysis, but could be more concentrated towards the center where the pressure can be significantly higher. This may lead to a higher value for the α in these cases, as per the above modeling.

A. Estimating the UEG Constant from Energy Source Model for a Solar-Mass Star

The Sun, which is the only star in our solar system, was used as the reference in the MLR of (1). Note that the mass of the Sun that has been historically deduced from measurement of orbital motions of all planets, in consistency with that of our own planet earth, is actually the equivalent gravitational mass of the Sun. Based on the UEG theory, introduced in the following section IV, the Sun may be considered an isolated body, for evaluation of its gravitational force acting on the planets in the solar system. This is because the Sun is an isolated star, and all the planets in the solar system are considerably much lighter than the Sun. Accordingly, the equivalent gravitational mass m_g of the Sun would be the sum of its inertial mass m and its UEG mass m_u (as defined in 2). This $m_g = m + m_u$ for the Sun needs to be equated to the equivalent mass m_e used here for energy source modeling, as well as to the m_g in the orbital modeling in section IV, for all solar-mass stars, in full consistency with the MLR of (1).

Applying the above solar condition $m_e = m + m_u$ in (7) leads to calculation of the m_u from the known value of the solar gravitational mass $m_g = m_e = 1.989 \times 10^{30} kg$ [9]. This calculated value of m_u can then be used in (2) to estimate the UEG constant γ, given the solar luminosity $L = L_0 = 3.828 \times 10^{26} W$ [9].

$$(m + m_u)^2 = m^2 + m_u^2 + 2mm_u = m(m + m_u e)$$
$$= m^2 + 3.60mm_u, m_u = 1.60m,$$
$$m_e = m + m_u = (1 + 1/1.60)m_u,$$
$$m_u = (1.60/2.60)m_e = 0.615m_e, m = 0.385m_e,$$
$$\gamma = m_u 4\pi Gc/L = 0.615m_e 4\pi Gc/L$$
$$= 0.804 \times 10^3 \, (m/s^2)/(J/m^3). \tag{8}$$

This estimate compares reasonably close to an accurate calculation of $\gamma = 0.6 \times 10^3 \, (m/s^2)/(J/m^3)$ from a particle physics model [1], with a difference of about 33%. Considering that the present estimation is based on some simple assumptions and formulations of the UEG effects on star luminosity, the above result is a reasonable support for the value of the UEG constant as well as for the UEG theory. With the accurate value of $\gamma = 0.6 \times 10^3$ $(m/s^2)/(J/m^3)$ from the particle physics model, the different mass parameters of (8) may be back-calculated as $m_u = 0.46m_e$, $m = 0.54m_e$, $m_u = 0.85m$, $m_u e = 2.85m_u$, with $\alpha = m_u e/m_u = 2.85$, which is within a reasonable

($\sim 26\%$) difference from the estimate of $\alpha = 3.60$ in (7). Further, using the accurate values of $m_u = 0.46m_e$ and $m = 0.54m_e$, the value of the effective mass that would be estimated using the estimated value of $\alpha = 3.60$ in (7), is equal to m_e(estimate) $= \sqrt{0.54(0.54 + 3.60 \times 0.46)}m_e = 1.09m_e$, which is within a small ($\sim 10\%$) difference from the actual m_e. Any such reasonable difference between the estimated and actual magnitudes of the equivalent mass may be accommodated (b) by using a more realistic energy-source distribution that is different from the ideal uniform distribution assumed in the present model, or (b) by adjusting the magnitude of the MLR (1) deduced from the energy source model of [4, 7] (Eddington's model) to be reasonably different from that from binary-star measurements, both of which we simply presumed to be identical. However, it is more significant to note the functional form of the equivalent mass (7), which would be shown in the following section IV to compare remarkably with an alternate relationship (19) derived from a binary-star model, for large m_u/m, that would provide a strong validation for the UEG theory.

Supported by the above estimations from the star-luminosity model, and to be supported even further by a UEG model of gravitation in a binary-star system in the following section IV, it is particularly significant to note the following consequence of the above results from the UEG theory. The inertial mass of the Sun might not be what we have been believing [8, 9], estimated based on the Newton's Laws of gravitation and motion [10, 11], using observation of planetary motions, including orbital motion of the earth around the Sun. We now find, as per the UEG theory, that the inertial mass m of the Sun could actually be about half ($m = 0.54m_e$) of what is calculated from the planetary motions based on the Newton's Laws. The approximately other half ($m_u = 0.46m_e$) is a result of the new UEG force due to the Sun's light. In other words, we are being pulled by the light of the Sun about as much as by the actual mass of the Sun! This would be a significant discovery, where the new UEG theory is shown to directly influence the gravitation in the solar system, and thus our common understanding of the basic nature of gravity that controls our own motion around the Sun.

IV. UEG MODEL FOR EFFECTIVE GRAVITATIONAL MASS OF A STAR IN A BINARY SYSTEM

A. Estimation of Distance Between Partner Stars in an Observed Eclipsing Binary System

The stellar mass-luminosity relation (MLR) is based on measurement survey of mostly eclipsing binary stars, where the partner stars are closely spaced from each other. Accordingly, in order to evaluate the MLR in relation to the new UEG theory, it would be useful to analytically estimate a typical or median value for the surface-

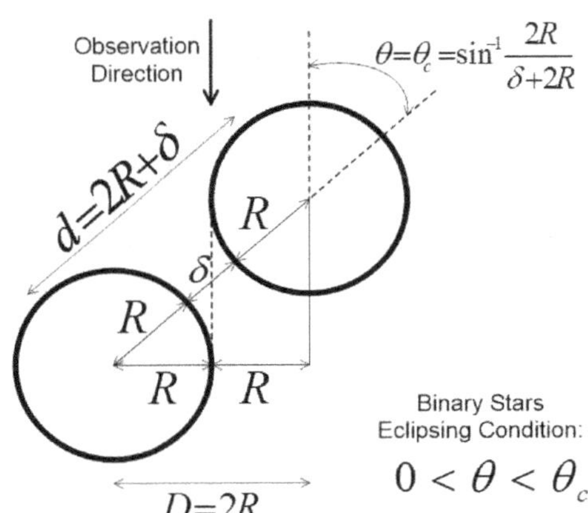

FIG. 1.

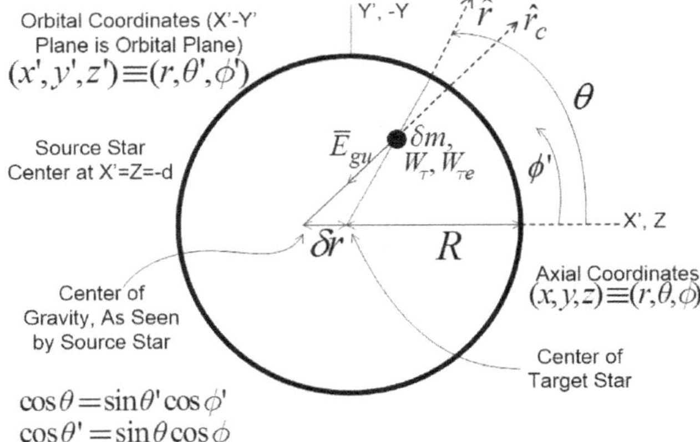

FIG. 2.

to-surface distance δ between the two partner stars. For simplicity the two stars may be assumed to be identical, each of radius R.

As shown in Fig.1, the critical angle $\theta = \theta_c$ between the orbital axis and the direction of observation, larger than which eclipsing would not be observed, may be expressed in terms of the surface-to surface distance δ and the star radius R. Assuming that orientation angle θ is equally likely between zero and $\pi/2$, stars with smaller θ_c (which is equivalent to a larger δ/R ratio), are less likely to be observed in a survey. A median probability $P > 0.5$ of observation would provide a useful estimate for the separation factor δ/R in an observed eclipsing binary system

$$P(0 < \theta < \theta_c) = \frac{2\theta_c}{\pi}, \ \sin\theta_c = \frac{2R}{2R+\delta} = \frac{D}{d} = \frac{1}{1+\frac{\delta}{2R}},$$

$$\frac{\delta}{2R} = (\csc\theta_c - 1);$$

$$\theta_c \geq \tfrac{\pi}{4}, \ P(0 < \theta < \theta_c) > 0.5, \ \delta \leq 2R(\csc\tfrac{\pi}{4} - 1) \simeq 0.8R,$$

$$\delta = \delta_m \simeq 0.4R \ . \tag{9}$$

B.　General Calculation of the UEG Force as a Function of the Equivalent Gravitational Mass

The additional gravitational force of attraction, as per the UEG theory, produced due to the light radiation from one star (source star) acting upon the other star (target star) in a binary system, would be directed towards a suitable center of gravity (CG). The distance δr (see Fig.2) of this CG from the center of the target star is determined by the effective gravitational mass mg of the target star and the inertial mass m of the source star.

$$\frac{m}{mg} = \frac{\delta r}{2R+\delta} = \frac{\delta r}{d}; \ mg >> m, \ \delta r << R, d \ . \tag{10}$$

The magnitude of the attraction upon an elemental mass δm, at a given location of the target star, is to be determined by the energy density W_τ reaching at the particular location due to radiation from the source star (presuming the target star was removed, or is transparent to the source-star's radiation). When the CG approaches the center of the target star (when $mg \to \infty$, $mg >> m$), we expect the total UEG force upon the target star to approach zero. In this limit, a mass-less source with any non-zero luminosity (finite or infinite) can not exert a non-zero force or acceleration upon a target of infinite mass. This condition may be empirically enforced by by redistribution of the energy-density function $W_\tau(r,\theta\phi$ into a new, effective energy-density function $W_{\tau e}(r,\theta,\phi)$ with appropriate symmetry. For a spherically symmetric target, this may be accomplished by simply using a constant $W_{\tau e}$, which is an average of the $W_\tau(r,\theta,\phi)$ over the entire target sphere. A less restrictive, general approach would be to define the effective energy density at a particular location as the average of the $W_\tau(r,\theta,\phi)$ over all θ and ϕ, for the same radial distance r of the given location. For further generality, we will choose an effective energy density $W_{\tau e}(r,\theta')$ which is cylindrically symmetric about the orbital axis (see Fig.2), calculated by taking an average of the $W_\tau(r,\theta',\phi')$ over all ϕ'.

$$W_{\tau e}(r,\theta,\phi) = W_{\tau e}(r',\theta'), \ r' = r, \ \theta' = \cos^{-1}(\sin\theta\cos\phi),$$

$$W_{\tau e}(r',\theta') = \frac{1}{2\pi}\int_{\phi'=0}^{2\pi} W_\tau(r',\theta',\phi')d\phi'$$

$$= \frac{1}{2\pi}\int_{\phi'=0}^{2\pi} \frac{L}{4\pi c(r'^2+d^2+2r'd\sin\theta'\cos\phi')}. \tag{11}$$

The gravitational acceleration $\overline{E}_{gu}$ due to the UEG effect may now be expressed using the $W_{\tau e}$ and the UEG constant γ.

$$\overline{E}gu(r,\theta,\phi) = -\hat{r}c\,Egu(r,\theta,\phi) = -\hat{r}c\gamma W_\tau e(r,\theta,\phi)$$

$$= -\hat{r}c\frac{1}{2\pi}\int_{\phi'=0}^{2\pi}\frac{Gm_u}{(r^2+d^2+2rd\cos\phi'\sqrt{1-\sin^2\theta\cos^2\phi})}d\phi',$$

$$m_u = \frac{\gamma L}{4\pi Gc}. \tag{12}$$

The total gravitational force $\overline{F}u$ towards the source star can be calculated by multiplying the $-\hat{z}$ component of the acceleration $\overline{E}gu$ with mass density ρvm, and integrating over the target sphere. An effective gravitational mass m_{ue} associated with the UEG force $\overline{F}u$ may be defined, and related to the source star luminosity L or its associated UEG mass m_u. The m_u is the equivalent gravitational mass of the source star in the limit of operating in isolation, when the mg of the target star approaches zero or the distance δ_{cg} approaches $-d/2$, which means the effective CG used in the evaluation of the UEG force is at the center of the source star.

$$\overline{F}u = -\hat{z}Fu = -\hat{z}\frac{Gm_{ue}m}{d^2},$$

$$Fu = \int_{r=0}^{R}\int_{\theta=0}^{\pi}\int_{\phi=0}^{2\pi}(-\overline{E}gu(r,\theta,\phi)\cdot\hat{z})\rho vm\,r^2\sin\theta\,d\phi d\theta dr$$

$$= \int_{r=0}^{R}\int_{\theta=0}^{\pi}\int_{\phi=0}^{2\pi}[E gu(r,\theta,\phi)\frac{r\cos\theta+\delta r}{\sqrt{r^2+\delta r^2+2r\delta r\cos\theta}}\rho vm$$

$$\times\,r^2\sin\theta\,d\phi d\theta dr],\quad \rho vm = \frac{m}{(4/3)\pi R^3}. \tag{13}$$

$$\frac{m_{ue}}{m_u} = \frac{Fu d^2}{Gmm_u} = \frac{d^2}{(4/3)\pi R^3}\int_{r=0}^{R}\int_{\theta=0}^{\pi}\int_{\phi=0}^{2\pi}[\frac{1}{2\pi}$$

$$\times\int_{\phi'=0}^{2\pi}\frac{1}{(r^2+d^2+2rd\cos\phi'\sqrt{1-\sin^2\theta\cos^2\phi})}d\phi']$$

$$\times\frac{r\cos\theta+\delta r}{\sqrt{r^2+\delta r^2+2r\delta r\cos\theta}}r^2\sin\theta\,d\phi d\theta dr. \tag{14}$$

C.   UEG Force of Attraction for a Large Equivalent Gravitational Mass

It may not be possible to evaluate the above general formulas analytically, requiring numerical integration for any general values of the source mass m and the target equivalent gravitational mass mg. However, when the mg is very large compared to the m, the CG would be close to the target star center, with the distance δr much smaller than the target radius R.

$$\frac{m}{mg} = \frac{\delta r}{2R+\delta} = \frac{\delta r}{d};\quad \delta r << R, d,\ mg >> m. \tag{15}$$

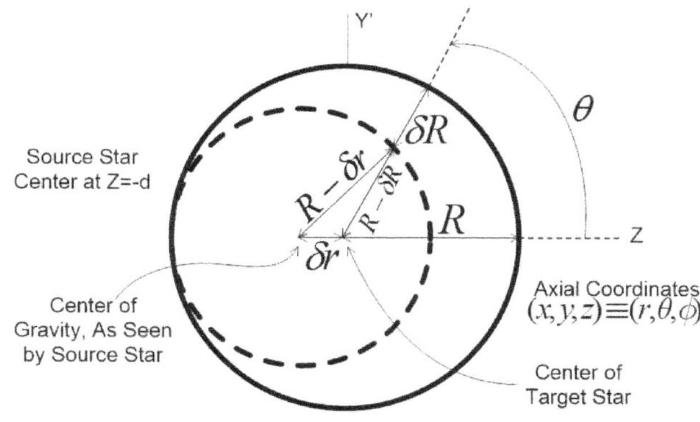

$$R - \delta r = \sqrt{(R-\delta R)^2 + (\delta r)^2 + 2\delta r(R-\delta R)\cos\theta}$$

$$\approx R - \delta R + \delta r\cos\theta,\ \delta R \approx \delta r(1+\cos\theta);\ \delta r, \delta R << R$$

FIG. 3.

The general formulas derived above can be simplified for this limiting case. For further simplicity of calculation, we would assume the energy density W_τ to be approximately uniform, equal to that at the center of the target star. Under this assumption, the gravitational force due to a maximal spherical region around the center of gravity with radius $R-\delta r$ (spherical region with dashed boundary, see Fig.3) would result in zero total force due to symmetrical cancellation of contributions from its elemental parts. Contributions from only the thin boundary shell (see Fig.3) with thickness $\delta R = \delta r(1+\cos\theta)$ would be needed to calculate the total force. The expression (14) may be simplified under the above approximations, requiring integration only over the shell region of variable thickness $\delta R = \delta r(1+\cos\theta)$, at $r \simeq R$. The only non-trivial integration in (14) over θ may be analytically evaluated. The resulting simple analytical expression for the limiting case would be useful for conceptual understanding, as well as for approximate validation of the general results for large mg.

$$\frac{m_{ue}}{m_u} \simeq \frac{3}{2}\int_{\theta=0}^{\pi}(\frac{dR}{R})\cos\theta\sin\theta\,d\theta$$

$$= \frac{3}{2}\int_{\theta=0}^{\pi}(\frac{\delta r}{R})(1+\cos\theta)\cos\theta\sin\theta\,d\theta = \frac{\delta r}{R}$$

$$= \frac{m}{mg}(\frac{d}{R}),\ m_{ue} = \frac{m_u m}{mg}(\frac{d}{R});\ \delta r, \delta R << d, R. \tag{16}$$

For a median distance $\delta r = 0.4R$, estimated for eclipsing close binaries in section IV A, the above limiting expression for the m_{ue} may be written as,

$$m_{ue} = \frac{m_u m}{mg}(\frac{\delta+2R}{R}) = 2.4\frac{m_u m}{mg}. \tag{17}$$

Based on the general derivation of section IV B, the ratio m_{ue}/m_u was computed using numerical integration

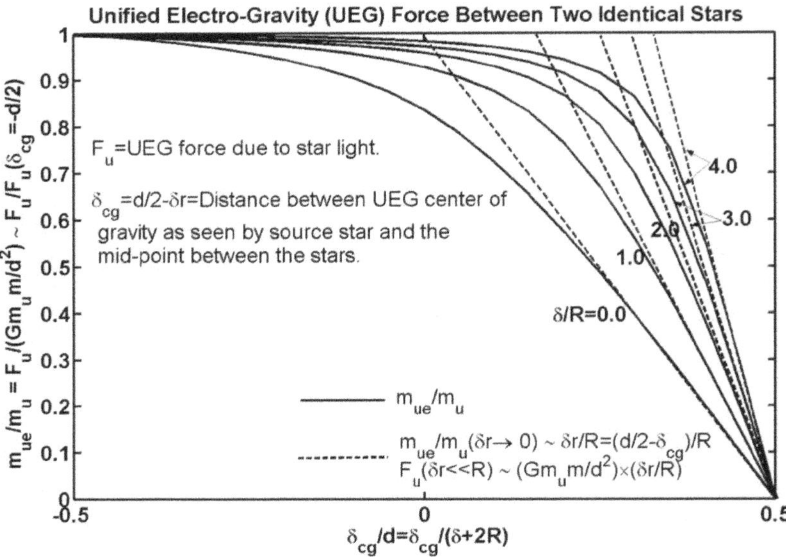

FIG. 4.

for different distances $\delta_{cg} = d/2 - \delta r$ of the CG (as seen by the source star) from the mid point between the source and target stars, for a fixed value of the surface-to-surface distance δ between the two stars. The computed ratio m_{ue}/m are plotted in Fig.4 as a function of the normalized distance δ_{cg}/R, for selected values of the normalized parameter δ/R. The computed results in the Fig.4 are compared with the limiting values of the m_{ue}/m_u, analytically derived above in section IV C. The general and the limiting plots in the Fig.4 are shown to validate each other when δr approaches small values (δ_{cg}/d approaches 0.5), or equivalently when the target-star's gravitational mass m_g is much larger than the source-star's inertial mass m, as expected. The effective UEG mass m_{ue} of the source star approaches its maximum value m_u when the CG moves to the center of the source star, or δ_{cg}/d approaches -0.5, as expected. The m_{ue} starts to drop significantly lower than the m_u after the CG moves beyond the mid point between the source and target stars ($\delta_{cg} > 0$), closer toward the target star. Note that the total effective gravitational mass m_{ge} of the source star is the sum of the inertial mass m and the effective UEG mass m_{ue}.

In a binary system, the same normalized plots of the Fig.4 would be applicable to model force from the first upon the second star, as well as from the second upon the first. In the former case, the m_{ue}, m_u, m and m_{ge} would be associated with the first star (referred to with a subscript 1), but the m_g would be associated with the second star (referred to with a subscript 2), where as for the later case the associations would be reversed. The final solutions for the m_{ue1}, m_{ge1}, m_{ue2}, m_{ge2} may be

established by equating $m_{g2} = m_{ge2} = m_{ue2} + m_2$ and $m_{g1} = m_{ge1} = m_{ue1} + m_1$. The process would be simpler when the two partner stars are identical, in which case the results of Fig.4 may be used for a final solution of the m_{ue} of each star, by enforcing the additional condition $m_g = m_{ge} = m_{ue} + m$ for mutual balance. For this condition, $\delta r/R = m/m_g = 1/(m_{ue}/m + 1)$ and therefore δ_{cg}/d would be directly dependent on the ratio m_{ue}/m, for a given parameter δ/R. Accordingly, for a given δ/R, the Fig.4 essentially provides m_{ue}/m_u as a function of m_{ue}/m, from which m_{ue}/m or $m_{ge}/m = m_{ue}/m + 1$ can be deduced for different values of m_u/m. These results are shown in Fig.5, for selected values of δ/R. These results are verified with those similarly deduced from the limiting expressions of m_{ue}/m_u in (16) applicable for sufficiently large m_{ue}/m, as follows.

The limiting expression for the m_{ue} in (16) is approximately equal to the $m_{ge} = m_{ue}+m$ because $m_{ue}/m >> 1$, or $m_{ue} >> m$. Accordingly, (16) may be solved for the symmetry condition $m_{ue} \simeq m_{ge} = m_g$, as prescribed earlier for a binary star with two identical partners.

$$mg = m_{ue} + m \simeq \sqrt{\frac{d}{R} m_u m} \, ,$$
$$\frac{mg}{m} = \frac{m_{ue}}{m} + 1 \simeq \sqrt{\frac{dm_u}{Rm}}. \tag{18}$$

For the estimated $\delta = 0.4R$ in (9,17), we get,

$$mg = m_{ue} + m \simeq \sqrt{2.4 m_u m} \, ,$$
$$\frac{mg}{m} = \frac{m_{ue}}{m} + 1 \simeq \sqrt{\frac{2.4 m_u}{m}}, \; \delta = \delta_m = 0.4R \, . \tag{19}$$

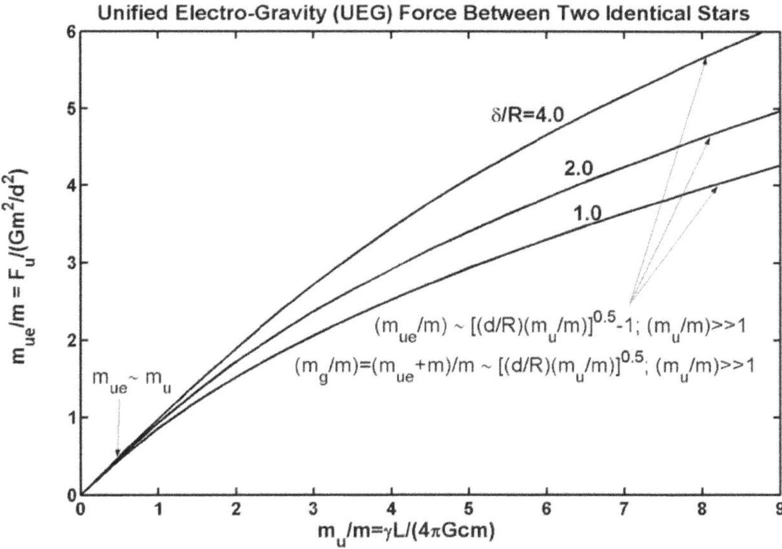

FIG. 5.

Note that the above limiting relation of (19) is in similar form as derived from the energy source model in section III, (7), for large m_u/m. This is a strong correlation between the two models, indicating a strong validation of the associated UEG theory. The factor d/R in (18) is functionally equivalent to the factor α deduced in (7). The expected value of $\alpha = 2.85$ in (7) (see section III A) is somewhat larger than the estimated factor $(d/R) \simeq 2.4$ in (19). Note that the factor (d/R) was estimated in section IV A, (9), based on a visual condition of orbital eclipsing where the R is the visual radius of a star, whereas the relation (18) was deduced from orbital dynamics where the R is the core radius of the star. Accordingly, the actual (d/R) for use in (18,19) should be somewhat larger than the estimate of 2.4 from (9), which would be consistent with the $\alpha = 2.85$ expected from the energy source model. Further, the above expected value of $\alpha = 2.85$ from section III A is valid only for a typical star like the Sun, with variations around this value for high and low intensity stars, which may be expected to track similar variations of the (d/R) factor, leading to the expected confirmation between the two models.

It may be noted, for a general case of gravitation between two different bodies, and therefore for the special case of two identical bodies as well, the basic theory of Newton's universal gravitation may need to be reviewed and revised in consistency with Newton's laws of mechanics, when one or both of the bodies are radiating. The UEG effects due to radiation as modeled above may be represented in terms of a revised equivalent gravitational constant G_u, substituting for the universal constant G for non-radiating bodies. The G_u is in general different from the G, and is different for two specific bodies dependent on their individual radiation, inertial mass and separation distance. This is presented in Appendix A, drawing particular attention to interesting special conditions that may arise in section A 2.

V. DERIVATION AND VALIDATION OF THE NEW MLR

In accordance with our equivalence modeling, the mass-term in the MLR of (1) is actually equal to the m_g for the orbital model of section IV, or the m_e for the energy-source model of section III. And, the luminosity L in the MLR (1) is proportional to the m_u as defined in (2). In other words, the MLR of (1) actually provides the relationship between (m_g, m_e) and m_u. This data, together with the theoretical relationship of Fig.5 between $m_{ue}/m = m_g/m - 1$ and m_u/m, may be used to deduce a new MLR (mass(actual inertial)-luminosity relation), based on the orbital model of section IV, as plotted in Fig.6 for $d/R = 2.85$.

Similarly, an alternate new MLR may be derived, using the theoretical relationship (7) between the equivalent mass m_e and m_u, based on the energy-source model of section III, and the (m_g, m_e) to m_u relationship of the MLR (1). This new MLR is plotted in Fig.6 for the parameter $\alpha = 2.85$, for comparison with its alternate MLR derived from the orbital model. As discussed earlier in section IV, the parameters α and (d/R) from the two models are functionally equivalent, and are estimated to have comparable values. The two new MLR's from the

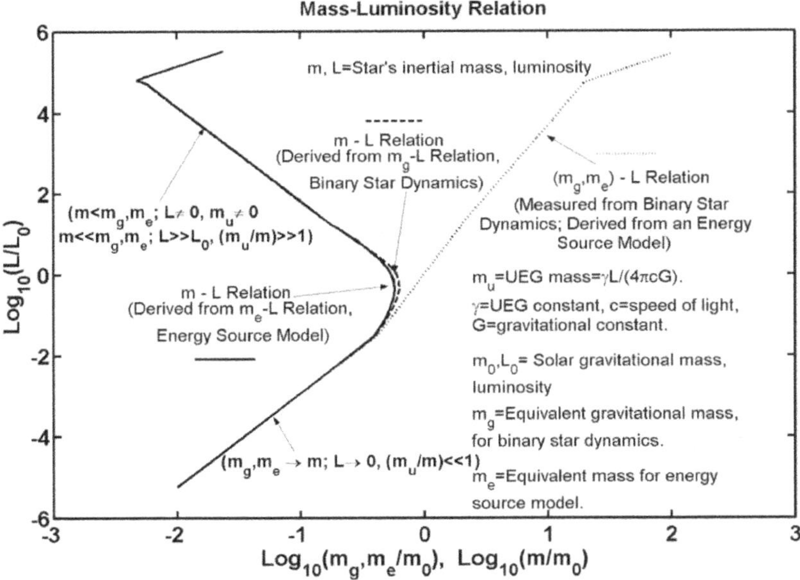

FIG. 6.

two independent models are seen to closely follow each other, but somewhat deviate in the region of solar-mass stars. Such agreement between the functional trends of the two models validate the two models as well as the associated UEG theory, over the entire range of low to high-luminosity stars. Note that the actual inertial mass deduced in a new MLR in Fig.6 is significantly less than what was believed (m_g or m_e) based on the existing MLR of (1) [4, 7]. Interestingly, for the mid-region of the MLR of Fig.6, the inertial mass m reduces for increasing luminosity, which may appear counter-intuitive based on a energy-source model [7] using Newtonian gravitation. The significantly different trends of the new MLR, as compared to the existing MLR (1), may prompt review of existing models of stellar evolution [12], which is beyond the scope of the present work.

The new MLR may be expressed in approximated analytical forms for high luminosity, using the relation between the normalized variables (m_g/m_0, m_e/m_0) and $L/L_0 = m_u/m_{u0}$ from (1) and the limiting relationship of (7,19) similarly normalized. For low luminosity with negligible m_u, the new MLR would remain approximately unchanged from the existing MLR (1).

$$\frac{L}{L_0} \simeq 0.23 \left(\frac{m}{m_0}\right)^{2.3}, \quad m < 0.43 m_0,$$

$$\simeq (1.5)^{-\left(\frac{2.0}{1.5}\right)} \left(0.46\alpha \frac{m}{m_0}\right)^{-\left(\frac{3.5}{1.5}\right)}, \quad 16 < \frac{L}{L_0} < 64000,$$

$$\simeq (3200)^2 \left(0.46\alpha \frac{m}{m_0}\right), \quad \frac{L}{L_0} > 64000. \qquad (20)$$

The parameter α is borrowed from the energy source model of (7), which is equivalent to the factor (d/R) from the orbital model of (18), and is expected to be about 2.85 for solar-mass stars with possible variation toward larger values for more luminous stars, as discussed in the end of section IV. The parameters $m_0 = m_{e0} = m_{g0}$, L_0 and m_{u0} refer to the solar mass (equivalent gravitational, not inertial), luminosity and UEG mass, respectively, and the factor 0.46 represents the expected ratio m_{u0}/m_{e0}.

VI.   DISCUSSION AND CONCLUSIONS

The UEG theory applied for stellar dynamics in a binary star system is found to be consistent with that for stellar energy-source model, as per comparison of the resulting mass-luminosity relation (MLR) with the existing MLR [3, 4, 7] from orbital measurement of binary stars as well as from the Eddington model of stellar energy-source. The "mass" in the existing MLR was assumed to be the inertial mass of a star which is equal to the gravitational mass as per the conventional Newtonian gravity, but it needs to be modified as per the UEG theory in different manners for the binary-star dynamics and for the stellar energy-soure model. However, the associated "equivalent-mass" parameters in the two cases happen to exhibit the same functional trend, with respect to actual inertial mass and luminosity (or the UEG mass) of the star. Accordingly, the existing MLR derived from the binary-star measurement and the Eddington's energy-source model were seen to agree with each other. This coincidence historically removed any doubt about the validity of the existing theories of [3, 4, 7]. We now know that mass term in the existing MLR is not really the actual mass (inertial) as has been assumed for long. The new MLR between the star's actual inertial mass and the light output is derived and plotted using the new UEG theory. As per the new theory, the inertial mass of the Sun or any other solar-mass star is actually about half of what has been believed all along! The Sun's gravitational force acting upon us on the earth is contributed in approximately equal parts by its inertial mass as by the UEG force due to its luminosity. This is a significant new finding, fundamentally changing our common understanding of the basic nature of gravity.

The effective gravitational mass of an individual star in a binary system, consisting of two stars of comparable mass and light intensity, would in general be different from that when the star operates as a single isolated star applying gravitational force on a nearby planet of significantly smaller mass, when the additional UEG effects are included. However, for observed binary systems with approximately two solar-mass stars, the equivalent gravitational mass in the binary-star system happened to be approximately equal to that of an isolated solar-mass star (equivalent gravitational mass of the Sun in our solar system), as well as equal to the equivalent mass needed in an energy-source model to produce its light output close to the solar luminosity. This coincidence of the data for the solar-mass stars in the existing MLR with the observed gravitation of the Sun in our solar system, also helped in removing any further doubt in the validity of the Newtonian gravitation. This, together with the other coincidence of the two MLRs mentioned earlier, may be considered interesting "conspiracies of nature" in the history of science, which possibly allowed to hide the new UEG theory of gravitation without suspicion for so long, till now!

Further, Einstein's equivalence principle in the general theory of relativity [6], together with Newton's third law of action-reaction equality [10], can be shown to require the gravitational mass of a source body to be equal to its inertial mass, with the gravitational constant G assumed be universally applicable to all bodies and locations. This fundamental requirement seemed to rule out possibility of the source gravitational mass of a radiating body to be any different from its inertial mass, also contributing to hiding the possibility of an additional UEG force for radiating bodies, without suspicion, as discussed above. However, all issues are shown in appendix A to be resolved, in full consistency with fundamental mechanical principles, if an equivalent gravitational constant G_u is allowed to be in general different for different pairs of gravitating bodies accounting for any additional UEG force due to radiation. This may limit the scope of the equivalence principle of the general relativity [6] to gravitation only between non-radiating bodies in a strictly "free-space" medium with no radiation-energy content, which the principle was fundamentally intended to. This

is a significant development, revising the Newton's law of universal gravitation and Einstein's principle of equivalence, extended to gravitation between general radiating bodies.

Starting with the remarkable success of the UEG theory in particle physics [1, 2], the further validation of the UEG theory in the present work of stellar orbital and energy-source physics to model the MLR, should now establish significant confidence in the theory, unifying its application in the small (elementary particles) as well as large (solar system and binary stars) dimensions, and spherically symmetric (elementary particle and an isolated single star) as well as asymmetric (binary star) structures.

Appendix A: UEG Theory of Gravitation for General Radiating Bodies, and Conservation of Momentum and Energy

The UEG theory of gravitation in a binary system, as modeled in this paper, expresses the gravitational accelerations in terms of new effective gravitational masses $m_{g1} = m_1 + m_{ue1}$ and $m_{g2} = m_2 + m_{ue2}$ of the two bodies in the system. This may lead to review of different concepts of mass, which may determine not only the gravitational field produced by a body, but also the mechanics of the body's motion in terms of its inertial mass, momentum and energy. In the process, we may need to identify the mass of a given body in distinct forms, which may or may not be equal under general conditions of a radiating body.

The gravitational mass of a body, which acts like a source or cause of the gravitational field the body produces in the surrounding medium, may be referred to as the source gravitational mass, m_g. As per the UEG theory of binary stars, the $m_g = m + m_{ue}$ is the source gravitational mass of a radiating body, which is clearly different from that, $m_g = m$, without the radiation. As per conventional theory of gravitation and mechanics (Newtonian or relativistic), in the absence of any radiation, a unique mass parameter m defines not only the body's gravitational field but also its inertial as well as internal energy ($E = mc^2$). In the presence of radiation, we need to review if the change in the body's source gravitational mass $m_g = m + m_{ue} \neq m$ may also change the body's inertia or energy. If any such change may violate certain fundamental principles, the UEG theory may have to be properly revised.

As per the UEG model, the m_{ue} is the additional source gravitational mass due to radiation from a given body, as seen by the other body in a particular binary system. The total gravitational acceleration, a'_{12} or a'_{21}, produced as per the new UEG theory by one body, 1 or 2, and experienced at the location of the other body, 2 and 1, respectively, is expressed as (see Fig.7):

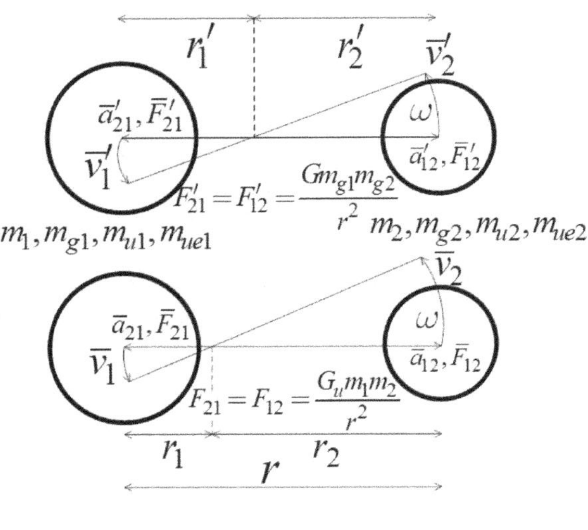

FIG. 7.

$$a'_{12} = \frac{Gm_{g1}}{r^2}, \; a'_{21} = \frac{Gm_{g2}}{r^2},$$

$$m_{g1} = m_1 + m_{ue1}, \; m_{g2} = m_2 + m_{ue2}. \qquad (A1)$$

Useful limiting conditions may be recognized. The m_{ue} of a radiating body would be less than or equal to its maximum value m_u, which would occur when the radiating body operates effectively in isolation, as the most dominant body with negligible or no gravitational influence from any surrounding body. In the other limit, m_{ue} of the radiating body would be zero, and consequently the source gravitational mass of the body would be equal to its Newtonian mass ($m_g = m + m_{ue} = m$), when it operates in the presence of a nearby dominant body, with the Newtonian mass of the source body much smaller than that of the dominant body. Further, when the two bodies are sufficiently far apart from each other, the m_{ue} of each body would be approximately equal to their respective maximum values, m_u.

$$m_{ue2} \to 0 \; (m_{u2} \neq 0), \; m_{g2} \to m_2, \; m_{ue1} \to m_{u1},$$

$$m_{g1} \to (m_1 + m_{u1}); \; m_1 >> m_2.$$

$$m_{ue1} \to m_{u1}, \; m_{ue2} \to m_{u2}; \; r \to \infty. \qquad (A2)$$

The above accelerations (A1) may be expressed in special coordinates (primed) (see Fig.7), which may be referred to as the UEG coordinates of the particular binary system, with reference origin located between the two bodies, at distances r'_1 and r'_2 from the bodies 1 and 2, respectively. This would be different from the coordinates (un-primed) used in a conventional modeling of the binary system using Newtonian gravity, where the respective distances of the reference origin would have been $r_1 = r \times m_2/(m_1 + m_2)$ and $r_2 = r \times m_1/(m_1 + m_2)$.

The accelerations a'_{21} and a'_{12} experienced by the bodies 1 and 2, and the respective velocities v'_1 and v'_2 along the individual circular orbits, may be expressed in terms of their common angular velocity ω and the radial distances r'_1 and r'_2. The v'_1 and v'_2 are directed opposite with respect to each other.

$$a'_{12} = \omega^2 r'_2, \; a'_{21} = \omega^2 r'_1,$$

$$\omega^2 (r'_1 + r'_2) = \omega^2 r = a'_{12} + a'_{21} = \frac{G(m_{g1}+m_{g2})}{r^2},$$

$$\omega = \sqrt{\frac{G(m_{g1}+m_{g2})}{r^3}},$$

$$P_2 = m_{g2}v'_2 = m_{g2}\omega r'_2 = \frac{m_{g2}a'_{12}}{\omega} = \frac{Gm_{g1}m_{g2}}{r^2\omega},$$

$$P_1 = m_{g1}v'_1 = m_{g1}\omega r'_1 = \frac{m_{g1}a'_{21}}{\omega} = \frac{Gm_{g1}m_{g2}}{r^2\omega},$$

$$P_1 = P_2, \; \overline{P}_1 = m_{g1}\overline{v}'_1, \; \overline{P}_2 = m_{g2}\overline{v}'_2,$$

$$\overline{P}_1 = -\overline{P}_2, \; \overline{P} = \overline{P}_1 + \overline{P}_2 = 0. \qquad (A3)$$

It is shown that total momentum $\overline{P} = \overline{P}_1 + \overline{P}_2$ of the binary system would be conserved as zero, if the momentum $\overline{P}_i$, $i = 1, 2$, of an individual body is defined as $\overline{P}_i = m_{gi}\overline{v}_i$, not $\overline{P}_i = m_i\overline{v}_i$ as conventionally defined in Newtonian mechanics. In other words, the inertial mass m_I of a radiating body may no longer be equal to its conventional inertial mass m, but could now be equal to its source gravitational mass m_g. Accordingly, the UEG theory would not only change the source gravitational mass m_g, but also the inertial mass m_I of a radiating body to be equal to $m_I = m_g = m + m_{ue}$. The inertial mass m_I would be equal to the conventional inertial mass m, only when there is no radiation ($m_u \to 0$).

$$m_{I1} = m_{g1} = m_{ue1} + m_1 \neq m_1;$$

$$m_{I1} = m_1, \; m_{ue1} = m_{u1} \to 0.$$

$$m_{I2} = m_{g2} = m_{ue2} + m_2 \neq m_2;$$

$$m_{I2} = m_2, \; m_{ue2} = m_{u2} \to 0. \qquad (A4)$$

To be consistent with the conserved momentum, the gravitational force may also have to be defined as the product of the corresponding gravitational acceleration and the new inertial mass m_I, not the conventional mass m. With this new definition of the gravitational force, the vector force, $\overline{F}'_{12}$, produced by one body acting upon the other would be equal in magnitude, but oppositely directed, to that, $\overline{F}'_{21}$, when the source and target bodies are interchanged. This would satisfy the Newton's third law of action and reaction, resulting in the total force in the system equal to zero, as should be expected.

$$F'_{12} = m_{g2}a'_{12} = \frac{Gm_{g1}m_{g2}}{r^2},$$

$$F'_{21} = m_{g1}a'_{21} = \frac{Gm_{g2}m_{g1}}{r^2},$$

$$F'_{12} = F'_{21}, \; \overline{F}'_{12} = -\overline{F}'_{21}, \; \overline{F}'_{12} + \overline{F}'_{21} = 0. \qquad (A5)$$

Clearly, the Newton's third law would not work if the mass of the target body were its conventional mass m, for radiating bodies with $m \neq m_g$ in general, resulting in a total non-zero force for the total system, which would also violate the principle of conservation of momentum.

$$F'_{12} = m_2 a'_{12} = \frac{G m_{g1} m_2}{r^2}, \ F'_{21} = m_1 a'_{21} = \frac{G m_{g2} m_1}{r^2},$$
$$F'_{12} \neq F'_{21}, \ \overline{F}'_{12} \neq -\overline{F}'_{21}, \ \overline{F}'_{12} + \overline{F}'_{21} \neq 0. \quad \text{(A6)}$$

The consistency of momentum and its conservation may be extended to the kinetic energy of the body, so that the energy may also be conserved as would be desired. Accordingly, the kinetic energy may also need to use the new inertial mass m_I. That is, the kinetic energy KE (non-relativistic) would be equal to $KE = (1/2)m_I v^2 = (1/2)(m + m_{ue})^2 \neq (1/2)mv^2$. This may lead to a fundamental dilemma. Extending the treatment of energy to special relativity, this may lead to a fictitious rest energy of $E_0 = m_I c^2$, which is different from the actual rest energy $E_0 = mc^2$ of the body when the radiation is turned off. This is contrary to the understanding, that the intrinsic energy of the body should not be different, if the radiation is suddenly turned on or off. However, the above new definitions for the gravitational mass, inertial mass, momentum, kinetic energy, as well as the rest mass (though appears non-physical), could still be mathematically consistent with each other, as shown in the above equations, in reference to the local UEG reference coordinates (primed coordinates). The above dilemma of rest energy may perhaps be ignored, by considering the rest mass simply as a reference value, and any difference between the total and the reference rest energy may still be consistently used for modeling and "book-keeping" of the kinetic energy.

1. Revised UEG model for General Radiating Bodies

The above modeling of gravitation and inertia may be consistently used, as discussed above, but only in a hypothetical situation of having the only two bodies in an ideal empty space, in complete isolation from any other bodies. The model may be untenable in a real physical situation with other surrounding bodies. If the above model is followed for a general multi-body system, each pairing of the multi-body system would be associated with two inertial masses for the two individual members of the pairing, but any particular body would in general carry a different inertial mass when it is associated with a different pairing. Consider an arbitrary three-body system, where any two pairings of the system would share a common member. The common member would be associated with a different inertial mass, and therefore different momentum and energy for a given velocity, in modeling the gravitational force it experiences from the other two different bodies

of the two pairings. Clearly, such non-unique values of the momentum and energy for the same particular body would not be fundamentally sensible, warranting suitable revision of the UEG model in order to reestablish order and consistency.

In order that the momentum or energy of a given body be uniquely defined and conserved, they must be proportional to the body's conventional mass m which remains unique under general conditions. This would be the case, if we require the gravitational force between two bodies to be proportional to the mass m of each body. We would maintain the same relative acceleration $a = a' = a'_{12} + a'_{21}$ between the two bodies in a binary system, defined in a new coordinate system (unprimed), such that the angular speed ω remains unchanged. In other words, the results of orbital periodicity from the original UEG model still remain valid through the following proposed revision.

$$a' = a'_{12} + a'_{21} = \frac{G(m_{g1} + m_{g2})}{r^2},$$
$$F_{12} = \frac{G_u m_1 m_2}{r^2} = F_{21},$$
$$a_{12} = \frac{F_{12}}{m_2} = \frac{G_u m_1}{r^2}, \ a_{21} = \frac{F_{21}}{m_1} = \frac{G_u m_2}{r^2},$$
$$a = a_{12} + a_{21} = \frac{G_u(m_1 + m_2)}{r^2}, \quad \text{(A7)}$$

$$\omega = \frac{a}{r^2} = \frac{a'}{r^2}, \ a = a',$$
$$G_u = G\frac{m_{g1} + m_{g2}}{m_1 + m_2} = G\frac{m_1 + m_{ue1} + m_2 + m_{ue2}}{m_1 + m_2}. \quad \text{(A8)}$$

The new model would satisfy all the Newton's law's of motion, as well as conservation of momentum and energy, with reference origin for orbital motion of the two stars same as that from Newtonian gravitation ($r_1 = r \times m_2/(m_1 + m_2)$, $r_2 = r \times m_1/(m_1 + m_2)$). However, each pair of bodies would now be associated with a different equivalent gravitational constant G_u, which is different from the Newtonian gravitational constant G. This is a significant new development, which may warrant review of orbital motions of two- and general multi-body systems, which may include radiating (stellar) and/or non-radiating (dark star or planets) elements.

2. Revised UEG Model for Gravitation in a Binary System Under Special Conditions

We may evaluate the equivalent gravitational constant G_u, under useful special conditions:

Case I: For the ideal case of a binary system with equal partner stars, the magnitudes of all the accelerations a_{12}, a_{21}, a'_{12} and a'_{21}, in the primed as well the unprimed coordinates would be equal.

$$Gu = G\frac{m+m_{ue}}{m}, \quad m_{ue1} = m_{ue2} = m_{ue}, \quad m_1 = m_2 = m,$$
$$a_{12} = a_{21} = a'_{12} = a'_{21}$$
$$= \frac{Gmg}{r^2} = \frac{G(m+m_{ue})}{r^2} = \frac{Gum}{r^2}. \quad (A9)$$

Case II: For a binary star system where the individual stars are sufficiently far apart, using the limiting condition of (A2) in (A7,A8), we have,

$$Gu = G\frac{m_1+m_{u1}+m_2+m_{u2}}{m_1+m_2},$$
$$m_{ue1} = m_{u1}, \quad m_{ue2} = m_{u2}, \quad r \to \infty. \quad (A10)$$

Case III: In the solar system, the gravitational acceleration between the Sun (body 1) and any of its planets (body 2) may be modeled by considering the Sun the most dominant body, as per the limiting condition (A2). In this case, the Newtonian gravitational constant G may be substituted by an effective gravitational constant Gu, which is larger than the G by the factor $m_{g1}/m_1 = (m_1 + m_{u1})/m_1$.

$$Gu \simeq G\frac{m_1+m_{u1}}{m_1} = G\frac{m_{g1}}{m_1}, \quad m_{ue1} = m_{u1}, \quad m_1 >> m_2,$$
$$(m_1 + m_{ue1}) = m_{g1} >> m_{g2} = (m_2 + m_{ue2}),$$
$$a_{21} \simeq \frac{Gum_2}{r^2} = \frac{Gm_{g1}m_2}{m_1 r^2} \neq \frac{Gm_2}{r^2},$$
$$a_{12} \simeq \frac{Gum_1}{r^2} = \frac{Gm_{g1}}{r^2}. \quad (A11)$$

Case IV: In contrast to the case III, the gravitation between a dominant luminous star (body 1) and a dominant massive but dark star (dark body 2) with little or no radiation, where $m_1 << m_2$, $m_{ue1} >> m_1, m_2$, would lead to an interesting situation. The dark star would exert much more acceleration on the luminous star, compared to that expected from its mass alone as per Newtonian gravity. It is as if the dark star has "acquired" the UEG mass m_{ue1} of the luminous star. Whereas, the luminous star would exert much less acceleration on the dark body, compared to that expected from its large effective UEG mass m_{ue1}. This concept may be referred to as "inversion." This results in complete opposite effect from what would be expected from a conventional stellar model, where a larger mass (source gravitational), and therefore a larger gravitational acceleration exerted upon the darker body, would be normally assumed (incorrectly) to be associated with the more luminous body. Although we establish only the limiting condition, as stated above (see (A12)), similar inversion conditions would apply also for any general unequal binary-star systems, where the more luminous star has lower mass. In light of this significant new result, some old controversies in astronomy such as the Algol Paradox [13, 14] in close binary systems and the mystery of the Sirus star system [15, 16] may need to be reevaluated.

$$Gu \simeq \frac{Gm_{ue1}}{m_2}, \quad m_{ue1} >> m_2 >> m_1, \quad m_{ue2} = 0,$$
$$a_{21} = \frac{Gum_2}{r^2} \simeq \frac{Gm_{ue1}}{r^2} >> \frac{Gm_2}{r^2},$$
$$a_{12} = \frac{Gum_1}{r^2} \simeq \frac{Gm_{ue1}m_1}{m_2 r^2} << \frac{Gm_{ue1}}{r^2} = a_{21}. \quad (A12)$$

Case V: Consider gravitation between a dominant massive body (body 1) with no or very little radiation, and a radiating body (body 2) of relatively small inertial or UEG mass compared to the body 1. This situation would be applicable to a planet like our earth, with a satellite or moon which may be naturally or artificially lighted. The gravitational force and acceleration in this case may be adequately modeled by using the conventional Newtonian gravitation, with $Gu \simeq G$. This is independent of the light radiation from the satellite or moon, even if its UEG mass m_{u2} or m_{ue2} is significant compared to its inertial mass m_2, or equivalently its source gravitational mass $m_{g2} = m_2 + m_{ue2}$ is significantly larger than its inertial mass m_2, as long as the m_{u2}, m_{ue2}, m_2 and m_{g2} are sufficiently smaller compared to the mass m_1 of the dominant body. In other words, the source gravitational mass m_{g2}, which should have proportionately increased the gravitational force as per the unrevised UEG model in (A5), would no longer determine the gravitational force in the revised model of (A7,A8), under the present conditions. Instead, the gravitation is modeled by the simple Newtonian gravitation, with the force proportional to the inertial mass m_2 not the source gravitational mass m_{g2}.

$$Gu \simeq G, \quad m_1 >> m_2, m_{u2}, m_{ue2};$$
$$m_{u1} = m_{ue1} << m_1 . \quad (A13)$$

---

[1] N. Das, "A New Unified Electro-Gravity (UEG) Theory of the Electron," Paper #1, pp.4-13, in "A Unified Electro-Gravity (UEG) Theory of Nature," (2018).

[2] N. Das, "A Generalized Unified Electro-Gravity (UEG) Model Applicable to All Elementary Particles," Paper #2, pp.14-30, in "A Unified Electro-Gravity (UEG) Theory of Nature," (2018).

[3] G. P. Kuiper, Astrophysical Journal **88**, 472 (1938).

[4] Wikipedia, "Mass-Luminosity Relation," **http://en.wikipedia.org/wiki/Mass-luminosity_relation**, Retrieved (2017).

[5] O. Y. Malkov, Astronomy and Astrophysics **402**, 1055

(2003).

[6] A. Einstein, Annalen der Physik **354**, 769 (1916).

[7] S. Lecchini, *How Dwarfs Became Giants* (Bern Studies in the History and Philosophy of Science [c/o Institut fur Philosophie, G Grasshoff], 2007).

[8] Wikipedia, "Sun," `http://en.wikipedia.org/wiki/Sun`, Retrieved (2017).

[9] D. R. Williams, "Sun Fact Sheet. NASA Gooddard Space Flight Center," `http://nssdc.gsfc.nasa.gov/planetary/factsheet/sunfact.html`, Retrieved (2017).

[10] S. I. Newton, *Principia: Mathematical Principles of Natural Philosophy. I. B. Cohen, A. Whitman and J. Budenz, English Translators from 1726 Original* (University of California Press, 1999).

[11] S. I. Newton and S. Hawking, *Principia* (Running Press, 2005).

[12] M.Salaris and S. Cassisi, *Evolution of Stars and Stellar Populations*, Vol. 88 (John Wiley and Sons, 2005).

[13] Wikipedia, "Algol Paradox," `http://en.wikipedia.org/wiki/Algol_paradox`, Retrieved (2017).

[14] I. Pustylnik, Astronomical and Astrophysical Transactions **15**, 357 (1998).

[15] D. Benest and J. L. Duvent, Astronomy and Astrophysics **299**, 621 (1995).

[16] Wikipedia, "The Sirius Mystery," `http://en.wikipedia.org/wiki/The_Sirius_Mystery`, Retrieved (2013).

Unified Electro-Gravity (UEG) Theory Applied to Spiral Galaxies

Nirod K. Das

*Department of Electrical and Computer Engineering, Tandon School of Engineering,
New York University, 5 Metrotech Center, Brooklyn, NY 11201*

(Dated: May 9, 2018)

The unified electro-gravity (UEG) theory, which has been successfully used for modeling elementary particles, as well as single and binary stars, is extended in this paper to model gravitation in spiral galaxies. A new UEG model would explain the "flat rotation curves" commonly observed in the spiral galaxies. The UEG theory is developed in a fundamentally different manner for a spiral galaxy, as compared to prior applications of the UEG theory to the elementary particle and single stars. This is because the spiral galaxy, unlike the elementary particles or single stars, is not spherically symmetric. The UEG constant γ, required in the new model to support the galaxies' flat rotation speeds, is estimated using measured data from a galaxy survey, as well as for a selected galaxy for illustration. The estimates are compared with the γ derived from a UEG model of elementary particles. The UEG model for the galaxy is shown to explain the empirical Tuly-Fisher Relationship (TFR), is consistent with the Modified Newtonian Dynamics (MOND), and is also independently supported by measured trends of galaxy thickness with surface brightness and rotation speed.

I. INTRODUCTION

Rotation curves of spiral galaxies [1] have been suspected not to confirm to gravitational forces due to galaxies' visible mass as per the Newton's law of gravitation, which is known to work well in our day-to-day experience on earth as well for planetary orbits in our solar system. In order to explain the observed rotation curves, it has been proposed and long believed that there is significant amount of invisible "dark matter" surrounding almost all spiral galaxies. There was no other existing theory which could explain the rotation behavior in a satisfactory manner, although modification of the laws of Newtonian dynamics has been proposed [2]. Recently, a new unified electro-gravity (UEG) theory is established, which has been successfully applied to model elementary particles [3, 4], where a new gravitational force, proportional to electromagnetic energy density, is introduced. This UEG theory has also been extended to model energy generation in single stars [5], which are spherically symmetric bodies like the elementary particles. However, the theory needed some basic modification when it was extended to model orbiting of a binary-star system [5], in order to accommodate the spherical asymmetry of the binary system. In this paper, the UEG theory would be applied to a spiral galaxy, which is another different non-spherical body. The energy density due to star lights in the galaxy would contribute to a new gravitational force, which could support the observed stellar rotation around the galaxy. A constant rotation speed beyond certain radial distance would require a $1/r$-dependent gravitational acceleration, in the given region. When the UEG theory is properly modified for the non-spherical structure of a spiral galaxy, the required $1/r$-dependent acceleration may result, although the stellar light radiation from the galaxy exhibit an approximate $1/r^2$ dependence, in the given region. This is possible, because the energy density of the actual light radiation may need to be redistributed,

based on the physical asymmetry of the spiral galaxy. The UEG field may be defined in proportion to the redistributed, effective energy density, so that the field may satisfy certain basic requirements and be self-consistent when applied to general problems.

The required UEG constant γ of proportionality, between the UEG field and the associated effective energy density, may be deduced from the new UEG model using measured data from galaxy survey as well as data for selected individual galaxies. The results may be compared with the UEG constant deduced from a UEG theory of elementary particles, for validation or verification of the new UEG model. The functional trends established from the new UEG model may be compared, for validation of the model, with those from the empirical Tully-Fisher Relation (TFR) [6] and the Modified Newtonian Dynamics (MOND) model [2, 7]. The trends predicted from the UEG model would explicitly depend upon the spiral galaxy's aspect ratio (ratio of the scale lengths in radius and thickness), because the new model is formulated based on the spherical asymmetry of the galaxy. This is distinct from the the MOND model, where there may not be such definitive interrelation between the galaxy's aspect ratio and the rotation speed. The functional dependence of the galaxy's aspect ratio on the surface brightness and rotation velocity, as required for the UEG galaxy model to reproduce the rotation curves, may be compared with available measurements, for another independent validation of the basic UEG galaxy model.

The formulation of the force-field in the UEG model of a spiral galaxy, which is a non-spherical body, is expected to be distinct from that for an elementary particle or an isolated star [3, 5], which are spherical structures. The galaxy's UEG force field is defined in proportion to an effective distribution of energy density, not the actual energy density of stellar radiation as was the case for the spherical structures. The effective energy density is obtained by suitable redistribution of the galaxy's light radiation, in proportion to the distribution of the Newtonian gravitation potential of the galaxy. The divergence of the resulting UEG force field surrounding the galaxy would be equivalent to having a fictitious "dark-matter" distribution, which may be needed in order to explain the observed rotation behavior of the spiral galaxies, as well as formation and evolution of the galaxies, on the basis of the conventional Newtonian gravitation [8]. Beyond a sufficiently large radial distance from the galactic center, the galaxy would "look" like a point source with a spherically symmetric distribution of the Newtonian potential, and with a $1/r^2$ dependence of its light intensity. In this far region the radial UEG field would also be spherically symmetric, and therefore the field would be directly proportional to the $1/r^2$-dependent light's energy density, without any need for redistribution of the energy density as per the proposed model. This spherically symmetric, $1/r^2$-dependent radial UEG field in the far region is associated with zero field divergence, and therefore with no dark matter. In contrast, the region sufficiently close to the center would in general be associated with a strong divergent UEG field, and therefore with a heavy dark-matter distribution. This region of heavy dark-matter presence would at least include the smallest spherical region which encloses most of the galaxy's mass and light sources, and may extend much farther.

Section II presents the theoretical concepts and an analytical formulation of the theory. The results for flat rotation velocity deduced from the model are validated with measured data for a galaxy survey as well as for an individual galaxy, in sections III, IV. The Tully-Fisher Relation (TFR) and the Modified Newtonian Dynamics (MOND) model are studied in section V, in relation to the present UEG galaxy model, for further validation of the model. This is followed by discussion and general conclusion from the study.

II.　THEORY

A.　The Basic Concept

As per the UEG theory, there exists a new gravitational force-field which is dependent on the electromagnetic energy density. For a simple spherical body, the new UEG field at any particular location is directly proportional to the energy density at the given location, and is directed toward the center of the body [3–5]. Such simple, direct relationship between the UEG field and the energy density may not be valid for a general non-spherical structure, with a non-spherical light distribution. Certain additional conditions may be established for a UEG force-field, which could be implicit in, or consistent with, the simple relationship for a spherical structure. But, the additional conditions may have to be explicitly applied for a general non-spherical structure. The Newtonian gravitational field in a spiral galaxy structure is not directed radially toward the center of the galaxy at every location, unlike that of a spherical structure which is radially directed at every location. Assuming an ideal disk structure for a spiral galaxy, which is independent of the azimuth (ϕ) coordinate, the Newtonian gravitational field may be shown to consist of only the radial (r) and elevation (θ) components, with no ϕ-component. Like the Newtonian gravitation field, the UEG field for a spiral galaxy may not be required to be strictly radial in direction, at all general locations. And, the UEG field for the galaxy may ideally be directed along the galaxy's Newtonian gravitational field with the $r-$ and $\theta-$ components.

We may assume the UEG field to be energy-conservative, which is defined as the gradient of an associated potential function. The desired non-radial (θ-) component of the UEG field for a spiral galaxy, as discussed above, would require the potential function, and accordingly the field, to maintain a gradient or a derivative along the $\theta-$direction. In other words, the distribution of the potential or the field on a spherical surface would be non-uniform in the θ variable. Such spherical asymmetry in the galaxy's UEG field or potential is in distinct contrast to the UEG field or potential for a spherical body, which is uniform on any spherical surface. We may define the UEG field for a spiral galaxy, on any spherical surface of a given radius, to be distributed in proportion to the galaxy's Newtonian potential on the spherical surface. This would ensure the gradients of the UEG and Newtonian potentials in the $\theta-$direction, or equivalently the $\theta-$components of the respective fields, to be in proportion to each other at all points on the surface of the given radius. Further, the gradients of the two potentials in the radial ($r-$) direction, and therefore the $r-$components of the respective fields, may be assumed to be proportionate to each other, at least in terms of their general functional trends on a first-order basis. Accordingly, the essentially proportionate components of the two fields would ensure the UEG and the Newtonian fields to be directed approximately parallel to each other, at all locations, which may be desired as discussed earlier. The above model may be formulated by having the radial UEG field to be proportional to a suitable distribution of an effective energy density, with the UEG constant γ [3, 4] as the constant of proportionality. The effective energy density at any given location is defined by redistribution of the actual energy density of the galaxy's stellar radiation on a spherical surface passing through the location, in proportion to the galaxy's Newtonian potential on the spherical surface. The redistribution would maintain the total integral of the actual and effective energy densities on the spherical surface to be equal to each other, which is a definite measure of the equivalent UEG mass (dark-mass) enclosed inside the sphere.

An additional fundamental condition may need to be enforced in any general UEG field. It would be reasonable to require the total UEG force due to a general distribution of energy density, produced due to the general distribution of its associated sources internal to a massive body, to be zero. Otherwise, a non-zero total force produced by a general source internal to a particular body, acting upon the given body itself, would not be fundamentally sensible. The above UEG model, as specifically proposed for a spiral galaxy, may be verified to enforce this basic condition of having zero total force. The azimuthal (ϕ) symmetry we assumed for an ideal spiral galaxy would ensure the total force to be zero, as required. However, it may also be ensured that this condition of zero total force may not be evidently violated when the UEG model is extended for a more general structure.

It may be argued, that the definition of the UEG field for a spiral galaxy, as proposed above and implemented in the following section II B, is perhaps not the unique or best way to define the desired field. For example, the UEG field could have been defined in direct proportion to the actual energy density, and been non-radially directed along the galaxy's Newtonian gravitation field as may be desired. Such a UEG field may also be shown to satisfy the above required condition of having zero total force. The actual energy density due to the star light in a disk galaxy is ideally independent of the azimuthal angle ϕ. All components of the above alternate UEG field for the disk galaxy, expressed in direct proportion to the galaxy's ϕ-independent actual energy density, may also be shown to produce a total zero force when the field acts upon an ideal ϕ-independent mass distribution of the galaxy. However, this alternate model would evidently fail to produce the required zero total force for a general condition, if either the mass or the light distribution were ϕ-dependent.

Such an alternate model, or any other similar proposition which would lead to such evident invalidity when extended to a general situation, is rejected. Whereas, the original UEG field as proposed earlier and formulated in the following section II B, particularly when the mass distribution is maintained to be symmetric in the azimuth (ϕ) coordinate, may be verified to properly enforce the required condition of having zero total force, for any general distribution of the radiation energy density. This would be based on the symmetry that is maintained in the proposed re-distribution model of energy density, which would result in a $\phi-$independent effective energy density, in proportion to the Newtonian potential of the $\phi-$independent mass distribution, and therefore a proportionate $\phi-$independent UEG field. The $\phi-$independent field, acting upon the ideal $\phi-$independent mass distribution, would produce the required total zero force. On the other hand, if the mass distribution was not ideally symmetric in the ϕ coordinate (with or without a $\phi-$symmetry of the energy density), the required condition of zero total force is expected to be closely established. The proposed UEG field tries to closely mimic the Newtonian gravitational field of the given mass distribution, as discussed before. Therefore, like the zero total force which is guaranteed from the

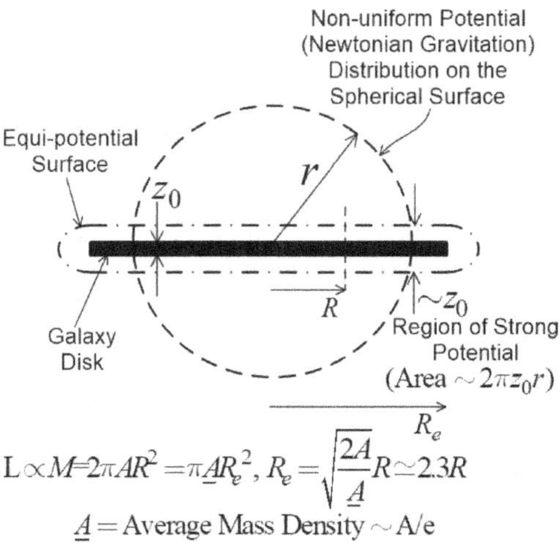

FIG. 1.

Newtonian gravitational field of any general mass distribution, acting upon its own mass distribution, the proposed UEG field would similarly establish the condition of zero total force, at least on a first order basis.

As suggested above, the proposed UEG model, as formulated in the following section (II B), may not be the most rigorous form of the UEG theory for general applications, even for the specific application to spiral galaxies. The model is intended as a first-order working hypothesis for the specific study of the flat rotation curves in spiral galaxies. However, the proposed UEG model is developed as a valuable theoretical framework, which satisfies expected fundamental conditions, ensures compatibility with all prior successful applications of the UEG theory in [3–5], while it foresees no evident contradiction for a general application. That is a significant scientific objective, to support future generalization of the UEG theory towards a rigorous and complete theory.

B. Analytical Model

The light radiation from a spherically distributed source, like a single isolated star for example, exhibits a $1/r^2$ dependence of its radiation energy density with radial distance r, external to the spherical source. Such $1/r^2$ dependence of radiation may also be seen for a non-spherical source, in an approximate form, outside of a spherical region of certain threshold radius. For a spiral galaxy, such a spherical region may be identified with a threshold radius equal to the galaxy's scale radius R. This means, the radiation of the galaxy establishes an approximate spherical symmetry beyond the radius R

A spherical source is defined by spherical equi-potential surfaces, which means all points on a spherical surface of radius r have the same potential. In contrast, the spiral galaxy may be represented as a thin disk of an average thickness z_0, with the z_0 much smaller than its disk radius $\sim R$. The equi-potential surfaces (as per Newtonian gravity) for the disk structure would be thin disk-like surfaces in the vicinity enclosing the source disk (see Fig.1). Such equi-potential surfaces exhibit spherical asymmetry inherent in the disk structure, and such asymmetry in the Newtonian potential distribution may effectively extend well beyond the scale radius R. This is unlike the light's energy density discussed above, which establishes a fairly spherical symmetry beyond the galaxy's scale radius.

Now, consider a spherical surface of radius r, with a common center as the disk galaxy, as shown in Fig.1. The distribution of the Newtonian gravitational potential on this surface would in general be non-uniform, with stronger potential values near the plane of the disk over a constant thickness $\sim z_0$ (independent of r), and weaker values in the rest of the spherical surface. As a first-order model, one may approximate the potential distribution to be uniform over its strong region of area $\sim 2\pi r z_0$ (Fig.1), and be negligible over the rest of the spherical surface. A uniform energy density W_τ of light radiation over the surface may be redistributed in proportion to the potential distribution, as approximated above, resulting in a stronger effective energy density $W_{\tau e}$ near the galaxy plane. The radial UEG force is proposed to be proportional to this effective energy density $W_{\tau e}$, not the actual energy density W_τ. In accordance with the above principle, the two energy densities would in principle be equal if the potential was spherically symmetric, with a uniform value everywhere on the spherical surface of Fig.1.

$$[W_\tau(r) \times 4\pi r^2] = [W_{\tau e}(r) \times (\sim 2\pi r z_0)],$$
$$W_{\tau e}(r) \propto \frac{r}{z_0} \times W_\tau(r);$$
$$W_\tau(r) \sim \frac{1}{r^2}, \; W_{\tau e}(r) \sim \frac{1}{r}, \; r > R. \qquad (1)$$

The original energy density W_τ with a $\sim 1/r^2$ dependence would transform into an effective energy density $W_{\tau e}$ with a $\sim 1/r$ dependence on the galaxy plane.

The gravitational potential distribution would exhibit closer spherical symmetry as one approaches towards the center, resulting in the effective density $W_{\tau e}$ to be close to the actual energy density W_τ in the central region. Accordingly, as a first-order estimate, the effective and actual energy densities may be assumed to be equal to each other for $r < R$. Based on this assumption and the above modeling (1), the effective and actual energy densities may be expressed as follows.

$$W_{\tau e}(r) = W_\tau(r), \; r < R;$$
$$W_\tau(r) = W_\tau(r = R)\frac{R^2}{r^2},$$
$$W_{\tau e}(r) = W_\tau(r = R)\frac{R}{r}, \; r > R. \qquad (2)$$

The energy density W_τ for $r > R$ may be approximated using the total luminosity L and the speed of light c, and assuming that the total light radiates in a spherically symmetric manner in the region, as if it radiates from a point source at the galaxy center. The total luminosity may be expressed using the surface density μ, which may be modeled with an exponential profile with amplitude μ_0 and scale radius R.

$$W_\tau(r) \simeq \frac{L}{4\pi r^2 c} = \frac{\mu_0 R^2}{2r^2 c}, \; W_\tau(r = R) \simeq \frac{\mu_0}{2c}, \; \mu(r) = \mu_0 e^{-r/R},$$
$$L = \int_0^\infty \mu(r) 2\pi r dr = \int_0^\infty \mu_0 e^{-r/R} 2\pi r dr = 2\pi\mu_0 R^2. \qquad (3)$$

The approximate energy density W_τ at $r = R$ can then be related to the light surface density μ at $r = R$, with $e/(2c)$ as the proportionality factor. For convenience of reference, the effective energy density function $W_{\tau e}(r > R)$ may be defined proportional to an equivalent effective surface density function $\mu_e(r)$, with the same above factor $e/(2c)$ of proportionality. Using the relation (2) between the $W_{\tau e}$ function and $W_\tau(r = R)$ in the proposed definition, the effective surface density function μ_e may be related to the actual surface-density function μ.

$$W_\tau(r = R) \simeq \frac{\mu_0}{2c} = \frac{e\mu(r=R)}{2c},$$
$$W_{\tau e}(r > R) = \frac{e\mu_e(r)}{2c} = W_\tau(r = R)\frac{R}{r}$$
$$\simeq \frac{e\mu(r=R) \times R}{2cr} = \frac{ea}{2cr},$$
$$a = \mu(r = R) \times R, \; \mu_e(r) = \frac{a}{r} = \frac{\mu(r=R) \times R}{r}. \qquad (4)$$

The effective surface density function $\mu_e(r)$ may be viewed as a $1/r$-functional fit to the actual surface-face density function $\mu(r)$, such that they are equal to each other at $r = R$. As mentioned above, the surface density function $\mu(r)$ is modeled as an exponential distribution with an amplitude μ_0 and a scale radius R. The amplitude a of the μ_e distribution may be related to the parameters μ_0 and R. Consequently, the total luminosity L in (3) may be expressed in terms of the parameters a and R.

$$\mu(r) = \mu_0 e^{-r/R}; \; \mu(r = R) = \frac{a}{R} = \mu_0 e^{-1}, \; \mu_0 = \frac{ea}{R},$$
$$L = 2\pi\mu_0 R^2 = 2\pi e a R. \qquad (5)$$

If the amplitude μ_0 is maintained to be approximately constant, then a would be proportional to R, or equivalently the luminosity L would be proportional to a^2. This may be the case for a large group of high surface brightness (HSB) galaxies, which were believed to confirm to the Freeman's Law [9] of having an approximately constant central brightness μ_0.

$$\mu_0 \sim \text{constant (Freeman's Law, HSB Galaxy)},$$
$$a \propto R, \; L \propto a^2. \qquad (6)$$

The radial UEG field $\overline{E}_{gu}$ may now be expressed proportional to the equivalent energy density $W_{\tau e}$, with the constant of proportionality equal to the UEG constant γ. The potential function associated with the above radial field could be obtained by integrating the field in the radial variable r, from which the θ component of the field may also be derived (in principle) as the θ-derivative of the potential function. However, we are interested here only on the radial UEG field, which completely determines the orbital acceleration on the central plane of the galaxy, because the $\theta-$ component of the UEG field on this plane would be zero. The magnitude E_{gu} of the radial UEG field on the central galaxy plane would be equal to the orbital acceleration v^2/r. The E_{gu} (for $r > R$) is proportional to the effective surface density $\mu_e(r) = a/r$, having the same $1/r$ dependence as the orbital acceleration. Accordingly, the rotation velocity v would exhibit a "flat" behavior for $r > R$, with v^2 **proportional to the constant amplitude 'a'.**

$$\bar{E}_{gu} = -\hat{r}E_{gu} = -\hat{r}\gamma W_{\tau e} = -\hat{r}\gamma\frac{e\mu e}{2c},$$
$$E_{gu}(r) = \frac{\gamma e\mu_e(r)}{2c} = \frac{\gamma ea}{2cr} = \frac{v^2}{r},$$
$$v^2 = \frac{\gamma ea}{2c}, \; r > R. \tag{7}$$

Combining (7,5), the luminosity L may be expressed in terms of the velocity v, radius R, and the UEG constant γ.

$$L = 2\pi eaR = \frac{4\pi Rv^2 c}{\gamma}, \; \gamma = \frac{4\pi Rv^2 c}{L}. \tag{8}$$

Accordingly, the UEG constant γ may be estimated from (8) using measured values of the L, v and R, available from a galaxy survey [10]. Alternatively, the amplitude a for the effective surface density $\mu_e(r)$ may be estimated directly from a measured surface-brightness profile $\mu(r)$ for a selected individual galaxy, and then the γ be estimated using the a and the measured flat rotation velocity v, as per (7,4). The estimation directly using measured data of an individual galaxy would complement the estimation from the galaxy survey, providing an explicit illustration of the UEG model. However, the estimation using an averaged data from the galaxy survey can, in principle, be more reliable than that using data for individual galaxies. Inaccuracies from astronomical measurements of individual galaxy parameters, as well as uncertainty due to deviation of individual galaxy characteristics from any ideal theoretical assumptions, can often be significant. The resulting inaccuracy or uncertainty in the estimation of the γ is expected to be minimized by using an "average" or a central data point among a survey of large number of sample galaxies.

III. ESTIMATION OF γ USING MEASURED DATA FROM GALAXY SURVEY

We first estimate the γ based on (8), using an average data point from the I-band measurement of the galaxy survey [10]. As suggested above, the data point is located approximately at the statistical center of the survey samples.

$$\text{(I-band data):}$$
$$L = 10^{10.4}L_0 = 3.828 \times 10^{36.4}W, \; v = 10^{5.2}\text{m/s},$$
$$R = 10^{0.5}\text{kpc} = 10^{0.5} \times 3.086 \times 10^{19}\text{m},$$
$$\gamma(\text{I-band}) = \gamma_I = \frac{4\pi\times3\times3.086\times10^{1.5}}{3.828}$$
$$= 0.96 \times 10^3[(\text{ms}^{-2})/(\text{Jm}^{-3})]. \tag{9}$$

Similarly, we estimate the γ from the K-band measurement of [10]. Note that an effective radius, R_e, is provided in [10] for the K-band measurements. The effective radius, defined as the radius of a sphere that encloses half of the total luminosity, would be 1.678 times the scale radius R used in our modeling, assuming an exponential light profile.

$$\text{(K-band data) :}$$
$$L = 10^{10.8}L_0 = 3.828 \times 10^{36.8}W, \; v = 10^{5.2}\text{m/s},$$
$$R_e = 10^{0.6}\text{kpc} = 10^{0.6} \times 3.086 \times 10^{19}\text{m}, \; R = R_e/1.678 ,$$
$$\gamma(\text{K-band}) = \gamma_K = \frac{4\pi\times3\times3.086\times10^{1.2}}{3.828\times1.678}$$
$$= 0.29 \times 10^3[(\text{ms}^{-2})/(\text{Jm}^{-3})]. \tag{10}$$

Measurements in the K-band overestimates the luminosity and the energy density, leading to underestimation of the γ. On the other hand, measurements in the I-band underestimates the energy density, leading to overestimation of the γ. Accordingly, the above results estimate a useful range for the value of the γ, which is consistent with the value of the $\gamma = 0.6 \times 10^3$ $(\text{ms}^{-2})/(\text{Jm}^{-3})$ deduced from the UEG model [3] of elementary particles.

$$0.29 \times 10^3 < \gamma < 0.96 \times 10^3[(\text{ms}^{-2})/(\text{Jm}^{-3})],$$
$$\gamma = 0.6 \times 10^3[(\text{ms}^{-2})/(\text{Jm}^{-3})]. \tag{11}$$

The best estimate for γ is assumed to be the average of the two estimates in the $I-$ and $K-$ bands.

$$\gamma \simeq \frac{(\gamma_I + \gamma_K)}{2} = 0.63 \times 10^3[(\text{ms}^{-2})/(\text{Jm}^{-3})]. \tag{12}$$

The above estimate closely agrees with the γ from the particle model [3]. Considering that we used a first-order approximation in the UEG modeling of (1,2), such agreement is remarkable. This means that the ideal conditions we assumed in the first-order UEG modeling of (1,2) are remarkably valid for the central data point of [10] used in our estimation.

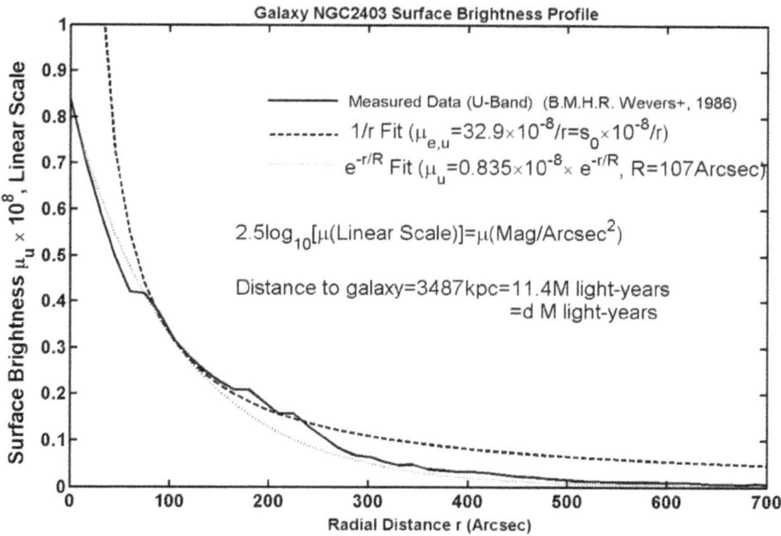

FIG. 2.

IV. ESTIMATION OF γ USING MEASURED DATA OF AN INDIVIDUAL GALAXY

Measured data for the surface brightness distribution $\mu(r)$ of a specific galaxy is first properly fitted with an exponential, and then an effective surface brightness distribution $\mu_e(r)$, as defined in (4). The data using mixed units, such as magnitude, arcsec, light-years, may be converted to suitable standard units. The μ_e distribution can then be related to the rotation velocity v using (7).

$$W_{\tau e} = \frac{e\mu_e}{2c} = \frac{s_0 \times 6.61 \times 10^{-13}}{r} J/m^3,$$

$$\text{UEG Acceleration(m/s}^2) = E_{gu}$$

$$= \gamma W_{\tau e} = \frac{\gamma s_0 \times 6.61 \times 10^{-13}}{r}$$

$$= \frac{v^2 \times 10^{10}}{rm} = \frac{v^2}{r \times d \times 4.6 \times 10^6}; \; v(10^5 m/s),$$

$$1(\text{lin-mag/arcsec}^2)_V = 1.46 \times 10^4 (W/m^2),$$

$$r(\text{arcsec})= r \times d \times 4.6 \times 10^{16}(m)$$

$$= r_m(m), \text{ at distance d(MLyr).} \qquad (13)$$

The UEG constant γ is deduced using the amplitude a, or its equivalent parameter s_0, of the effective surface brightness distribution $\mu_e(r)$, the flat rotation velocity v and the distance d of the galaxy. Suitable correction factors may be needed to relate the K- and U-band measured magnitudes to a common reference of solar visible magnitude of 4.83. This assumes the solar magnitudes in the K- and U-bands are 3.28 and 5.56, respectively.

$$\gamma = \frac{v^2 \times 10^7}{s_0 d \times 6.61 \times 4.6} = \frac{v^2 \times 10^6}{s_0 d \times 3.04} [(\text{ms}^{-2})/(\text{Jm}^{-3})] \text{ (Visible)},$$

$$\gamma = \frac{\Delta_u \times v^2 \times 10^6}{s_0 d \times 3.04} [(\text{ms}^{-2})/(\text{Jm}^{-3})] \text{ (U-Band)},$$

$$\gamma = \frac{\Delta_k \times v^2 \times 10^6}{s_0 d \times 3.04} [(\text{ms}^{-2})/(\text{Jm}^{-3})] \text{ (K-Band)};$$

$$v(10^5 m/s), \; d(MLyr),$$

$$\Delta_k = 10^{(4.83-3.28)/2.5}$$

$$= 4.17 = \text{K-Band correction factor,}$$

$$\Delta_u = 10^{(4.83-5.56)/2.5}$$

$$= 0.51 = \text{U-Band correction factor.} \qquad (14)$$

Using the U-band (assumed $\simeq$ U'-band) surface-brightness data [11] for the galaxy NGC-2403, presented in Fig.2, we estimate the amplitude parameter $s_0 = 32.9$. This parameter, together with the galaxy's distance $d = 11.4$MLyr [12] and flat rotation velocity $v = 1.35 \times 10^5$m/s [13], would provide an estimate for the $\gamma_u = 0.81 \times 10^3$ $(\text{ms}^{-2})/(\text{Jm}^{-3})$, using the above relation (14). Similarly, using the K-band data [14] for the same galaxy NGC-2403, presented in Fig.3, we estimate the amplitude parameter $s_0 = 430$. This would provide an estimate for the $\gamma_k = 0.51 \times 10^3$ $(\text{ms}^{-2})/(\text{Jm}^{-3})$, using (14). An average of these two estimates for the γ would lead to the best estimate for the $\gamma = 0.66 \times 10^3$ $(\text{ms}^{-2})/(\text{Jm}^{-3})$ from the available data for the galaxy NGC-2403. This is close to the $\gamma = 0.63 \times 10^3$ $(\text{ms}^{-2})/(\text{Jm}^{-3})$ deduced from the galaxy survey in (12) or the $\gamma = 0.60 \times 10^3$ $(\text{ms}^{-2})/(\text{Jm}^{-3})$ from particle model [3]. Such remarkable agreement implies that any deviation from the basic model of (1-4) due to

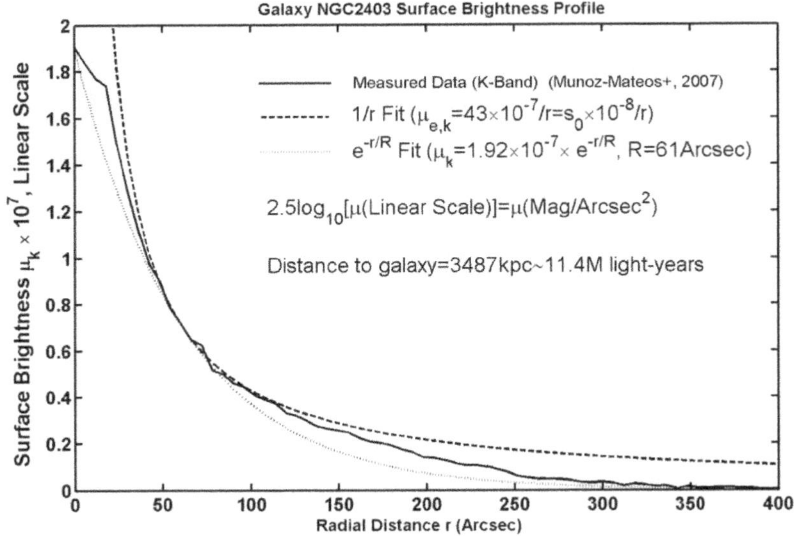

FIG. 3.

differences in the surface brightness μ_0 (see section V)) of the individual galaxy NGC-2403 from the "average" galaxy used in the estimation (12), is minimal. The $\mu_{0,k}$ are estimated to be roughly equal to 16.75 (mag/arcsec^2) in both cases ([10], Fig.3), which is consistent with the above expectation.

NGC-2403:

$$\gamma_u = 0.81 \times 10^3 (\text{ms}^{-2})/(\text{Jm}^{-3}) \ (\text{U-Band}),$$
$$\gamma_k = 0.51 \times 10^3 (\text{ms}^{-2})/(\text{Jm}^{-3})(\text{K-Band}),$$
$$\gamma = (\gamma_v + \gamma_k)/2$$
$$= 0.66 \times 10^3 (\text{ms}^{-2})/(\text{Jm}^{-3}) \ (\text{Best Estimate}). \quad (15)$$

V. THE TULLY-FISHER RELATION (TFR) AND THE MODIFIED NEWTONIAN DYNAMICS (MOND) MODEL, DERIVED FROM THE UEG MODEL

Combining (5,7) and assuming an approximately constant μ_0, a Tully-Fisher Relation (TFR) [6] may be deduced, where the total luminosity L would be proportional to the fourth power of the flat rotation velocity v. As mentioned before, the above condition of an approximately constant μ_0 is satisfied by a large group of high surface brightness (HSB) galaxies that were believed to confirm to the Freeman's Law [9].

$$L = 2\pi\mu_0 R^2 = \frac{2\pi e^2 a^2}{\mu_0} = \frac{8\pi v^4 c^2}{\mu_0 \gamma^2}, \ \mu_0 = \frac{ea}{R},$$
$$L \propto v^4 \ (\text{TFR}),$$
$$\mu_0 \sim \text{constant (Freeman's Law, HSB Galaxy).} \quad (16)$$

However, the Freeman's Law is no longer believed to strictly valid, and galaxies are measured to exhibit a broad range of amplitudes μ_0 covering variations among the HSB galaxies as well as extending to low surface brightness (LSB) galaxies with lower values of μ_0. For a general treatment to closely model the variation in the amplitude μ_0, we may introduce a new parameter α for fitting the $1/r$ profile of μ_e with the exponential profile of μ in (4). The unit reference value of α is expected to apply for an "average" HSB galaxy, as assumed in the basic model of (4) and in the estimations of (12,15). The μ_e may be adjusted to a smaller or larger value, relative to the $\mu(r = R)$, with a proportional adjustment of the parameter α, which would represent a smaller or large value of the UEG force, respectively, as per (7).

The variable factor α is accommodated in the gravitational potential model of (1,2), Fig.1, by recognizing the galaxy thickness z_0 to be an active variable, like the scale radius R or the surface brightness μ_0, for parametrization of galaxy characteristics. In the potential model of (1), an approximately uniform (spherically) potential would be established for all radial distances less than a variable threshold radius R_t, dependent on a variable thickness z_0, not less than the ideal fixed threshold radius $r = R$ assumed in (2). Accordingly, the effective energy density $W_{\tau e}$ would match with the actual energy density W_τ for all the radial distances less than the variable threshold radius, not the ideal reference threshold $r = R$ assumed in (2). Consequently, the $W_{\tau e}(r = R)$ would no longer be equal to $W_\tau(r = R)$ as ideally assumed in (2), but now be equal to $\alpha W_\tau(r = R)$, with the variable factor α proportional to the normalized galaxy thickness R/z_0.

The model of (1,2) may be revised as follows, as explained above.

$$W_{\tau e} \propto W_\tau \times \frac{r}{z_0} = W_\tau \times \frac{r}{R} \times \frac{R}{z_0}; \ W_{\tau e} \sim \frac{1}{r}, \ W_\tau \sim \frac{1}{r^2}.$$
$$W_{\tau e}(r) \propto W_\tau(r = R) \times \frac{R}{r} \times \frac{R}{z_0}, \ r > R;$$
$$W_{\tau e} = W_\tau, \ r < R_t \propto z_0. \tag{17}$$

Using the above revisions and (3), the relation (4) between the surface density μ and effective surface density μ_e, and the resulting expression for the luminosity L (5) using (7), may also be revised.

$$\mu_e(r) = \frac{a}{r} = \alpha \times \frac{\mu(r=R)R}{r}, \ \alpha \propto \frac{R}{z_0},$$
$$\frac{a}{R} = \alpha \times \mu(r = R) = \alpha\mu_0 e^{-1}, \ \mu_0 = \frac{ea}{\alpha R},$$
$$L = 2\pi\mu_0 R^2 = \frac{2\pi e^2 a^2}{\alpha^2 \mu_0} = \frac{8\pi v^4 c^2}{\alpha^2 \mu_0 \gamma^2}. \tag{18}$$

The TFR (16), which was established based on the simple assumption of an approximately constant μ_0, would still be valid for a range of different surface brightness μ_0, if $\mu_0\alpha^2$ in (18) is approximately a constant. This condition, of having a larger value of the α for a lower μ_0, means there would be relatively more contribution from the UEG force as the surface brightness μ_0 reduces. This trend better represents observed characteristics among the HSB galaxies, extending to LSB galaxies as well. The higher UEG contribution for a lower surface brightness μ_0 would be equivalent to having relatively more "dark matter" contribution for a LSB galaxy [15], as per the current dark-matter paradigm.

$$L \propto v^4 \ \text{(MOND, TFR)},$$
$$\mu_0\alpha^2 = \text{constant}, \ \alpha \propto \frac{1}{\sqrt{\mu_0}}; \ \alpha \propto \frac{R}{z_0}, \ \mu_0 \propto \left(\frac{z_0}{R}\right)^2,$$
$$\alpha \ \text{(LSB Galaxy)} > \alpha \ \text{(HSB Galaxy)} \sim 1,$$
$$\text{Dark Matter (LSB)} > \text{Dark Matter (HSB)},$$
$$\frac{z_0}{R}\text{(LSB)} < \frac{z_0}{R}\text{(HSB)}. \tag{19}$$

The above TFR of having the luminosity proportional to the fourth power of the velocity v, is also consistent with prediction from an alternate model using a modified Newtonian dynamics (MOND) [2, 7].

As derived in (17,18), the parameter α, which proportionately represents the equivalent distribution $W_{\tau e}$ or μ_e, is proportional to the normalized galaxy scale R/z_0. Accordingly, the condition (19) of a constant factor $\mu_0\alpha^2$, required for the validity of the TFR or MOND, would be satisfied if the normalized scale parameter (z_0/R) is

proportional to the square-root of the surface brightness μ_0. This general trend, of having the normalized galaxy thickness z_0/R to be smaller for a lower surface brightness μ_0, may seem to be a sensible characteristic. The specific required relationship between the galaxy thickness and the surface brightness may be compared and verified with the measured data in [16].

Using the above required relationship (19) between the μ_0 and the normalized scale z_0/R in (18,7) would translate to another galaxy scaling relationship between the absolute thickness z_0 (not normalized to R) and the flat rotation velocity v.

$$\mu_0 = \frac{ea}{\alpha R}, \ v^2 = \frac{\gamma ea}{2c} = \frac{\gamma\mu_0\alpha R}{2c} = \frac{\gamma(\mu_0\alpha^2)R}{2c\alpha} \propto z_0,$$
$$\mu_0\alpha^2 = \text{constant}, \ \alpha \propto \frac{R}{z_0}. \tag{20}$$

Accordingly, the galaxy thickness z_0 is required to be proportional to the square of the flat rotation velocity v. This required relationship is clearly verified from the measured data of [16]. It is significant to note that the above two required relations (a) between the galaxy normalized thickness z_0/R and the surface brightness μ_0, and (b) between the thickness z_0 and the flat rotation velocity v, are independently predicted from the UEG model of (17,18), based on the observed TFR (19,16), but could not have been anticipated either from the TFR of [6] or the MOND [2, 7]. Verification of the above predictions from [16] is a significant development, which strongly validates the new UEG model of (1,17), as applied to the non-spherical structure of a galaxy.

A.   Refinement in the Tully-Fisher Relation

Some refinement in the above TFR (19) may be needed, in order to confirm to the measured data [6, 10] more accurately, where the luminosity seems to be proportional to a smaller exponent (than the ideal value of 4 in (19)) of the velocity v. This trend may be empirically established from (19) by having the factor $\mu_0\alpha^2$ to be weakly dependent on the velocity v (proportional to a relatively small exponent of v), instead of the ideal constant factor $\mu_0\alpha^2$ suggested above. This may be represented by suitable refinement in the required relation in (19) between the galaxy normalized thickness z_0/R and the surface brightness μ_0.

$$\mu_0\alpha^2 \sim v^b, \ 0 < b < 0.5;$$
$$L \sim v^{4-b} = v^d, \ 3.5 < d < 4 . \tag{21}$$

However, this refined TFR does not confirm to the MOND, where the luminosity is definitively required to be proportional to the fourth power of the velocity v. It is not clear if the above refinement (21) is really fundamental or is simply due to selection bias in the measurements of [6, 10], resulting in a limited range in the data over which the exponent d is estimated with a smaller value $d < 4$.

The total luminosity and surface brightness profile are usually proportional to the total baryonic mass and its mass distribution, respectively, in which case the TFR would work as well if the luminosity is interchanged with the baryonic mass. The proportionality between the baryonic mass and the luminosity may not, however, strictly extend to all LSB galaxies, having smaller luminosity and rotation velocity. In this case, the measured data follow a TFR more accurately, if the total baryonic mass M_b is used in the relation (19,21), instead of the total luminosity L. The revised relation is referred to as the Baryonic Tully-Fisher Relation (BTFR) [17]. The baryonic mass M_b would be proportional either to the fourth power or to a smaller exponent of the velocity, if the baronic mass substitutes the luminosity in the TFR versions (19) or (21), respectively. The former version of the BTFR is consistent with MOND which, to fundamentally begin with, relates the baryonic mass to the fourth power of the velocity v.

The deviation from the original TFR may be partly attributed to the larger contribution to the rotation velocity v from the Newtonian gravity due to the proportionately larger regular mass (baryonic), in the lower-luminosity LSB galaxies. More significantly, the revised trend may be empirically accommodated by properly adjusting the parameter α in (18) to be dependent on both the surface brightness μ_0 and an equivalent baryonic surface mass density A_b of the galaxy. This would be consistent with the basic principles of the present UEG model in (1- 5,17), where the gravitational potential function that determines the redistribution of the energy density W_τ into the effective density $W_{\tau e}$ (see Fig.1) may be recognized to depend upon both the Newtonian gravitation (related to mass profile) as well as the UEG field due to the light profile of a galaxy. However, more specific physical explanation behind such an empirical trend, leading to the preference of the baryonic mass over the luminosity in the BTFR, is at this point unclear, and is beyond the scope of the present work.

$$M_b = L \times \frac{M_b}{L} = \frac{8\pi v^4 c^2}{\alpha^2 \mu_0 \gamma^2} \times \frac{M_b}{L}$$

$$= \frac{8\pi v^4 c^2}{\alpha^2 (\mu_0^2/A_b)\gamma^2}, \quad \frac{M_b}{L} = \frac{A_b}{\mu_0},$$

$$M_b \propto v^4, \quad \alpha^2 \times (\mu_0^2/A_b) = \text{constant}. \tag{22}$$

Accordingly, for a given surface luminosity μ_0, a larger value of the baryonic mass density A_b is expected to result in a tighter confinement of the gravitational potential near the galaxy surface (smaller z_0), resulting in a larger α. The two refinements (21,22) may need to be studied together, which may be associated with interdependent and/or mutually compensating physical effects.

VI.   CONCLUSION

The estimate of the UEG constant γ from measured data from a galaxy survey [10], based on the new UEG model, agrees well with an accurate value derived from the UEG model of elementary particles [3, 4]. This is based on a statistically average data point from the survey samples. Direct analysis of measured brightness profile and rotation curve of a specific selected galaxy is also illustrated to provide a similar estimate for the γ, that is consistent with the estimate from the galaxy survey. Further, the UEG galaxy model confirms to the TFR [6, 17] for varying range of galaxy amplitudes, and is consistent with results from a modified Newtonian dynamics (MOND) [2, 7] model. The required condition for the agreement between the UEG model, TFR and MOND is supported by measured relations of the galaxy thickness with the surface brightness and the rotation velocity [16], which may be considered as an independent validation of the UEG model. The above studies strongly support validity of the new UEG model, established for the non-spherical structure of a disk galaxy. The UEG theory is intended to serve as a theoretical substitute for the current "dark-matter" hypothesis.

The UEG theory, which has been successfully applied for elementary particles [3, 4] as well as single and binary stars [5], and is now supported as well for galaxy modeling, may provide a new unified theoretical paradigm for a broad range of physical concepts, covering both small and large size scales of nature, and spherically symmetric as well as asymmetric structures.

---

[1] V. Rubin, N. Thonard, and J. W. K. Ford, Astrophysical Journal, Part 1 **238**, 471 (1980).

[2] M. Milgrom, Astrophysical Journal, Part 1 **270**, 365 (1983).

[3] N. Das, "A New Unified Electro-Gravity (UEG) Theory of the Electron," Paper #1, pp.4-13, in "A Unified Electro-Gravity (UEG) Theory of Nature," (2018).

[4] N. Das, "A Generalized Unified Electro-Gravity (UEG) Model Applicable to All Elementary Particles," Paper #2, pp.14-30, in "A Unified Electro-Gravity (UEG) Theory of Nature," (2018).

[5] N. Das, "Unified Electro-Gravity (UEG) Theory Applied to Stellar Gravitation, and the Mass-Luminosity Relation (MLR)," Paper #4, pp.44-58, in "A Unified Electro-

Gravity (UEG) Theory of Nature," (2018).

[6] R. B. Tully and J. R. Fisher, Astronomy and Astrophysics **54**, 661 (1977).

[7] M. Milgrom, Astrophysical Journal, Part 2 **270**, 371 (1983).

[8] A. Borriello and P. Salucci, Monthly Notices of the Royal Astronomical Society **323**, 285 (2001).

[9] K. C. Freeman, Astrophysical Journal **160**, 811 (1970).

[10] S. Courteau, A. A. Dutton, F. C. van den Bosch, L. A. MacArthur, A. Dekel, D. H. McIntosh, and D. A. Dale, Astrophysical Journal **671**, 203 (2007).

[11] B. M. H. R. Weavers, P. C. van der Kruit, and R. J. Allen, Astronomy and Astrophysics Supplement Series **66**, 505 (1986).

[12] NED, "Nasa Extragalactic Database, Results for NGC-2403," `http://ned.ipac.caltech.edu`, Retrieved (2017).

[13] K. Begeman, PhD Thesis, University of Groningen, Netherlands (2006).

[14] J. Munoz-Mateos, A. G. de Paz, S. Boissier, J. Zamorano, T. Jarrett, J. Gallego, and B. F. Madore, Astrophysical Journal **658**, 1005 (2007).

[15] W. J. G. de Blok and S. S. McGaugh, Monthly Notices of the Royal Astronomical Society **290**, 533 (1997).

[16] D. Bizyaev and S. Kajsin, The Astrophysical Journal **613**, 886 (2004).

[17] S. S. McGaugh, J. M. Schombert, G. D. Bothun, and W. J. G. de Blok, The Astrophysical Journal **533**, L99 (2000).

A Unified Electro-Gravity (UEG) Model as a Substitute for Super-Massive Black Holes (SMBH) at Galactic Centers

Nirod K. Das

Department of Electrical and Computer Engineering, Tandon School of Engineering,
New York University, 5 Metrotech Center, Brooklyn, NY 11201

(Dated: May 9, 2018; Revised April 30, 2019)

The UEG model for rotation in a disk galaxy is extended in this paper to model gravitation in a galaxy's central region. The strong gravitational effects at the centers of many galaxies, observed in the form of fast stellar orbits or velocity dispersion near the center, may be explained using the UEG theory, without having to invoke the hypothesis of super-massive black holes (SMBH).

I. INTRODUCTION

The UEG theory of [1, 2] was extended in [3] to successfully model rotation around disk galaxies, without need for any "dark-matter". The UEG theory for the disk region of a disk galaxy may be extended as well into the galaxy's bulge, in order to model gravitation near the galactic center. This may provide a substitute theory for the super-massive black holes (SMBH), that are currently hypothesized to exist at the centers of most galaxies. In the absence of an alternate scientific theory, the SMBH hypothesis is invoked in order to explain fast stellar orbits that is directly observed near the central nuclear region of our own Milky Way galaxy [4], as well as indirectly deduced from Doppler measurements in the central region of many other galaxies [5]. The stars in the central galactic region of our own Milky Way galaxy are known to be significantly brighter, on average as well as in individual terms, as compared to the stars in the galaxy's outer periphery [6]. Such distribution of bright stars in the Milky Way galaxy is likely to extend to other galaxies. The UEG field due to the light radiation from a reasonable number of individual bright stars, or due to integrated light intensity over a suitable volume around the central region, may support the high magnitude of acceleration associated with the fast stellar motions near the galaxy centers.

In addition to the high magnitude of acceleration, the fast motions in the galactic centers are also deduced to follow conventional Keplerian orbits [4]. Accordingly, in addition to supporting the high magnitudes of acceleration, the proposed UEG field would also be required to justify a $1/r^2$ dependence of the field with respect to the radial distance r from the galaxy center, in order to support the Keplerian orbits. The required $1/r^2$ dependence of the UEG field near the nucleus could be supported by presence of a single star or a few stars with sufficiently high total luminosity, at or very close to the nucleus of the galaxy. Farther from the nucleus, the same $1/r^2$ dependence of the UEG field is also assumed to be effectively maintained, produced due to radiation from the high concentration of stars in the region, in presence of high extinction. Alternatively, the required $1/r^2$ dependence may be explained using a suitable UEG model, where the UEG field is determined by an effective distri-

bution of energy density, which is obtained by proper re-distribution of the light density in the galactic core. The energy re-distribution is in proportion to the density of a non-spherical mass distribution, that is expected to exist in the central core region, possibly in the form of galactic jets or bars that might originate from this region. The UEG theory, in its simple form in the presence of a uniform or spherically symmetric mass distribution, or with suitable adjustment to account for any non-spherical mass distribution in a central region, would establish a suitable M-sigma relation [5, 7] between the equivalent mass of the SMBH in the central nucleus and the velocity dispersion or rotation velocity in the galaxy's bulge. This includes both disk as well as elliptical galaxies.

II. THEORY

We will follow the UEG theory [3] that was developed to model gravitation in the external disk region of a spiral galaxy, with reasonable assumptions for analytical simplicity and extension of the model into the galactic bulge. In the most of the internal region of the bulge, the effective energy density $W_{\tau e}$ would be equal to the actual energy density $W_\tau(r)$, which is assumed to be approximately uniform, produced due to a uniform distribution of stellar sources. However, the uniformity of the effective energy density may not be valid in a core region of radius r_0, where the effective energy density may be modeled differently.

$$W_{\tau e}(r) = W_\tau(r) = W_{\tau 0} = \frac{a}{R_0}, \ r_0 < r < R_0;$$

$$= \frac{b}{r^2}, \ r < r_0;$$

$$r_0 = \alpha_0 R_0, \ \frac{b}{r_0^2} = \frac{a}{R_0}, \ b = \frac{a r_0^2}{R_0} = a \alpha_0^2 R_0. \quad (1)$$

The effective energy density $W_{\tau e}$ in the core region is modeled with a $1/r^2$ variation, as discussed later in the section III. This results in a proportional radial component E_{ur} of the UEG acceleration with the $1/r^2$ variation, where the constant of proportionality is the UEG constant γ. This would be equivalent to having a mass m_0 as per the Newtonian gravitation. In the rest of the bulge the UEG acceleration is proportional to the effective energy density, which is equal to the actual energy density $W_\tau(r) = W_{\tau 0}$. The uniform UEG acceleration in this region would be equal to the circular orbital acceleration v^2/R_0 at the boundary of the bulge. We assume that the central velocity dispersion σ in the bulge is equivalent to the circular velocity v at the boundary of the bulge $r = R_0$. Accordingly, the equivalent mass m_0 for the core region may be related to the flat rotation speed v, based on the model (1).

$$E_{ur}(r < r_0) = \gamma W_{\tau e}(r < r_0) = \frac{\gamma b}{r^2} = \frac{Gm_0}{r^2}, \ m_0 = \frac{\gamma b}{G},$$

$$E_{ur}(r = R_0) = \gamma W_{\tau e}(r = R_0) = \gamma W_{\tau 0} = \frac{\gamma a}{R_0} = \frac{v^2}{R_0},$$

$$v^2 = \gamma a = \gamma W_{\tau 0} R_0, \ b = a\alpha_0^2 R_0,$$

$$m_0 G = v^2 \alpha_0^2 R_0, \ m_0 = \frac{v^2 \alpha_0^2 R_0}{G}. \tag{2}$$

We may also assume that the average surface brightness $\mu_0 \simeq \mu(r)$, or its associated energy density $W_{\tau 0}$, is constant, as a first-order approximation for simplicity. This would include a large group of galaxies, which in case of disk galaxies would confirm to the Freeman's Law of High Surface-Brightness (HSB) galaxies [8]. With this assumption, from (2) the bulge radius R_0 may be shown to be proportional to the square of the rotation velocity v $(R_0 \propto (v^2/W_{\tau 0}))$. This is similar to the relation between the disk scale length R of a disk galaxy and its flat rotation speed v in the outer disk region, when the galaxy's surface brightness is approximately constant (Freeman's Law) [3]. This also leads to a Tully-Fisher Relation (TFR) for the disk galaxies, where the galaxy's luminosity is proportional to the fourth power of the velocity v, as shown in [3]. The equivalent relation, the Faber-Jackson Law [9], may be established for an elliptical galaxy.

Any deviation from the ideal trend, due to deviation of the UEG acceleration E_{ur} in (2) as the surface brightness deviates from an ideal reference value, is assumed to be empirically balanced by suitable counter-effects in the UEG acceleration. This may include dependence of the UEG acceleration with the bulge's aspect ratio in mass or light distribution (or effective radius), having a counter dependence with the surface brightness. Similar countering UEG effect due the thickness of a disk galaxy was discovered in the [3], in the modeling of the galaxy's rotation curve. Any further specific study in this direction, particularly for an elliptical galaxy, is beyond the scope of this work.

An equivalent luminosity L_c of the star lights enclosed inside the core of radius r_0, which produces the $1/r^2$-dependent effective energy density $W_{\tau e} = b/r^2$ in the core region, would be equal to $L_c = 4\pi r_0^2 c W_{\tau e}(r = r_0) = 4\pi bc$. The c is the speed of light in free space. Similarly, an equivalent luminosity L_b in the total bulge region of radius R_0 would be equal to $L_b = 4\pi R_0^2 c W_{\tau e}(r = R_0) = 4\pi R_0 ac$. It may be reasonable to assume that the L_c is

proportional to the L_b: larger is the total luminosity of the star lights in the galaxy's bulge, more likely there would be bright stars of proportionately larger luminosity to be found in the core region inside the bulge, to support the $1/r^2$-dependent UEG field in the core region. Based on this assumption $L_c \propto L_b$, we would have $b \propto R_0 a$. Using this result in the model (2), it may also be reasonable to assume that the core radius r_0 is proportional to the bulge radius R_0, which is equivalent to having the parameter α_0 to be a constant.

Under the above conditions ($R_0 \propto v^2$, Freeman's Law, and constant α_0, $L_c \propto L_b$), the M-Sigma relation [5] would be established, where the equivalent SMBH mass $M = m_0$ is shown to be proportional to the fourth power of the velocity dispersion or the flat rotation velocity $\sigma = v$ [7]. With a reasonable variation of the above model, where the r_0 is proportional to the 5/4 power of the R_0 ($\alpha_0 \propto R_0^{0.25}$), an empirically more accurate version of the M-sigma relation could be established, where the m_0 is proportional to the fifth power of the velocity v [5, 7].

$$\text{M-Sigma Relation :}$$
$$m_0 \propto v^4, \ R_0 \propto v^2 (\text{Freeman's Law}), \ \alpha_0 \sim (\text{constant}),$$
$$m_0 \propto v^5, \ R_0 \propto v^2, \ \alpha_0 \propto R_0^{0.25}, \ r_0 \propto R_0^{1.25}. \tag{3}$$

The core radius r_0 may be estimated for the Milky Way galaxy.

$$\text{For Milky-Way:}$$
$$m_0 = 4 \times 10^6 M_{\text{sun}},$$
$$M_{\text{sun}} = 1.989 \times 10^{30} \text{kg},$$
$$v = 100 \,\text{km/s},$$
$$R_0 \sim 10000 \,\text{Lyr} = 9.4 \times 10^{19} \text{m} \tag{4}$$
$$G = 6.67 \times 10^{-11} \,\text{Nm}^2/\text{kg}^2,$$
$$\alpha_0 = \sqrt{\frac{m_0 G}{v^2 R_0}} = \sqrt{\frac{4 \times 1.989 \times 6.7}{9.4}} \times 10^{-2} = 2.38 \times 10^{-2},$$
$$r_0 = \alpha_0 R_0 \sim 238 \,\text{Lyr} = 73 \,\text{parsec}. \tag{5}$$

This radius is comparable to the size of the Milky Way's central region, where high concentration of bright stars have been observed [6]. Such bright stars in the central region of the Milky Way, and presumably in the central region of other galaxies as well, would provide the required high energy density and the associated high acceleration, as anticipated in the proposed UEG model.

III.   UEG MODEL IN THE CORE REGION

The $1/r^2$ dependence of the UEG acceleration in the galactic core region, as assumed in the above UEG model (2), may be established in following possible ways:
(**I**) A single bright star, or few stars closely together, of sufficiently high total luminosity, is(are) assumed to exist at or near the nucleus. The bright star(s) may yet to be

discovered in the nuclear region of the Milky Way, likely undetectable due to high extinction in its radiation spectrum. Or, the luminosity of one or a few of the known stars near the nucleus of the Milky Way are actually sufficiently bright, but their luminosities have been underestimated. Such bright sources at or near the nucleus would exhibit the conventional $1/r^2$-dependent light radiation, like a central point source, which would support the $1/r^2$-dependent UEG acceleration of sufficient magnitude, as required. After all, stars with luminosity close to 8 million solar luminosity, needed to emulate the central SMBH of the Milky Way as per the UEG theory, have been discovered elsewhere in our galactic neighborhood (star R136a1 has 8 million solar luminosity [10]). Stars of comparable luminosity have also been discovered in the Milky Way within $\sim$ 1pc of the galactic center (WR102ka and WR102c have about 3 million solar luminosity each [6]). It is quite likely that a single star or a few stars with the required total high luminosity (comparable to one R136a1 or three WR102ka-type stars), but radiating mostly in the visible spectrum, is(are) already present in or near the nuclear region, but remain(s) undetected due to the high extinction in the visible spectrum. In the core region, farther away from the nucleus, the same $1/r^2$ dependence of the UEG acceleration is also assumed to be maintained, effectively, determined by distribution of star radiation and extinction characteristics in the region.

It may be mentioned, a star could attain the required high luminosity (8 million solar luminosity) with mass comparable to only a solar-mass, as per the UEG model of stars [11]. It is feasible to attain even much higher stellar luminosity, with only reasonably larger level of stellar mass, without any un-physical requirement of mass or mass concentration. Presence of such brighter stars would be needed, as per the UEG theory, to support much higher acceleration, or equivalently to emulate much heavier SMBH, measured at the centers of other galaxies.

The theory in the above first scenario is based on a simple UEG model [1], where the UEG acceleration is proportional to the energy density of radiation, assuming that the mass distribution in the core region is approximately uniform or spherically symmetric.

(II) In a second scenario, the UEG theory may need to be applied differently in the galactic core, taking into account suitable non-spherical mass distribution in the core region ($r < r_0$), possibly forming jets or handle-bars. The new model can provide the required $1/r^2$-dependent acceleration, while the actual energy density of stellar light is approximately uniform in the central nuclear region. This possibility is theoretically interesting, and could be physically quite likely, considering that galaxies are known to exhibit jet or handle-bar formations near the galactic center, and such non-uniform mass formations may originate from the nuclear region as assumed in the present scenario.

It may be noted, that the above proposed model for a non-spherical mass distribution in the galactic core re-

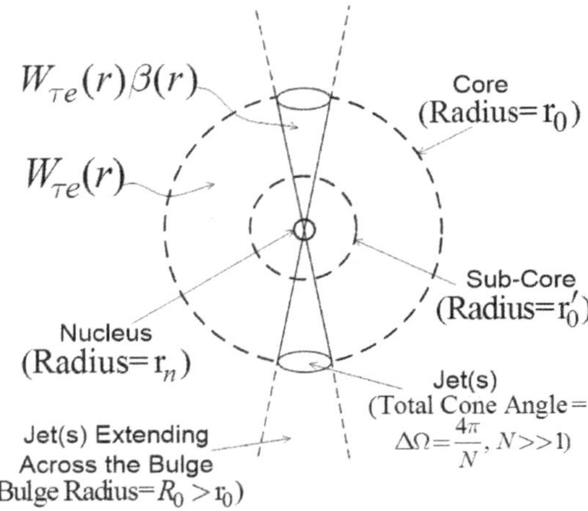

FIG. 1.

gion, is similar in principle to the UEG model of [3] for the non-spherical mass distribution in the disk region of a disk galaxy. Particular differences are in the specific mass distribution and the region of interest in the two cases. The UEG field in the thin disk region, which is the region of higher mass(baryonic) concentration as compared to the large external halo, supports the flat rotation behavior in the disk. Whereas, the UEG field in the region outside of a narrow jet in the galactic core, which is the region of lower mass concentration as compared to the narrow jet, supports the fast stellar motion in the galactic core.

The required $1/r^2$ dependence of the acceleration is achieved in the region outside a small nucleus of radius r_n at the galactic center, and external to a narrow conical jet of solid angle $\Delta\Omega = 4\pi/N$ (or a combination of more than one jet of the same total solid angle), likely with $N \gg 1$. This is achieved by establishing in the region an effective energy density $W_{\tau e}(r)$ with the $1/r^2$ variation, while the actual energy density, W_τ, of the light is assumed to be approximately uniform in the vicinity of the central nucleus (see Fig.1). This would be possible if the mass density in the jet region is larger than the surrounding region by a suitable jet density factor $\beta(r) > 1$, which is assumed to be physically realistic for formation of the jets.

$$W_{\tau e}(r)(4\pi - \Delta\Omega) + W_{\tau e}(r)\beta(r)\Delta\Omega = 4\pi W_\tau(r),$$

$$W_{\tau e}(r) = \frac{W_\tau(r)N}{(N-1)+\beta(r)}, \quad \Delta\Omega = \frac{4\pi}{N}. \tag{6}$$

The energy density of stellar radiation is approximately uniform in a sub-core region $r < r_0'$, with sufficiently large magnitude. This maybe produced by a high-density distribution of luminous stars in the sub-core region. As mentioned, the stars may possibly be radiating in the visible or ultraviolet region, and may remain undetectable due to high extinction in the galactic center. Due to the high extinction, the energy density may sharply drop just outside of the sub-core region ($r'_0 < r < r_0$), from its high uniform value $W_{\tau n}$ in the sub-core region $r < r'_0$, to its ideal constant value $W_{\tau 0}$ outside the core region $R_0 > r > r_0$.

$$W_\tau(r) = W_{\tau n}, \ r < r'_0;$$
$$\simeq W_{\tau 0} + \frac{W_{\tau n} - W_{\tau 0}}{r_0 - r'_0}(r_0 - r), \ r'_0 < r < r_0;$$
$$= W_{\tau 0}, \ r_0 < r < R_0. \tag{7}$$

From (6,7,2), the density factor $\beta(r)$ would be unity at the nucleus $r = r_n$, and have a r^2 dependence towards the sub-core boundary $r = r'_0$ if the sub-core radius is much larger than the nucleus ($r'_0 >> r_n$). The density factor would have a reasonable value ($1 < \beta < N$) in the region $r_0 < r < R_0$ outside the core, which may ideally be assumed to be a constant β_0. In the transition region, $r'_0 < r < r_0$, the density factor would have a suitable variation as per (6), related to the energy density $W_\tau(r)$ of (7) in the transition region and the $1/r^2$-dependent effective energy density $W_{\tau e}(r)$ assumed in the SMBH model of (2).

$$W_{\tau e}(r = r_n) = W_\tau(r = r_n) = W_{\tau n}, \ \beta(r = r_n) = 1;$$
$$W_{\tau e}(r_0 < r < R_0) \simeq W_\tau(r_0 < r < R_0) = W_{\tau 0},$$
$$\beta(r_0 < r < R_0) = \beta_0, \ 1 < \beta_0 << N;$$
$$W_{\tau e}(r) = \frac{W_{\tau n} r_n^2}{r^2} = \frac{W_{\tau 0} r_0^2}{r^2} = \frac{b}{r^2}, \ r_n < r < r_0; \tag{8}$$

$$W_{\tau e}(r) \simeq \frac{W_\tau(r) N}{\beta(r)}, \ \beta(r) >> N,$$
$$W_{\tau e}(r) \simeq \frac{W_{\tau n} N}{\beta(r)} = \frac{W_{\tau n} r_n^2}{r^2},$$
$$\beta(r'_0 > r >> r_n) = N \frac{r^2}{r_n^2} >> N. \tag{9}$$

Note that a SMBH has not been located at the center of each and every galaxy. Accordingly, the above proposed UEG models are not likely to be applicable universally for all galaxies. One model may be more likely than the other in an elliptical or a disk galaxy. For galaxies that are associated with a central SMBH, either of two proposed models, or possibly a combination of parts of the two models, may be generally applicable, leading to the M-Sigma relation (3) for these galaxies.

IV.   CONCLUSION

The UEG theory, either in its simple form [1, 2] in a uniform material environment, or in a modified form [3] in a non-uniform environment of narrow jets or handlebars, can successfully model the strong stellar acceleration, with a Keplerian orbit, that is observed in the core region of many galaxies, including the Milky Way. With suitable simplifications, the UEG model deduces the empirical M-Sigma relation, thus validating the proposed model. The hypothesis that there is a SMBH at the center of many galaxies may no longer be necessary, in order to explain the strong central accelerations observed in the galaxy core. Instead, the hypothetical SMBH is emulated in the form of an equivalent UEG acceleration of sufficiently high magnitude, and with the required $1/r^2$ dependence for the Keplerian motion.

The strong magnitude of the UEG force is possible due to star lights from sufficiently bright stars that are assumed to exist, in the form of a few individual bright stars or in an integrated form due to distributed stars, in the galactic core of most galaxies. This is consistent with the presence and distribution of bright stars in the core region of our own Milky Way galaxy. The high UEG acceleration is possible without any un-physical, high mass concentration at the galactic nucleus, as might be required based on the conventional Newtonian gravitation. The un-physicality of the mass concentration, as per the Newtonian gravitation, required to support the fast stellar motion very close to the galactic center, is often invoked to "predict" the presence of SMBH at the centers of most galaxies, which may no longer be justified. Further, a recent observation of radio signals generated from fast-moving charged particles much closer to a galaxy's center [12], which apparently suggested an "event-horizon" of a presumed central SMBH, could as well be explained in terms of the high central acceleration due to radiation from the bright central stars, as per the UEG theory. This would neither require a super-massive body, nor a black hole, but simply bright stellar (or quasi-stellar) objects at the galactic center, having relatively small mass (Newtonian, baryonic) as per [11], which exhibit black-hole-like characteristics with a large UEG-based central acceleration. The bright stellar light coming from the galaxy's center, presumed in the UEG theory, would actually contradict presence of a central black hole from which the light supposedly should not have escaped.

The UEG theory was successfully applied to elementary particles [1, 2] as well as single stars [11], which are ideal spherical structures. The UEG theory was also successfully applied with suitable modification to model non-spherical structures such as a binary star [11], as well as the disk region of a spiral galaxy [3]. The UEG model of [3] is now extended to model gravitation in the galactic core, which may not consist of spherically uniform mass distribution, as a substitute for the SMBH hypothesis currently believed. The UEG theory, with suitable extensions to general problems, may provide a unified paradigm to model diverse physical phenomena in small as well as large size scales, in structures with ideal spherical as well as non-spherical distributions.

[1] N. Das, "A New Unified Electro-Gravity (UEG) Theory of the Electron," Paper #1, pp.4-13, in "A Unified Electro-Gravity (UEG) Theory of Nature," (2018).

[2] N. Das, "A Generalized Unified Electro-Gravity (UEG) Model Applicable to All Elementary Particles," Paper #2, pp.14-30, in "A Unified Electro-Gravity (UEG) Theory of Nature," (2018).

[3] N. Das, "Unified Electro-Gravity (UEG) Theory Applied to Spiral Galaxies," Paper #5, pp.59-68, in "A Unified Electro-Gravity (UEG) Theory of Nature," (2018).

[4] A. M. Ghez, S. Salim, S. D. Hornstein, A. Tanner, J. R. Lu, M. Morris, E. E. Becklin, and G. Duchene, The Astrophysical Journal **620**, 744 (2005).

[5] L. Ferrarese and D. Merritt, Astrophysical Journal **539**, L9 (2000).

[6] A. Barniske, L. M. Oskinova, and W. R. Hamann, Astronomy and Astrophysics **486**, 971 (2008).

[7] Wikipedia, "M-Sigma Relation," `http://en.wikipedia.org/wiki/M-sigma_relation`, Retrieved (2013).

[8] K. C. Freeman, Astrophysical Journal **160**, 811 (1970).

[9] S. M. Faber and R. E. Jackson, The Astrophysical Journal **204**, 668 (1976).

[10] P. A. Crowther, O. Schnurr, R. Hirschi, N. Yusof, R. J. Parker, and S. P. G. H. A. Kassim, Monthly Notices of Royal Astronomical Society **408**, 731 (2010).

[11] N. Das, "Unified Electro-Gravity (UEG) Theory Applied to Stellar Gravitation, and the Mass-Luminosity Relation (MLR)," Paper #4, pp.44-58, in "A Unified Electro-Gravity (UEG) Theory of Nature," (2018).

[12] T. E. H. T. Collaboration, The Astrophysical Journal **875** (2019).

The Unified Electro-Gravity (UEG) Theory Applied to Cosmology

Nirod K. Das

Department of Electrical and Computer Engineering, Tandon School of Engineering,
New York University, 5 Metrotech Center, Brooklyn, NY 11201
(Dated: May 9, 2018; Revised April 30, 2019)

The Unified Electro-Gravity (UEG) theory is extended for the unique conditions of cosmology, which may support a possible reversal of the current expansionary phase of the universe, explain the current accelerated expansion of the universe without need for any dark energy, and also explain the signatures of the baryon acoustic oscillation (BAO) in the cosmic microwave background (CMB) and in the correlation function of galaxy distribution, without any dark matter. UEG effects due to the the CMB radiation in the recent universe, and in the ionized environment before recombination, as well as those due to anticipated star lights in the future universe, are modeled with suitable cosmological assumptions. This may provide a new theoretical paradigm, which can potentially answer some of the most fundamental questions in cosmology today.

I. INTRODUCTION

The Unified Electro-Gravity (UEG) Theory has been successfully applied to model elementary particles [1, 2], quantum mechanics [3], stars [4] and galaxies [5]. In the simplest form, the UEG theory introduces a new gravitational field in proportion to the energy density of radiation [1], with the UEG constant γ as the constant of proportionality. This simple form applies only for small levels of energy density, having an ideal spherical symmetry. Suitable modification is needed to model non-spherical distributions of energy density in a binary star [4], and a spiral galaxy [5], or for higher levels of energy density seen in elementary particles [2]. Based on the past successes of the UEG theory under the diverse conditions, we may expect that the UEG theory, with suitable extensions to account for the unique conditions of cosmology, would help to answer different unresolved questions in cosmology today. A fundamental question may be opened: is the big bang just a fortuitous one-time event for our universe, or it could be only one of the natural sequence of big bounces in a cyclic universe (e.g. [6]), with periodic expansion and contraction? The answer to this question would hinge on a satisfactory theory that could support reversal of the current expansion of the universe, back to a contracting phase, to be followed by a natural big crunch and a bounce, which the cyclic model would presume. Another basic question would be, what is the physical basis for the apparent accelerated expansion [7, 8] of the current universe? Any new physics is expected to emulate the hypothetical dark energy, which is invoked by scientists today to explain the accelerated expansion [7, 8]. The new physics is also expected to emulate the hypothetical dark matter, which apparently explains the signature of the baryon acoustic oscillations (BAO) in the cosmic microwave background (CMB) [9–11] as well as in the large-scale correlation function of galaxy distribution [12]. With the success of the UEG theory in modeling the flat rotation curves in spiral galaxies [5], without any need for the hypothetical dark matter, the current theory for the BAO and CMB signatures based on the dark matter may no longer be tenable.

We attempt in this paper to answer some of the basic questions, based on the UEG theory, with suitable assumptions and extensions to accommodate unique cosmological conditions, which might not have been encountered in the other problems [1]-[5] solved by the UEG theory. We would assume an ideal homogeneous, isotropic universe, and propose a cyclic universe that anticipates future events. The present expansionary state of the universe is assumed to have been adjusted over repeated cycles in the past, such that together with the future anticipated events it would result in a reversal of its current expansion, leading to a complete cyclic process. Any energy density associated with the CMB radiation, or with any present and future star lights, would produce new UEG forces. These new forces, in addition to the Newtonian gravity due to conventional matter content of the universe, would constitute the complete physical basis for the current expansion, possible future contraction, and the geometry of the universe, without need for any fictitious dark energy or dark matter. The new UEG model could potentially explain important cosmological observations, such as (a) the supernova distance-redshift measurements [7, 8] without any dark energy or dark matter, and (b) the basic BAO signature in the CMB [10, 11] without any dark matter, as well as (c) support a possible reversal of the current expansion of the universe, in order that the universe can contract and then cycle back to maintain a periodic process. The regime of big-bang nucleo-synthesis (BBN) [13, 14], when nuclei of light elements are believed to have been synthesized in the early universe, is assumed to be unaffected by the UEG theory. This is possibly because in the BBN regime the photons in the cosmic radiation would remain tightly coupled to the highly ionized material environment, which may not contribute to any significant UEG forces. In addition, in this regime when the universe is dominated by radiation, any UEG effect may have been highly diluted over a larger effective region of universe far beyond the observable universe. Accordingly, all successful predictions of the BBN may remain largely unaffected by the new UEG theory.

All the above proposed physics is expected to be based

on a UEG theory that is applicable at a relatively low level of energy density. The theory in principle may be extended in the regime of high energy density, as was the case for modeling elementary particles, to model very early universe. The UEG theory may be extended to the highest level of energy density, beyond the levels applicable to model elementary particles, where the gravitation may transition from its usual attractive to a new repulsive nature. This reversal of gravitation could provide a definitive physical basis for the reversal from a previously contracting (big crunch) to the currently expanding (big bounce) universe, supporting an inflation-like [15] or any other suitable form of expansion (or contraction) in the transitional phase.

We have used available cosmological parameters for different estimations in this paper, that may have been adopted from the Wilkinson Microwave Anisotropy Probe (WMAP) 9 year results [10] or from early Planck Mission (2013) results [11], as appropriate and adequate for particular purposes. All parameters are specified, for proper interpretation of results with respect to variation of the parameters. Any variations based on more recent results of the Planck Mission (2015) [16] may not materially change the results or conclusions from the study.

II.   BASIC THEORY

A.   UEG Acceleration Due to the CMB Radiation

The UEG acceleration a_u, associated with the energy density of the current CMB radiation at temperature $T = 2.725^0 K$ may be estimated, assuming a nominal value of the UEG constant $\gamma_0 = 0.6 \times 10^3$ $(\text{m/s}^2)/(\text{J/m}^3)$ derived from a UEG model of elementary particles [1, 2].

$$a_u = \gamma_0 W_\tau = \gamma_0 (4\sigma/c)T^4 = 2.5 \times 10^{-11} \text{m/s}^2,$$
$$\gamma_0 = 0.6 \times 10^3 (\text{m/s}^2)/(\text{J/m}^3),$$
$$\sigma = 5.670 \times 10^{-8} \text{W}/(\text{m}^2\text{K}^4), \ \text{T=}2.725^0\text{K}. \quad (1)$$

The σ is the Stefan-Boltzman constant, and the c is the speed of light in empty space. The UEG acceleration a_u may be compared with the cosmological acceleration a_0 at the boundary of the observable universe of radius $R \simeq 46.3 \ GLy$ [17], approximated using the current value of the Hubble constant $H \simeq 67.8$ (km/s)/Mpc.

$$a_0 = \tfrac{1}{2}H^2 R = 1.057 \times 10^{-9} \text{m/s}^2,$$
$$H = 67.8 \text{ (km/s)/Mpc, R=}46.3 \text{ BLy,}$$
$$\text{Mpc=}3.0857 \times 10^{22}\text{m, 1 BLy=}9.4607 \times 10^{24}\text{m.} \quad (2)$$

The a_u is smaller than the a_0 by about a factor of 40. Assuming the matter (baryonic) density of the universe to be 4.9% of the critical density to maintain the current expansion rate associated with the Hubble constant H_0, we may estimate the acceleration a_g at the boundary of the observable universe $r = R$, attributed to the Newtonian gravitation. The UEG acceleration a_u due to the CMB radiation is about half of the Newtonian acceleration a_g at $r = R$ due to matter (baryonic) content of the universe. The a_u is a fundamental parameter, which would shape any cosmological model based on the UEG theory.

$$a_g = (0.049) \times a_0 = 5.179 \times 10^{-11}\text{m/s}^2,$$
$$a_u = (2.5/5.179)a_g = 0.483 a_g. \quad (3)$$

B.   UEG Acceleration Due to any Present or Future Star Lights

The Newtonian acceleration a_g may be directly expressed using Newton's law of gravitation, in terms of the energy density $w = \rho_v c^2$ associated with the matter density ρ_v.

$$a_g = \frac{4\pi G \rho_v R}{3} = 1.36w, \ w = \rho_v c^2,$$
$$G = 6.67 \times 10^{-11}(\text{m}^3/\text{s}^2)/\text{kg},$$
$$\text{R=}46.3 \text{ BLy} = 4.409 \times 10^{26}\text{s.} \quad (4)$$

About 3/4-th of the matter content of the universe is made of hydrogen [13, 18], and only a negligible percentage of the hydrogen have been used for hydrogen fusion in the stars. Most of the hydrogen content remain unused outside of the stars in inter-stellar and intergalactic space, waiting for possible right conditions to locally collapse and light up in the form of stars and galaxies of the future. If we ideally allow all the hydrogen to, at once, form light radiation through hydrogen fusion today, the density of the light radiation would be about 0.7% of the energy density [19] $(3/4)w = (3/4)\rho_v c^2$ associated with the hydrogen mass density $(3/4)\rho_v$. The UEG acceleration a'_u produced by this star radiation may be expressed in terms of the w, and then compared with the Newtonian acceleration a_g of (4).

$$a'_u = w \times 0.007 \times \gamma_0 \times 0.75 = 3.15w,$$
$$a'_u = (3.15/1.36)a_g = 2.3 a_g = (2.3/0.483)a_u = 4.8 a_u,$$
$$a'_u = 4.8 \times 2.5 \times 10^{-11} = 1.2 \times 10^{-10}\text{m/s}^2. \quad (5)$$

The UEG acceleration a'_u due to light radiation of the possible future stars is 2.3 times the Newtonian acceleration a_g at $r = R$ due to matter (baryonic) content of the universe. Like the UEG acceleration $a_u = 0.483 a_g$ due to the CMB radiation, the $a'_u = 2.3 a_g = 4.8 a_u$ due to the future star lights is also a fundamental parameter, which would shape any cosmological model based on the UEG theory. Assuming that only a negligible fraction of the total primordial hydrogen has so far been used in all the stars, the UEG acceleration due to all the current star lights is negligible compared to the a'_u or the a_g.

C. Equivalent UEG Mass and Energy for Cosmological Modeling

The UEG accelerations a_u and a'_u would be uniform everywhere, in proportion to the associated uniform energy densities W_τ and W'_τ, respectively, as per the UEG theory applied in a simple form [1]. In contrast, the acceleration a_g due to the Newtonian gravitation increases linearly with distance, assuming a uniform mass density. Accordingly, the simple UEG model would produce much larger acceleration at smaller distances, compared to the Newtonian acceleration, leading to a possible non-uniform expansion which would be clearly incompatible with the fundamental assumption of a uniform, isotropic universe. The simple UEG theory may have to be properly revised for cosmology, requiring basic UEG parameters to be properly redistributed in proportion to the respective parameters from the Newtonian gravity. Equivalently, there may be some new physics at cosmological scale, which would transform the basic non-uniform expansion due to the UEG gravitation into the expected uniform expansion, leading to effectively the same results as the redistribution model suggested above.

We will follow a redistribution model for the UEG theory, which would confirm to the fundamental assumption of a uniform or homogeneous universe. Basic UEG parameters, such as equivalent UEG mass and energy, may be redistributed in proportion to the respective quantities expected from the Newtonian gravity, such that certain total measure of the UEG parameters are conserved.

A simple objective measure of conservation may be to ensure the total integration of a UEG parameter over the volume of the observable universe of radius $r = R$ to remain fixed. Here, the volume of the observable universe is a naturally objective region. However, the above measure of conservation would truncate the integration of the conserved parameter abruptly at $r = R$, which may seem arbitrary. Instead, conserving a weighted integration over the observable universe, with the weighting factor at a location proportional to the red-shift factor associated with the location, may be physically meaningful. The weighting factor would gradually de-emphasize the conserved integrand from its reference unit value at the center $r = 0$, to zero at the edge of the observable universe.

The equivalent mass density associated with the uniform UEG acceleration a_u has a ρ_0/r distribution. This may be redistributed with a uniform mass density ρ_{uv}, such that the total mass M_u integrated over the observable universe with a weighting function $(1 - r/R)^2$ is conserved. The selected weighting function may be shown to be the red-shift factor for an ideal universe with a critical material density, which is assumed to be approximately valid for the proposed redistribution. The equivalent UEG mass density ρ_{uv} may now be compared with the material density ρ_v, which is related to the Newtonian acceleration a_g at $r = R$. The relation (3) between the a_u and a_g may be used here. The weighted material

mass M enclosed in the sphere of radius $r = R$ would be related to the M_u by the same ratio between the respective mass densities ρ_v and ρ_{uv}.

$$M_u = \int_0^R (\frac{\rho_{u0}}{r})(1 - \frac{r}{R})^2 4\pi r^2 dr = \int_0^R \rho_{uv}(1 - \frac{r}{R})^2 4\pi r^2 dr$$

$$= \frac{4\pi}{12}\rho_{u0}R^2 = \frac{4\pi}{30}\rho_{uv}R^3, \quad \rho_{uv} = \frac{5\rho_{u0}}{2R} = \frac{5a_u}{4\pi GR},$$

$$a_u = \frac{G}{R^2}\int_0^R (\frac{\rho_{u0}}{r})4\pi r^2 dr = 2\pi G\rho_{u0}, \tag{6}$$

$$\rho_v = \frac{3a_g}{4\pi GR}, \quad \rho_{uv} = \frac{5a_u\rho_v}{3a_g} = (5/3) \times 0.483\rho_v = 0.8\rho_v,$$

$$M = \int_0^R \rho_v(1 - \frac{r}{R})^2 4\pi r^2 dr = \frac{4\pi}{30}\rho_v R^3, \quad M_u = 0.8M. \tag{7}$$

Similarly, the equivalent uniform mass density ρ'_{uv} associated with the UEG acceleration a'_u, and its weighted mass M'_u may also be expressed, and compared with respective material parameters ρ_v and M.

$$\rho'_{uv} = \frac{5a'_u\rho_v}{3a_g} = (5/3) \times 2.3\rho_v = 3.83\rho_v, \quad M'_u = 3.83M. \tag{8}$$

Using the same weighting factor used above for calculating equivalent cosmological mass parameters, we may also find equivalent kinetic energy parameters of expansion W_u, W'_u and W, associated with the UEG masses M_u, M'_u and the material mass M, respectively.

$$W_u = \int_0^R \frac{1}{2}v^2 \frac{\rho_{u0}}{r}(1 - \frac{r}{R})^2 4\pi r^2 dr$$

$$= \int_0^R \frac{1}{2}(Hr)^2 \frac{\rho_{u0}}{r}(1 - \frac{r}{R})^2 4\pi r^2 dr$$

$$= \frac{4\pi}{120}H^2\rho_{u0}R^4 = \frac{1}{10}(HR)^2 M_u = \frac{1}{10}(H \times 46.3BY)^2 M_u c^2$$

$$= \frac{1}{10}(\frac{67.8}{3.0587} \times 10^{-19} \times 1.46 \times 10^{18})^2 M_u c^2 = 1.048 M_u c^2,$$

$$W'_u = 1.048 M'_u c^2. \tag{9}$$

The relationship in (6) between M_u and the UEG mass-density coefficient ρ_{u0} is used in the above derivation. Similarly,

$$W = \int_0^R \frac{1}{2}v^2 \rho_v(1 - \frac{r}{R})^2 4\pi r^2 dr$$

$$= \int_0^R \frac{1}{2}(Hr)^2 \rho_v(1 - \frac{r}{R})^2 4\pi r^2 dr$$

$$= \frac{4\pi}{210}H^2\rho_v R^5 = \frac{1}{7}(HR)^2 M = \frac{1}{7}(H \times 46.3BY)^2 Mc^2$$

$$= \frac{1}{7}(\frac{67.8}{3.0587} \times 10^{-19} \times 1.46 \times 10^{18})^2 Mc^2$$

$$= 1.496 Mc^2. \tag{10}$$

The W_u, W'_u and W are the kinetic energies of the current universe at the expansion velocity v, associated with a critical mass density ρ_{vc}. It may be useful to find the corresponding kinetic energies, W_{u0}, W'_{uo} and W_0, if the expansion velocity were $v_0 = \sqrt{0.049} \times v$. The v_0 is the expansion velocity associated with the current material density ρ_v, which is about 4.9% of the critical mass density ρ_{vc}.

$$W_{u0} = 0.049 W_u = 1.048 M_u c^2 \times (0.049),$$
$$W'_{u0} = 0.049 W'_u = 1.048 M'_u c^2 \times (0.049),$$
$$W_0 = 0.049 W = 1.496 M c^2 \times (0.049),$$
$$v_0^2 = v^2 \times (0.049) . \tag{11}$$

III. A UEG MODEL IN ANTICIPATION OF A FUTURE CONTRACTION OF THE UNIVERSE

As mentioned, the universe may be anticipating future star light due to fusion of existing hydrogen content, mostly unused to date. If the star burst ideally happens today, all at once, the total mass content would be $M + M_u + M'_u$, consisting of the UEG masses M_u and M'_u due to CMB radiation and star light, in addition to the material mass M. This would be associated with a critical expansion velocity v'_0, which may be related to the velocity v_0 defined in (11). The critical velocity v'_0 is the threshold velocity less than which eventual contraction would be possible. We assume that that UEG acceleration would reduce as $1/\alpha^{4.5}$, as the scale factor α increases, in contrast with a $1/\alpha^2$ variation for the Newtonian acceleration. Integration of the acceleration with the scale factor would be proportional to the the respective contributions to the squared critical velocity, which would be associated with integration coefficients $1/3.5$ and 1, respectively. This fundamentally assumes that the equivalent mass/energy of the UEG field due to radiation is modeled as pressure-less, unlike the mass/energy of conventional radiation which is associated with radiation pressure. Otherwise, the above integration coefficient for the UEG contribution would have been 1, the same as that for the Newtonian gravitation due to conventional matter.

$$v'^2_0 = (1 + \frac{M_u + M'_u}{M} \times \frac{1}{3.5}) v_0^2$$
$$= (1 + \frac{\rho_{uv} + \rho'_{uv}}{\rho_v} \times \frac{1}{3.5}) v_0^2 = 2.32 v_0^2. \tag{12}$$

The $1/\alpha^{4.5}$-dependence of the UEG acceleration, assumed above, may be explained as follows. As the universe expands, the energy density of radiation would reduce with a $1/\alpha^4$ variation, which would directly contribute to the reduction of the UEG acceleration. The horizon of the observable universe is assumed to expand in excess of the scale factor, proportional to $\alpha^{0.5}$, which may contribute to an additional factor of $1/\alpha^{0.5}$ in the reduction of the UEG acceleration, according to the redistribution model of section II C to determine the UEG

acceleration. The $\alpha^{0.5}$ dependence of the horizon in excess of the scale factor is valid for an ideal condition of a matter-only, flat universe, but is assumed to be approximately valid in the present model, representing a small exponent in the UEG acceleration in addition to the primary $1/\alpha^4$ dependence.

The total kinetic energy W'_0 associated with the threshold velocity v'_0 may be expressed as,

$$W'_0 = 2.32(W_0 + W_{u0} + W'_{u0}) = 2.32 W_0 \times (1 + \frac{W_u + W'_u}{W})$$
$$= 2.32 W_0 \times (1 + \frac{1.048(M_u + M'_u)}{1.496 M})$$
$$= 2.32 \times 0.049 W \times (1 + 3.24)$$
$$= 0.482 W = 0.73 M c^2. \tag{13}$$

Now, the total energy W_2 available in the future universe at the threshold of possible contraction, after the ideal star burst phase, may be calculated. This is obtained by adding the threshold kinetic energy W'_0 to the equivalent mass-energies of the Newtonian mass M, and of the UEG masses M_u, M'_u due to the CMB radiation and star lights, respectively. Similarly, the total energy W_1 in the current universe may be obtained, by adding the kinetic energies W and W_u to the mass-energies associated with the Newtonian mass M and the UEG mass M_u due to the CMB radiation.

$$W_2 = (M + M_u + M'_u)c^2 + W'_0$$
$$= (M + M_u)c^2 + 3.83 M c^2 + 0.73 M c^2,$$
$$W_1 = (M + M_u)c^2 + W + W_u$$
$$= (M + M_u)c^2 + 1.496 M c^2 + 1.048 \times 0.8 M c^2,$$
$$W_2 > W_1, \ \gamma = \gamma_0 = 0.6 \times 10^3 (m/s^2)/(J/m^3). \tag{14}$$

Note that the W_2 is greater then the W_1, which means the excess kinetic energy in the current universe may not be enough to guarantee continuation of the expansion. The above calculations assume a nominal value of $\gamma = \gamma_0$. We may trace the above calculations with $\gamma = \alpha \gamma_0$, and find the required γ for the current universe to lead to a future universe just at the threshold of possible contraction, as per the ideal model, by solving a quadratic equation of α.

$$W_2 = W_1, \ \gamma = \alpha \gamma_0,$$
$$1.496 M c^2 + 1.048 \times 0.8 \alpha M c^2$$
$$= 3.83 M c^2 \alpha + 0.049 \times 1.496(1 + 1.32\alpha)(1 + 3.24\alpha) M c^2,$$
$$1 + 0.56\alpha = 2.56\alpha + 0.049(1 + 1.32\alpha)(1 + 3.24\alpha),$$
$$0.21\alpha^2 + 2.22\alpha - 0.951 = 0,$$
$$\alpha = \frac{-2.22 + \sqrt{4.93 + 0.8}}{0.42} = 0.41,$$
$$\gamma > \alpha \gamma_0 = 0.41 \gamma_0 = 0.25 \times 10^3 (m/s^2)/(J/m^3). \tag{15}$$

Essentially, the above model predicts a lower limit of the $\gamma > 0.25 \times 10^3$ $(m/s^2)/(J/m^3)$, in anticipation of a future contraction that would lead to a cyclic universe. The predicted lower limit is consistent with the the $\gamma = \gamma_0$ deduced from a UEG model of elementary particles [1, 2]. Conversely, if the value of the γ is given to be equal to γ_0, the above model may be extended into the future for estimation of an effective timing for the anticipated star-burst event in the future.

IV. A UEG MODEL FOR THE ACCELERATED EXPANSION OF THE UNIVERSE

We will model the expansion velocity v as it changes with the scale factor $\alpha < 1$, or its associated redshift factor $z > 0$, of the universe. The velocity v may be normalized with its unit reference equal to the total velocity of the current universe, at time $t = t_0$.

$$v = \frac{\dot{\alpha}}{\dot{\alpha}(t=t_0)} = \frac{\dot{\alpha}}{H_0}, \ \dot{\alpha} = \frac{d\alpha}{dt},$$
$$v^2(z) = v_g^2(z) + v_u^2(z) + v_\Delta^2(z), \ \alpha = \frac{1}{1+z}. \quad (16)$$

The squared-velocity v^2 may be expressed consisting of three parts. The first two parts, v_g^2 and v_u^2, are contributed from the critical velocities that could be supported by the Newtonian gravity and the new UEG field, respectively. The contribution from the Newtonian gravity of conventional matter is $\Omega_b(1+z)$, where $\Omega_b = 0.049$ is the fractional density of the conventional matter, with respect to the critical density necessary to support the observed expansion of the current universe. The functional dependence of the UEG contribution v_u^2 was explained in section III.

$$v_g^2(z) = \Omega_b(1+z),$$
$$v_u^2(z) = \Omega_u(1+z)^{3.5} = \frac{\rho_{uv}}{\rho_v}\Omega_b\frac{(1+z)^{3.5}}{3.5},$$
$$\Omega_u = \frac{\rho_{uv}}{\rho_v} \times \frac{1}{3.5}\Omega_b = 0.8 \times \frac{1}{3.5}\Omega_b = 0.23\Omega_b. \quad (17)$$

The third term v_Δ^2 in (16) is the contribution of the excess velocity v_Δ. The v_Δ^2 is the total squared-velocity in excess of the first two terms that are critically supported by the Newtonian gravity and the UEG field, respectively. The excess squared-velocity is $1 - \Omega_b - \Omega_u$ at $t = t_0$, and is required to change with the scale factor with the following basic condition. The kinetic energy associated with the excess velocity, enclosed inside a co-moving spherical volume, with its radius changing in proportion with the scale factor, with a current reference radius equal to the current horizon distance, is required to be conserved independent of the scale factor. The kinetic energy over any given spherical volume is defined such that the ratio of the kinetic energy to the mass in the volume at a given time, for a unit reference velocity at the spherical boundary, is equal to that over the entire volume of the observable universe, at the particular

time. The ratios $W/M = 1.496c^2$ and $W_u/M_u = 1.048c^2$ between the kinetic energies and the respective masses for the conventional gravity and the UEG field, respectively, as derived in (9,10) for the current universe, would apply for all scale factors for a unit normalized squared-velocity (normalized to a unit value for the current universe at r=R). Accordingly, the excess kinetic energies W_Δ and $W_{u\Delta}$ may be expressed in terms of the associated masses M and M_u, respectively, proportional to the excess squared-velocity v_Δ^2

$$W_\Delta(z) + W_{u\Delta}(z) = 1.496M(z)c^2v_\Delta^2(z) + 1.048M_u(z)c^2v_\Delta^2(z)$$
$$= W_\Delta(z=0) + W_{u\Delta}(z=0)$$
$$= 1.496M(z=0)c^2v_\Delta^2(z=0) + 1.048M_u(z=0)c^2v_\Delta^2(z=0),$$
$$v_\Delta^2(z) = v_\Delta^2(z=0) \times \frac{1.496M(z=0)+1.048M_u(z=0)}{1.496M(z)+1.048M_u(z)}$$
$$= (1 - \Omega_b - \Omega_u) \times \frac{1+0.7M_u(z=0)/M(z=0)}{1+0.7M_u(z)/M(z=0)}. \quad (18)$$

The relationship (7) between the M_u and M in the current universe, and the associated relationship (17) between the Ω_b and Ω_u, may be used in the above expression. The conventional mass M in the observable universe, which is associated with a $1/\alpha^2 = (1+z)^2$ dependence of its acceleration due to Newtonian gravity, remains constant with the scale factor α. Whereas, the equivalent UEG mass M_u, which is associated with a $1/\alpha^{4.5} = (1+z)^{4.5}$ dependence of the UEG acceleration, would change with a $1/\alpha^{2.5} = (1+z)^{2.5}$ dependence.

$$v_\Delta^2(z) = (1 - 1.23\Omega_b) \times \frac{1+0.7\times0.8}{1+0.7\times0.8(1+z)^{2.5}}$$
$$= \Omega_\Delta \times \frac{1.56}{1+0.56(1+z)^{2.5}},$$
$$M(z) = M(z=0), \ M_u(z) = M_u(z=0)(1+z)^{2.5},$$
$$M_u(z=0) = 0.8M(z=0),$$
$$\Omega_\Delta = 1 - \Omega_b - \Omega_u = 1 - 1.23\Omega_b = 0.94 . \quad (19)$$

Combining (19,17) in (16), the total normalized velocity $v(z)$ may be expressed.

$$v^2(z) = \Omega_b(1+z) + \Omega_u(1+z)^{3.5}$$
$$+ (1 - \Omega_b - \Omega_u)[\frac{1.56}{1+0.56(1+z)^{2.5}}]$$
$$= 0.049(1+z) + 0.011(1+z)^{3.5}$$
$$+ 0.94[\frac{1.56}{1+0.56(1+z)^{2.5}}]. \quad (20)$$

The above derivations assumes a specific set of available cosmological parameters, with the Hubble constant $H_0 = 67.8$ (km/s)/Mpc and $\Omega_b = 0.049$. Any variations due to changes of the parameters may be similarly traced by introducing additional factors for the different parts, in terms of fractional changes of the appropriate parameters, which may be expressed in terms of the fractional change $h_{67.8}$ of the measured Hubble constant H_0 with respect to the best value of $H_0 = 67.8$ (km/s)/Mpc currently available.

$$v^2(z) = \Omega_b h_{67.8}^{-2}(1+z) + \Omega_u h_{67.8}^{-1}(1+z)^{3.5}$$
$$+ (1 - \Omega_b h_{67.8}^{-2} - \Omega_u h_{67.8}^{-1})[\frac{1+0.56 h_{67.8}}{1+0.56 h_{67.8}(1+z)^{2.5}}]$$
$$= 0.049 h_{67.8}^{-2}(1+z) + 0.011 h_{67.8}^{-1}(1+z)^{3.5}$$
$$+ (1 - 0.049 h_{67.8}^{-2} - 0.011 h_{67.8}^{-1})[\frac{1+0.56 h_{67.8}}{1+0.56 h_{67.8}(1+z)^{2.5}}],$$
$$h_{67.8} = \frac{H_0}{67.8 \text{ kms}^{-1}\text{Mpc}^{-1}}. \qquad (21)$$

The normalized squared-velocity v^2 as derived above is compared in Fig.1 with those from the standard cosmological model, where $v^2 = \Omega_M(1+z) + \Omega_\Lambda/(1+z)^2 + (1 - \Omega_M - \Omega_\Lambda)$. The acceleration in the standard model due to the dark-energy term, with its fractional density Ω_Λ, is emulated in the UEG model without any need for the hypothetical dark-energy. Further, only the conventional matter with the fractional density Ω_b is used in the UEG model, without need for any additional dark matter. Whereas, the standard model uses the mass fraction of $\Omega_M = \Omega_b + \Omega_{dm}$, which includes the density Ω_b of the conventional baryonic mass and additional density Ω_{dm} of dark matter. Unlike the mass M due to the conventional baryons or dark matter, the equivalent UEG mass M_u is reduced as the universe expands. This results in an effective outward acceleration as the universe expands, so that the kinetic energy in the observable universe due to the excess velocity is conserved, as the UEG model requires. This effective acceleration is seen only in the current and recent past of the universe ($z < 1$ from Fig.1) when the excess velocity is significantly larger than the critical velocity that can be supported by the conventional and UEG masses. In the past, the UEG mass M_u was larger, and consequently the excess velocity to conserve the excess kinetic energy was smaller. In sufficient past, the smaller excess velocity, as compared to the critical velocity in the current universe, was even much smaller than the larger critical velocity that could be supported at the time. This would result in having the effective outward acceleration associated with the smaller excess velocity, due to the kinetic-energy conservation discussed above, to be much smaller than the normal gravitational deceleration (inward acceleration) in the sufficient past associated with the larger critical velocity supported at the time. Accordingly, the expansion of the universe was effectively decelerating in the sufficient past ($z > 1$ from Fig.1), while it is accelerating only currently and in recent past ($z < 1$ from Fig.1), as per the UEG model, which would be consistent with the standard model with $\Omega_\Lambda \sim 0.76$.

The luminosity distance D_L [20] derived from the velocity function $v(z)$ is plotted in Fig.2, which shows the UEG model with $\Omega_b = 0.49$ is comparable to the standard model with $\Omega_\Lambda = 0.76$, for $z < 2$. The results from the UEG model and the standard model with the $\Omega_\Lambda = 0.76$,

are plotted in Fig.3 in relative magnitudes with respect to a nearly empty universe with $\Omega_M = 0.2$, $\Omega_\Lambda = 0$, which are consistent with measurements of high-z supernovae from [7]. The theoretical results from the UEG and standard models over a larger range of redshift are shown in Fig.4, which maybe similarly compared with results from [21] that include measurements of gamma-ray bursts (GRB). In summary, the UEG model with no dark matter or dark energy is shown to be consistent with measurements of high-z supernovae, and possibly GRBs, emulating the standard model with the hypothetical dark matter and dark energy. That is a remarkable development.

It may be noted that, unlike the conventional matter which is associated with a definitive mass density, the equivalent UEG mass density is not a definitive quantity, but is modeled in relation to the horizon distance of the observable universe, as per the redistribution model developed in section II C. The above derivations use an approximate formulation for the dependence of the horizon distance of the observable universe on the scale factor. We assume that the horizon distance expands with a $\alpha^{0.5}$ dependence as an excess factor, multiplied to the scale factor α of normal expansion of the universe. This dependence is the ideal case for a matter-only universe. It is used in the derivations only as an effective dependence of the horizon, as a good reference, which may work in an overall average sense over a range of the scale factor. A more accurate formulation may require the above dependence to be modeled with a variable exponent of the scale factor, that varies as a function of the scale factor. Refinement of the reference analysis may be possible by estimating the exponent under different specific conditions, and revising the associated formulations accordingly. However, it may require a involved numerical computation process, in order to rigorously model the horizon distance and incorporate it into the UEG model.

V. A UEG MODEL FOR THE ACOUSTIC HORIZON AND DARK MATTER BEFORE RECOMBINATION

Based on the comparisons with the standard model, in consistency with the current observations, the above model for the UEG mass based on the size of the observable universe appears to be reasonably valid in the recent universe, covering redshifts of the order of $z \sim 10$ possibly even larger. However, for much larger redshifts questions may arise about the fundamental validity of the redistribution model of section II C, based on the size of the observable universe. The radial distance of the observable universe may be referred to as the "matter horizon", which is the farthest distance the matter produced in the earliest universe would appear to be located to a current observer. The universe is assumed to be expanding with a gravitational deceleration (or acceleration toward the reference origin), due to the conventional

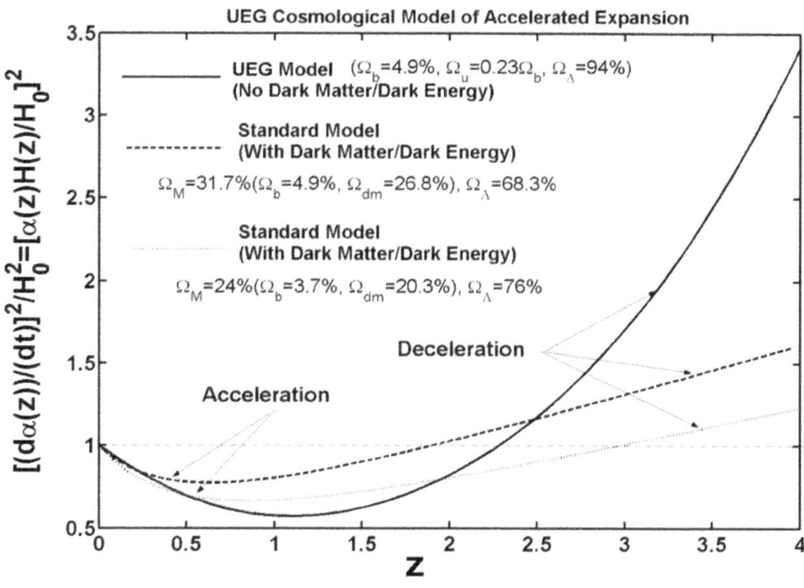

FIG. 1.

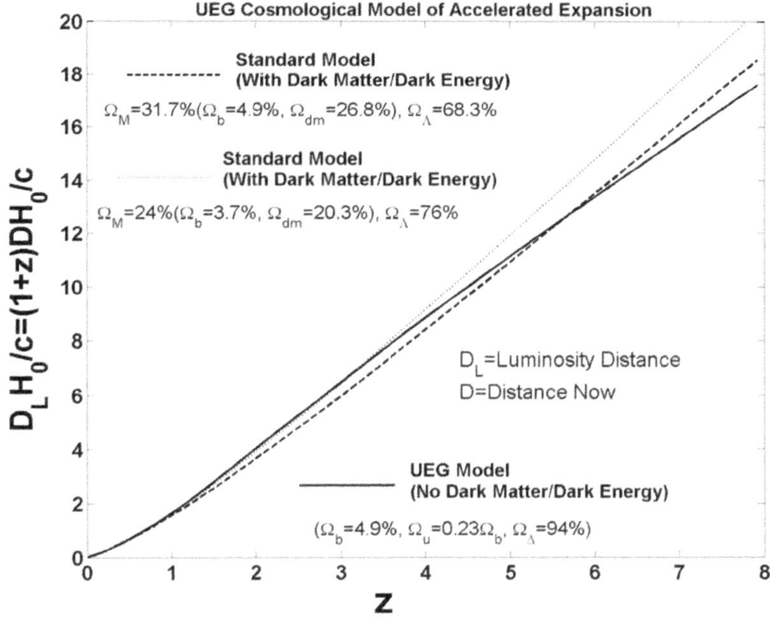

FIG. 2.

attractive form of gravity, since the time of the earliest matter formation. However, before the era of matter formation, the earliest radiation-only universe might have undergone an inflationary phase [15] with gravitational acceleration (away from the reference origin), possibly following a big crunch, and supported by a form of repulsive gravity based on a UEG theory at the highest level of energy density. The horizon associated with this gravitationally repulsive phase of accelerated expansion, which may be referred to as the "radiation horizon," is expected to be much farther than the "matter horizon". It is conceivable that the effective UEG mass may have to be modeled differently for different scale factor of expansion, based on the matter horizon, or the radiation

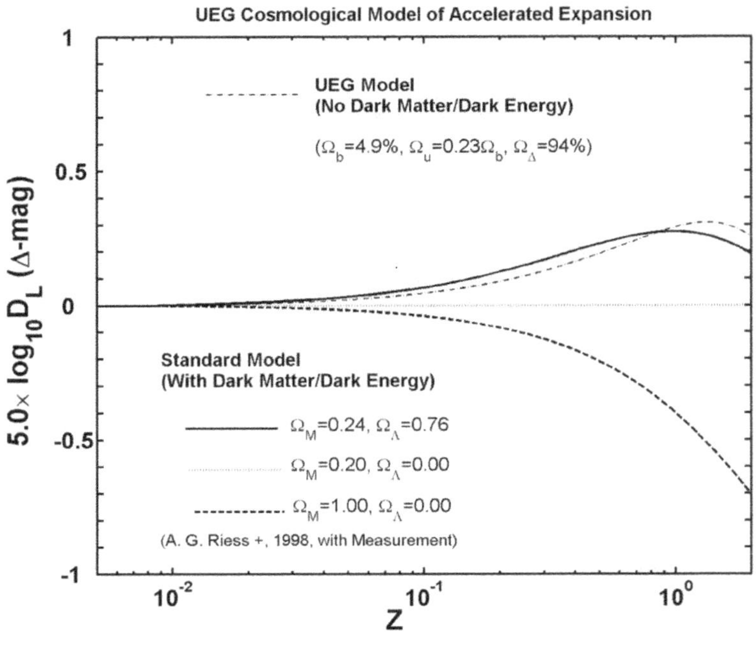

FIG. 3.

horizon, or possibly a combination of the both, depending on the relative matter and radiation contents of the universe. In the current universe, which is matter dominated, the conventional matter horizon appear to determine the UEG physics accurately. However, as one gets close to the scale of recombination ($z \sim 1100$), the radiation density would be comparable to the matter (baryonic) density, in which case the UEG model applicable in the current universe may not be valid.

The UEG model in the time frame around the recombination may require the knowledge of the radiation horizon, which is not available without a definitive model of the inflationary phase. However, considering that the radiation horizon would be much farther than the matter horizon, it may be assumed that the effective UEG mass in this time frame would be much smaller than that modeled using the matter horizon, as it was done in the UEG model for the current universe. The effective UEG mass at the recombination may emulate the hypothetical dark matter in the standard model. Accordingly, we may assume the effective UEG mass enclosed inside the matter universe, or its associated matter density, to be larger than the respective baryonic parameters by a factor of $\Omega_{dm}/\Omega_b = 0.268/0.049 = 5.47$, as a reference, effective over the duration of recombination. The Ω_b and Ω_{dm} are the baryonic and dark matter fractions of the current universe, respectively, used in the standard model. The ratio of the baryonic and dark matter is assumed to remain constant over all different time scales, in accordance with the dark-matter characteristic of the standard model.

The above effective UEG mass density is assumed to be valid just after and sufficiently during the recombination process. However, before the recombination the universe was ionized and opaque to radiation. Therefore, unlike in the current universe, there would not have been any CMB radiation available before the recombination to produce UEG forces. Accordingly, the effective UEG mass density sufficiently before the recombination would have been zero, but it increased to be effectively about 5.47 times the baryonic matter density after the recombination, which may be considered a relatively abrupt process. This is similar to the possible increase of UEG effects in the current universe due to anticipated future star lights, modeled in section III. As the similar case in the current universe, the expansion velocity before the recombination would have been larger than the critical velocity that could be supported by the baryonic and radiation mass densities, in anticipation of the increased UEG mass and associated kinetic energy after the recombination. We will follow a formulation similar to that in section III, in order to find the expansion velocity before the recombination.

For convenience, all parameters used in the following modeling will refer to the recombination time scale as the current reference with zero redshift or unit scale factor, and the final results may be properly scaled back to the actual current universe as needed. Distinct from the actual current universe, the universe at the recombination would have appreciable mass density of radiation (photon) and neutrino, as compared to the baryon mass density, and all parameters associated with the conventional photon radiation would be referred to with a subscript r', and those associated with total relativistic

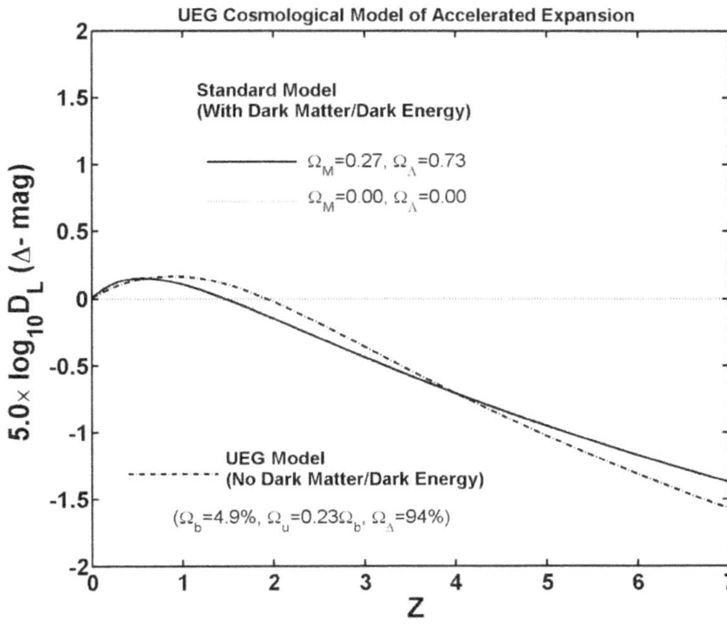

FIG. 4.

particles (photon and neutrino) with a subscript r. v_0 is the reference critical velocity supported by the baryonic matter content, and the associated kinetic energy of the baryons is W_0. Unlike the matter horizon, the radiation horizon can be shown to expand proportional to the scale factor. Assuming that the UEG model at the recombination would be based dominantly on the radiation horizon, as discussed earlier, all special adjustments (with 0.5 exponent of scale factor used for modeling in the current universe) to account for variation of the horizon distance may not be needed for modeling in the recombination phase. Accordingly, the UEG acceleration, associated critical squared velocity which is obtained by integration of the UEG acceleration with the scale factor α, and the effective UEG mass or mass density, would have a $1/\alpha^4$, $1/(3\alpha^3)$, and $1/\alpha^2$ dependence for modeling in the recombination phase. This is in contrast with the $1/\alpha^{4.5}$, $1/(3.5\alpha^{3.5})$, and $1/\alpha^{2.5}$ for the respective dependencies used for modeling in the current universe. Further, the distance to the radiation horizon, which is assumed to be the effective horizon for the UEG modeling in the recombination phase, is much farther than the conventional matter horizon. Therefore, in the recombination phase, the effective kinetic energy due to the expansion velocity, which linearly increases with distance, would be much larger than the mass-energy enclosed by the effective horizon. Accordingly, different mass-energies may be ignored in the computation of the total energy enclosed by the horizon, for the present derivation in the recombination phase.

The squared-velocity $v_0'^2$ just after recombination, which is the total critical squared-velocity supported by the baryonic and radiation masses, and any equivalent UEG mass due to the radiation at the recombination, may be expressed in terms of the v_0^2. As discussed above, the squared-velocity due to the UEG mass would require a factor 1/3. This is the factor needed in the derivation of the squared-velocity, implemented as the integration of the $1/\alpha^4$-dependent UEG acceleration with the scale factor.

$$v_0'^{\,2} = (1 + \tfrac{M_r}{M} + \tfrac{M_u}{M} \times \tfrac{1}{3})v_0^2 = (1 + \tfrac{\rho_{rv}}{\rho_v} + \tfrac{\rho_{uv}}{\rho_v} \times \tfrac{1}{3})v_0^2$$
$$= (1 + \tfrac{\Omega_r}{\Omega_b} + \tfrac{\Omega_{dm}}{\Omega_b} \times \tfrac{1}{3})v_0^2. \qquad (22)$$

The $\Omega_{dm}/\Omega_b = 5.47$ is the ratio of the dark and baryonic masses, whose value is maintained independent of the scale factor, and $\Omega_r/\Omega_b = 25/12$ is the ratio of the radiation (photon and neutrino) and baryonic masses at the scale of recombination. The kinetic energy of expansion W_0' after the recombination may be expressed in terms of the kinetic energy W_0 of the baryonic matter associated with the reference velocity v_0. The W_0' is also approximately equal to the total energy W_2 after the recombination. The same relationships (9,10) between the energy W and mass M for the baryonic mass, and the W_u and M_u for the UEG mass (equivalent to dark matter content at recombination), in the current universe is also used here as a rough estimate, although the associated redistribution weighting factor (see section II C) may not apply as well at the recombination phase.

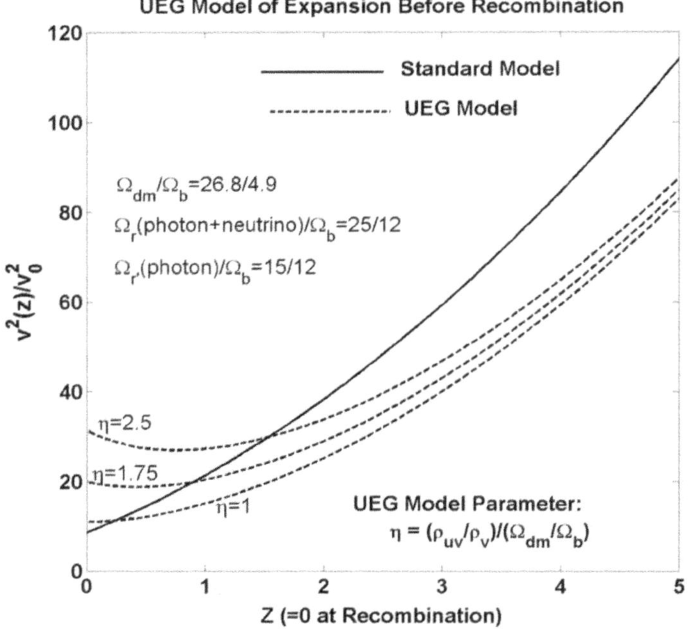

FIG. 5.

$$W_0' = \frac{v_0'^2}{v_0^2}W_0 \times (1 + \frac{M_r}{M} + \frac{1.048M_u}{1.496M})$$

$$= \frac{v_0'^2}{v_0^2}W_0 \times (1 + \frac{\Omega_r}{\Omega_b} + \frac{1.048\Omega_{dm}}{1.496\Omega_b}), \ W_2 = W_0'. \quad (23)$$

The squared-velocity $v^2(z)$ may be expressed as a function of the redshift $z > 0$, with reference zero redshift at the recombination. It consists of two principal parts, which are the critical squared-velocities supported by the baryonic and radiation contents, and the additional term v_Δ^2 in excess of the principal parts. The total energy W_1 just before recombination ($z = 0^+$), which is approximately equal to the total kinetic energy as discussed, may be expressed using the $v^2(z = 0^+)$.

$$v^2(z > 0) = v_0^2(1 + z) + v_0^2\frac{\Omega_r}{\Omega_b}(1 + z)^2 + v_\Delta^2(z),$$

$$v^2(z = 0^+) = v_0^2 + v_0^2\frac{\Omega_r}{\Omega_b} + v_\Delta^2(z = 0), \quad (24)$$

$$W_1 = \frac{v^2(z=0^+)}{v_0^2}W_0 \times (1 + \frac{M_r}{M})$$

$$= \frac{v^2(z=0^+)}{v_0^2}W_0 \times (1 + \frac{\Omega_r}{\Omega_b}). \quad (25)$$

The excess squared-velocity $v_\Delta^2(z = 0)$ just before recombination may be solved by enforcing energy conservation with $W_2 = W_1$.

$$W_2 = W_1, \ \frac{v_0'^2}{v_0^2}W_0 \times (1 + \frac{\Omega_r}{\Omega_b} + \frac{1.048\Omega_{dm}}{1.496\Omega_b})$$

$$= \frac{v^2(z=0^+)}{v_0^2}W_0 \times (1 + \frac{\Omega_r}{\Omega_b}),$$

$$(1 + \frac{\Omega_r}{\Omega_b} + \frac{\Omega_{dm}}{\Omega_b} \times \frac{1}{3})(1 + \frac{\Omega_r}{\Omega_b} + \frac{1.048\Omega_{dm}}{1.496\Omega_b})$$

$$= (1 + \frac{\Omega_r}{\Omega_b} + \frac{v_\Delta^2(z=0)}{v_0^2})(1 + \frac{\Omega_r}{\Omega_b}),$$

$$\frac{v_\Delta^2(z=0)}{v_0^2} = \frac{(1+\frac{\Omega_r}{\Omega_b}+\frac{\Omega_{dm}}{\Omega_b}\times\frac{1}{3})(1+\frac{\Omega_r}{\Omega_b}+\frac{1.048\Omega_{dm}}{1.496\Omega_b})}{(1+\frac{\Omega_r}{\Omega_b})}$$

$$- (1 + \frac{\Omega_r}{\Omega_b}). \quad (26)$$

The sum of the kinetic energies $W_\Delta(z)$ and $W_{r\Delta}(z)$ of the baryonic and radiation masses, respectively, associated with the excess velocity $v_\Delta(z)$ may be required to be conserved for all redshifts. This would lead to expressing the z-dependence of the squared-velocity $v_\Delta^2(z)$, in terms of the $v_\Delta^2(z = 0)$ solved above. Using this result in (24) would provide a complete expression for the $v^2(z > 0)$ before recombination.

$$W_\Delta(z) + W_{r\Delta}(z) = \frac{v_\Delta^2(z)}{v_0^2}(W_0 + W_0\frac{\Omega_r}{\Omega_b}(1 + z))$$

$$= W_\Delta(z = 0) + W_{r\Delta}(z = 0)$$

$$= \frac{v_\Delta^2(z=0)}{v_0^2}(W_0 + W_0\frac{\Omega_r}{\Omega_b}), \quad (27)$$

$$v_\Delta^2(z) = v_\Delta^2(z=0)\frac{(1+\frac{\Omega_r}{\Omega_b})}{(1+\frac{\Omega_r}{\Omega_b}(1+z))}. \qquad (28)$$

In the above derivation we ideally assumed the ratio of the UEG and baryonic masses or the respective mass densities $M_u/M = \rho_{uv}/\rho_v$ to be equal to Ω_{dm}/Ω_b, abruptly after the recombination, and equal to zero in the ionized environment before the recombination. However, in reality the UEG effect would gradually transition as the ionization changes during this phase. In order that this transitional UEG effect emulates the effect of the dark matter of the standard model, which is maintained at its constant value throughout the phase, the above ratio of the UEG and baryoninc masses may have to be sufficiently larger than the ratio Ω_{dm}/Ω_b by a factor $\eta > 1$. With introduction of this factor, the complete function $v^2(z > 0)$ is expressed as follows.

$$v^2(z>0) = v_0^2(1+z) + v_0^2\frac{\Omega_r}{\Omega_b}(1+z)^2 + v_\Delta^2(z)$$

$$= v_0^2(1+z) + v_0^2\frac{\Omega_r}{\Omega_b}(1+z)^2$$

$$+ v_0^2\left[\frac{(1+\frac{\Omega_r}{\Omega_b}+\eta\frac{\Omega_{dm}}{\Omega_b}\times\frac{1}{3})(1+\frac{\Omega_r}{\Omega_b}+\eta\frac{1.048\Omega_{dm}}{1.496\Omega_b})}{(1+\frac{\Omega_r}{\Omega_b})} - (1+\frac{\Omega_r}{\Omega_b})\right]$$

$$\times\left[\frac{(1+\frac{\Omega_r}{\Omega_b})}{(1+\frac{\Omega_r}{\Omega_b}(1+z))}\right]. \qquad (29)$$

For comparison, the squared-velocity function $v^2(z)$ from the standard model is expressed in the following form.

$$v^2(z>0) = v_0^2(1+z) + v_0^2\frac{\Omega_{dm}}{\Omega_b}(1+z)$$

$$+ v_0^2\frac{\Omega_r}{\Omega_b}(1+z)^2, \qquad (30)$$

where $\Omega_r/\Omega_b \sim 25/12$ is the ratio of the radiation (photon and neutrino) and baryon masses at the time of recombination.

Fig.5 shows the normalized velocity function $v^2(z)/v_0^2$ of (29) for different values of the parameter η, that are compared with the corresponding function (30) from the standard model.

The sound horizon distance r_s at the recombination, scaled back in the current universe, may be derived using the $v(z)/v_0$ functions of (29,30), in terms of the Hubble constant $H_0 = 67.8$ (km/s)/Mpc and the fractional matter content $\Omega_b = 0.049$ in the current universe, the scale factor $\alpha_c = 1/(1+z_c) = 1/1100$ at the recombination, and the sound speed $c_s(z)$ in the photon-baryon plasma.

$$r_s = \frac{1}{H_0\sqrt{0.049(1+z_c)}}\int_{z=0}^{\infty}\frac{c_s(z)dz}{[v(z)/v_0](1+z)},$$

$$c_s(z) = \frac{c}{\sqrt{3(1+\frac{3\Omega_b}{4\Omega_{r'}(1+z)})}}, \qquad (31)$$

where $\Omega_{r'}/\Omega_b = 15/12$ is the ratio of radiation (photon) and baryon mass densities at the recombination. The values of the r_s from the UEG model with variable UEG mass-density, defined by the parameter $\eta = (\rho_{uv}/\rho_v)/(\Omega_{dm}/\Omega_b)$, are compared in Fig.6 with those from the standard model with the fixed parameter $\Omega_{dm}/\Omega_b = 5.47$ for the dark matter. The reference value for the parameter $\eta = 1$ corresponds to $\rho_{uv}/\rho_v = \Omega_{dm}/\Omega_b = 5.47$. The results show that the UEG model using only baryon and radiation contents, and UEG effect of the radiation, but without any dark matter, would emulate the standard model that includes the baryon and radiation, and additional dark-matter, with a reasonable adjustment of the parameter $\eta \sim 1.75, \eta > 1$, as we expected.

The agreement of the sound horizon r_s from the standard model with the UEG model for $\eta \sim 1.75$ means that all signatures of the baryon acoustic oscillation (BAO) in the current universe (in the CMB [10, 11] and in the correlation distance of galaxy density [12]) predicted by the standard model, that are based on the horizon distance r_s as a reference "ruler", would be emulated in the UEG model for the given η. In addition, this value of $\eta \sim 1.75$, which is reasonably larger than unity, means that the UEG mass during the transition phase of recombination could potentially emulate the effective gravity of the dark matter in acoustic oscillations before the recombination. Therefore, the signature of the dark matter in the CMB could also be replicated by the UEG effects. The characteristics of the BAO in the ionized environment before recombination [22] needs to be reviewed, by properly including the new UEG effects, in order to make a more definitive evaluation. In any case, the present results indicate that all essential signatures of the BAO observed in the current universe could be potentially explained by the UEG theory without need for any dark matter, in consistency with the standard model predictions that require the hypothetical dark matter. That is a significant development.

Furthermore, a somewhat different value of the Hubble constant $H_0 \neq 67.8$(km/s)/Mpc, that can be consistent with the CMB observations as well as recent measurement of the H_0 in the local universe [23, 24], could also be accommodated in the present UEG theory, by suitable adjustment of the parameter η. This is significant as well, in order to overcome any tension between the CMB signature and the local H_0 measurement, which is getting increasingly difficult to resolve based on a conventional dark-energy model using a cosmological constant [23, 24].

VI. DISCUSSION AND CONCLUSION

The UEG theory, originally developed for modeling elementary particles [1, 2], is applied under special conditions to cosmology. The new theory explains the accelerating expansion of the recent universe, consistent with supernova measurements [7, 8]; explains the expansion of

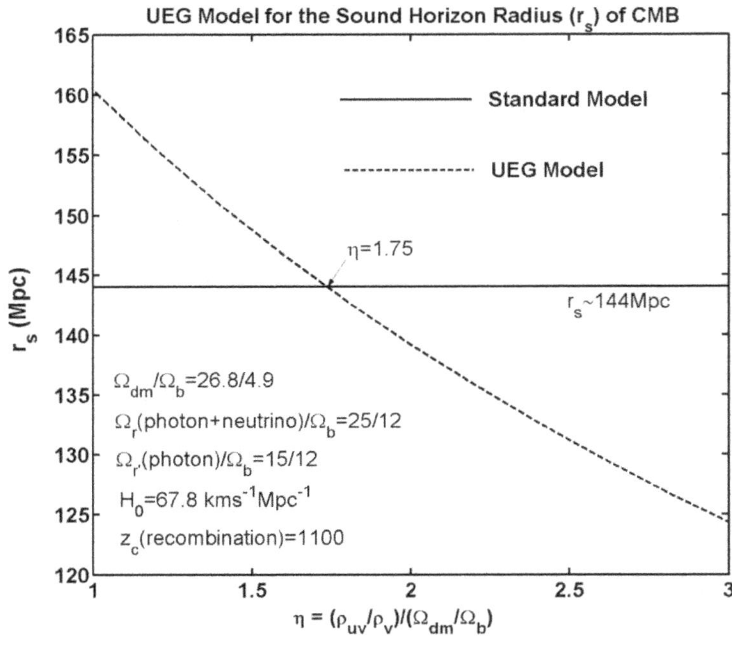

FIG. 6.

the universe before recombination, consistent with measured signatures of BAO in galaxy distributions [12] and in the CMB [10, 11]; could resolve a potential tension between different measured values of the Hubble constant, consistent with the CMB signatures as well as recent local measurements of the H_0 [23, 24]; and the theory supports a future contraction of the universe presumably leading to a cyclic process. The theory is based on gravitation of conventional matter in the universe, with additional acceleration and equivalent mass due to new UEG effects of the CMB radiation and any future star lights, without need for hypothetical dark matter or dark energy. As per the UEG theory, the energy density associated with any radiation, such as the CMB radiation or star lights, would produce new gravitational acceleration. The new UEG acceleration is modeled in terms of an equivalent mass distribution, just like conventional gravitational acceleration is modeled in terms of a conventional mass distribution as its source. The UEG mass distribution may also be treated like any distribution of conventional inertial mass, and accordingly be associated with its rest as well as kinetic mass-energy based on special relativity. These are significant new understandings on the basic principles of gravity, mass and energy, in the context of the new UEG theory.

The above new UEG effects are to be adopted in consistency with the basic cosmological assumption of a homogeneous and isotropic universe. However, the UEG theory, when applied in its simple form, would lead to a uniform acceleration independent of the radial distance from a center of observation. The uniform acceleration is associated with a uniform energy distribution of the CMB radiation, or with a uniform distribution of star lights produced from a uniform galaxy distribution. The equivalent mass associated with the uniform UEG acceleration, based on a simple UEG theory, can be shown to be non-uniform in distribution. This would be in contradiction with a uniform mass distribution, with associated gravitational acceleration linearly increasing with radial distance, that would be expected in consistency with the basic cosmological assumption of a homogeneous universe. In order that the UEG theory be consistent with the basic cosmological assumption, suitable adjustment in the simple UEG theory is needed. A new model is proposed and implemented in the paper, in the form of an effective UEG model for cosmology. Based on the success of the proposed approach, validated in consistency with measured observations, the effective model might be accepted as a fundamental new UEG theory for cosmology. Alternatively, some new physical process in the cosmological scale may allow readjustment of the expansion and mass distribution of the universe, in response to the uniform UEG accelerations supported by the simple UEG theory, which may ultimately lead to the same outcome as predicted from the effective UEG model. Both the above possibilities would be theoretically equivalent to each other.

The effective UEG model proposes suitable redistribution of the UEG mass and energy enclosed inside a spherical volume, defined by a "particle horizon" associated with first creation of conventional matter, or possibly by a "radiation horizon" (much farther than the particle horizon) associated with the early radiation-dominated inflationary universe, or even by a suitable combination of the above two horizons based on the mass and radiation content of the universe at a given time. The particle or radiation horizon would carry fundamental significance in the proposed UEG theory of cosmology, having critical theoretical as well as philosophical implications. The effective UEG model in the present work is implemented using a physically reasonable redistribution model, that may be adequate for certain objectives. However, further theoretical or observational development may be needed for a more definitive and rigorous UEG redistribution model. In addition, the physics of the BAO [22] may need to be re-evaluated based on the proposed UEG model, in order to properly account for any UEG effects on the CMB signature. The UEG effects in the ionized environment before recombination could potentially emulate effects of the hypothetical dark matter, as we have assumed in section V. A focused study of the BAO physics, based on the new UEG theory, would be needed for a rigorous understanding and analysis, beyond the scope of the present work.

Aside from the possible fundamental advancement in the proposed UEG theory of cosmology, as discussed above, some analytical or numerical refinement in the proposed UEG model could be implemented in principle. For analytical simplicity we may have assumed certain functional variation for the horizon distance of the observable universe, at different scale lengths or associated red-shifts. These assumptions may be effective in an average sense over a range of scale lengths, with adequate validity for the specific results presented. For accurate results in general applications, the functional variation of the horizon distance may have to be accurately tracked, using a more involved numerical computation.

With evident success in answering some of the key questions in cosmology today, as presented in this paper, the UEG theory may provide a new theoretical framework for any future advancement in physical cosmology. With successful prior application of the UEG theory in particle physics [1, 2], quantum mechanics [3], and stellar and galactic modeling [4, 5], the present extension of the UEG theory to cosmology may help to establish a complete, unified theory of physics, fundamentally integrating gravity, electromagnetics, as well as quantum mechanical concepts, with validity in in the smallest (elementary particles) to the largest (cosmology) domains of the nature.

[1] N. Das, "A New Unified Electro-Gravity (UEG) Theory of the Electron," Paper #1, pp.4-13, in "A Unified Electro-Gravity (UEG) Theory of Nature," (2018).

[2] N. Das, "A Generalized Unified Electro-Gravity (UEG) Model Applicable to All Elementary Particles," Paper #2, pp.14-30, in "A Unified Electro-Gravity (UEG) Theory of Nature," (2018).

[3] N. Das, "Unified ElectroGravity (UEG) Theory and Quantum Electrodynamics," Paper #3, pp.31-42, in "A Unified Electro-Gravity (UEG) Theory of Nature," (2018).

[4] N. Das, "Unified Electro-Gravity (UEG) Theory Applied to Stellar Gravitation, and the Mass-Luminosity Relation (MLR)," Paper #4, pp.44-58, in "A Unified Electro-Gravity (UEG) Theory of Nature," (2018).

[5] N. Das, "Unified Electro-Gravity (UEG) Theory Applied to Spiral Galaxies," Paper #5, pp.59-68, in "A Unified Electro-Gravity (UEG) Theory of Nature," (2018).

[6] P. J. Steinhardt and N. Turok, New Astronomy Reviews **49**, 43 (2005).

[7] A. G. Riess, A. V. Filippenko, P. Challis, A. Clocchiatti, *et al.*, The Astronomical Journal **116**, 1009 (1998).

[8] S. Perlmutter, G. Aldering, G. Goldhaber, R. A. Knop, *et al.*, The Astrophysical Journal **517**, 565 (1999).

[9] A. A. Penzias and R. W. Wilson, Astrophysical Journal **142**, 419 (1965).

[10] G. Hinshaw, D. Larson, E. Komatsu, D. N. Spergel, *et al.*, "Nine-Year Wilkinson Microwave Anisotropy Probe (WMAP) Observations: Cosmological Parameter Results," The Astrophysical Journal, Supplement Series, Vol.208 (2), p.19-43, October (2013).

[11] P. A. R. Ade, N. Aghanim, C. Armitage-Caplan, M. Arnaud, *et al.*, "Planck 2013 Results, Planck Collaboration, XVI: Cosmological Parameters," Astronomy and Astrophysics, Special Feature, Vol. 571 (A16), p.1-66, November (2014).

[12] D. J. Eisenstein, I. Zehavi, D. W. Hogg, R. Scoccimarro, *et al.*, Astrophysical Journal **633**, 560 (2005).

[13] G. Steigman, Annual Review of Nuclear and Particle Science **57**, 463 (2007).

[14] R. A. Alpher, H. Bethe, and G. Gamow, Physical Review **73**, 803 (1948).

[15] A. H. Guth, Physical Review D **23**, 347 (1981).

[16] P. A. R. Ade, N. Aghanim, M. Arnaud, M. Shdown, *et al.*, "Planck 2015 Results, Planck Collaboration, XII: Cosmological Parameters," Astronomy and Astrophysics, Special Feature, Vol.594 (A13), p.1-63, October (2016).

[17] P. Halpern and N. Tomasello, Advances in Astrophysics **1** (2016).

[18] H. Suess and H. Urey, Reviews of Modern Physics **28**, 53 (1956).

[19] E. Bohm-Vitense, *Introduction to Stellar Astrophysics (Ch.8)* (Cambridge University Press, 1992).

[20] S. M. Caroll, W. H. Press, and E. L. Turner, Annual Review of Astronomy and Astrophysics **30**, 499 (1992).

[21] E. L. Wright, arXiv:astro-ph/0701584v3 (2007).

[22] W. Hu, Annals of Physics **303**, 203 (2003).

[23] A. G. Riess, S. Casertano, W. Yuan, *et al.*, The Astrophysical Journal **861**, 126 (2018).

[24] A. G. Riess, L. M. Macri, S. L. Hoffman, *et al.*, The Astrophysical Journal **826**, 56 (2016).

Part-III: Derivation of Maxwell's Equations of Electromagnetic Theory from First Principles, which Supersede Newtonian Mechanics

A New Approach to Teaching Maxwell's Equations, as Derived from Simple Relativistic Transformation Principles: A Tutorial

Nirod K. Das

Department of Electrical and Computer Engineering

Tandon School of Engineering, New York University, Five Metrotech Center, Brooklyn NY 11201

(Dated: August, 2016)

Abstract

In this paper we present a simple, rigorous approach to introduce electromagnetic theory, based on basic relations for relativistic space-time transformation, and a new general principle of charge invariance. Basic space-time transformation equations are introduced reasonably quickly, using two independent methods: one is based on mathematical deduction, and the other on a physical analysis. More elaborate interpretation of the space-time transformation equations, and any further advancement into relativistic mechanics, such as mass and force transformation, are not necessary in the entire development. The space-time transformation equations are then used to derive basic transformation relations for electric current and charge densities, which enforce continuity or conservation of the electric charge. This is followed by derivation of the transformation relations for Gauss' laws for electric and magnetic fields, leading to Ampere's and Faraday's laws, respectively, which together constitute Maxwell's equations. The material is intended to fill an educational need to introduce modern relativity theory in teaching engineering electromagnetics. This is intended to provide an alternative interpretation as well as a complete "derivation" of Maxwell's equations, that can be adopted in an early, basic level of teaching. The approach would be suitable for a senior (even junior) undergraduate or an introductory graduate engineering class.

1. Introduction

1.1. Background. The concept of Ampere's law relating magnetic field to conduction and displacement currents, and the concept of Farady's law relating electric field to a time-varying magnetic field, were established historically through practical experimentation and gradual generalization. The general findings were formalized in suitable mathematical forms for analytical use, with only limited physical and philosophical rationalization. Ampere and Faraday's laws, in their most generalized forms, constitute Maxwell's equations [1], which are known to supersede all other basic circuit as well as field laws, such as Kirchoff's Current Law (KCL), Kirchoff's Voltage Law (KVL), Biot-Savart's law, and Gauss' laws of electric and magnetic fields. Such consistency with other pre-existing laws, as well as their success in understanding and predicting practical experiments, develop remarkable confidence in Maxwell's equations. They have so far stood the test of time, and are now accepted to be valid with farthest universal reach, except possibly in the nuclear and quantum-mechanical domains. In spite of all the remarkable generality and success of the theory, the underlying concepts of Maxwell's equations, or equivalently Ampere and Faraday's laws, may appear quite "mysterious" to basic human intuition. Without some form of logical explanation of the principles, one has to accept them solely on the basis of confidence in the experimental observations, and their consistent validity to date. This may not be fully satisfactory and insightful.

Later on, Einstein's theory of special relativity was established as an independent physical principle [2, 3]. This is founded upon the basic assumption that the speed of light or any electromagnetic wave, propagating in a uniform free-space medium, is a fixed constant when measured from any reference frame. Further, if the reference frames are "unbiased" (referred to as inertial reference frames,) then the light would propagate with the fixed invariant speed, along any given straight-line path. The theory also assumes that any "fundamental" physical experiment, designed to establish a particular "fundamental" physical principle or parameter, would lead to the same conclusion when measured or observed from any of the inertial frames of reference. This led to new transformation equations, relating the space and time coordinates of two inertial reference frames, that are consistent with the basic assumptions in the principles of relativity. In this paper, we will use the new space-time transformation relations to deduce Maxwell's equations from Gauss' laws of electric and magnetic fields. The deduction is intended to serve as an alternate explanation or validation for Ampere's and Faraday's laws.

In basic intuitive terms, the relativistic transformation principles may not be that easy to accept or understand, as compared with the standard non-relativistic principles one gathers through common, day-to-day experiences. However, with proper interpretation and logical understanding, they are arguably much less "mysterious" to reason than the principles of Ampere's and Faraday's laws. Similarly, Gauss's laws for electric and magnetic fields, which are fundamentally established in integral forms, at first may not seem to be readily acceptable in intuitive terms. However, they can be explained as logical and philosophical generalization from the basic, more intuitive concept of Coulomb's law, and therefore accepted to be much less mysterious than Ampere's and Faraday's laws. Accordingly, the deduction of Ampere's and Faraday's laws, or equivalently Maxwell's equations, from Gauss' laws through the relativistic transformation is as well expected to be much less "mysterious." Such a deduction would be much easier to logically comprehend, and therefore be intellectually satisfying, in contrast with simply accepting Maxwell's equations based on experimental observation. In this sense, the deduction would be considered philosophically or logically fundamental.

Traditionally, the basic level texts on engineering electromagnetics [4, 5, 6] have used Maxwell's equations under different special, simplified conditions, or in the complete form, as the starting point to study various electromagnetic fields and radiation problems. However, connecting Maxwell's equations to the relativity theory is not usually explored in the basic engineering texts. Simple relativistic treatment of the electromagnetic fields are available in some physics text books [7, 8] which are meant only to initiate an interesting, alternate mode of reasoning, but not really to provide a comprehensive development of Maxwell's equations from the relativistic theory. More involved relativistic treatments of Maxwell's equations at higher levels are available in [8, 9, 10], which can be mathematically and/or conceptually tasking, making them inaccessible to introductory, even some advanced level students. All the available approaches assume a descent level of prior study of the theory of special relativity, including mass, momentum and force transformation relations. That may be fine for advanced physics students, but usually not for introductory - even advanced - level engineering students. For the varied reasons, the available approaches have been rarely used in introductory engineering classrooms. Useful contributions in in the general context of introducing special relativity to engineering electromagnetics, particularly for teaching at the undergraduate level, include [11]-[12].

1.2. **Objective.** It would be valuable for students of introductory engineering electromagnetics to study the theory of special relativity at some essential level, and learn its direct connection to Maxwell's equations to provide a modern, alternative perspective of the electromagnetic principles. The new perspective would enrich the introductory learning process, leading to modern, creative thinking, possibly leading to insightful design applications as well. The potential benefits may justify introduction of the new teaching, only if the material can be presented economically in a simple, comprehensive manner, with minimal distraction into the involved mechanical principles of the special relativity. This is particularly considering the limited time and resources available for the engineering electromagnetics in a typical undergraduate electrical engineering curriculum.

To this end, we develop comprehensive material to introduce the concepts of the special relativity at an early, basic level of teaching engineering electromagnetics. This is intended to provide an alternate interpretation as well as a complete "derivation" of Maxwell's equations. We accomplish this with mathematical as well as conceptual simplicity and economy, so that the material could be widely adopted. Use of differential operators such as curl and divergence are even avoided in the main derivation. The summation or integral principles are used instead, which are mathematically simpler and intuitive, so that the material can be introduced in an earliest possible, basic level of teaching.

We first introduce the space-time transformation equations of the relativity theory. They can developed reasonably quickly with minimal effort, using two independent approaches, which might appeal to diverse student mindsets. One is based on simple mathematical deduction, whereas the other is based on intuitive physical analysis. More elaborate interpretation of the space-time transformation equations, and any further advancement into relativistic mechanics, are not needed. The space-time transformation equations are then used to derive basic charge-current transformation relations, by enforcing continuity of the charge. This is followed by derivation of suitable transformation relations for Gauss' laws for electric and magnetic fields, which leads to Ampere's and Faraday's laws, respectively.

A simple transformation from Gauss' laws to Ampere's and Faraday's laws is possible by using a new general kind of principle of invariance of charge, as measured or seen from different inertial reference frames (see section 6). As mentioned, this approach needs only the simple space-time relativistic transformation relations, and is not dependent upon more advanced concepts of relativistic mechanics, and associated transformation relations for mass, momentum and force. In contrast, the common theoretical approaches to develop or interpret Maxwell's equations from special relativity in [7]-[10] are based on a more restrictive principle of invariance for the source and test charges, and on the transformation relations for mass, momentum and force [13, 14]. In these approaches, the mechanical transformation relations need to be first developed from the principle of momentum and energy conservation, which must be assumed to be valid for any relative uniform velocity of the inertial frame of observation. This process could consume significant valuable time and attention in the initial development of the relativistic transformation relations, and understanding the involved mechanical concepts, which can be a major distraction from an introductory engineering electromagnetics class. Further, in contrast to the present proposed approach, the use of the mechanical transformation relations in the derivation of Maxwell's equations often leads to significant mathematical complexity, requiring restrictive assumptions or intricate conceptual arguments. This makes the material inaccessible or unsatisfactory to basic as well as advanced level engineering, even physics students. Contributions in the general context of introducing special relativity to engineering electromagnetics include [11]-[12].

2. SPACE-TIME TRANSFORMATION

Consider two frames of reference, as shown in Fig.1. The time and space coordinates of a particular event, as measured in one reference frame, are represented by four variables (x, y, z, t). The respective coordinates of the event, as measured in the second reference frame, are represented by primed variables (x', y', z', t'), Accordingly, the first and the second reference frames may be informally referred to as the "un-primed" and the "primed" reference frames or reference coordinates, respectively. The four variables may be referred to as the space-time coordinates of the event, and the event may be referred to as a particular space-time point in a coordinate system. Now, assume that the primed reference frame is moving with a uniform velocity V in the x direction, with respect the unprimed coordinates. Also assume that at time $t = 0$, the origins of the two coordinate systems are aligned. That is, at $t = 0$, the space coordinates $x' = y' = z' = 0$ in the primed system coincide with the space coordinates $x = y = z = 0$ in the unprimed system. Further, at this instant the clock in the primed coordinate system is initialized with that of the unprimed coordinate system with $t' = 0$.

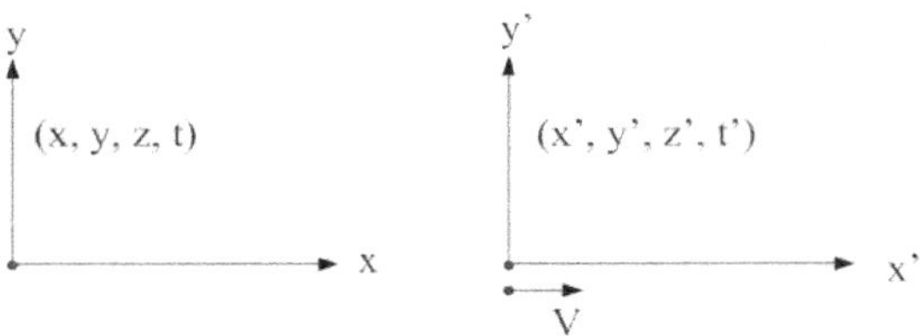

FIGURE 1

2.1. **Non-Relativistic Transformation.** If one uses a conventional or "common-sense" coordinate transformation, referred to as non-relativistic transformation, the space-time coordinates of the event in the two reference frames can be be related as follows:

$$y = y', \ z = z', \ x = x' + Vt, \ t = t'. \tag{1}$$

This transformation would also lead to relating any incremental changes in the coordinates, represented by a pre-fix Δ:

$$\Delta y = \Delta y', \ \Delta z = \Delta z', \ \Delta x = \Delta x' + V\Delta t, \ \Delta t = \Delta t'. \tag{2}$$

Accordingly, the components of the velocity of the point in different directions may also be related by dividing respective incremental distance by incremental time:

$$v_y = \frac{\Delta y}{\Delta t} = \frac{\Delta y'}{\Delta t'} = v'_y,$$

$$v_z = \frac{\Delta z}{\Delta t} = \frac{\Delta z}{\Delta t'} = v'_z,$$

$$v_x = \frac{\Delta x}{\Delta t} = \frac{\Delta x' + V\Delta t'}{\Delta t'} = \frac{\Delta x'}{\Delta t'} + V = v'_x + V. \tag{3}$$

Notice that the two time variables t and t' are assumed to be equal. This means, such standard transformation implicitly assume that the flow of time is "absolute," meaning it is independent of the relative motion between the frames. In addition, t is equal to t', independent of the space coordinates of the event being observed. However, the above two assumptions do not have any concrete physical basis, and should be open to review and adjustment based on any advanced understanding or experimental observation.

2.2. Special Nature of Light, and Incompatibility with Non-Relativisitc Transformation. In the non-relativistic transformation, we see that the x-directed velocity in the unprimed reference frame can be obtained from that in the primed reference frame by simply adding the relative velocity V between the frames. Accordingly, any x-directed velocity measured in one coordinate frame would not be equal to that measured in the other, for a non-zero value of the relative velocity V. Further, the magnitude of the total velocity, which is the speed, defined as the square-root of the sum of squares of the individual velocity components in the three directions x, y and z, would also not be equal when measured in the two reference frames.

Now, let us apply the standard common-sense, non-relativistic transformation to a light signal propagating in free-space. As per the transformation rules discussed above, the speed of light in free-space would be measured with different results in the two reference frames. With some insight on the special nature of light, this conclusion may be brought to question, which would lead to invalidating the non-relativistic transformation for general applications.

The speed of light is different from that of any common material substance such as a rock or a bullet. Light is not "thrown" off a light bulb like a rock thrown from someone's hand or a bullet from a gun. Therefore, unlike a rock or a bullet, the speed of light can not be fixed as a given value with respect to its source, and the given speed could not be changed as one desires by employing more strength or energy of its source. Instead, light is generated as a wave from the bulb, more like a sound wave generated from a flute, or more like the water ripples generated when a rock is dropped in a lake. Once the wave is generated by its source, it is physically detached from its source and its propagation speed is supposed to be determined by the medium, independent of the source. However, unlike a mechanical wave, such as the sound or water wave, the light wave does not require a material medium for propagation. Light can propagate in free-space. It would bring challenges in the understanding, when light propagation in an ideal free-space is considered.

The water wave propagates as a disturbance of the water particles, and the disturbance propagates with respect to the body of the water. Therefore, the body of the water, or equivalently the body of the solid ground around the lake with respect to which the water is assumed to be stationary, is the natural frame of reference. The speed of the water wave is derived from the material properties of the water, and is clearly defined with respect this natural frame of reference. Similarly, for the sound wave, the solid earth with respect to which the surrounding air is assumed to be stationary, is the natural reference frame. The speed of the sound wave is a known constant (as determined from the physical parameters of the air), clearly defined with respect to the earth or the surrounding stationary air. Once the speed of the water wave or the sound wave is definitively known, with respect to its natural, or "preferred," reference frame as discussed, pointed in any specific direction, the wave velocity with respect to any other reference frame may be determined by using velocity transformation rule. In distinct contrast, an ideal free-space in which light propagates, as per the very philosophical nature of the free-space, does not have a natural or "preferred" reference frame. Unlike the water in a lake or the air surrounding earth, the free-space is not "attached" to any definite body of reference. Therefore, to begin with, there is no preferred reference frame with respect to which we can define and fix the speed of light in free-space. Accordingly, the standard procedure of starting with a known value of the speed, pointed in any specific direction, with respect to a naturally preferred reference frame, and then calculating the velocity with respect to other references using velocity transformation, may not be as evident for light propagation in free-space. In this process, if one would start by fixing a certain value of the speed to any particular reference frame, that may appear arbitrary without proper logical basis.

2.3. Theory of Relativity and the Speed of Light in Free-Space. We may, however, look at the above situation from a new perspective. From the earlier discussion, we understand that there is no naturally preferred reference frame for propagation of light in free-space. To put it a bit differently, all reference frames should be equally preferred for treatment of the propagation of light in free-space. Accordingly, if one may start with a fixed value for the speed of light in free-space in one reference frame, arbitrarily chosen, then there would be no reason why the same value could not have been fixed in any other reference frame. This is an important philosophical argument, leading to the conclusion that, whatever is the speed of light in an ideal free-space, it may have to be the same universal constant for all reference frames of measurement. Further, if the reference frame is also "unbiased," then the light would propagate with the same speed along any given direction, with no biased preference to deflect the propagation direction to one side or other. This was postulated in Einstein's theory of relativity as a universal principle. This conclusion is also established through practical experiments.

The new theory of relativity would clearly contradict the principles of the non-relativistic transformation. The basic rule of non-relativistic transformation discussed earlier - that the speed of a given physical event would necessarily have unequal values, when measured in two reference frames moving with a non-zero relative velocity V - is clearly violated for light propagation in free-space. The transformation relations would then have to be revised in order to be consistent with the new theory of relativity. We will show in the following how this can be achieved, using two approaches: (1) mathematical analysis, and (2) physical experimentation. The first approach mainly uses mathematical arguments for the derivation of the new transformation relations. Whereas, the second approach derives the transformation relations based on a more intuitive understanding of a physical measurement process using light. The two approaches may be used equally effectively, or may be used in complementary ways, in order to develop an understanding of the new transformation relations. The new transformation relations, as derived in the following, are referred to as the relativistic transformation relations.

In order that the new relativistic transformation relations are to be universal in scope, in scientific consistency, they should be applicable not just for light in free-space, but for all physical phenomena. They would have significant implications when applied to the mechanics of material bodies. However, when the relative velocity V is much smaller than the speed of light in free-space, which is usually the case in our "common-sense" world, the new relativistic relations are seen to approach the standard non-relativistic relations. Accordingly, the non-relativistic relations are accurate enough for common day-to-day observations, as normally expected. Physical mechanics, under general conditions of relative motion, is to be revised based on the new theory of relativity and transformation relations. The reader may be referred to textbooks on modern physics for further study on this topic. Development of mechanics under the revised relativistic conditions may have indirect implications to the electromagnetic theory, but it is not the goal of the present study. Here, we would focus on the applications of the relativistic transformation specifically to the development and understanding of Maxwell's equations.

2.4. Relativistic Transformation: Mathematical Analysis. The two reference frames in Fig.1 are assumed to be moving with a relative velocity V in the x direction. The relative motion in the x direction is not expected to alter the y and z coordinates of an event, when seen from the two frames, assuming that the two frames and the free-space medium are equally unbiased in the y and z directions. That is, we have $y = y'$ and $z = z'$. This leaves the transformation of the only space coordinate along the x axis, and the time coordinate. Accordingly, in the following we may represent an event with only two variables, (x, t) or (x', t').

Consider that the primed space-time coordinates (x', t') are linearly related to the respective unprimed coordinates (x, t).

$$x' = ax + bt,$$
$$t' = px + qt, \tag{4}$$

where a, b, p and q are now unknown constants, to be determined. Let us mathematically see if transformation relations in the above form can be established, which would be consistent with the requirements of the relativity theory. The above relationships, to begin with, already satisfied the initial conditions we have assumed. From the above equations, we have $x' = 0$ when $t = 0$ and $x = 0$. That means, at time $t = 0$, the origin of the unprimed coordinate system $(x = 0)$ coincides with that of the primed coordinate system $(x' = 0)$. At the same instant, that is when $x = x' = t = 0$, we would also have $t' = 0$ from the above equations. In other words, the clock in the primed coordinate system located at $x' = 0$ is initialized with $t' = 0$, when the origins of the two reference frames coincide, which is the same instant when the clock in the unprimed coordinate system is also initialized to zero $t = 0$. In addition to the initial conditions, we need other basic conditions to be enforced in order for the transformation relations to be logically valid, and meet the physical constraints of the relativity theory. These additional conditions would determine the values of the constants in the transformation equations (4).

At time $t = 0$ the origins of the two frames coincide. We also know, the origin of the primed coordinate system moves with a given velocity V as seen from the origin of the unprimed coordinate system. Accordingly, for $x' = 0$, we have to have $x = Vt$. Using this constraint in (4) we get,

$$x' = 0 = ax + bt, \ x = -\tfrac{b}{a}t = Vt,$$
$$\tfrac{b}{a} = -V. \tag{5}$$

One basic expectation in the relativity transformation is that, if one observer sees a second observer to move with a velocity V, then the second observer should see the first moving with a velocity $-V$. We just explained that the origin of the primed coordinate system moves with a velocity V as seen by an observer at the origin of the unprimed coordinate system. Therefore, the origin of the un-primed coordinate system, that is $x = 0$, should be seen by an observer at the origin of the primed coordinates to be moving with a velocity $-V$. Accordingly, for $x = 0$, we have to have $x' = -Vt'$ Using this constraint in (4) we get,

$$t' = qt, \ x' = bt; \ x = 0,$$
$$x' = bt = \tfrac{b}{q}t' = -Vt',$$
$$\tfrac{b}{q} = -V. \tag{6}$$

The above constraints we have enforced are quite elementary, and are not particularly unique to the relativity theory. What would be new or unique to the relativity theory is the following. Consider a point (x, t) in the unprimed coordinate system, which is seen as a point (x', t') in the primed coordinate system. Consider that the point is moving in the x direction with a speed equal to the speed of light c, as seen in the unprimed coordinates. That is, $\frac{\Delta x}{\Delta t} = c$. Then, the speed of the same point, as measured by the primed coordinates, would also be equal to the speed of light c. That is, $\Delta x'$ and $\Delta t'$, corresponding to the incremental distance and time Δx and Δt, respectively, would be such that $\frac{\Delta x'}{\Delta t}$ is also equal to the speed of light c. Using this condition in (4)

$$\Delta x' = a\Delta x + b\Delta t,$$
$$\Delta t' = p\Delta x + q\Delta t,$$
$$\tfrac{\Delta x'}{\Delta t'} = \tfrac{a\Delta x + b\Delta t}{p\Delta x + q\Delta t} = \tfrac{a\frac{\Delta x}{\Delta t} + b}{p\frac{\Delta x}{\Delta t} + q},$$
$$c = \tfrac{ac + b}{pc + q}, \ pc^2 + qc = ac + b,$$
$$pc^2 + (q - a)c - b = 0. \tag{7}$$

Using (5,6) in (7)

$$pc^2 = b. \tag{8}$$

For $x = 0$, we have $t' = qt$. Accordingly, for $x' = 0$ we should also expect $t = qt'$. This is a basic symmetry condition between times in the two coordinates. Using this symmetry condition in (4),

$$x' = 0 = ax + bt, \quad x = -\tfrac{b}{a}t,$$
$$t' = px + qt = -\tfrac{pb}{a}t + qt = t(q - p\tfrac{b}{a}) = \tfrac{t}{q},$$
$$q^2 - pq\tfrac{b}{a} = 1. \tag{9}$$

Now, the constants a, b, p and q can be solved from the equations (5-9)

$$a^2 - pb = 1 = a^2 - \tfrac{b^2}{c^2} = a^2 - a^2\tfrac{V^2}{c^2} = 1,$$
$$a = \frac{1}{\sqrt{1-\frac{V^2}{c^2}}} = q,$$
$$b = -Va = \frac{-V}{\sqrt{1-\frac{V^2}{c^2}}},$$
$$p = \tfrac{b}{c^2} = \frac{-\frac{V}{c^2}}{\sqrt{1-\frac{V^2}{c^2}}},$$
$$x' = ax + bt = \tfrac{x - Vt}{\alpha},$$
$$t' = px + qt = \frac{-\frac{Vx}{c^2}+t}{\alpha},$$
$$\alpha = \sqrt{1 - \tfrac{V^2}{c^2}}. \tag{10}$$

2.5. Relativistic Transformation: Physical Experimentation. We will use simple physical processes employing light signals in free-space to measure time and distance. A particular process using a light signal is measured from two different reference frames. The results of measurement in the two frames can then be compared to establish transformation relations between the space and time coordinates of the two frames.

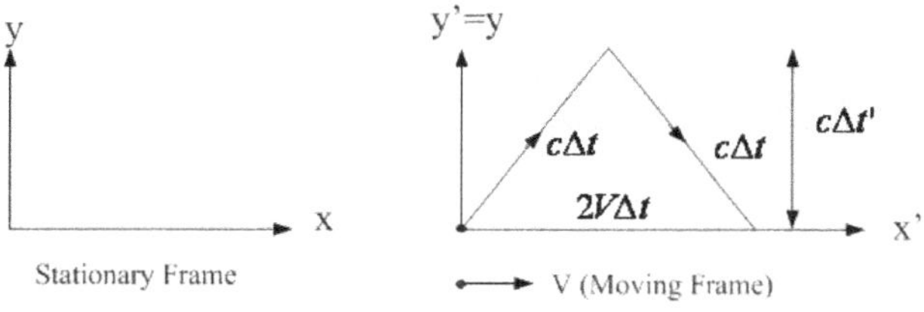

$$\text{F{\scriptsize IGURE} } 2$$

2.5.1. *Time Transformation.* First, let us measure time by bouncing a light through a fixed distance Δy in the y-direction. The round-trip delay experienced by the light to cover a fixed distance may be used as a proportionate measure of the time. Consider such a time-measurement process conducted in the primed reference frame (at the origin $x' = 0$). This same process is observed in the unprimed reference frame, and compared with another identical time-measurement process conducted at the origin of the unprimed reference frame. The relative velocity V in the x direction is assumed not to change the y dimension in the two reference frames. Accordingly, $\Delta y = \Delta y'$. Let $2\Delta t'$ be the round-trip time taken by the light, as measured in the primed reference frame, to cover a reference distance $\Delta y = \Delta y'$.

$$\Delta y = \Delta y' = c\Delta t'. \tag{11}$$

This light-bouncing experiment conducted in the primed frame, when observed from the un-primed frame, would appear to take a longer route (see Fig.2). The round-trip time would be measured $2\Delta t$, as compared with its local timing process conducted in the unprimed frame. Accordingly, Δt is referred to as "equivalent" to $\Delta t'$, as observed from the unprimed reference frame. As a definition, an incremental interval between a pair of time measurements, with given starting and end points, is referred to be "equivalent" or "simultaneous" to that between another pair, as observed from a particular reference frame, under the following condition. If the reference starting points of the two pairs coincide with each other (if they happen to occur simultaneously, or by introducing a suitable delay between their observations,) then the corresponding end points would also be observed in coincidence, or "simultaneously," from the given frame. In reference to the Fig.2, one can now geometrically relate Δt with $\Delta t'$ in terms of the the speed of light c and the relative velocity V.

$$c^2\Delta t^2 = c^2\Delta t'^2 + V^2\Delta t^2, \tag{12}$$

$$\Delta t' = \Delta t(1 - \frac{V^2}{c^2})^{\frac{1}{2}} = \Delta t\alpha. \tag{13}$$

The above geometric analysis assumes that the two reference frames are ideally unbiased, from which the light is observed to propagate along straight lines. Also, as per the theory of relativity, we have assumed the same value c for the speed of light as observed in either of the two reference frames. Equation (13) is a simple relationship between an incremental time $\Delta t'$ measured at the origin of the primed coordinate system, and the corresponding incremental time Δt as measured and observed to be equivalent in the unprimed coordinate system. Now, as we have assumed before, the times t' and t are initialized to zero when the origin $x' = 0$ coincides with the origin $x = 0$. With this initialization, the above proportionality relationship between the equivalent incremental times would apply to the corresponding reference times t' and t. The time t' measured at the origin $x' = 0$ of the primed coordinates is determined to be equivalent or "simultaneous" to the time t as measured and observed in the unprimed coordinates. These equivalent times t' and t are related as follows.

$$t' = t(1 - \frac{V^2}{c^2})^{\frac{1}{2}}, \; x' = 0. \tag{14}$$

Note that the time t' is specified in association with a particular location of measurement $x' = 0$. This is important. If the particular location x' at which the original experiment is conducted is changed, the relationship between the equivalent times t' and t would be different. If the point x' is fixed in the primed coordinate frame (independent of t'), but not at the origin $x' = 0$, the relationship between the equivalent incremental times in (13) would still be valid, whereas the relationship (14) between the actual reference times t' and t would not (requiring some time offset). Also, as we have stated, the above relationship assumes that the t' and t are determined to be equivalent or "simultaneous" as observed from the unprimed reference frame. Instead, if the determination of equivalence or simultaneity is made as observed from the primed reference frame, the relationship would be different. For example, if the experiment is conducted at the origin of the unprimed coordinates, and the observation of simultaneity is made from the primed reference frame, it can be shown (by principle of symmetry between the frames) that the relationship between the equivalent times t and t' can be expressed using (14), but with the variables t' and t switched. These concepts of equivalence or simultaneity should be clearer from a complete space-time transformation relationship between (x, t) and (x', t').

2.5.2. Space-Time Transformation. The above experiment established relationship between equivalent times t and t' in the two frames of measurement. Now we will conduct another light experiment, using which we can measure the distance and time of a particular "event" as observed in the two reference frames. Let a light signal be initiated from the origin of the unprimed coordinate system at time $t = t_1$. Let the light signal be aimed towards a particular event-point in space, as shown in the Fig.3, whose space-time coordinates (x, t) and (x', t') we are interested to determine as measured from the two reference frames. The signal passes through the origin of the primed reference frame at time t_2, reaches the particular point of interest at time t_3, reflects and returns towards the starting point, passes again through the origin of the primed reference frame on its way at time t_4, and reaching finally at the origin of the unprimed reference frame at time t_5. All the above times are as measured with respect to the unprimed coordinate system. The corresponding equivalent times measured at the origin of the primed reference frame can be obtained using the above relationship (14). The space and time coordinates (x, t) and (x', t'), as measured with respect to the two reference frames, can be determined and related from the above timing information.

The distance x of the event is determined from the time delay $t_5 - t_1$. The time $t = t_3$ of the event is determined as the average of t_5 and t_1.

$$x = (t_5 - t_1)\frac{c}{2}, \tag{15}$$

$$t = t_5 - \frac{x}{c} = t_5 - \frac{t_5 - t_1}{2} = \frac{t_1 + t_5}{2} = t_3. \tag{16}$$

From the above two equations, the measured x and t can be related to the initial time t_1.

$$-x + ct = ct_1. \tag{17}$$

The distance x' of the event is determined from the time delay $t'_4 - t'_2$. The time $t' = t'_3 = \alpha t_3$ of the event is determined as the average of t'_4 and t'_2.

$$x' = (t'_4 - t'_2)\frac{c}{2}, \tag{18}$$

$$t' = t'_4 - \frac{x'}{c} = t'_4 - \frac{t'_4 - t'_2}{2} = \frac{t'_2 + t'_4}{2}. \tag{19}$$

The above (x', t') are expressed in terms of $t'_4 = t_4\alpha$ and $t'_2 = t_2\alpha$. Equation (17) relates (x, t) to t_1. Accordingly, in order to relate (x', t') with (x, t), we may need to relate t_2 and t_4 with t_1. This can be accomplished as follows. The distance covered by the light signal during time $t_2 - t_1$ is equal to distance Vt_2 between the reference frames at time t_2. Solving from this information, t_2 may be related with t_1

$$c(t_2 - t_1) = Vt_2, \quad t_2 = \frac{t_1 c}{c - V}. \tag{20}$$

Similarly, the distance covered by the light signal during time interval $t_4 - t_1$ is equal to round-trip distance $2x$ of the event point minus the distance Vt_4 between the reference frames at time t_4. Solving from this information, t_4 may be related with t_1 and x.

$$c(t_4 - t_1) = 2x - Vt_4, \ \ t_4 = \frac{2x + ct_1}{c + V}.$$

(21)

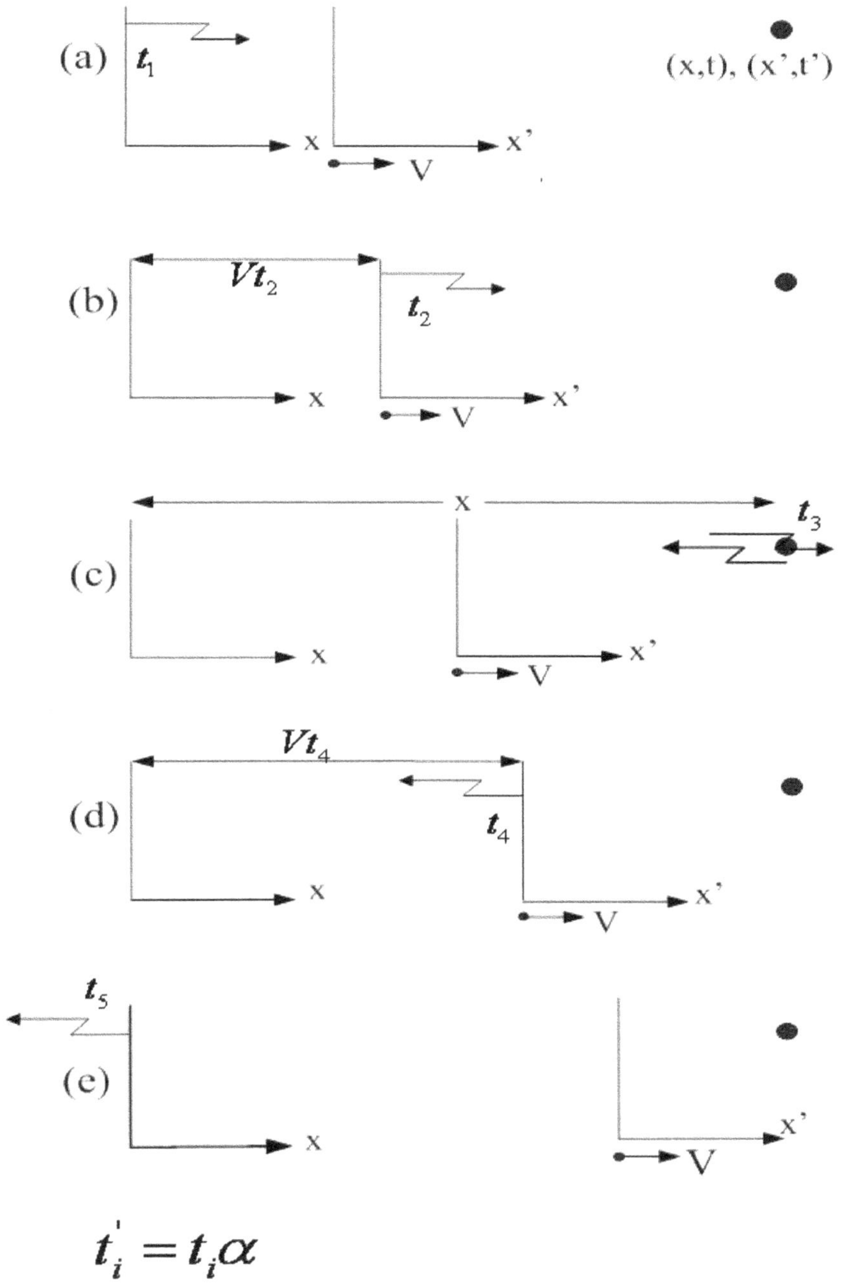

$$t_i' = t_i \alpha$$

FIGURE 3

Using (17) in (20,21), we can relate t_2 and t_4 with x and t .

$$t_2 = \frac{ct - x}{c - V}, \quad t_4 = \frac{2x + (ct - x)}{c + V} = \frac{ct + x}{c + V}, \tag{22}$$

$$t_4 - t_2 = \frac{-2cVt + 2cx}{c^2 - V^2}, \quad t_2 + t_4 = \frac{2c^2t - 2Vx}{c^2 - V^2}. \tag{23}$$

Use (23) in (18,19) to relate (x', t') to (x, t).

$$x' = (t_4 - t_2)c\frac{\alpha}{2} = \frac{(c^2x - c_2Vt)\alpha}{c^2 - V^2} = \frac{x - Vt}{\alpha},$$

$$t' = \frac{t_2 + t_4}{2}\alpha = \frac{\alpha(c^2t - Vx)}{c^2 - V^2} = \frac{t - \frac{Vx}{c^2}}{\alpha}. \tag{24}$$

The above transformation relations (24), derived here using a complete physical analysis, are the same relations in (10) which were derived on a mathematical basis. Both are valid and complementary approaches to establish the relativistic transformation.

Using the above transformation relations, it can be shown that a straight-line path of light propagation along any general orientation in space, as originally observed from one of the unbiased frames, would be seen with a deviated orientation in the other frame. The amount of the deviation would be dependent on the magnitude V of the relative velocity between the two frames. The relative orientation of the light path seen in the second frame, would obviously depend on the direction of the relative velocity $\overline{V}$ between the frames. Therefore, if the velocity $\overline{V}$ (magnitude and/or direction) varies in time, the resulting light path with its variable orientation in time would appear as a curved path, as seen in the second frame. This would contradict the unbiased nature of the two reference frames, that we assumed in the above analyses, which expects any observed light path to be strictly a straight line. Therefore, the unbiased nature of the two frames would require the relative velocity $\overline{V}$ between the frames to be constant in time, as a necessary fundamental condition.

3. Relativistic Transformation of Current and Charge Density

3.1. **Current Along the Relative Velocity.** Let us first consider only an x-directed current. An experiment is conducted in the primed reference frame to verify the continuity of current and charge conservation (Fig.4). The experiment may be mathematically expressed as follows.

$$\Delta\tau'[J'_x(x' + \Delta x'/2, t') - J'_x(x' - \triangle x'/2, t')]\Delta A = -\frac{\partial \triangle Q'}{\partial t'}\Delta\tau' = -\frac{\partial \rho'_v}{\partial t'}(x', t')\Delta\tau'\Delta A\Delta x',$$

$$\frac{J'_x(x' + \Delta x'/2, t') - J'_x(x' - \triangle x'/2, t')}{\Delta x'} = -\frac{\partial \rho'_v}{\partial t'}(x', t'),$$

$$\frac{\partial J'_x}{\partial x'} = -\frac{\partial \rho'_v}{\partial t'}. \tag{25}$$

The same experiment is observed from the unprimed coordinate frame, as shown in the Fig.4. Let us find relationships between the space $(\Delta x, \Delta x')$ and time $(\Delta t, \Delta t')$, $(\Delta\tau, \Delta\tau')$ increments observed in the two reference frames. The experiment was performed in the (x', t') coordinates with measurements done at the two ends of the volume $x' - \Delta x'/2$ and $x' + \Delta x'/2$ at the same time t'. This means $\Delta t' = 0$ at the two ends. In the (x, t) reference frame, the corresponding increments (Δx and Δt) may be related with each other and with $\Delta x'$ using relativistic transform relations (10,24).

$$t' = \frac{t - xV/c^2}{\alpha}, \ x' = \frac{x - Vt}{\alpha},$$

$$\triangle t' = \frac{\triangle t - \triangle x V/c^2}{\alpha} = 0, \ \triangle t = \triangle x V/c^2,$$

$$\triangle x' = \frac{\triangle x - \triangle t V}{\alpha} = \frac{\triangle x - \triangle x V^2/c^2}{\alpha} = \alpha \triangle x,$$

$$\triangle x = \frac{\triangle x'}{\alpha}, \ \triangle t = \triangle x V/c^2 = \frac{\triangle x'}{\alpha} V/c^2. \tag{26}$$

The charge ΔQ and $\Delta Q'$ in the two frames would be equal. We also assume that the transverse cross-section area ΔA is the same in both frames. Because the lengths $\Delta x'$ and Δx are different when measured in the two frame, the same charge enclosed between the lengths would appear as different charge densities. Let ρ_{v0} be the charge density of the volume element as observed in the unprimed frame.

$$\Delta Q = \Delta Q' = \rho_v' \Delta A \Delta x' = \rho_{v0} \Delta A \Delta x,$$

$$\rho_{v0} = \rho_v' \times \frac{\Delta x'}{\Delta x} = \rho_v' \alpha. \tag{27}$$

The time increment $\Delta \tau'$ is an arbitrarily small interval between two instants of measurements performed at a given $x' (\Delta x' = 0)$. The corresponding time interval in the (x, t) reference frame is $\Delta \tau = \Delta \tau'/\alpha$.

As per a basic principle of the theory of relativity, the outcome of the basic, physical experiment conducted in the primed reference frame at a given $t', \Delta t' = 0$, and that observed from the other reference frame should be the same. The current continuity experiment, as observed in the (x, t) frame can be expressed as follows.

$$\Delta \tau [J_x(x + \Delta x/2, t + \Delta t/2) - J_x(x - \Delta x/2, t - \Delta t/2)] \Delta A$$

$$= -\frac{\partial \Delta Q}{\partial t} \Delta \tau = [-\frac{\partial \rho_{v0}}{\partial t}(x, t)\Delta x \Delta A]\Delta \tau,$$

$$(J_x + \frac{\partial J_x}{\partial x}\Delta x/2 + \frac{\partial J_x}{\partial t}\Delta t/2) - (J_x - \frac{\partial J_x}{\partial x}\Delta x/2 - \frac{\partial J_x}{\partial t}\Delta t/2) = -\frac{\partial \rho_{v0}}{\partial t}(x, t)\Delta x,$$

$$\frac{\partial J_x}{\partial x} + \frac{\partial J_x}{\partial t}\frac{V}{c^2} = -\frac{\partial \rho_{v0}}{\partial t},$$

$$\int \frac{\partial J_x}{\partial x}\partial t + \frac{V}{c^2}J_x = -\rho_{v0}. \tag{28}$$

When the velocity $V = 0$, we know $\rho_{v0} = \rho_v$. Using this condition in the above equation, the integral term can be recognized as $-\rho_v$.

$$\rho_{v0} = \rho_v'\alpha = \rho_v - \frac{V}{c^2}J_x = \rho_v + \Delta\rho_v,$$

$$\Delta\rho_v = -\frac{V}{c^2}J_x, \ \frac{\partial \rho_v}{\partial t} = -\frac{\partial J_x}{\partial x}. \tag{29}$$

ρ_v is the charge density the observer in the (x, t) frame normally estimates (at a given $t, \Delta t = 0$) and ρ_{v0} is the charge density the same observer would estimate in the transformed current continuity experiment (at a given $t', \Delta t' = 0$). These two parameters differ, with the difference $\Delta\rho_v$ dependent on the current density J_x. If the current is charge free as seen in the (x', t') frame, then the transformed experiment would yield $\rho_{v0} = 0 = \alpha\rho_v' = \rho_v - J_x\frac{V}{c^2}$. This means $\rho_v = J_x\frac{V}{c^2}$. In other words, a charge free current in the (x', t') frame would look charged in the (x, t) frame. This is an important observation.

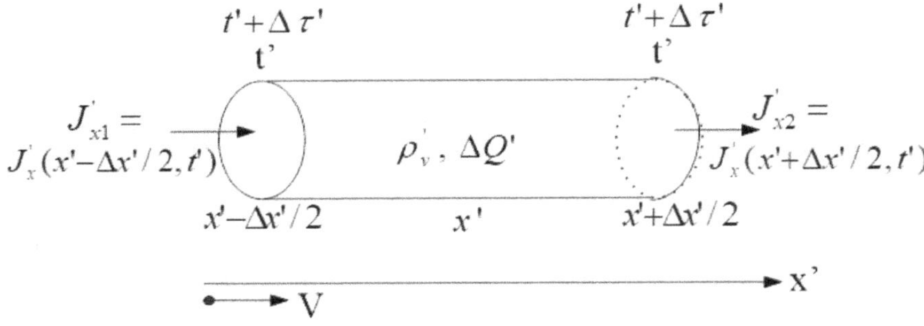

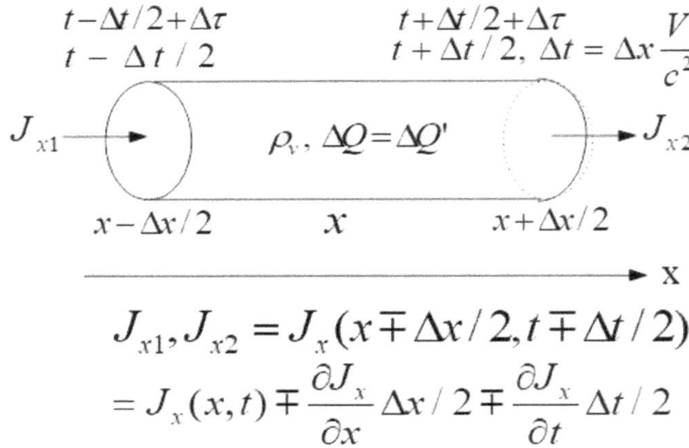

$$J_{x1}, J_{x2} = J_x(x \mp \Delta x/2, t \mp \Delta t/2)$$

$$= J_x(x,t) \mp \frac{\partial J_x}{\partial x} \Delta x/2 \mp \frac{\partial J_x}{\partial t} \Delta t/2$$

FIGURE 4

3.2. Current in Arbitrary Direction. In the above derivation, for simplicity we have considered only x-directed current (along the relative velocity). If the current is along an arbitrary direction, with x, y and z components, the above derivation may be extended. It can be shown that the same relationship between the charge density and current would be valid for the general case as well. It may not be necessary to present all derivation steps for the general case with all current directions. We will provide a conceptual picture, and discuss necessary changes in the above derivation.

For the general treatment, the volume element in the above experiment (Fig.4) may now be considered to be a rectangular box with dimensions Δx, Δy and Δz in the three rectangular coordinates. The space-time coordinates for the center of the box is (x, y, z, t). The volume element would consist of six rectangular faces, defined by the coordinates $(x \pm \Delta x/2, y, z, t \pm \Delta t/2)$, $(x, y \pm \Delta y/2, z, t)$, and $(x, y, z \pm \Delta z/2, t)$. The additional currents J_y and J_z would flow through the xz and xy faces, respectively. Let us consider changes to the equations (28) and (29), when the current continuity experiment is observed in the unprimed coordinates. The experiment is conducted in the primed reference frame ($\Delta t' = 0$). Incremental lengths $\Delta y'$ and $\Delta z'$ in the y and z directions would be observed in the unprimed frame with equal lengths ($\Delta y' = \Delta y$ and $\Delta z' = \Delta z$), at the same instant ($\Delta t = 0$). This is in distinct contrast with the dimensions in the x direction, which are observed in the unprimed frame with incremental time differences. Accordingly, the time increment

Δt would be zero for treatment of currents J_y and J_z in the xz and xy surfaces. With this in mind, the modified version of the equation (28) can be expressed as follows.

$$\Delta\tau\Big[\big(J_x(x+\Delta x/2,t+\Delta t/2)-J_x(x-\Delta x/2,t-\Delta t/2)\big)\Delta y\Delta z$$

$$+\big(J_y(y+\Delta y/2,t)-J_y(y-\Delta y/2,t)\big)\Delta x\Delta z$$

$$+\big(J_z(z+\Delta z/2,t)-J_z(z-\Delta z/2,t)\big)\Delta x\Delta y\Big]=-\tfrac{\partial\Delta Q}{\partial t}\Delta\tau=[-\tfrac{\partial\rho_{v0}}{\partial t}\Delta x\Delta y\Delta z]\Delta\tau,$$

$$\tfrac{\partial J_x}{\partial x}+\tfrac{\partial J_x}{\partial t}\tfrac{V}{c^2}+\tfrac{\partial J_y}{\partial y}+\tfrac{\partial J_z}{\partial z}=-\tfrac{\partial\rho_{v0}}{\partial t},$$

$$\int\big(\tfrac{\partial J_x}{\partial x}+\tfrac{\partial J_y}{\partial y}+\tfrac{\partial J_z}{\partial z}\big)\partial t+\tfrac{V}{c^2}J_x=-\rho_{v0}. \tag{30}$$

When the velocity $V=0$, we know $\rho_{v0}=\rho_v$. Using this condition in the above equation, the integral term can be recognized as $-\rho_v$.

$$\rho_{v0}=\rho_v'\alpha=\rho_v-\tfrac{V}{c^2}J_x=\rho_v+\Delta\rho_v,$$

$$\Delta\rho_v=-\tfrac{V}{c^2}J_x,\quad \tfrac{\partial\rho_v}{\partial t}=-\tfrac{\partial J_x}{\partial x}-\tfrac{\partial J_y}{\partial y}-\tfrac{\partial J_z}{\partial z}. \tag{31}$$

Equation (31), derived here for the general case with current in arbitrary direction, establishes the same relationship (29) we had derived for the simple case with only J_x current. $\Delta\rho_v$, which is the difference between $\rho_{v0}=\alpha\rho_v'$ and ρ_v, depends only on the J_x component of the current. The above general equation is a useful transformation relation between current and charge densities in two reference frames. Note that ρ_v' as observed in (x',t') coordinates ($\Delta t'=0$) depends both on ρ_v and J observed in the (x,t) reference frame. A similar expression can be written relating ρ_v to ρ_v' and J', by switching ρ_v and ρ_v', and replacing V by $-V$. This is equivalent to switching the frame in which the current continuity experiment is conducted and the frame in which it is observed.

$$\rho_v\alpha=\rho_v'+\frac{V}{c^2}J_x'. \tag{32}$$

Substituting ρ_v' in the above equation using (31), a relationship between J_x', ρ_v and J_x can be obtained.

$$J_x'=\tfrac{c^2}{V}(\rho_v\alpha-\rho_v')=\tfrac{c^2}{V}(\rho_v\alpha-\tfrac{\rho_v}{\alpha}+J_x\tfrac{V}{c^2\alpha}),$$

$$J_x'\alpha=J_x-\rho_vV. \tag{33}$$

A similar expression can also be written relating J_x to J_x' and ρ_v'. This is obtained by replacing the primed with corresponding unprimed variables, and replacing V by $-V$. This is equivalent to switching the reference frames of measurement and observation.

$$J_x\alpha=J_x'+\rho_v'V. \tag{34}$$

The equations (31-34) constitute the relativistic transform relations between current and charge densities in different reference frames. Out of the above four relations, any two can be used independently, from which the other two can be derived. The relations appear very much similar to the transform relations between space-time coordinates. The current density represents timing information, and the charge density represents dimensional information (length) for charge distribution.

4. Relativistic Transformation of Gauss' Law for the Electric Field: Ampere's Law

$$t' = \frac{t - x\dfrac{V}{c^2}}{\alpha}, \quad \Delta t' = 0, \quad \Delta t = \Delta x \frac{V}{c^2}$$

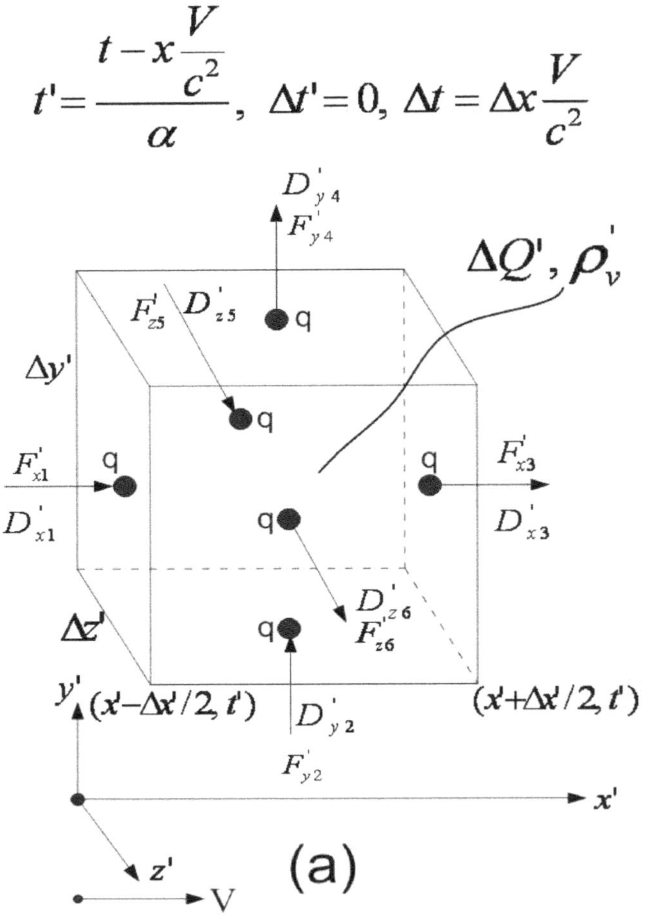

Figure 5

4.1. Gauss' Law for the Electric Field, in the Primed Coordinates.
Consider Gauss' law for the electric field, applied in the primed coordinate system (x', y', z', t') to a closed surface S'.

$$\sum_{S'} \overline{D}'_i \cdot \overline{\Delta S}'_i = \Delta Q', \tag{35}$$

where $\Delta Q'$ is the total charge inside the surface S'. In reference to the Fig.5a, the above form of Gauss' law may be applied to a closed surface S' consisting of six faces of an elemental rectangular box of dimensions $\Delta x' \times \Delta y' \times \Delta z'$. The equation (35) may be expressed using normal components of the flux density $\overline{D}_i$ at the center of the six faces of the box, and the internal charge density ρ'_v

$$(D'_{x3} - D'_{x1})\Delta y'\Delta z' + (D'_{y4} - D'_{y2})\Delta x'\Delta z' + (D'_{z6} - D'_{z5})\Delta y'\Delta x'$$
$$= \Delta Q' = \rho'_v \Delta x'\Delta y'\Delta z'. \tag{36}$$

$$D_{x1}, D_{x3} = D_x(x \mp \Delta x/2, t \mp \Delta t/2) =$$

$$D_x(x,t) \mp \frac{\partial D_x}{\partial x} \Delta x/2 \mp \frac{\partial D_x}{\partial t} \Delta t/2$$

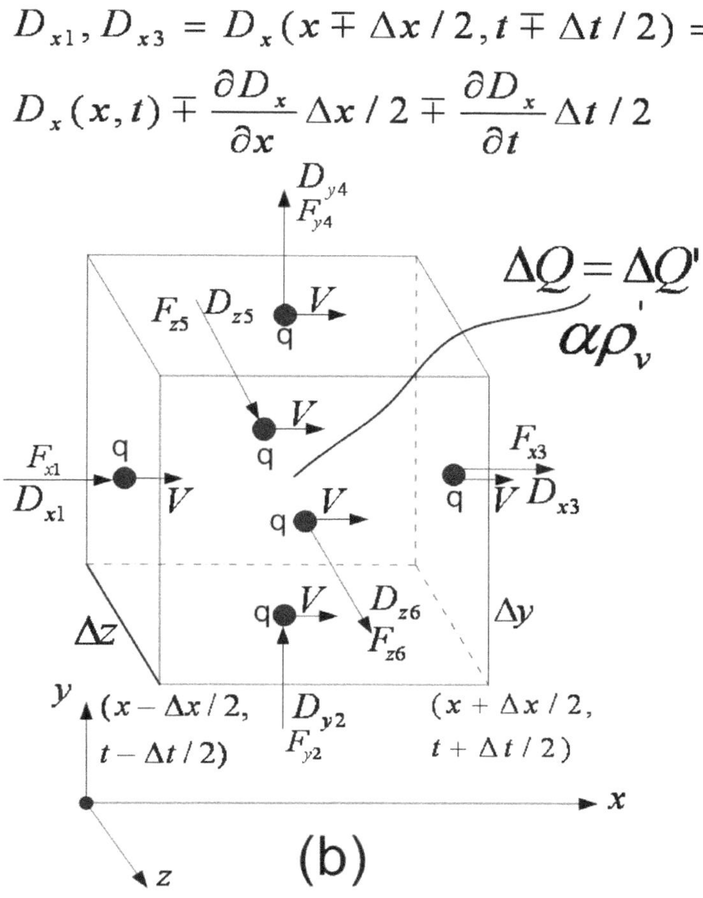

FIGURE 5. (a) Electric field divergence (Gauss' law) experiment in the (x',y',z',t') reference frame, and (b) the same experiment as seen by an observer from the (x,y,z,t) reference frame.

The above summation form of Gauss' law may also be expressed equivalently using derivatives of the flux density $\overline{D}'$ at the center of the box.

$$(D'_{x3} - D'_{x1})\Delta y'\Delta z' + (D'_{y4} - D'_{y2})\Delta x'\Delta z' + (D'_{z6} - D'_{z5})\Delta y'\Delta x' = (\rho_v')\Delta x'\Delta y'\Delta z'$$

$$= \frac{\partial D'_x}{\partial x'}\triangle x'\Delta y'\Delta z' + \frac{\partial D'_y}{\partial y'}\triangle y'\Delta x'\Delta z' + \frac{\partial D'_z}{\partial z'}\triangle z'\Delta y'\Delta x' = \rho_v'\Delta x'\Delta y'\Delta z',$$

$$\frac{\partial D'_x}{\partial x'} + \frac{\partial D'_y}{\partial y'} + \frac{\partial D'_z}{\partial z'} = \rho_v'. \tag{37}$$

4.2. A Basic Gauss' Law Experiment as Measured from Two Reference Frames. Let an observer in the primed coordinate system conduct an experiment to verify or validate Gauss' law for the rectangular box, placed in a free-space medium. The observer would need to measure the normal component of the electric field $\overline{E}_i$ for each of the six faces, $i = 1, .., 6$, of the rectangular box, from which the corresponding normal component of the flux density $\overline{D}_i = \epsilon_0 \overline{E}_i$ can be calculated. The electric field and the flux density are fundamentally defined in terms of the force experienced by a given stationary charge q.

$$\overline{F}' = q\overline{E}' = \frac{q}{\epsilon_0}\overline{D}', \quad \overline{D}' = \frac{\epsilon_0}{q}\overline{F}'.\tag{38}$$

Accordingly, in order to validate Gauss' law, the observer may place a reference stationary charge q at the center of each face of the rectangular box, and then measure the force $\overline{F}'_i$ experienced by the charge using an appropriate measurement technique. Now, Gauss' law in the summation form of equation (36) may be expressed in terms of the measured normal components of the force and the charge density ρ'_v as follows.

$$\frac{\epsilon_0}{q}(F'_{x3} - F'_{x1})\Delta y'\Delta z' + \frac{\epsilon_0}{q}(F'_{y4} - F'_{y2})\Delta x'\Delta z' + \frac{\epsilon_0}{q}(F'_{z6} - F'_{z5})\Delta y'\Delta x'$$
$$= \rho'_v\Delta x'\Delta y'\Delta z'.\tag{39}$$

The above experiment in the primed coordinates is conducted at a given time t'. In other words, all the above force measurements are conducted simultaneously in the primed coordinate system, with time difference $\Delta t'$ between experiments at different faces equal to zero. Now, let the experiment be observed from the unprimed coordinate system. The force measurements on the six faces, performed simultaneously in the primed coordinates ($\Delta t' = 0$), would not be observed simultaneously in the unprimed coordinates ($\Delta t \neq 0$). Using the relativistic transformation relations (10,24) one may relate the time (Δt) and location (Δx) parameters of observation in the unprimed reference frame. The timing would be independent of the y and z coordinates. In other words, Δt would only depend on Δx, not on Δy or Δz.

$$t' = \frac{t - xV/c^2}{\alpha}, \quad x' = \frac{x - Vt}{\alpha},$$
$$\Delta t' = \frac{\Delta t - \Delta x V/c^2}{\alpha} = 0, \quad \Delta t = \Delta x V/c^2,$$
$$\Delta x' = \frac{\Delta x - \Delta t V}{\alpha} = \frac{\Delta x - \Delta x V^2/c^2}{\alpha} = \alpha\Delta x, \quad \Delta x = \frac{\Delta x'}{\alpha},$$
$$y = y', \quad z = z', \quad \Delta y = \Delta y', \quad \Delta z = \Delta z'.\tag{40}$$

Accordingly, the forces $\overline{F}'_i$ measured simultaneously in the primed coordinate system would be measured as $\overline{F}_i$ in the unprimed coordinates at different times. The corresponding charge density, as observed from the unprimed frame, would be $\rho_{v0} = \rho'_v\Delta x'/\Delta x = \rho'_v\alpha$. This is shown in the last section, and is different from the charge density ρ'_v, normally measured in the primed reference frame at a given time $t', \Delta t' = 0$. As derived in the last section, in equations (29,31), ρ_{v0} would also be different from the charge density ρ_v one would normally measure in the unprimed coordinates at a given time $t, \Delta t = 0$,

$$\rho_{v0} = \rho_v + \Delta\rho_v = \rho_v - J_x V/c^2.\tag{41}$$

As per the general principle of relativity, any "basic" experiment conducted in one coordinate system should lead to the same conclusion when measured or observed from another coordinate system, moving with an uniform velocity with respect to each other. The Gauss' law experiment, which establishes the basic defining relationship for the charge, may be considered one such basic experiment. This assumes that a given charge, as fundamentally defined by Gauss' law, is relativistically invariant, which means the value of the charge is independent of the relative velocity of the charge and the observer. Accordingly, the results of measurement in (39) would lead to the following relationship between the forces $\overline{F}_i$ and the charge density ρ_v

$$\frac{\epsilon_0}{q}(F_{x3} - F_{x1})\Delta y \Delta z + \frac{\epsilon_0}{q}(F_{y4} - F_{y2})\Delta x \Delta z + \frac{\epsilon_0}{q}(F_{z6} - F_{z5})\Delta y \Delta x$$

$$= (\rho_v + \Delta\rho_v)\Delta x \Delta y \Delta z = (\rho_v - J_x V/c^2)\Delta x \Delta y \Delta z. \tag{42}$$

4.3. Recognizing the Need for a New Force Field. Let us first assume that the force on a reference charge in the unprimed frame is produced due to the electric force, in a conventional sense. With this assumption, the forces $\overline{F}_i$ and the equivalent flux densities at different faces of the test box (see Fig.5) may be related to the flux density $\overline{D}$ at the center of the box (x, y, z, t) using derivatives. Remember that the flux densities in the above experiment at different locations are measured in the unprimed coordinates at different times, as per the space-time relations (40).

$$F_{x1} = \frac{q}{\epsilon_0}D_{x1} = \frac{q}{\epsilon_0}D_x(x - \triangle x/2, t - \triangle t/2) = \frac{q}{\epsilon_0}(D_x - \frac{\partial D_x}{\partial x}\Delta x/2$$

$$- \frac{\partial D_x}{\partial t}\Delta t/2) = \frac{q}{\epsilon_0}(D_x - \frac{\partial D_x}{\partial x}\Delta x/2 - \frac{\partial D_x}{\partial t}\frac{V}{c^2}\Delta x/2),$$

$$F_{x3} = \frac{q}{\epsilon_0}D_{x3} = \frac{q}{\epsilon_0}D_x(x + \triangle x/2, t + \triangle t/2) = \frac{q}{\epsilon_0}(D_x + \frac{\partial D_x}{\partial x}\Delta x/2$$

$$+ \frac{\partial D_x}{\partial t}\Delta t/2) = \frac{q}{\epsilon_0}(D_x + \frac{\partial D_x}{\partial x}\Delta x/2 + \frac{\partial D_x}{\partial t}\frac{V}{c^2}\Delta x/2),$$

$$F_{y2} = \frac{q}{\epsilon_0}D_{y2} = \frac{q}{\epsilon_0}(D_y - \frac{\partial D_y}{\partial y}\Delta y/2),$$

$$F_{y4} = \frac{q}{\epsilon_0}D_{y4} = \frac{q}{\epsilon_0}(D_y + \frac{\partial D_y}{\partial y}\Delta y/2),$$

$$F_{z5} = \frac{q}{\epsilon_0}D_{z5} = \frac{q}{\epsilon_0}(D_z - \frac{\partial D_z}{\partial z}\Delta z/2),$$

$$F_{z6} = \frac{q}{\epsilon_0}D_{z6} = \frac{q}{\epsilon_0}(D_z + \frac{\partial D_z}{\partial z}\Delta z/2). \tag{43}$$

Note that there is no time difference between the measurements at the center of the faces 4 and 2, and similarly those of faces 6 and 5. This is because they differ only in their y and z coordinates with respect to the center of the box. The time difference Δt of observation at two locations is dependent only on the x coordinates of the locations. Now, using the force expressions of (43) in the equation (42), we get,

$$\frac{\partial D_x}{\partial x} + \frac{\partial D_x}{\partial t}\frac{V}{c^2} + \frac{\partial D_y}{\partial y} + \frac{\partial D_z}{\partial z} = \rho_{v0} + \Delta\rho_v = \rho_v - J_x\frac{V}{c^2}. \tag{44}$$

The above measurement for Gauss' law for the electric field was originally performed in the primed coordinates, which was then observed from the unprimed coordinates. The experiment may also be duplicated in the unprimed reference frame itself. In this case, the measurements in the different faces of the box is to be performed simultaneously in the unprimed coordinates $\Delta t = 0$. The results of this experiment may be obtained from the equivalent expression (37) in the primed coordinates, by simply substituting the primed variables by the corresponding unprimed variables. This would be the differential form of Gauss' law in the unprimed rectangular coordinates.

$$\frac{\partial D_x}{\partial x} + \frac{\partial D_y}{\partial y} + \frac{\partial D_z}{\partial z} = \rho_v. \tag{45}$$

Equation (44) would be clearly inconsistent with the equation (45) for general conditions with a non-zero current density $\overline{J}$ and/or a time-varying electric flux density $\overline{D}$. Let us examine the possible source of this inconsistency. We assume that Gauss' law for electric field applies universally in all reference frames. This means the equivalent expressions of Gauss' law in (35-39) for the primed coordinates, and in (45) for the unprimed coordinates, must be correct. We also assume that the basic postulate of relativity, which requires that a validation experiment for a basic theory should lead to equivalent conclusions when conducted in one reference frame, and when the experiment is observed from another frame moving with a constant relative velocity. Accordingly, the deduction of the equations (42) through relativistic transformation of Gauss' law in (39) must also be correct. This leaves equations (43,44) to be examined for any deficiency. The total forces on the reference charges, which are expected to satisfy the relationship (42), may not have been properly characterized in the equations (43,44).

Note that the reference charges q in the experiment are assumed to be stationary in the primed coordinates, in which the experiment was originally conducted. This experiment in the primed coordinates is described by the force and field equations (35-39). These equations are based on Gauss' law and on the definition of the electric field as the total force on a unit stationary reference charge. However, when the experiment is observed from the unprimed coordinates, the reference charges are no longer stationary, and are moving with a velocity V along the x direction. The total forces experienced by these moving reference charges in the unprimed coordinates have been established also using the electric fields through the equations (43,44). Now, the forces in (35-39), where the charges are stationary, are assumed to be valid, leading also to the validity of the force equation in (42). Whereas, those in (43,44), where the charges are moving, we suspect could be wrong. Therefore, one would conclude that the forces in (43,44) will have to be corrected with additional parts that must dependent on the velocity of the reference charge q.

The essential conclusion is that, the force experienced by a moving charge may have to be characterized differently from that by a stationary charge. The total force on a stationary charge is determined as the product of the charge and the electric field, as per the very definition of the electric field. Having defined the force on a stationary charge this way, the total force on a moving charge may not also be characterized in the same way - as the product of the charge and the electric field - by simply ignoring possible contributions due to its velocity. Additional force effects that depend on the velocity of the charge may have to be introduced. Otherwise, the forces on an electric charge would be relativistically inconsistent and incomplete, as we have now encountered. This is an important basic finding.

4.4. **Force Correction, the Magnetic Field, and Ampere's Law.** As per the above discussion, we seek to adjust the forces in the equations (43,44), such that the total forces would satisfy (42), as well as be consistent with (45). Note that the differences between the equations (44) and (45) are linear with velocity V. This suggests, in order that the revised versions of (43,44) be consistent with (45), any new motion-dependent force that needs to be added to (43,44) should be linearly dependent on the charge velocity. Further, the new force might possibly be directed along or perpendicular to the charge velocity. However, if one would proceed by adding a new force directed along the charge velocity V, it can be shown not to resolve the above inconsistency. The new force $\overline{\Delta F}$ will have to be directed perpendicular to the charge velocity. With the charge velocity along the $\hat{x}$ direction, this means $\overline{\Delta F}$ may only have a non-zero $\hat{y}$ or $\hat{z}$ component ($\triangle F_z \neq 0$, $\triangle F_y \neq 0$), with its $\hat{x}$ component equal to zero ($\triangle F_x = 0$). Accordingly, in reference to the Fig.5b, we need to revise the normal-force equations (43,44) by adding new normal forces ΔF_{y2}, ΔF_{y4}, ΔF_{z5} and ΔF_{z6}, respectively for the faces 2, 4, 5 and 6. These would be in addition to the conventional normal forces due to the electric field. Whereas, no new normal force would be added for the faces 1 and 3. This is because, for these two surfaces the normal directions are $\pm\hat{x}$, along which the new force would be zero ($\Delta F_x = 0$), as we explained.

$$F_{x3} = \tfrac{q}{\epsilon_0} D_{x3},$$

$$F_{x1} = \tfrac{q}{\epsilon_0} D_{x1},$$

$$F_{y4} = \tfrac{q}{\epsilon_0} D_{y4} + \Delta F_4,$$

$$F_{y2} = \tfrac{q}{\epsilon_0} D_{y2} + \Delta F_2,$$

$$F_{z6} = \tfrac{q}{\epsilon_0} D_{z6} + \Delta F_6,$$

$$F_{z5} = \tfrac{q}{\epsilon_0} D_{z5} + \Delta F_5,$$

$$\Delta x \Delta y \Delta z \left(\tfrac{\partial D_x}{\partial x} + \tfrac{\partial D_x}{\partial t}\tfrac{V}{c^2}\right) + \Delta x \Delta z \left[\tfrac{\partial D_y}{\partial y}\Delta y + (\Delta F_{y4} - \Delta F_{y2})\tfrac{\epsilon_0}{q}\right]$$

$$+\Delta x \Delta y \left[\tfrac{\partial D_z}{\partial z}\Delta z + (\Delta F_{z6} - \Delta F_{z5})\tfrac{\epsilon_0}{q}\right] = (\rho_v - J_x \tfrac{V}{c^2})\Delta x \Delta y \Delta z. \tag{46}$$

Combining the equations (45,46), we get

$$\Delta x \Delta y \Delta z \tfrac{\partial D_x}{\partial t}\tfrac{V}{c^2} + \Delta x \Delta z (\Delta F_{y4} - \Delta F_{y2})\tfrac{\epsilon_0}{q} + \Delta x \Delta y (\Delta F_{z6} - \Delta F_{z5}) = -J_x \tfrac{V}{c^2}\Delta x \Delta y \Delta z,$$

$$\Delta y \Delta z \left(\tfrac{\partial D_x}{\partial t} + J_x\right)\tfrac{V}{c^2} = (\Delta F_{y2} - \Delta F_{y4})\tfrac{\epsilon_0}{q}\Delta z + (\Delta F_{z5} - \Delta F_{z6})\tfrac{\epsilon_0}{q}\Delta y,$$

$$\Delta y \Delta z \left(\tfrac{\partial D_x}{\partial t} + J_x\right) = [(\Delta F_{y2} - \Delta F_{y4})\Delta z + (\Delta F_{z5} - \Delta F_{z6})\Delta y]\tfrac{\epsilon_0 c^2}{qV}. \tag{47}$$

For analytical convenience, one may define a new vector $\overline{H}$, using which any additional force $\overline{\Delta F}$ is indirectly expressed in terms of the charge velocity $\bar{v}$ as follows:

$$\frac{q}{\epsilon_0 c^2}\bar{v} \times \overline{H} = \overline{\Delta F} = q\mu_0 \bar{v} \times \overline{H}, \quad \mu_0 = \frac{1}{\epsilon_0 c^2}. \tag{48}$$

The force is defined proportional to the cross product of the velocity vector with $\overline{H}$. This would ensure that the magnitude of the force is proportional to the velocity, and the force is directed normal to the direction of the velocity, as per our expectation discussed earlier. The components of the new force that are normal to different faces of the test box may be related to appropriate components of the new vector $\overline{H}$.

$$\overline{\Delta F}_2 = q\mu_0 V \hat{x} \times \overline{H}_2, \ \Delta F_{y2} = \hat{y} \cdot \overline{\Delta F}_2 = -q\mu_0 V H_{z2},$$

$$\overline{\Delta F}_4 = q\mu_0 V \hat{x} \times \overline{H}_4, \ \Delta F_{y4} = \hat{y} \cdot \overline{\Delta F}_4 = -q\mu_0 V H_{z4},$$

$$\overline{\Delta F}_5 = q\mu_0 V \hat{x} \times \overline{H}_5, \ \Delta F_{z5} = \hat{z} \cdot \overline{\Delta F}_5 = q\mu_0 V H_{y5},$$

$$\overline{\Delta F}_6 = q\mu_0 V \hat{x} \times \overline{H}_6, \ \Delta F_{z6} = \hat{z} \cdot \overline{\Delta F}_6 = q\mu_0 V H_{y6}. \tag{49}$$

Now combine equations (47) and (49) .

$$\Delta y \Delta z \left(\tfrac{\partial D_x}{\partial t} + J_x\right) = -H_{z2}\Delta z + H_{z4}\Delta z + H_{y5}\Delta y - H_{y6}\Delta y$$

$$= \sum_{\Delta C} \overline{H}_i \cdot \overline{\Delta l_i} , \tag{50}$$

$$\left(J_x + \frac{\partial D_x}{\partial t}\right)\Delta S = \sum_{\Delta C} \overline{H}_i \cdot \overline{\Delta l_i} = \left(\overline{J} + \frac{\partial \overline{D}}{\partial t}\right) \cdot \overline{\Delta S}. \tag{51}$$

The loop ΔC refers to a closed rectangular loop parallel to the face 3 of the rectangular box in Fig.5b, passing through the center of the box. This is shown separately in the Fig.6. Further, the orientation of the path of the loop ΔC is such that the normal direction to the enclosed surface vector $\overline{\Delta S}$, as per the right-hand rule, is along the normal to the face 3 of the box (that is, along $+\hat{x}$).

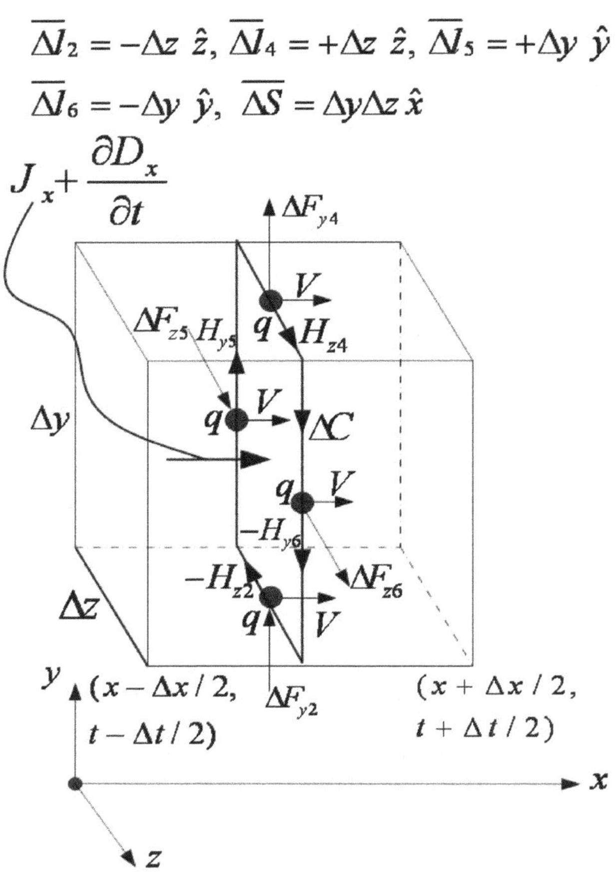

FIGURE 6. Deduction of Ampere's law from the Electric field divergence (Gauss' law) experiment of Fig.5, as seen by an observer from the (x,y,z,t) reference frame.

We have found a relationship (51) for the new force field $\overline{H}$, such that the equation (42) is satisfied for the total forces, as observed in the unprimed reference frame. This means that the Gauss' law experiment in the primed coordinates would now be consistent or equivalent when observed from the unprimed coordinates, as fundamentally required. The orientation of ΔC, and the normal to the enclosed surface $\overline{\Delta S}$, used in the above derivation of (51) are established by the direction of the relative motion between the primed and unprimed frames of reference. We happened to have selected the direction of the relative velocity $\overline{V}$ to be along $\hat{x}$. In general, by doing the analysis with velocity $\overline{V}$ in an arbitrary direction, it may be recognized that the equation (51) would apply for an elemental closed loop ΔC, and its enclosed surface $\overline{\Delta S}$, having any arbitrary orientation.

$$\sum_{\Delta C} \overline{H}_i \cdot \overline{\Delta l_i} = (\overline{J} + \frac{\partial \overline{D}}{\partial t}) \cdot \overline{\Delta S}. \tag{52}$$

The equation (52) is Ampere's law expressed for an elemental loop. The new force field described by the vector $\overline{H}$, which we have defined in (48), may be recognized as the magnetic field. The above relationship (52) may also be expressed using the curl operator.

$$\sum_{\Delta C} \overline{H}_i \cdot \overline{\Delta l_i} = (\overline{\nabla} \times \overline{H}) \cdot \overline{\Delta S} = (\overline{J} + \frac{\partial \overline{D}}{\partial t}) \cdot \overline{\Delta S}, \ \overline{\nabla} \times \overline{H} = \overline{J} + \frac{\partial \overline{D}}{\partial t}. \tag{53}$$

The obvious implication of the derivation is that Ampere's law no longer has to be established as an independent law. It can be derived as a direct consequence of Gauss' law for the electric field, through relativistic transformation. Interestingly, the magnetic field, which relates to the electric current and flux density through Ampere's law, may be interpreted as a new "synthesized" field. This synthesized field will have to be added in order that Gauss' law for the electric field is generalized across reference frames through the principle of relativistic equivalence. This unique interpretation of the magnetic field, from the view point of the relativistic transformation, is a significant development.

5. Relativistic Transformation of Gauss' Law for the Magnetic Field: Faraday's Law

The new magnetic field $\overline{H}$ was introduced in order that Gauss' law for the electric field is relativistically consistent. Now, analogous to the electric flux density and flux, we define a magnetic flux density to be $\overline{B} = \mu_0 \overline{H}$, using which magnetic flux over a given surface can be determined. Further, like Gauss' law for the electric field, we may establish Gauss' law for the magnetic field in terms of the magnetic flux. This defines the total flux over a closed surface to the total charge enclosed by the surface. The charge in this case is referred to as the magnetic charge Q_m from which the magnetic field is supposed to originate or diverge from. However, no magnetic charge has been found to exist naturally, in which case the magnetic charge used in Gauss' law for the magnetic field would be zero. In any case, like Gauss' law for the electric field, Gauss' law for the magnetic field may also be considered to be the basic governing relationship for the magnetic field, which is relativistically invariant. Accordingly, let Gauss' law for the magnetic field be "observed" from different relativistic frames, in order to see what additional relationship the magnetic field will have to satisfy so that it is relativistically consistent. We will closely follow the process employed in the last section for Gauss' law for the electric field, but suitably extended to Gauss' law for the magnetic field. This is presented in the following, leading to Faraday's law as an additional relationship that must be established between the magnetic and electric fields.

5.1. Gauss' Law for the Magnetic Field, in the Primed Coordinates.

Consider Gauss' law for the magnetic field, applied in the primed coordinate system (x', y', z', t') to a closed surface S'.

$$\sum_{S'} \overline{B}'_i \cdot \overline{\Delta S}'_i = 0. \tag{54}$$

As mentioned above, this is similar to Gauss' law for the electric field, except that the magnetic charge is assumed here to be zero for real-word phenomena. One may sometimes find hypothetical or equivalent magnetic charges included in electromagnetic modeling. Such magnetic charges are used only for useful analytical manipulations, and should not be confused to be physically realistic. Such hypothetical magnetic charges can be included in Gauss' law for analytical generality. In this case, the right side of the Gauss' law equation (54) is simply replaced by the total equivalent

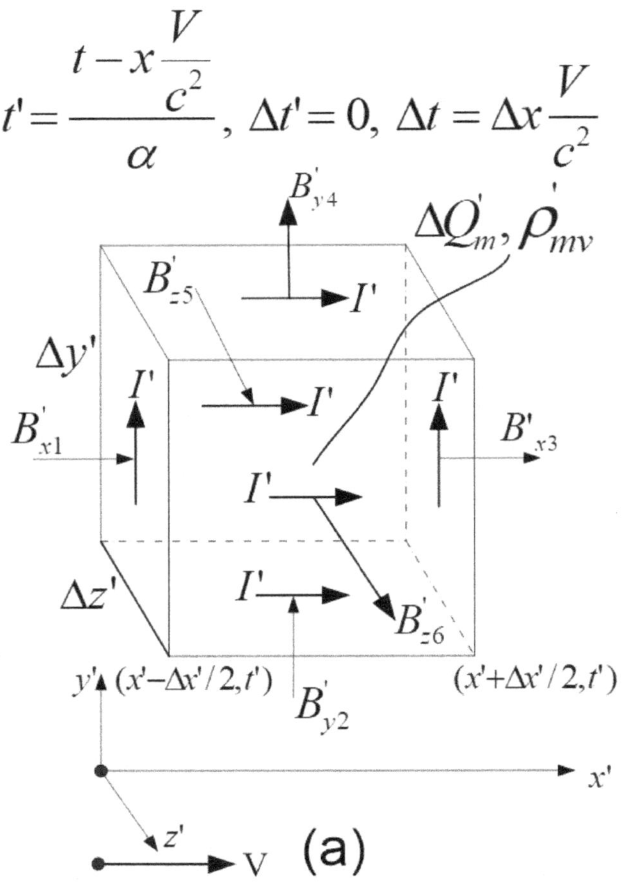

FIGURE 7

magnetic charge $\Delta Q'_m$ inside the closed surface S'. For all analytical considerations, the magnetic charge would be treated analogous to the electric charge. The magnetic charge would be assumed to be relativistically invariant. All derivations and relationships established for electric charge and current in the last sections, can also be equivalently extended for magnetic charge and magnetic current.

$$\sum_{S'} \overline{B}'_i \cdot \overline{\Delta S}'_i = \Delta Q'_m. \tag{55}$$

In reference to the Fig.7a, the above form (55) of Gauss' law may be applied to a specific closed surface S', consisting of six faces of an elemental rectangular box of dimensions $\Delta x' \times \Delta y' \times \Delta z'$. For this case, the equation (55) may be expressed using normal components of the flux density $\overline{B}_i$ at the center of each of the six faces of the box, and the equivalent magnetic charge density ρ'_{mv} at the center of the box. The magnetic charge $\Delta Q'_m$ is expresses as $\rho'_{mv}\triangle x'\triangle y'\triangle z'$, which is the product of the equivalent magnetic charge density and the the elemental volume of the box.

$$B_{x1}, B_{x3} = B_x(x \mp \Delta x/2, t \mp \Delta t/2)$$

$$= B_x(x,t) \mp \frac{\partial B_x}{\partial x}\Delta x/2 \mp \frac{\partial B_x}{\partial t}\Delta t/2$$

$$\Delta l_1 = \Delta l_3, \quad \Delta l_2 = \Delta l_4 = \Delta l_5 = \Delta l_6$$

$$I_1 = I_3, \quad I_2 = I_4 = I_5 = I_6$$

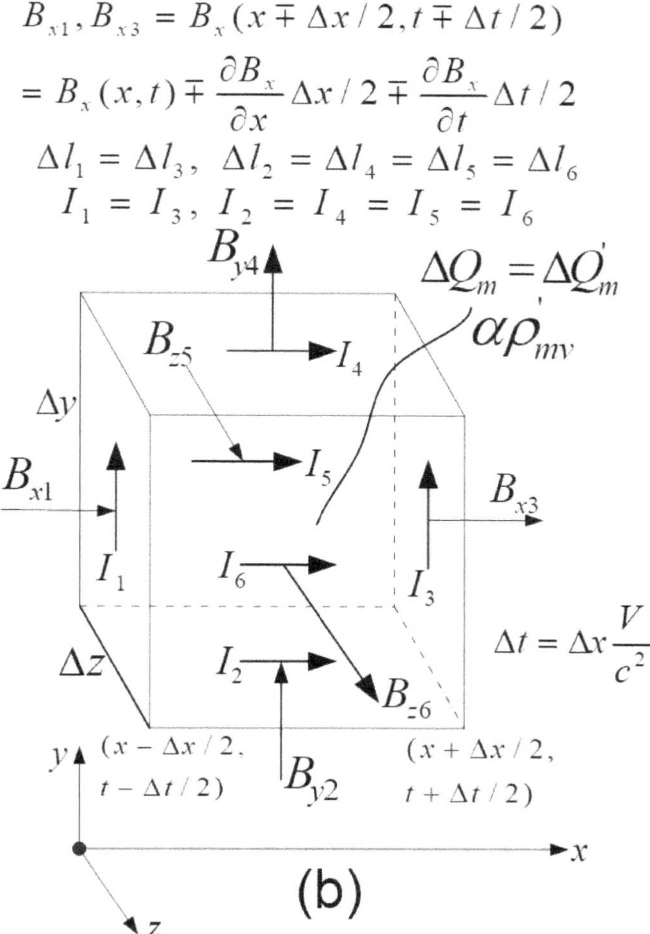

FIGURE 7. (a) Magnetic field divergence (Gauss' law) experiment in the (x',y',z',t') reference frame, and (b) the same experiment as seen by an observer from the (x,y,z,t) reference frame.

$$(B'_{x3} - B'_{x1})\Delta y'\Delta z' + (B'_{y4} - B'_{y2})\Delta x'\Delta z' + (B'_{z6} - B'_{z5})\Delta y'\Delta x' = \Delta Q'_m$$
$$= \rho'_{mv}\triangle x'\triangle y'\triangle z'. \tag{56}$$

The above summation form of Gauss' law may also be expressed using derivatives of the flux density $\overline{B}'$ at the center of the box.

$$(B'_{x3} - B'_{x1})\Delta y'\Delta z' + (B'_{y4} - B'_{y2})\Delta x'\Delta z' + (B'_{z6} - B'_{z5})\Delta y'\Delta x' =$$
$$\frac{\partial B'_x}{\partial x'}\triangle x'\Delta y'\Delta z' + \frac{\partial B'_y}{\partial y'}\triangle y'\Delta x'\Delta z' + \frac{\partial B'_z}{\partial z'}\triangle z'\Delta y'\Delta x' =$$
$$\rho'_{mv}\triangle x'\triangle y'\triangle z',$$
$$\frac{\partial B'_x}{\partial x'} + \frac{\partial B'_y}{\partial y'} + \frac{\partial B'_z}{\partial z'} = \rho'_{mv}. \tag{57}$$

5.2. **A Basic Gauss' Law Experiment in the Primed Reference Frame.** Let an observer in the primed coordinate system conduct an experiment to verify or validate Gauss' law for the rectangular box, placed in a free-space medium. With reference to the Gauss' law expression of (56), the observer would need to measure the normal components of the flux density $\overline{B}_i = \mu_0 \overline{H}_i$ for each of the six faces, $i = 1, .., 6$, of the rectangular box S'. The magnetic field $\overline{H}_i$ or the flux density $\overline{B}_i$ are fundamentally defined in terms of the force experienced by a given current element $\overline{I}'$ of a given length $\Delta l'$. This is equivalent to the definition of (48), applied in the primed frame, where $q\overline{v}' = \overline{I}' v' \Delta t = \Delta l' \overline{I}'$.

$$\overline{F}' = \Delta l' \overline{I}' \times \overline{B}' = \mu_0 \Delta l' \overline{I}' \times \overline{H}'. \tag{58}$$

Accordingly, one may measure the force on a reference current element, from which a particular component of the magnetic field or flux density can be deduced. As per the equation (58), the component of the magnetic field which is aligned along the current element would not contribute to the total force. Therefore, one can not deduce the the component of the magnetic field along the current element from the force measurement. This implies, in order to measure the normal component of the magnetic field on a particular face of the elemental box, as needed in the validation experiment, one would like to place the reference current element parallel to the face. With this in mind, let us choose the reference currents on faces 1 and 3 to be along the y direction, but along the x direction for all other faces. For simplicity, let us select the magnitude of each reference current to be the same.

Accordingly, a conducting wire is placed centered on each face of the rectangular box, directed along the x direction for faces 2, 4, 5 and 6, but along the y direction for faces 1 and 3. Each wire is excited with a current of magnitude I'. The forces $\overline{F}'_i$ experienced by a given section $\Delta l'$ of the current wire is then measured using an appropriate technique. The actual length of the reference current, over which the force measurement is conducted, is not really critical, because we are interested in the magnetic field or flux density, which is defined in terms of the force per unit length. However, for simplicity, we have specified the reference sections of the currents over which the fore is measured on each face to be of equal length $\Delta l'$. Now, the normal magnetic field components on each face are related to appropriate force components, as per (58).

$$\overline{F}'_1 = \Delta l' I' \hat{y} \times \overline{B}'_1, \quad -F'_{z1} = \Delta l' I' B'_{x1}, \quad B'_{x1} = -\frac{F'_{z1}}{\Delta l' I'},$$

$$\overline{F}'_3 = \Delta l' I' \hat{y} \times \overline{B}'_3, \quad -F'_{z3} = \Delta l' I' B'_{x3}, \quad B'_{x3} = -\frac{F'_{z3}}{\Delta l' I'},$$

$$\overline{F}'_2 = \Delta l' I' \hat{x} \times \overline{B}'_2, \quad F'_{z2} = \Delta l' I' B'_{y2}, \quad B'_{y2} = \frac{F'_{z2}}{\Delta l' I'},$$

$$\overline{F}'_4 = \Delta l' I' \hat{x} \times \overline{B}'_4, \quad F'_{z4} = \Delta l' I' B'_{y4}, \quad B'_{y4} = \frac{F'_{z4}}{\Delta l' I'},$$

$$\overline{F}'_5 = \Delta l' I' \hat{x} \times \overline{B}'_5, \quad -F'_{y5} = \Delta l' I' B'_{z5}, \quad B'_{z5} = -\frac{F'_{y5}}{\Delta l' I'},$$

$$\overline{F}'_6 = \Delta l' I' \hat{x} \times \overline{B}'_6, \quad -F'_{y6} = \Delta l' I' B'_{z6}, \quad B'_{z6} = -\frac{F'_{y6}}{\Delta l' I'}. \tag{59}$$

The Gauss' law equation (56) can be expressed in terms of the measured force components in (59).

$$(B'_{x3} - B'_{x1})\Delta y' \Delta z' + (B'_{y4} - B'_{y2})\Delta x' \Delta z' + (B'_{z6} - B'_{z5})\Delta y' \Delta x' =$$

$$\frac{1}{I'\Delta l'}[(-F'_{z3} + F'_{z1})\Delta y' \Delta z' + (F'_{z4} - F'_{z2})\Delta x' \Delta z' (-F'_{y6} + F'_{y5})\Delta x' \Delta y'] =$$

$$\Delta Q'_m = \rho'_{mv} \Delta x' \Delta y' \Delta z'. \tag{60}$$

The above equation (60) is a form of Gauss' law for the magnetic field, expressed in terms of the force components on the reference current elements. For a known charge density ρ'_{mv}, this relationship can be experimentally verified by measuring the force components, for given values of the reference currents and the length elements, It may be noted that the above experiment is conducted in the primed coordinates, at a fixed time t'. In other words, all the above force measurements are conducted simultaneously in the primed coordinate system, with time difference $\Delta t'$ between measurements at different faces equal to zero.

5.3. The Experiment as Observed from the Unprimed Frame.

Now, let the above physical experiment, originally conducted in the primed frame, be "observed" from the unprimed coordinate system, as shown in Fig.7b. As per the general principle of relativity, any "basic" physical experiment conducted in one reference frame should lead to the same conclusion when the experiment is observed or measured from another coordinate frame, moving with an uniform velocity with respect to each other. The Gauss' law experiment may be considered one such basic experiment. It establishes a fundamental relationship between the measured forces experienced by reference current elements and any enclosed equivalent magnetic charges. Accordingly, the governing relationship (60) for the experiment performed in the primed frame is expected to remain invariant when the frame of observation is switched. In other words, the governing equation (60) should remain valid, when the different parameters in (60) are properly substituted by their new values of measurement, when the same physical experiment is observed from the unprimed frame.

$$\left[(-\frac{F_{z3}}{I_3\Delta l_3} + \frac{F_{z1}}{I_1\Delta l_1})\Delta y\Delta z + (\frac{F_{z4}}{I_4\Delta l_4} - \frac{F_{z2}}{I_2\Delta l_2})\Delta x\Delta z + (-\frac{F_{y6}}{I_6\Delta l_6} + \frac{F_{y5}}{I_5\Delta l_5})\Delta x\Delta y\right] = \Delta Q_m. \quad (61)$$

We will examine all the unprimed variables in (61), in contrast with the corresponding primed variables in (60). Fundamental and analytical implications of observing the physical experiment from the unprimed frame will have to be properly understood.

The length element Δx would be different from $\Delta x'$, as per the transform relation (40). Length measurements only along the direction of relative velocity change through relativistic transformation. Whereas, those along directions orthogonal to the relative velocity remain the same. Accordingly, $\Delta y = \Delta y'$ and $\Delta z = \Delta z'$. The timing of measurement on locations with different x coordinates would be different ($\Delta t \neq 0$), whereas those with different y or z, but the same x coordinates would be simultaneous ($\Delta t = 0$). Using the relativistic transformation relations (10,24), one may relate the differential time (Δt) and location (Δx) parameters of observation in the unprimed reference frame. This would lead to the relationship (40) deduced in the last section.

$$\Delta t = \Delta x V/c^2, \ \Delta x' = \alpha\Delta x,$$
$$\Delta y' = \Delta y, \ \Delta z' = \Delta z. \quad (62)$$

Accordingly, the forces on the faces 1 and 3, which differ in their x coordinates, would be measured in the unprimed frame at different times. Whereas, those on all other faces 2, 4, 5, and 6 would be measured simultaneously, because the x coordinates at the center of all these faces have the same x coordinates. The forces $\overline{F}_i$ on a given face maybe in general assumed to be different in magnitude from $\overline{F}'_i$ on the corresponding face.

As we have indicated before, for simplicity of the original measurement in the primed frame, the reference currents I' and their length elements $\Delta l'$ were selected with equal magnitude on all faces. However, they are substituted in (61) with distinct variables I_i and Δl_i, $i = 1, ..., 6$, for the six faces. This is because the reference currents having equal magnitude in the unprimed frame may no longer be equal when measured in the unprimed frame. If desired, these reference currents and length elements can be related to I' and $\Delta l'$, and consequently with each other, using space-time transform relations. The final outcome of our present derivation happens to be independent of their actual magnitudes. Therefore, we choose to keep them as distinct variables just to be technically correct, without any further analysis or simplification.

The equivalent magnetic charge and current parameters, as seen in the two frames, can be treated analogous to electric charge and current parameters. The total magnetic charge $\Delta Q'_m = \rho'_{mv}\triangle x'\triangle y'\triangle z'$ is assumed to be invariant to the frame of observation, and, therefore, should be equal to the charge ΔQ_m as observed from the unprimed frame. One may like to define ΔQ_m in terms of a new equivalent charge density ρ_{mv0}, as observed from the unprimed frame, such that $\Delta Q_m = \rho_{mv0}\triangle x\triangle y\triangle z$. Accordingly, we can relate ρ_{mv0} and ρ'_{mv} by equating ΔQ_m and $\Delta Q'_m$: $\rho_{mv0} = \rho'_{mv}\triangle x'/\triangle x = \rho'_{mv}\alpha$. This derivation uses the transformation equation (62) to relate the dimensional variables. Now, ρ'_{mv} or ρ_{mv0} may also be related to the charge density ρ_{mv} one would normally measure in the unprimed coordinates at a given time $t, \Delta t = 0$. We may extend the derivations in the last sections (3,4), equations (29,31,41), to magnetic charges.

$$\rho_{mv0} = \rho'_{mv}\alpha = \rho_{mv} + \Delta\rho_{mv} = \rho_{mv} - M_x V/c^2, \tag{63}$$

where the parameter M represents magnetic current density, which is analogous to J used for the electric current density. By combining (63) with (61), we get,

$$\left[(-\frac{F_{z3}}{I_3\Delta l_3} + \frac{F_{z1}}{I_1\Delta l_1})\Delta y\Delta z + (\frac{F_{z4}}{I_4\Delta l_4} - \frac{F_{z2}}{I_2\Delta l_2})\Delta x\Delta z + (-\frac{F_{y6}}{I_6\Delta l_6} + \frac{F_{y5}}{I_5\Delta l_5})\Delta x\Delta y\right] =$$
$$\Delta Q_m = \rho_{mv0}\triangle x\triangle y\triangle z = (\rho_{mv} - M_x V/c^2)\triangle x\triangle y\triangle z. \tag{64}$$

5.3.1. *Charged Reference Currents.* Now, let us examine the forces experienced by the electric current elements $I_i\Delta l_i$, and relate them to suitable field components measured in the unprimed frame. Before we can characterize the forces on the new current elements, we need to examine the nature of these current elements $I_i\Delta l_i$ as seen in the unprimed coordinates. The reference current elements $I'\Delta l'$ used in the original experiment are assumed to be free of charge, so that the forces experienced by the current elements in the primed reference frame are contributed only due to the magnetic fields. That allowed us to directly relate the magnetic fields in Gauss' law to the total forces on the current element, which can be measured. Otherwise, the basic governing equation (60) for the experiment would have been invalid. However, when these charge-free currents are observed from the unprimed frame, they would look charged if the current is directed along x, but remain charge free if directed along y or z. This is governed by the derivations in section 3. An x-directed current I_x and its observed line-charge density ρ_l in the unprimed frame may be related using (29,31,41).

$$\rho'_v\alpha = \rho_v - J_x V/c^2,$$
$$\rho'_l\alpha = \rho_l - I_x V/c^2 = 0, \quad \rho_l = I_x V/c^2,$$
$$\rho'_l = \triangle A\rho'_v = 0, \quad \rho_l = \triangle A\rho_v, \quad I_x = J_x\triangle A. \tag{65}$$

The volume distributions ρ'_v, ρ_v and J_x, in (29,31,41) are substituted in terms of the corresponding line distributions ρ'_l, ρ_l, and I_x, respectively, leading to the above relationship (65). ΔA is the small cross-sectional area of the current element, which approaches zero for an ideal line current. ρ'_v is assumed zero, because the current element is chosen to be charge free in the primed frame. This is equivalent to having ρ'_l also to be zero.

5.3.2. *Force Transformation Using Electric and Magnetic Fields.* With the understanding of the nature of the reference current elements and other relativistic considerations, discussed above, let us characterize the forces components of the Gauss' law equation (64) using different field components measured in the unprimed coordinates. Let us classify the forces in two separate groups, based on the timing of the force measurement and the nature of their reference currents used. The two groups are, (a) forces for the faces 1 and 3, and (b) the forces for the faces 2, 4, 5 and 6. We will discuss the force modeling for these two groups separately.

For the two faces in the first group, the test current elements are directed along y, and therefore do not appear charged, as we have discussed earlier. Consequently, the forces experienced by these current elements may be expressed using magnetic field alone. This group of faces differ in their x coordinates, and therefore the forces measured on these faces in the primed coordinates at a given time $(t', \Delta t' = 0)$ are observed in the unprimed coordinates at different times t, $\Delta t \neq 0$. This is in accordance with the differential space-time relationship (62), as discussed before. Now, the different components of the force and magnetic flux density, as measured in the unprimed frame, can be related using an extension of (59) as follows. The primed variables in (59) are replaced by the corresponding unprimed variables, and the space and time coordinates for different parameters in (59) are specified at the center of corresponding face (see Fig.7b). Further, the fields at the center of the faces are related to those at the center of the box using partial derivatives, and equation (62) is used to relate differential space ($\triangle x$) and time ($\triangle t$) variables.

$$\overline{F}_1 = \Delta l_1 I_1 \hat{y} \times \overline{B}_1, \quad -F_{z1} = \Delta l_1 I_1 B_{x1} = \Delta l_1 I_1 B_x(x - \triangle x/2, t - \triangle t/2)$$
$$= \Delta l_1 I_1 \left(B_x(x,t) - \frac{\triangle x}{2}\frac{\partial B_x(x,t)}{\partial x} - \frac{\triangle t}{2}\frac{\partial B_x(x,t)}{\partial t} \right)$$
$$= \Delta l_1 I_1 \left(B_x(x,t) - \frac{\triangle x}{2}\frac{\partial B_x(x,t)}{\partial x} - \frac{\triangle x V}{2c^2}\frac{\partial B_x(x,t)}{\partial t} \right),$$
$$\overline{F}_3 = \Delta l_3 I_3 \hat{y} \times \overline{B}_3, \quad -F_{z3} = \Delta l_3 I_3 B_{x3} = \Delta l_3 I_3 B_x(x + \triangle x/2, t + \triangle t/2)$$
$$= \Delta l_3 I_3 \left(B_x(x,t) + \frac{\triangle x}{2}\frac{\partial B_x(x,t)}{\partial x} + \frac{\triangle t}{2}\frac{\partial B_x(x,t)}{\partial t} \right)$$
$$= \Delta l_3 I_3 \left(B_x(x,t) + \frac{\triangle x}{2}\frac{\partial B_x(x,t)}{\partial x} + \frac{\triangle x V}{2c^2}\frac{\partial B_x(x,t)}{\partial t} \right). \tag{66}$$

On the other hand, for the second group of faces 2, 4, 5 and 6, the reference currents are directed along x, and therefore they would appear charged, as discussed earlier. Equation (65) can be used to relate the observed line charge density ρ_l to the corresponding line current density I_x. Consequently, the force experienced by these currents are to be expressed using both the magnetic and electric fields. The centers of measurement for the four faces have the same x coordinates. Therefore, as discussed before, the experiment in the primed coordinates at a fixed time $(t', \Delta t' = 0)$ are observed in the unprimed coordinates also at a fixed time t, $\Delta t = 0$. This is in accordance with equation (62). With these above issues in mind, the different components of the force, as measured in the unprimed frame, can now be modeled by adding two contributions: the force due to the magnetic field using an extension of (59), added with the force on the charges on the current elements using appropriate electric field components.

$$\overline{F}_2 = \Delta l_2 I_2 \hat{x} \times \overline{B}_2 + \Delta l_2 \rho_{l2} \overline{E}_2, \quad F_{z2} = \Delta l_2 I_2 B_{y2} + \Delta l_2 \rho_{l2} E_{z2}$$
$$= \Delta l_2 I_2 \left(B_y - \frac{\triangle y}{2}\frac{\partial B_y}{\partial y} \right) + \Delta l_2 I_2 \frac{V}{c^2} E_{z2},$$
$$\overline{F}_4 = \Delta l_4 I_4 \hat{x} \times \overline{B}_4 + \Delta l_4 \rho_{l4} \overline{E}_4, \quad F_{z4} = \Delta l_4 I_4 B_{y4} + \Delta l_4 \rho_{l4} E_{z4}$$
$$= \Delta l_4 I_4 \left(B_y + \frac{\triangle y}{2}\frac{\partial B_y}{\partial y} \right) + \Delta l_4 I_4 \frac{V}{c^2} E_{z4},$$
$$\overline{F}_5 = \Delta l_5 I_5 \hat{x} \times \overline{B}_5 + \Delta l_5 \rho_{l5} \overline{E}_5, \quad -F_{y5} = \Delta l_5 I_5 B_{z5} - \Delta l_5 \rho_{l5} E_{y5}$$
$$= \Delta l_5 I_5 \left(B_z - \frac{\triangle z}{2}\frac{\partial B_z}{\partial z} \right) - \Delta l_5 I_5 \frac{V}{c^2} E_{y5},$$
$$\overline{F}_6 = \Delta l_6 I_6 \hat{x} \times \overline{B}_6 + \Delta l_6 \rho_{l6} \overline{E}_6, \quad -F_{y6} = \Delta l_6 I_6 B_{z6} - \Delta l_6 \rho_{l6} E_{y6}$$
$$= \Delta l_6 I_6 \left(B_z + \frac{\triangle z}{2}\frac{\partial B_z}{\partial z} \right) - \Delta l_6 I_6 \frac{V}{c^2} E_{y6}. \tag{67}$$

The contribution in (67) from the magnetic field have been obtained by replacing the primed variables in (59) by the corresponding unprimed variables. The magnetic field components are measured at the center of particular faces (see Fig.7), which are then related to those at the center of the box using partial derivatives. The force contribution in (67) due to the charges on the current elements is expressed as product of the electric field and the charge. The equation (65) is used for simplification relating line charge density to the line current.

5.4. Faraday's Law, Deduced from the Force Transformation. Now, using the equations (66,67) in the force equation (64)), we get a relationship between the electric and magnetic fields in the unprimed reference frame.

$$\left[(\tfrac{\partial B_x}{\partial x} + \tfrac{V}{c^2}\tfrac{\partial B_x}{\partial t})\Delta x\Delta y\Delta z + (\tfrac{\partial B_y}{\partial y}\Delta y + \tfrac{V}{c^2}E_{z4} - \tfrac{V}{c^2}E_{z2})\Delta x\Delta z + \right.$$

$$\left.(\tfrac{\partial B_z}{\partial z}\Delta z - \tfrac{V}{c^2}E_{y6} + \tfrac{V}{c^2}E_{y5})\Delta x\Delta y\right] = (\rho_{mv} - M_x V/c^2)\Delta x\Delta y\Delta z,$$

$$(\tfrac{\partial B_x}{\partial x} + \tfrac{\partial B_y}{\partial y} + \tfrac{\partial B_z}{\partial z} + \tfrac{V}{c^2}\tfrac{\partial B_x}{\partial t})\Delta x\Delta y\Delta z + \tfrac{V}{c^2}\left[(-E_{y6} + E_{y5})\Delta x\Delta y\right.$$

$$\left. + (E_{z4} - E_{z2})\Delta x\Delta z\right] = (\rho_{mv} - M_x V/c^2)\Delta x\Delta y\Delta z. \tag{68}$$

We have established Gauss' law for the magnetic field in the primed coordinates, which is expressed in the summation form (56) or a differential form (57). The fields used in these expressions are measured simultaneously in the primed frame at a given t', $\Delta t' = 0$. Gauss' law for the magnetic field may be independently established in the unprimed frame as well, using fields that are measured simultaneously in the unprimed frame at a given t, $\Delta t = 0$. Let us rewrite the differential form of Gauss' law in (57) for the unprimed frame. This is accomplished by simply replacing the unprimed variables in (57) by the corresponding primed variables.

$$\frac{\partial B_x}{\partial x} + \frac{\partial B_y}{\partial y} + \frac{\partial B_z}{\partial z} = \rho_{mv}. \tag{69}$$

Using (69) in (68) we would get,

$$\tfrac{V}{c^2}\tfrac{\partial B_x}{\partial t}\Delta x\Delta y\Delta z + \tfrac{V}{c^2}\left[(-E_{y6} + E_{y5})\Delta x\Delta y + (E_{z4} - E_{z2})\Delta x\Delta z\right]$$

$$= -M_x\tfrac{V}{c^2}\Delta x\Delta y\Delta z,$$

$$\left[-E_{y6}\Delta y + E_{y5}\Delta y + E_{z4}\Delta z - E_{z2}\Delta z\right] = -(\tfrac{\partial B_x}{\partial t} + M_x)\Delta y\Delta z. \tag{70}$$

The above relation (70) may be recognized in terms of line and surface integrals over an elemental rectangular loop ΔC and its enclosed surface $\overline{\Delta S}$, respectively.

$$\sum_{\Delta C} \overline{E}_i \cdot \overline{\Delta l}_i = -(\tfrac{\partial B_x}{\partial t} + M_x)\Delta y\Delta z = -(\tfrac{\partial \overline{B}}{\partial t} + \overline{M}) \cdot \overline{\Delta S}. \tag{71}$$

The loop ΔC refers to a closed rectangular loop parallel to the face 3 of the rectangular box in Fig.7b, passing through the center of the box. This is separately shown in the Fig. 8. Further, the orientation of the path of the loop ΔC is such that the normal direction to the enclosed surface vector $\overline{\Delta S}$, as per the right-hand rule, is along the normal to the face 3 of the box (that is, along $+\hat{x}$).

Equation (71) is Faraday's law as applied to an elemental loop ΔC. The obvious implication of the above derivation is that Faraday's law no longer has to be established as an independent law. It is derived from Gauss' law for the magnetic field in a free-space medium, through relativistic transformation. Accordingly, Faraday's law (71) may be interpreted as a necessary condition, so that Gauss' law for the magnetic field is consistent through relativistic transformation across reference frames. This is a significant development. The elemental loop ΔC in the above derivation

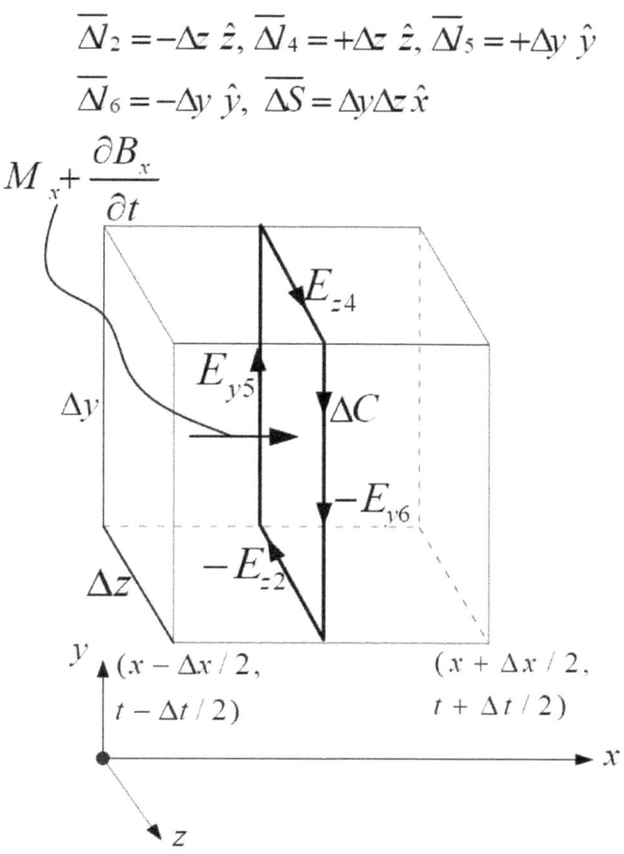

FIGURE 8. Deduction of Faraday's law from the magnetic field divergence (Gauss' law) experiment of Fig.7, as seen by an observer from the (x,y,z,t) reference frame.

is oriented with its normal along the x direction, which is parallel to the relative velocity between the frames. The choice of the direction of the relative velocity is arbitrary. If the analysis was performed with relative velocity in a general direction, the expression (71) for Faraday's law can be shown to apply to an elemental loop with any general orientation.

$$\sum_{\Delta C} \overline{E}_i \cdot \overline{\Delta l}_i = -(\tfrac{\partial \overline{B}}{\partial t} + \overline{M}) \cdot \overline{\Delta S}. \tag{72}$$

The above equation (72) for Faraday's law may also be expressed using the curl operator.

$$\sum_{\Delta C} \overline{E}_i \cdot \overline{\Delta l}_i = (\overline{\nabla} \times \overline{E}) \cdot \overline{\Delta S} = -(\overline{M} + \tfrac{\partial \overline{B}}{\partial t}) \cdot \overline{\Delta S},\ \overline{\nabla} \times \overline{E} = -\overline{M} - \frac{\partial \overline{B}}{\partial t}. \tag{73}$$

6. Discussions

6.1. Application in a Material Medium. It may be noted, that we have explicitly assumed a free-space medium for the derivations of Ampere's law in (51,53), as well as Faraday's law in (72,73). The derivations, in principle, are theoretically complete. The results may be extended to any material medium by substituting the material with equivalent current loops and charge dipoles, that are properly arranged in the free-space as the background. These equivalent currents and dipoles would represent the internal structure of the material, that are influenced by the electric and magnetic fields. The basic forms of Ampere's and Faraday's laws in (51,53) and (72,73), respectively, can be shown to be valid for the material medium as well, by properly defining the electric and magnetic fields and flux densities inside the medium, and relating them using suitable permittivity and permeability parameters.

6.2. A New form of Gauss' Laws and Charge Invariance. The conventional Gauss' laws (equations (37,57)) are valid in the primed frame, that are verified in the respective Gauss' law experiments (equations (39,60)) using suitable force measurements. The conventional Gauss' laws would also be valid in the unprimed reference frame (equations (45,65)), that may be similarly verified using force measurements all conducted independently in its own unprimed frame. All the measurements in the conventional Gauss' law experiments are conducted simultaneously, at a given time, in the respective independent frames.

In addition, a new form of Gauss' laws are introduced, implemented in the experiments (42,61). Here, a Gauss' law experiment originally conducted in the primed frame at a given time t', $\Delta t' = 0$, is invariant as observed from the unprimed frame with different timing ($\Delta t \neq 0$) for the individual measurements. These new Gauss' law experiments, definitively timed in a particular frame (primed frame), unambiguously measure the same amount of charge (electric or equivalent magnetic), assuming the charge is invariant to any relative motion. On the other hand, the conventional form of the Gauss' law experiments are not guaranteed to measure the same amount of charge in two frames, because a part of the charge may be moving and might escape from the measurement box during the different, independent timings in the two frames. In other words, the new form of Gauss' laws is the only unambiguous way to ensure invariance of charge (electric or equivalent magnetic) across reference frames, and therefore is more fundamental.

Enforcing this new fundamental form of Gauss' laws naturally allows a simple "derivation" of Ampere's and Faraday's laws (51,72), as additional required conditions for the enforcements. This is a significant discovery.

6.3. Mechanical Principles Derived from the Electromagnetic Theory. We succeeded to derive Maxwell's equations (Ampere's and Faraday's laws) from Gauss' laws, by additionally employing only the space-time relativistic transformation equations. This does not require the transformation relations for force, mass and momentum, or their related mechanics of momentum and energy conservation. However, once Maxwell's equations are rigorously established, they can always be solved for the fields and the associated forces in a given problem (two stationary electric charges in the free-space, for example), as seen by two inertial frames. The relationships between the solved forces in the two frames would in turn provide the required force-transformation formulas in the two frames.

Conventionally, the force-transformation formulas in special relativity are deduced starting from basic Newton's laws of force, momentum and energy, by employing the space-time relations of the special relativity [15]. This leads to transformation relations for the mass, momentum and energy as intermediate steps, leading to the force transformation relations. Now that the force transformation relations are available directly from Gauss' laws through Maxwell's equations, one can then retrace backwards the conventional derivations of relativistic mechanics. Accordingly, one could derive the transformation relations for the mass, momentum and energy, leading to the "derivation" of Newton's laws as well as the related principles of conservation of momentum and energy. This would be a significant development, where the basic concepts of an electric and magnetic charge (as defined through their respective fields, Gauss' laws and charge invariance) would completely describe all electromagnetic as well as material phenomena of nature, making the conventional mechanics of matter (as defined through mass, Newton's laws and momentum/energy conservation principles) theoretically redundant. What it means is that all mechanical principles and parameters may not be fundamental after all, but are somehow intrinsic to the basic definitions of electric and magnetic charge, and their invariance, and concepts of space and time.

REFERENCES

[1] James Clark Maxwell. *A Treatise on Electricity and Magnetism, Vol. I and II (Reprint from 1873)*. Dover Publications, 2007.

[2] Albert Einstein and Anna Beck (English Translator). *The Collected Papers of Albert Einstein, Volume 2: The Swiss Years: Writings 1900-1909 (see Documents 23 and 24)*. Princeton University Press, 1989.

[3] Albert Einstein. Zur Elektrodynamik bewegter Körper (On the Electrodynamics of Moving Bodies). *Annalen der Physik*, 322(10):891–921, 1905.

[4] D. K. Cheng. *Fundamentals of Engineering Electromagnetics*. Addison-Wesley Publishing, 1993.

[5] Jr. D. H. Hayt. *Engineering Electromagnetics*. McGraw-Hill, New York, 1995.

[6] N. N. Rao. *Elements of Engineering Electromagnetics*. Prentice Hall, New Jersey, 2000.

[7] E. M. Purcell. *Electricity and Magnetism (Berkeley Physics Course, Vol.2, 2 Ed.)*. Prentice Hall, New Jersey, 1984.

[8] Richarrd P. Feynman, Robert B. Leighton, and Mathew Sands. *Lectures on Physics, Vol.II, Ch.25,26*. Addision Wesley, 1964.

[9] J. D. Jackson. *Classical Electrodynamics, 2 Ed.* John Wiley and Sons, New York, 1975.

[10] R. S. Elliott. *Electromagnetics: History, Theory and Applications*. Wiley-IEEE Press, 1999.

[11] J. R. Bray. From Maxwell to Einstein: Introduction of the Time-Dialation Property of Special Relativity in Undergraduate Electromagnetics. *IEEE Antennas and Propagation Magazine*, 48(3):109–114, June 2006.

[12] J. W. Arthur. The Fundamentals of Electromagnetic Theory Revisited. *IEEE Antennas and Propagation Magazine*, 50(1):19–65, February 2008.

[13] D. H. Frisch and L. Wilets. Development of the Maxwell-Lorentz Equations from Special Relativity and Gauss' Law. *American Journal of Physics*, 24(8):574–579, November 1956.

[14] J. R. Tessman. Maxwell - Out of Newton, Coulomb and Einstein. *American Journal of Physics*, 34(11):1048–1055, November 1966.

[15] Ray Skinner. *Relativity for Scientists and Engineers*. Dover Publications, Inc., 1982.

Deriving Newton's Laws from Maxwell's Equations - Basic Concepts of Charge and Space-Time Supersede All Mechanical Principles

Nirod K. Das

Department of Electrical and Computer Engineering

Tandon School of Engineering, New York University, Five Metrotech Center, Brooklyn NY 11201

(Dated: August, 2016. Revised July, 2020)

Abstract

The basic principles of Newton's laws, and related concepts of conservation of momentum and energy, are derived from Maxwell's equations. The electric and magnetic fields produced by an electric charge in uniform motion, as derived from Maxwell's equations, are used to find the force it exerts on another charge, as measured in two inertial frames. These force transformation relations in the two frames are extended to apply to any general physical problem involving force. The force transformation relations are then used, together with the space-time relations of special relativity, to derive Newton's laws of motion applicable for velocity v much smaller than the speed of light c ($v << c$), as well as general expressions for the mass, momentum and energy, applicable for any velocity $v \leq c$. Further, the momentum or energy as expressed in one inertial frame, can be linearly related to the momentum and the energy expressed in another inertial frame. This result, when applied to a closed system with no external interaction, proves the momentum and the energy to be conserved. Fundamental and philosophical implications of the results and derivations are discussed. The principles of invariant electric and magnetic charge, upon which all electromagnetic concepts of Maxwell's equations are based, are recognized to be complete, more general and fundamental than Newton's laws, making the mechanical or material principles theoretically redundant.

1. Introduction

It has been recently established in [1, 2] that Maxwell's equations [3] can be derived from basic principle of invariance of the electric and magnetic charges, as fundamentally defined by Gauss' laws for the electric and magnetic fields, respectively, using only the space-time relations of special relativity [4, 5]. The principle of invariance of the charges, unambiguously defined using Gauss' laws applicable across reference frames, allows a simple, direct derivation of Maxwell's equations from the basic charge principle, without requiring Newton's laws of motion or the principles of momentum and energy conservation.

Once Maxwell's equations are established, they can be independently solved for the fields and the associated forces in any given problem in two reference frames. The relationships between the solved forces in the two frames would establish the required relativistic force-transformation formulas in the two frames, without any need for Newton's laws. Instead, Newton's laws can now be derived from the established force-transformation formulas.

Conventionally, the force-transformation formulas in special relativity are deduced starting from basic Newton's laws and principles of momentum and energy conservation, by employing the space-time relations of special relativity [5]. This process derives the velocity-dependent functions for the mass, momentum and energy as intermediate steps, leading to the force transformation relations. Now that the force transformation relations are available directly from Maxwell's equations, one can then essentially retrace backwards the conventional derivations of the relativistic mechanics. Accordingly, one could derive the functional forms for the mass, momentum and energy, leading to the "derivation" of Newton's laws and the associated principles of momentum and energy conservation.

In this paper we will follow such a derivation, starting with a simple electrical problem having simple solutions for Maxwell's equations. Theoretical and philosophical significance of the different results and derivations are addressed. The fundamental nature of the electromagnetic principles, in contrast with the basic material principles of Newton's laws, are discussed.

2. Force Transform Relations Derived From the Forces Between Two Charges

Consider two charges of equal magnitude Q are stationary with respect to each other. Their fields and mutual forces are measured in two reference frames, one (primed frame) where the charges are at rest with respect to the observer, and the other (unprimed frame) where the charges are moving with respect to the observer at a constant velocity V along the z direction, as shown in Fig.1. This is equivalent to having individual observers in the unprimed and the primed frames, who see the other observer moving with a uniform velocity V in the $+z$ and $-z$ directions, respectively. The origins of both the frames are aligned with the location of one of the charges at time $t = t' = 0$, whereas the other charge is located at (x', y', z') in the primed frame, or at (x, y, z) in the unprimed frame, timed at $t = 0$ in the unprimed frame.

2.1. Choice of Electromagnetically "Unbiased" Frames. The two frames, moving with uniform velocity with each other, are assumed to be naturally "unbiased" in a uniform free-space medium. Due to the special nature of propagation of light (any electromagnetic wave) in a uniform free-space medium, the speed of the propagation is required to be a fixed constant, with no rational preference to any frame of reference of an observer, as well as to any location or time of observation [1, 2]. Specifically for an unbiased frame, in addition to having the fixed speed, the light needs to propagate only in straight-line paths, because there is no biased preference to deflect from a given straight-line path to one side or another.

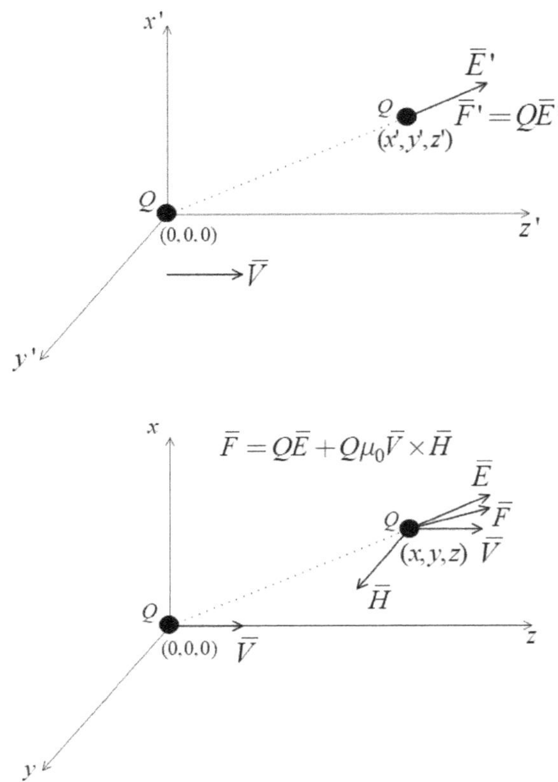

FIGURE 1. Two charges, that are stationary with respect to each other, but located at different positions in space. The fields produced by one charge (source charge), acting upon the second charge (test charge), as seen in two different reference frames. The primed frame is moving with a velocity V along the z axis with respect to the unprimed frame.

Further, a straight-line path of light propagation along any given orientation in space, as originally observed from one unbiased frame, would be observed with a deviated orientation in a second frame. This is because, the magnitude V of the relative velocity between the two frames is expected to change the two components - along and orthogonal to the direction of the relative velocity - of light's velocity, as observed in the second frame, with two different scaling factors. The relative orientation of the light path observed in the second frame, would obviously depend on the direction of the relative velocity $\bar{V}$ between the frames. Therefore, if the relative velocity $\bar{V}$ (magnitude and/or direction) varies in time, the resulting light path with its variable orientation in time, as observed in the second frame, would appear as a curved path. This would contradict the fundamental nature of an unbiased frame, which expects any observed light path to be strictly a straight line. In other words, if any two frames are to be both unbiased in nature, they are allowed to maintain only a uniform relative velocity $\bar{V}$ between them, as a necessary fundamental condition.

Maxwell's equations are valid only in unbiased reference frames, which are required to maintain a uniform relative velocity, as discussed above. Therefore, the two frames in Fig.1 are assumed to be both unbiased frames, maintaining a uniform velocity between each other, so that Maxwell's equations can be applied to solve for the force fields in both the frames, and the resulting forces in the frames be related.

2.2. Electromagnetic Force Calculations in the Two Frames.
We will find the electric and magnetic fields produced by the charge at the origin, moving with velocity V along z direction in the unprimed frame. The fields seen in the primed frame is a specific case of that in the unprimed frame, when the velocity is substituted as $V = 0$ and the coordinates are changed from the unprimed to the respective primed variables. Using these fields due to the charge at the origin, we can find the total force applied on the second charge at the general location, for the two cases with observers in the primed and unprimed frames. Relating the components of the two forces $\bar{F}'$ and $\bar{F}$ would establish the required force transformation between the frames. These force transform relations, although derived for the specific simple situations of the two charges, would be applicable to a general physical problem involving force, and considered fundamental relations with universal scope.

The electric $\bar{E}(x, y, z)$ and magnetic $\bar{H}(x, y, z)$ fields observed at $t = 0$ in the unprimed frame, due to the charge Q located at the origin and moving in uniform velocity V along the z axis, can be solved from Maxwell's equations. One simple approach is to express the moving charge as a superposition or integration of Fourier current distributions on a plane parallel to the charge velocity (xz-plane). The individual Fourier currents would produce uniform plane waves propagating or evanescent in the $\pm y$ directions [6, 7], the fields of which are one of the simple solutions of Maxwell's equations (in the uniform free-space medium, observed in an unbiased reference frame). The total fields can then be obtained by Fourier integration of the plane-wave fields. We will provide here the final results, which are also available from physics and engineering texts [8, 9]. Now, the special case for a stationary charge (in the primed frame) consists of only the electric field given by Coulomb's law, with a zero magnetic field. This may be verified from the general results with any uniform velocity V in the unprimed frame, by simply substituting $V = 0$ and changing the unprimed to the primed coordinate parameters.

$$\bar{E}(x, y, z) = \frac{Q}{4\pi\varepsilon_0 r'^3 \alpha}(x\hat{x} + y\hat{y} + z\hat{z}),$$

$$\bar{E}'(x, y, z) = \frac{Q}{4\pi\varepsilon_0 r'^3}(x'\hat{x} + y'\hat{y} + z'\hat{z}),$$

$$\bar{H}(x, y, z) = \frac{QV}{4\pi r'^3 \alpha}(-y\hat{x} + x\hat{y}), \quad \bar{H}'(x', y', z') = 0,$$

$$r' = (x^2 + y^2 + z'^2)^{1/2}, \quad x' = x, \quad y' = y, \quad z' = \frac{z}{\alpha}, \quad \alpha = (1 - \frac{V^2}{c^2})^{1/2}, \tag{1}$$

$$\bar{F}(x, y, z) = Q\bar{E} + Q\mu_0(V\hat{z} \times \bar{H}) = \frac{Q^2}{4\pi\varepsilon_0 r'^3 \alpha}(\alpha^2 x\hat{x} + \alpha^2 y\hat{y} + z\hat{z}),$$

$$\bar{F}'(x', y', z') = Q\bar{E}' + Q\mu_0((v = 0)\hat{z} \times \bar{H}') = \frac{Q^2}{4\pi\varepsilon_0 r'^3}(x'\hat{x} + y'\hat{y} + z'\hat{z}), \tag{2}$$

$$F_x = \alpha F'_x, \quad F_y = \alpha F'_y, \quad F_z = F'_z. \tag{3}$$

2.3. Generality of the Force Transform Relations, Extended to Any Physical System Involving Force.
The above result (3), although is derived for a simple problem, may be properly interpreted and extended for a general configuration. The charge at the origin is the "source" charge, which produces all the force fields we derived that act upon the second charge, called the "test" charge. The same result (3) would apply for any arbitrary location of the source charge, as well as for any arbitrary values of the source and test charges

that may not be equal to each other. By principle or superposition, the same final result (3) would be obtained as well for an arbitrary spatial distribution of the source charges, producing an arbitrary distribution of the force field $\bar{F}(x, y, z)$. Further, the result (3) requires the velocity of the test charge to be directed along the z axis, with a magnitude equal to zero and V as seen in the primed and unprimed frames, respectively, only at the time of observation $t = 0$. The same result (3) would be valid for any arbitrary path and velocity function of the test charge, with any other velocity $\bar{v}(t)$ at times $t \neq 0$ before or after the observation. This is because, the force (2) acting upon the test charge is dependent only on the location and velocity of the test charge at the time of observation $t = 0$, independent of all time-derivatives of the velocity at $t = 0$ or of the velocity function $\bar{v}(t)$ of the test charge at other times $t \neq 0$.

In summary, the force-transform relationship (3) would work for a general force field as well as a general path or velocity function of the test body, with the body's reference velocity equal to zero and $V\hat{z}$ as seen in the primed and unprimed frames, respectively, only at the time of observation $t = 0$. Considering such generality, the above relations between the forces in the two frames may be declared to be valid for a physical problem involving any possible force field and motion of the test body, with the above choice for the reference velocity of the body.

As an alternate approach, the general force transformation relations (3) could be established directly from an invariant form of Gauss' law, required to be relativistically valid across reference frames, from which Maxwell's equations are originally derived [1, 2]. As per the invariance of Gauss' law, the total force-flux over any closed surface (that may or may not enclose any charge, electric or magnetic), originally measured at a fixed time in a reference frame (primed frame) using only stationary charges at different locations of the closed surface, must remain invariant when the measurements are observed from any other reference frame (unprimed frame). An elemental force-flux over a unit area at any particular location of the closed surface, is defined as the component of the force, directed normal to the area element, experienced by a unit charge placed at the given location. Enforcement of the invariance condition of the force-flux, for all arbitrary closed surfaces, using space-time relations across the reference frames, would establish the force transformation relations (3).

$$F_x \Delta y \Delta z = F_x' \Delta y' \Delta z', \ \ F_x = \alpha F_x',$$
$$F_y \Delta x \Delta z = F_y' \Delta x' \Delta z', \ \ F_y = \alpha F_y',$$
$$F_z \Delta x \Delta y = F_z' \Delta x' \Delta y', \ \ F_z = F_z',$$
$$\Delta x = \Delta x', \ \Delta y = \Delta y', \ \Delta z = \Delta z'/\alpha; \ \Delta t' = 0. \tag{4}$$

However, an additional condition for the measured forces would still have to be independently confirmed through Maxwell's equations. That is, all the forces on the test charges are completely defined by the electric and magnetic fields of Maxwell's equations, and therefore are determined only by the velocity of each charge, irrespective of any higher order motion of the charge. Accordingly, the general transformation relation (4) for the forces on a test body would be applicable, as long as the velocity of the test body is zero and $V\hat{z}$ in the primed and unprimed frames, respectively, irrespective of any higher-order motion (first or higher time-derivative of the velocity) of the test body.

3. Fundamental Definition of Force, in Relation to Motion

3.1. Zero Force on a Stationary Body, and the Principle of an Inertial Frame.
Consider a stationary body placed at any specific location (origin), as observed from any

one of the unbiased frames (primed or unprimed). Due to the "unbiased" natures of the reference frames and the surrounding free-space medium, which we assumed in the above analysis to begin with, the body is expected to naturally remain stationary at the specified location, without any force, because there is no intrinsic "bias" or force for its movement in any one way or another. Accordingly, any valid definition of force must be associated with the above basic condition. That is, the force must be defined such that it would be zero for a stationary body observed in an unbiased frame.

Accordingly, an observer attached to an unbiased reference frame, would also naturally remain fixed at the origin of the frame as a stationary body, without any influence of force. In other words, the reference frame may be considered to be naturally "free-floating" in space. In this sense, the reference frame may be called an "inertial frame," in reference to the mechanical concept of inertia of the observer, with its natural tendency to maintain its fixed position in absence of any force.

The "unbiased" nature of the frame, originally defined electromagnetically in section 2.1, is now explained to be equivalent to its free-floating, "inertial" nature, defined in mechanical terms. Because two electromagnetically unbiased frames are allowed to move only with a uniform relative velocity with respect to each other, as explained in section 2.1, two mechanically inertial frames also would be allowed to move only with a uniform relative velocity. This is a fundamental deduction of the mechanical nature of force and motion, from the original electromagnetic nature. It maybe noted, the above conclusion about the uniform relative velocity between two unbiased, inertial frames could not have been independently established, on the basis of only the mechanical nature. This is because, the observation of the uniform motion (or any motion) of the second frame could as well have been perceived (incorrectly) as certain mechanical bias in one of the observation frames.

3.2. Definition of Force in a Unbiased or Inertial Frame.

A force applied on a given body is meant to be an agent to produce change in motion of the body, as time passes. Accordingly, the amount of the applied force $\bar{F}$ may be defined as the time-derivative of certain physical quantity, called the momentum $\bar{p}$, associated with the body in general motion. The momentum and force are vector quantities, representing the directed, vector nature of the motion and its change. Accordingly, the component of the force vector in any given direction is equal to the time derivative of the component of the momentum vector in the particular direction. For mathematical generality, the time variation of the momentum may be expressed in the form of a general momentum function dependent on the position $\bar{r}$, velocity $\bar{v}$, acceleration $\bar{a}$ and all higher-order time-derivatives of the velocity.

$$\bar{F}(t) \triangleq \frac{d\bar{p}(t)}{dt}, \quad \bar{F}'(t) \triangleq \frac{d\bar{p}'(t)}{dt'},$$

$$\bar{p}(t) = \bar{p}(\bar{r}, \bar{v}, \bar{a}, \bar{a}_1, \bar{a}_2, \ldots), \quad \bar{p}'(t') = \bar{p}(\bar{r}', \bar{v}', \bar{a}', \bar{a}'_1, \bar{a}'_2, \ldots),$$

$$\bar{r} = x\hat{x} + y\hat{y} + z\hat{z}, \quad \bar{r}' = x'\hat{x} + y'\hat{y} + z'\hat{z},$$

$$\bar{v} = \frac{d\bar{r}}{dt} = v_x\hat{x} + v_y\hat{y} + v_z\hat{z}, \quad \bar{v}' = \frac{d\bar{r}'}{dt'} = v'_x\hat{x} + v'_y\hat{y} + v'_z\hat{z},$$

$$\bar{a}_n = \frac{d^n\bar{a}}{dt^n} = \frac{d^{n+1}\bar{v}}{dt^{n+1}}, \quad \bar{a}_0 = \bar{a} = \frac{d\bar{v}}{dt}, \quad \bar{a}'_n = \frac{d^n\bar{a}'}{dt'^n} = \frac{d^{n+1}\bar{v}'}{dt'^{n+1}}, \quad \bar{a}'_0 = \bar{a}' = \frac{d\bar{v}'}{dt'},$$

$$\bar{F} = F_x\hat{x} + F_y\hat{y} + F_z\hat{z}, \quad \bar{F}' = F'_x\hat{x} + F'_y\hat{y} + F'_z\hat{z},$$

$$\bar{p} = p_x\hat{x} + p_y\hat{y} + p_z\hat{z}, \quad \bar{p}' = p'_x\hat{x} + p'_y\hat{y} + p'_z\hat{z}. \tag{5}$$

For the naturally stationary body at a given location in any one of the unbiased/inertial frames, with no spatial motion as time progresses, there would be no time variation of the momentum $\bar{p}'$ or $\bar{p}$, and therefore the associated force $\bar{F}'$ or $\bar{F}$ be zero, as per the above definition of (5). This is consistent with the required condition of force in an unbiased/

inertial frame established earlier. However, it may be realized that such a definition of force is to be applicable only in an unbiased, inertial frame. A stationary body in a biased/non-inertial frame would instead require a force in order to maintain its stationary position, in which case the force definition (5) would be clearly invalid.

4. Dependence of the Momentum of a Body on its Motion, Derived from the Force-Transformation Relations

Any specific dependence of the momentum in (5) on parameters of motion of a body can be deduced from the fundamental force-transformation relations of (3), based on the space-time transformation relations of special relativity. Any specific dependence, deduced for one of the unbiased frames (primed or unprimed), would apply as well for the other frame, with no special preference for one unbiased frame over the other.

We will primarily consider a simple case with a force $\bar{F} = F_z \hat{z}$ in the z direction, resulting in motion with changing position $\bar{r}(t) = z(t)\hat{z}$ and velocity $\bar{v}(t) = v_z(t)\hat{z}$ only along the z direction, as seen by an observer in the unprimed frame. The corresponding motion observed in the primed frame maybe deduced from the above motion in the unprimed frame, using space-time transformation between the frames. We will derive results for this simple case of linear motion, based on the general force transformation relations (3). The results for the simple motion can be extended as well for a general motion.

4.1. Position Independence of the Momentum.
A naturally stationary body in the primed frame would be seen in the unprimed frame with a uniform velocity V in the z direction, having no acceleration or other time-derivatives of its velocity. As per the force transformation relation (3), the force F_z seen in the unprimed frame is required to be zero, given that the force F_z' for the naturally stationary body in the primed frame is known to be zero. In other words, the body must not need any force in order to sustain a uniform linear motion, as observed in the unprimed frame.

$$F_z = \frac{dp_z}{dt} = \frac{dp_z}{dz}\frac{dz}{dt} = \frac{dp_z}{dz}V, \ \frac{dz}{dt} = v_z = V,$$
$$F_z' = \frac{dp_z'}{dt'} = \frac{dp_z'}{dz'}\frac{dz'}{dt'} = 0, \ \frac{dz'}{dt'} = v_z' = 0,$$
$$F_z = F_z' = 0, \ \frac{dp_z}{dz} = 0. \tag{6}$$

The above conclusion regarding the body in uniform linear motion, specifically deduced in the unprimed frame, which is an unbiased or inertial frame, may be generally stated for validity in any inertial frame. That is, a body would maintain a uniform linear motion in an inertial frame, without any assistance of force.

Mathematically, the above conclusion (6), derived using (3) and (5), is equivalent to having the momentum p_z to be independent of the position z. This leaves the momentum p_z to be a function of its remaining variables - the velocity v_z, acceleration a_z, and other higher-order time-derivatives of the v_z (see (5)).

Using a general analysis in (6), by including force components in the transverse (x, y) directions, and relating them based on (3), that is $F_{x,y} = \alpha F_{x,y}' = 0$, we would also have the respective momentum components $p_{x,y}$ to be independent of the position z. By functional symmetry to the deduced independence of p_z and $p_{x,y}$ with z, we will also have independence of $p_{x,y}$ and p_z with (x, y), respectively. In other words, all momentum components and the associated forces would be independent of the location of observation, all other parameters of motion remaining the same. This would be consistent with the uniform nature of the surrounding free-space medium, which is assumed to be independent of the location of observation.

4.2. Independence of Momentum With All Time-Derivatives of Velocity, and Newton's First Law.

The position independence of momentum established that a stationary body or a body with uniform velocity does not require a force. We would like to know other possible motions, if any, that also may not require force.

Consider the linear motion along the z axis, with a non-zero acceleration a_z' in the primed frame, having the velocity v_z' and all time derivatives of the velocity v_z', except the first derivative (or acceleration a_z'), to be zero. The force component F_z and F_z' along the z direction, as seen in the two frames, defined in (5) as time-derivatives of the momentum p_z or p_z' in the respective frames, must satisfy the transform relations (3), when the uniform velocity V is equal to v_z at the time of observation. This would require the momentum p_z to be independent of all time derivatives of the v_z.

The space-time relations of special relativity may be used to deduce relations for the velocity, as well as for its time-derivatives, in the unprimed frame with those in the primed frame. It may be shown that all time-derivatives of the velocity v_z in the unprimed frame would be non-zero functions of $v_z = V \neq 0$, even though only the first time-derivative (acceleration a_z') of the velocity v_z' is non-zero in the primed frame. This is due to the non-linear nature of the relativistic relation (9) between the velocities v_z' and v_z in the two frames. Further, the time-derivatives of the velocity v_z of increasingly higher order (a_{nz}) can be shown to be proportional to increasing exponents of the acceleration a_z' ($a_z'^{n+1}$), with non-zero coefficients ρ_n of the proportionality for all $n \geq 0$. The above conditions, applied with the force transformation relations (3) in the two frames, would lead to the independence of the momentum p_z with all time-derivatives of the velocity v_z.

$$F_z = \frac{dp_z}{dt} = \frac{dp_z}{dz}v_z + \frac{dp_z}{dv_z}a_z + \sum_{n=0}^{\infty} \frac{dp_z}{da_{nz}}a_{n+1z} =$$

$$\frac{dp_z}{dv_z}\rho_0(v_z)a_z' + \sum_{n=0}^{\infty} \frac{dp_z}{da_{nz}}\rho_{n+1}(v_z)a_z'^{\,n+2},$$

$$a_{nz} = \frac{d^{n+1}v_z}{dt^{n+1}} = \rho_n(v_z)a_z'^{\,n+1}; \; a_{0z} = a_z = \frac{dv_z}{dt}, \; \rho_n(v_z = V \neq 0) \neq 0, \; n \geq 0,$$

$$F_z' = \frac{dp_z'}{dt'} = \frac{dp_z'}{dv_z'}a_z', \; a_z' = a_{0z}' = \frac{dv_z'}{dt'}, \; a_{nz}' = \frac{d^{n+1}v_z'}{dt'^{n+1}} = 0, \; n \geq 1,$$

$$F_z' = F_z, \; \frac{dp_z}{da_{nz}} = 0, \; n \geq 0. \tag{7}$$

In the above derivation, the F_z' is expressed proportional to the a_z', with no dependence on higher exponents of the a_z'. The F_z' expression may be viewed as a power-series of the a_z', with only one term involving the first-exponent of the a_z'. On the other hand, the F_z is expressed as a power-series of the a_z', involving all exponents of the a_z'. The expressions of F_z and F_z' must be equated, as required by the force transformation relations (3). This would require the individual terms in the power-series expressions of the F_z and F_z', with different exponents of the a_z', to be equated. Given that the coefficients ρ_n are expected to be non-zero for all $n \geq 0$, as explained earlier and discussed further in the following section, the above process leads to requiring the momentum p_z to be independent of all time-derivatives of the velocity v_z.

Like the position independence of the momentum deduced earlier, the independence of the momentum with all time-derivatives of the velocity is also a significant result from the force conditions (3) deduced from the electromagnetic theory. This leaves the momentum to be dependent only upon the velocity. Using the definition of force in (5), this means that a non-zero force would be required only when the velocity of a massive body is changed. In other words, a stationary body would remain stationary, and a body in uniform motion would maintain the uniform motion, without any force, whereas an accelerating body would certainly require a non-zero force. However, any change in the acceleration would not require any additional force. This is Newton's first law of motion, although the first law does not specify that higher-order time derivatives of velocity beyond the first derivative (acceleration) do not require additional force. This aspect is specified only through Newton's second law, to be derived in the following.

4.3. Functional Dependence of the Momentum with Velocity.

As explained above, the momentum function p_z is left with the velocity v_z as its only valid variable. The functional expression of p_z with the variable v_z can be deduced from the above result (7), by using the expression of the ρ_0 derived from the space-time relations of special relativity.

$$F_z = F'_z, \quad \frac{dp_z}{dv_z} = \frac{1}{\rho_0}\frac{dp'_z}{dv'_z} = \frac{1}{\alpha^3}\frac{dp'_z}{dv'_z} = \frac{1}{(1-\frac{v_z^2}{c^2})^{3/2}}\frac{dp'_z}{dv'_z},$$

$$p_z(v_z) = \frac{m_0 v_z}{(1-\frac{v_z^2}{c^2})^{1/2}}, \quad m_0 = \frac{dp'_z}{dv'_z}\Big|_{v'_z=0} = \frac{dp_z}{dv_z}\Big|_{v_z=0}, \tag{8}$$

$$x = x', \quad y = y', \quad z = \frac{z'+Vt'}{\alpha}, \quad t = \frac{t'+z'V/c^2}{\alpha},$$

$$v_x = \frac{v'_x \alpha}{(1+Vv'_z/c^2)}, \quad v_y = \frac{v'_y \alpha}{(1+Vv'_z/c^2)}, \quad v_z = \frac{v'_z+V}{(1+Vv'_z/c^2)},$$

$$dt = \frac{dt'}{\alpha}, \quad dv_x = \alpha(dv'_x), \quad dv_y = \alpha(dv'_y), \quad dv_z = \alpha^2(dv'_z); \quad v'_z = v'_x = v'_y = 0,$$

$$\frac{dv_z}{dt} = \rho_0 \frac{dv'_z}{dt'} = \alpha^3 \frac{dv'_z}{dt'}; \quad v'_z = 0, \quad \rho_0 = \alpha^3. \tag{9}$$

Relations between the higher order time-derivatives of the velocity v_z in the unprimed frame and the acceleration in the primed frame can be similarly obtained by further differentiating the above relations between the velocities in the two frames. This would provide the expressions for all other ρ_n, $n > 0$, which are non-zero functions of $v_z = V$ as we needed in the above derivation (7).

$$\frac{d^n a_z}{dt^n} = \rho_n(v_z)\left(\frac{dv'_z}{dt'}\right)^{n+1}, \quad \rho_n(v_z = V, v'_z = 0) = (-1)^n(2n+1)!!\left(\frac{V}{c^2}\right)^n \alpha^{n+3},$$

$$(2n+1)!! = (2n+1)(2n-1)(2n-3)\cdots(1). \tag{10}$$

4.4. Expressions in the Small-Velocity Limit, and Newton's Second Law.

Note that we have "derived" the expression (8) for the momentum component p_z, as a function of the velocity component v_z, starting from Maxwell's equations. In the limit of a small velocity, the expression of momentum in (8), and the associated force defined in (5), would take the form of Newton's second law. In the small-velocity limit, the momentum is shown to be proportional to velocity, with the constant of proportionality m_0 recognized as the rest mass. The force, defined in (5) as the time-derivative of the momentum, is therefore equal to the rest mass times the acceleration (time-derivative of the velocity), in the small-velocity limit. This is the most basic mechanical formula constituting Newton's second law [10] of motion for a body of constant rest mass m_0. Accordingly, we have "derived" Newton's second law of motion, from the electromagnetic theory based on Maxwell's equations. This is a significant development.

$$p_z(v_z) = \frac{m_0 v_z}{(1-\frac{v_z^2}{c^2})^{1/2}}, \ \ p_z(v_z \to 0, \ v_z << c) = m_0 v_z,$$

$$F_z = \frac{dp_z}{dt} = \frac{d(m_0 v_z)}{dt} = m_0 \frac{dv_z}{dt} = m_0 a_z; \ \ v_z << c,$$

$$p_z(v_z) = m(v_z)v_z = \frac{m_0 v_z}{(1-\frac{v_z^2}{c^2})^{1/2}}, \ \ m(v_z) = \frac{m_0}{(1-\frac{v_z^2}{c^2})^{1/2}}. \tag{11}$$

4.5. Relativistic Mass.

In consistency with the momentum expression in the small-velocity limit, which we deduced above to be the product of the velocity v_z and the rest mass m_0, the general expression of the momentum $p_z(v_z)$ in (8) may also be expressed as a product of the velocity v_z and a general mass term $m(v_z)$. This new mass term, as shown in (11), is a function $m(v_z)$ of the velocity v_z of motion, unlike a fixed mass m_0 assumed in Newton's second law. Further, this velocity-dependent mass, referred to as the relativistic mass, would increase indefinitely as the velocity v_z increases approaching the speed of light c. We have succeeded to derive the required velocity function of the relativistic mass, directly from Maxwell's equations.

The same dependence of the relativistic mass, as a function of the velocity v_z for the linear motion along z, is extended in the following to apply as well for a general motion along any arbitrary path, where v_z may be substituted with the magnitude v of the general velocity vector $\bar{v}$.

4.6. Generalization to Motion in the Three Dimensions.

The above derivations assumed a simple linear motion along the z axis. The direction of motion along the z axis for the simple motion is an arbitrary choice. Similar results would work as well for a motion along any general direction. Accordingly, the result in (8) may be used to relate the magnitude of a general momentum function $\bar{p}(\bar{v})$ to the magnitude of the velocity vector $\bar{v}$. The small-velocity limit for the general case would be an extension of the equivalent limit (11) for the simple case. Further, consistent with the small-velocity limit, the general momentum vector is also directed along the velocity $\bar{v}$.

The momentum vector in the general direction can then be decomposed into its individual components p_x, p_y and p_z in the x, y and z directions, respectively.

$$\bar{p}(\bar{v}) = m(v)\bar{v}, \ \ p(v) = m(v)v = \frac{m_0 v}{(1-\frac{v^2}{c^2})^{1/2}}, \ \ m(v) = \frac{m_0}{(1-\frac{v^2}{c^2})^{1/2}},$$

$$\bar{p}(\bar{v}) = m\bar{v} = m(v_x\hat{x} + v_y\hat{y} + v_z\hat{z}) = \frac{m_0(v_x\hat{x}+v_y\hat{y}+v_z\hat{z})}{(1-\frac{v^2}{c^2})^{1/2}},$$

$$p_x = \frac{m_0 v_x}{(1-v^2/c^2)^{1/2}}, \ \ p_y = \frac{m_0 v_y}{(1-v^2/c^2)^{1/2}}, \ \ p_z = \frac{m_0 v_z}{(1-v^2/c^2)^{1/2}},$$

$$v^2 = v_x^2 + v_y^2 + v_z^2, \tag{12}$$

$$p_z(v_z) = m_0 v_z, \ \ p_x(v_x) = m_0 v_x, \ \ p_y(v_y) = m_0 v_y; \ \ v_x, v_y, v_z << c,$$

$$\bar{p}(\bar{v}) = p_x\hat{x} + p_y\hat{y} + p_z\hat{z} = m_0(v_x\hat{x} + v_y\hat{y} + v_z\hat{z}) = m_0\bar{v}; \ \ v << c,$$

$$m_0 = \frac{dp_x}{dv_x}\Big|_{v=0} = \frac{dp_y}{dv_y}\Big|_{v=0} = \frac{dp_z}{dv_z}\Big|_{v=0} = \frac{dp}{dv}\Big|_{v=0}. \tag{13}$$

We derived the above general expressions (12) for the momentum components, starting with a simple motion along the z direction. This derivation explicitly satisfied the required transform relationship (3) only between the force components F_z and F'_z, for the simple case, which led to relating the momentum p_z to the velocity v_z in (8), also for the simple case. The results were then generalized to (12) for motion along a general direction by reorienting the velocity axis, from which the expressions for the individual momentum components $p_{x,y,z}$ were decomposed. The required transform relationships (3) for all three force components were expected to be satisfied by the deduced expressions of the momentum components of (12), implicitly through the coordinate reorientation. This is a theoretically simple, valid approach.

However, the expressions for the individual momentum components in (12) may also be explicitly verified to satisfy the required transform relationships (3) for all three force components. This is possible by first differentiating the momentum components in (12) with respect to the individual velocity components. The results are then used to relate respective force components in the two frames using the velocity-space-time relationships (9), leading to verification of the force transform relations (3).

$$dp_{x,y} = \frac{m_0}{(1-v^2/c^2)^{1/2}}dv_{x,y}, \;\; dp_z = \frac{m_0}{(1-v^2/c^2)^{3/2}}dv_z,$$

$$\frac{\partial p_x}{\partial v_{y,z}} = \frac{\partial p_y}{\partial v_{x,z}} = \frac{\partial p_z}{\partial v_{x,y}} = 0; \;\; v_{x,y} = 0, \;\; v_z = v = V,$$

$$F_{x,y} = \Big(\frac{dp_{x,y}}{dv_{x,y}}\Big)\Big(\frac{dv_{x,y}}{dt}\Big) = \frac{m_0}{(1-v^2/c^2)^{1/2}}\frac{\alpha(dv'_{x,y})}{(dt'/\alpha)} = \alpha F'_{x,y},$$

$$F_z = \Big(\frac{dp_z}{dv_z}\Big)\Big(\frac{dv_z}{dt}\Big) = \frac{m_0}{(1-v^2/c^2)^{3/2}}\frac{\alpha^2(dv'_z)}{(dt'/\alpha)} = F'_z,$$

$$F'_{x,y,z} = \Big(\frac{dp'_{x,y,z}}{dv'_{x,y,z}}\Big)\Big(\frac{dv'_{x,y,z}}{dt'}\Big) = m_0\frac{dv'_{x,y,z}}{dt'}; \; v'_{x,y,z} = v' = 0. \qquad (14)$$

Further, following the same steps of the analysis (7), but to relate the force components $F_{x,y}$ and $F'_{x,y}$ in the two frames, the respective momentum components $p_{x,y}$ - like the momentum p_z - would be independent of all time-derivatives of the velocity component v_z. Further extending the analysis of (7), by inserting a non-zero acceleration component $a'_{x,y}$ in the primed frame in addition to the a'_z, it can also be similarly shown that each momentum component would be independent of all time-derivatives of the velocity component $v_{x,y}$. These results would be consistent with the momentum expressions of (12), that are dependent only on the velocity components, not any of their time-derivatives.

4.7. Energy Expression Derived From the Force and Momentum.

Now, let us derive the expression for the energy of a moving body, adopting the conventional definition of energy used in the Newtonian mechanics. The derivation would make use of the momentum expression we established above. At this point, we do not question any reasoning behind the choice of the definition of energy. The definition is likewise introduced in the Newtonian mechanics, without any justification for its special form. It is simply expected without "proof" that the conventional energy definition would provide a useful conserved quantity, which is one of the foundational principles in the Newtonian mechanics. The validity of definition of the energy used, and the proof of its conserved nature, will be addressed in the section 5.2.

$$dW = \overline{F} \cdot \overline{ds} = \frac{d\overline{p}}{dt} \cdot \overline{ds} = d\overline{p} \cdot \overline{v} = v_x dp_x + v_y dp_y + v_z dp_z \tag{15}$$

$$= \frac{m_0(v_x dv_x + v_y dv_y + v_z dv_z)}{(1-v^2/c^2)^{3/2}} = \frac{(m_0/2)d(v^2)}{(1-v^2/c^2)^{3/2}},$$

$$W = \int \frac{(m_0/2)d(v^2)}{(1-v^2/c^2)^{3/2}} = \frac{m_0 c^2}{(1-v^2/c^2)^{1/2}} = mc^2. \tag{16}$$

We have now established the basic mass-energy relationship $W = mc^2$, derived directly from Maxwell's equations. Accordingly, all forms of energy and mass may be treated in equivalent terms using (16). This would allow mechanical treatment of general systems which may include conventional massive bodies as well as electromagnetic radiation. Any exchange of energy and momentum between the conventional bodies and the radiation may be implemented using concepts of electromagnetic field-mass/energy and field-momentum [11].

5. ENERGY AND MOMENTUM CONSERVATION IN A CLOSED SYSTEM

5.1. Momentum-Energy Transformation Relations in the Two Frames. Let us express the momentum (12) in two inertial frames, moving with velocity V with respect to each other along the z direction. This is possible using the space-time relations (9) of special relativity. The momentum in the unprimed frame can now be linearly related with that in the primed frame in terms of the energy expression of (16) in the primed frame. Using symmetry of results between the two frames, an equivalent relationship between the momenta in the two frames and the energy in the unprimed frame can also be obtained by interchanging the primed and unprimed variables, and replacing V with $-V$.

$$\overline{p} = \frac{m_0 \overline{v}}{(1-\frac{v^2}{c^2})^{1/2}}, \quad \overline{p}' = \frac{m_0 \overline{v}'}{(1-\frac{v'^2}{c^2})^{1/2}},$$

$$p_x = p'_x, \quad p_y = p'_y, \quad p_z = \frac{p'_z + m'V}{\alpha} = \frac{p'_z + W'V/c^2}{\alpha}, \quad p'_z = \frac{p_z - mV}{\alpha} = \frac{p_z - WV/c^2}{\alpha}, \tag{17}$$

$$v_x = \frac{v'_x \alpha}{1+v'_z V/c^2}, \quad v_y = \frac{v'_y \alpha}{1+v'_z V/c^2}, \quad v_z = \frac{v'_z + V}{1+v'_z V/c^2},$$

$$\left(1 - \frac{v^2}{c^2}\right) = \left(1 - \frac{v_x^2 + v_y^2 + v_z^2}{c^2}\right) = \frac{\alpha^2}{(1+v'_z V/c^2)^2}\left(1 - \frac{v_x'^2 + v_y'^2 + v_z'^2}{c^2}\right)$$

$$= \frac{\alpha^2}{(1+v'_z V/c^2)^2}\left(1 - \frac{v'^2}{c^2}\right), \quad \alpha = (1 - V^2/c^2)^{1/2}. \tag{18}$$

The energy expression of (16) in the unprimed frame can be similarly related to that in the primed frame in terms of the z directed momentum in the primed frame. An equivalent relationship in terms of the momentum component in the unprimed frame can also be obtained by interchanging primed and unprimed variables and replacing V by $-V$. This is by symmetry of results between the two frames.

$$W = mc^2 = \frac{m_0 c^2}{(1-\frac{v^2}{c^2})^{1/2}}, \ \ W' = m'c^2 = \frac{m_0 c^2}{(1-\frac{v'^2}{c^2})^{1/2}},$$

$$W = \frac{m_0 c^2 (1+\frac{v'_z V}{c^2})}{\alpha(1-\frac{v'^2}{c^2})^{1/2}} = \frac{m'c^2(1+\frac{v'_z V}{c^2})}{\alpha} = \frac{(W'+p'_z V)}{\alpha},$$

$$W' = \frac{(W-p_z V)}{\alpha}. \tag{19}$$

5.2. Concept of Energy as a Conserved Parameter.

The transformation relation (3) simply requires that a given body with no external force, as observed in any one inertial frame, would also be observed with no external force in any other inertial frame. However, the body could consist of an arbitrary number of internal parts, having general forces of interaction and relative motion between them, but with the sum of all the forces equal to zero. Therefore, the above simple condition (3) needs to be consistently expanded to require that any such set of zero-sum forces to be as well measured with the same zero-sum condition in all the inertial frames. This would be independent of the constitution of the individual parts and the nature of their interacting forces.

Now, consider a system with all its individual forces added to zero, as seen by the primed inertial frame. As discussed above, the system would also be seen with the zero total force in the unprimed inertial frame, which is moving with a uniform velocity V along the $-z$ axis with respect to the primed frame. Although the total force is zero, the system is free to undergo any change of state of its individual parts, produced due to the forces of interactions between the parts. This would be characterized by change of velocity, momentum and energy of the individual parts.

Based on the basic definition of force (5), having the total force zero would mean that the total change of momentum $\Delta\bar{p}$ and $\Delta\bar{p}'$ of all constituent parts of the system, over any time interval, would also be zero. Given the required momentum expressions of (12) and their relationships (17) in the two frames, it would additionally require the energy of (16) to be conserved ($\Delta W' = \Delta W = 0$).

$$\sum \bar{F}' = 0, \ \Delta\bar{p}' = 0; \ \sum \bar{F} = 0, \ \Delta\bar{p} = 0,$$
$$\Delta p_x = \Delta p'_x = 0, \ \Delta p_y = \Delta p'_y = 0, \ \Delta p_z = \Delta p'_z = 0,$$
$$\Delta p_z = \frac{\Delta p'_z}{\alpha} + \frac{(\Delta W')V/c^2}{\alpha} = 0, \ \Delta W' = 0; \ \Delta p'_z = \frac{\Delta p_z}{\alpha} - \frac{(\Delta W)V/c^2}{\alpha} = 0, \ \Delta W = 0. \tag{20}$$

This is a significant result, which proves that the energy, as conventionally defined in the Newtonian mechanics using the incremental form (15), is in fact conserved in a system with zero total force. The conservation of energy for a zero-force system no longer needs to be accepted as a foundational mechanical principle, without proof, simply based on theoretical and observational success of the principle. Conversely, if we are looking for a useful scalar parameter to be conserved in a system with zero total force, then the conventional definition of energy (15) (written in incremental form) is now theoretically proved to be one such conserved quantity. Other possible expressions of the energy one might think of may not succeed to maintain the desired energy conservation, consistent with the force transform relations (3) and special relativity.

5.3. Momentum Conservation in a Closed System, and Newton's Third Law.

Now consider a system physically contained inside a definite volume of space, identified with an entirely closed surface boundary, with no interaction with the external free space across the boundary surface. And, this is the case as seen by any inertial observer (primed and unprimed frames). The non-interaction condition across the closed boundary may be characterized in terms of no flow of energy, or its mass equivalent as per (16), across any part of the boundary. Accordingly, the total energy or equivalent mass would remain constant inside the system ($\Delta W = \Delta W' = 0$). This assumes that no energy or mass can spontaneously appear or disappear at any locaation inside the closed system, without a definite trace of flow of the energy occurring across the closed boundary surface.

Under the above condition, it may be shown from (19) that the total momentum p_z, p'_z inside the closed system in each frame would remain unchanged ($\Delta p'_z = 0 = \Delta p_z$). The choice of the z direction is arbitrary in the above discussion of the energy conservation in the closed system. Therefore, component of the momentum along any direction, or equivalently the total momentum vector, would remain unchanged ($\Delta \bar{p} = 0 = \Delta \bar{p}'$). This is the principle of momentum conservation in a closed system.

Further, because the total momentum would remain unchanged, the total of all forces in the closed system would be zero, as per the definition of force in (5). Equivalently, every force in the closed system would be balanced by a counter reaction force that is equal in magnitude but oppositely directed. This is Newton's third law of motion. We have now proved Newton's third law from the electromagnetic theory and special relativity.

$$\Delta W = \Delta W' = 0, \ \ \Delta W = \frac{\Delta W'}{\alpha} + \frac{V\Delta p'_z}{\alpha} = 0, \ \ \Delta p'_z = 0,$$
$$\Delta W' = \frac{\Delta W}{\alpha} - \frac{V\Delta p_z}{\alpha} = 0, \ \ \Delta p_z = 0, \ \ \Delta \bar{p}' = \Delta \bar{p} = 0,$$
$$\Delta \bar{p}' = 0, \ \ \sum \bar{F}' = 0; \ \ \Delta \bar{p} = 0, \ \ \sum \bar{F} = 0. \tag{21}$$

It may be noted, that the two results (20) and (21) are mutually complementary to each other. That is, the condition of zero total force, or equivalently the conservation of total momentum, would require the total energy to be conserved. And conversely, the conservation of the total energy would require the total momentum to be conserved, as well as the total force to be zero.

5.4. **Conservation of Total Energy and Momentum in the Universe.** Consider the entire universe, which in principle contains all physical space there is, and therefore does not have any other external space across which any energy or mass can be exchanged with. Accordingly, the entire universe is in principle a closed system. Therefore, as per the above deductions, the total momentum as well the energy in the entire universe must be conserved, with every possible force in the universe balanced by an opposing force of equal magnitude, at all times. This is the universal principle of conservation of energy and momentum.

6. DISCUSSION: BASIC CONCEPTS OF ELECTRO-MAGNETIC CHARGE AND SPACE-TIME SUPERSEDE NEWTON'S LAWS

We have succeeded to derive all basic mechanical principles of Newton's laws from Maxwell's equations. Further, we known that Maxwell's equations can be established [1, 2] directly from the basic principles of electric and magnetic charge and their invariance, using only the space-time concepts of the special relativity. Accordingly, the principles of the electric and magnetic charge and the space-time relativistic transformation relations, constitute a complete set of basic rules or laws to govern the electrical *as well as* mechanical characteristics of the nature.

In other words, we have established that the basic concepts of electro-magnetic charge and space-time are complete, which "supersede" all mechanical principles making them theoretically redundant. This interpretation may at first seem counter-intuitive. This is because we come to be educated about the mechanical principles first, which are more instinctively experienced as we come in contact with our physical world on a daily basis. Based on the mechanical principles, we are then gradually educated about more advanced principles of the electrical or magnetic forces, and their associated fields. This learning process leads to a common impression that the mechanical principles that are academically established first must be independent of, and therefore fundamentally supersede, the more advanced electromagnetic principles we learn later on. As we now understand, this impression is misleading.

The mechanical principles are introduced based only on our common-sense faith in Newton's laws without any objective "proof", by essentially relying on our everyday experiences and experimental observations. Although the electromagnetic principles, in the form of Maxwell's equations, are established later based upon these mechanical principles, with deeper insights we come to understand that the electromagnetic principles could be more fundamental. The governing basic principles of invariant electric and magnetic charges are recognized to be complete and minimal, and the underlying mechanical concepts will now have to be constrained in order to be consistent with the fundamental electromagnetic concepts. These constraints provide the desired "proof" or explanation for Newton's laws and the associated momentum and energy conservation, which no longer have to be accepted only on faith in their agreement with experimental observations and common-sense experiences. This is a significant, new scientific view.

References

[1] N. Das. Introducing Maxwell's Equations as Derived from Simple Relativity Transformation Principles. *IEEE Antennas and Propagation Magazine (to appear)*, June 2020.

[2] N. Das. A New Approach to Teaching Maxwell's Equations, as Derived from Simple Relativistic Transformation Principles: A Tutorial. *Paper #8, pp.88-120, in "A Unified Electro-Gravity (UEG) Theory of Nature"*, 2018.

[3] James Clark Maxwell. *A Treatise on Electricity and Magnetism, Vol. I and II (Reprint from 1873)*. Dover Publications, 2007.

[4] Albert Einstein and Anna Beck (English Translator). *The Collected Papers of Albert Einstein, Volume 2: The Swiss Years: Writings 1900-1909 (see Documents 23 and 24)*. Princeton University Press, 1989.

[5] Ray Skinner. *Relativity for Scientists and Engineers*. Dover Publications, Inc., 1982.

[6] N. N. Rao. *Elements of Engineering Electromagnetics, Ch.4,8*. Prentice Hall, New Jersey, 2000.

[7] R. F. Harrington. *Time Harmonic Electromagnetic Fields, Ch.2,3*. John Wiley and Sons; IEEE Press, 2001.

[8] L. B. Felsen and N. Marcuvitz. *Radiation and Scattering of Waves (Ch.4)*. Prentice Hall, 1973.

[9] Richarrd P. Feynman, Robert B. Leighton, and Mathew Sands. *Lectures on Physics, Vol.II, Ch.25,26*. Addision Wesley, 1964.

[10] Sir Isaac Newton. *Principia: Mathematical Principles of Natural Philosophy. I. B. Cohen, A. Whitman and J. Budenz, English Translators from 1726 Original*. University of California Press, 1999.

[11] Richarrd P. Feynman, Robert B. Leighton, and Mathew Sands. *Lectures on Physics, Vol.II, Ch.27,28*. Addision Wesley, 1964.